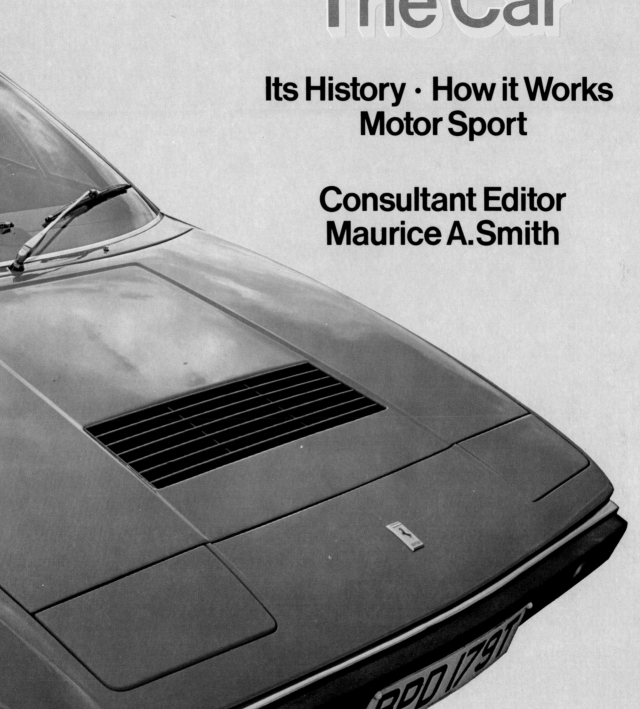

The Car

Its History · How it Works
Motor Sport

Consultant Editor
Maurice A. Smith

Contents

First published in 1980 by
Octopus Books Limited
59 Grosvenor Street, London W1
© 1979 Hennerwood Publications Limited
ISBN 0 7064 1090 4

Produced by Mandarin Publishers Limited
22A Westlands Road, Quarry Bay
Hong Kong

Printed in Hong Kong

J. Doyle del.^t et lithog.

A Sk

MR GURNEY'S NEW

As it appeared at Hounslow on the 12.th of August, with a Barouche attac

Pub.^d by J. Dickinson

Ancestry

... of

... TEAM CARRIAGE.

... containing the Duke of Wellington and other Persons of Distinction.

New Bond S.

1 The Horseless Carriage

Although four centuries have elapsed since the search began for some way of making a road carriage move without horses, it is only during the past 100 years that man's efforts have been crowned with lasting success. As long ago as 1645 there were reports of plans to build carriages powered by 'wonderful springs'; and in 1680 Sir Isaac Newton proposed a steam carriage propelled by a high-pressure steam jet from a rear-pointing spout, which was little more than a huge kettle mounted on a wheeled undercarriage and was quite impracticable. About that time, too, a Jesuit missionary, Father Verbiest, built a toy steam carriage for the emperor of China. The first crude attempts to make an internal combustion engine, with a piston displaced by the explosion of a charge of gunpowder, proved unworkable.

Before steam or internal combustion were properly harnessed, experimenters relied on gearing operated either by powerful springs or by men concealed within the body of the machine. Such a vehicle, it seems, was that demonstrated by Christopher Holtum 'at the 7 Stars under the Piazzas in Covent Garden' in early 1711. It was described as 'a chariot in the which a man may travel without horses, the like never made nor seen before in England: it will go for 5 or 6 miles an hour [8 or 9.5 km/h] and measure the miles as it goes'. Even the power of the wind was tried. Some of the later sail-carriages, such as George Pocock's 1826 *Charvolant* drawn by kites, were surprisingly sophisticated, with the claimed ability to move forward against virtually a headwind. Yet although they could move at speeds of 24–32 km (15–20 mph) when the wind blew hard enough, they were powerless when it stopped.

Harnessing steam

So the way was left open for 'King Steam, with his whistle and scream', the great motive power of the Industrial Revolution. In 1784 James Watt patented a steam carriage, but failed to put his design into practice. Watt may well have been actuated by envy at the successful experiments with model steam carriages carried out by his engineer, William Murdock. He probably wanted to prevent Murdock succeeding further and leaving the company.

England would lead the way in the development of the steam carriage, even though a full-size steam vehicle already existed in France. This had been built, with state backing, in 1770 by a military engineer named Nicholas Joseph Cugnot in order to assess its potential as an artillery tractor. It proved inefficient, for the boiler was too short-winded to propel the vehicle for more than 12–5 minutes at a time; the machine was badly balanced and almost

impossible to steer. It is now in the Conservatoire National des Arts et Métiers in Paris.

The first successful steam carriage appeared in 1801. It was the work of a 30-year-old Cornishman, Richard Trevithick, a pioneer in the use of high-pressure steam, who was described by a contemporary as 'the tall and strong young man who cared not for Watt'. Trevithick was the leading mining engineer in West Cornwall, and in his spare time built a number of small model carriages, the first of which was completed in 1796–7. The success of these encouraged him to proceed with a full-size vehicle, which was assembled in a blacksmith's shop in Camborne, Cornwall.

On Christmas Eve 1801 it made its first public runs. According to a local newspaper report, it 'carried several persons, amounting to at least a ton and a half weight, against a hill of considerable steepness at the rate of four miles an hour; and when upon a level road, of eight or nine miles an hour'. Four days later, a run of 5 km (3 miles) was made, when the carriage met with a minor mishap which prevented it from travelling further. Trevithick and his cousin and backer, Andrew Vivian, pushed it under a lean-to and adjourned to a nearby inn for 'a roast goose and proper drinks'. Meanwhile, the carriage boiled dry, caught fire, and destroyed both itself and the lean-to. It had proved its viability, however, and within weeks Trevithick and Vivian were in London to secure a patent on Trevithick's engine, with special emphasis on its application 'to give motion to wheel-carriages on common roads'.

In the spring of 1803 Trevithick commenced

Nicholas Joseph Cugnot's *fardier* of 1770 is generally held to be the first self-propelled steam-powered vehicle. Cugnot's obituary said of the *fardier* that the 'excessive violence of its movements prevented its being steered and, as early as its first trial, a length of wall which got in its way was knocked down'.

Preceding two pages 19th-century steam on the road: one of Goldsworthy Gurney's steam 'drags' of the 1830s. The railway pioneer Robert Stephenson is sitting beside Gurney in the driving seat; the Duke of Wellington is standing in the barouche behind.

work on an improved steam carriage, which was shipped to London to be fitted with wheels and coachwork. For many weeks Trevithick and Vivian ran the carriage about London, sometimes reaching speeds of up to 13–4 km/h (8–9 mph). As so often in Trevithick's career, however, money ran out, the carriage was sold – its engine was later used in a hoop-iron rolling mill – and the roads saw no more of 'Trevithick's dragons' (although the Cornishman later pioneered development of the steam railway locomotive).

There followed a period of experiment, when some wholly unsuccessful steam carriages were built. These included Brunton's 1813 'Traveller', pushed along by steam-operated legs, and David Gordon's steam carriage driven by a 2.7 m (9 ft) diameter wheel, inside which ran a tiny steam locomotive.

More rational designs appeared, too. In 1829 Goldsworthy Gurney's steam carriage accomplished the journey from London to Bath after numerous breakdowns – the first long-distance run by a self-propelled road vehicle. Gurney (1793–1875) went on to build far more successful light steam vehicles called 'drags', which were used to pull light carriages. But the most successful of all the steam-carriage pioneers was Walter Hancock, of Stratford, near London, who over a 12-year period built a number of carriages which provided regular services for limited periods, mainly in the London area. Hancock, however, proved a far better engineer than a businessman: he was bilked by many who pretended to back him, and was eventually forced to abandon his experiments.

Opposition to steam

Steam carriages aroused great hostility in Britain among those whose livelihoods were in some way connected with horses, especially trustees of toll roads and the stage-coach proprietors. To subvert the imagined threat from horseless carriages, bills were hurried through Parliament that imposed huge tolls on steam vehicles. On the Liverpool and Prescot road, for instance, a steam carriage had to pay a toll of the equivalent of £2.40 while a loaded stage coach paid only 20p. Although an 1831 Parliamentary select committee came to a largely favourable opinion on the merits of steam carriages and recommended that the heavy tolls be lifted, no action was taken. So most of the engineers abandoned their experiments, and by the early 1840s the golden age of steam on the road was over. Europe was soon in the grip of 'railway mania', and it became obvious that there were far greater fortunes for speculators in promoting railway companies than

there had ever been in steam-carriage companies.

Elsewhere, too, experiment with steam road vehicles had declined. In the 1780s in the United States, for instance, Oliver Evans (1755–1819) had obtained an exclusive licence for the manufacture and operation of steam carriages in the state of Maryland. He built his first self-propelled carriage, the clumsy 20-ton Amphibious Digger, in 1805. Thereafter, Evans devoted most of his time to the development of industrial steam engines.

Above Richard Trevithick's steam coach which was successfully demonstrated in London in 1803.

Below Gurney's steam carriage of 1829. The leg-like appendages in front of the back wheels are 'propellers' – powered levers to aid hill-climbing.

Early steam carriages were an irresistible target for satirists. This lampoon of 1829 by 'A Sharpshooter' was captioned 'By-and-bye a Man will go a-hunting after breakfast upon his Tay-kettle'.

Experiments with gas and petrol

A new method of propulsion, potentially far more suitable for road carriages, made its first appearance at the beginning of the 19th century. This was the gas engine, and as early as 1807 a Swiss, Isaac de Rivaz, had patented a crude powered trolley driven by a simple gas engine that had managed to travel across a room. One factor limiting its future development was that its exhaust valve had to be manually operated. But the potential of the gas engine was soon recognized. A patent 'gas-and-vacuum, engine powered Samuel Brown's road carriage, which in May 1826 climbed Shooter's Hill in London 'to the astonishment of numerous spectators', although it proved too expensive to operate commercially. The first practicable gas engine was patented in 1853 by two Italians, Eugenio Barsanti and Felice Matteucci, who claimed that 'before long the power of steam will be replaced by a perfect, inexpensive motive force'; but they failed to carry through any of their designs.

In 1859 a company with a capital of 2 million francs was formed in Paris to exploit the invention of the Belgian-born engineer, J-J-Étienne Lenoir. It was described as 'an engine dilated by the combustion of gas', and although early examples of the power unit were extremely inefficient – an 18-litre Lenoir engine developed only 2 hp – as early as 1860 the inventor was proposing to build a motor carriage, illustrations of which appeared in the journal *Le Monde Illustré* that year. The machine appears to have run successfully only in 1863, when Lenoir claimed to have often made the 9 km (5.5 mile) journey from Paris to the village of Joinville-le-Pont, taking three hours for the round trip 'if we avoided the usual breakdown'. Lenoir apparently sold this car to Tsar Alexander II of Russia, although its eventual fate is unknown.

Lenoir's engine inspired a German clerk, Nikolaus August Otto, to develop an internal-combustion engine which could be used where steam was impracticable. In conjunction with a wealthy engineer, Eugen Langen, Otto developed a 'free-piston' engine which was patented in 1866 and went into production in 1872. The company that Otto and Langen formed was reorganized as the Deutz Gas Engine Factory – an early Otto engine still stands in the Otto-platz at Deutz, a suburb of Cologne – and a 38-year-old engineer named Gottlieb Daimler became factory manager with his protégé, Wilhelm Maybach, as chief designer.

Although commercially successful, the Otto engine was noisy and inefficient, and needed an overhead clearance of some 4 m (13 ft) to allow for the movement of the piston rod which turned the flywheel through a rack and pinion gear. When sales began to decline, Daimler and Maybach were ordered to develop a 'petroleum engine' as a replacement, and Otto's chief engineer, Franz Rings, had a prototype running in the autumn of 1876. It used the four-stroke cycle of induction-compression-explosion-exhaust which Otto had first tried but abandoned in 1861–2. In an attempt to monopolize the gas-engine industry, Otto patented the four-stroke cycle (see drawing on p.100), forcing other experimenters to concentrate on the less efficient two-stroke system or risk prosecution. In 1886 his patent was overthrown after two years of litigation on the grounds that an obscure French civil engineer, Alphonse Beau de Rochas, had patented the four-stroke cycle and had described it in a pamphlet which he distributed to the press in 1862.

Benz and Daimler

This left the way open for inventors who were attempting to find a suitable power source for a self-propelled vehicle. Most prominent were Gottlieb Daimler, who had broken with Otto in 1881, and Karl Benz, another German, who owned a machine shop at Mannheim. Benz built his first two-stroke engine in 1879, and by 1884 was planning to build a complete motor vehicle. When it became apparent that Otto's master patent would be ruled invalid, Benz began work on a four-cycle engine for his 'vehicle with gas-engine drive'. This appeared in 1885–6, and made its first public runs in the summer of 1886. A spidery three-wheeler, it was the first purpose-designed

Right A model of Nikolaus Otto's original production engine of 1872. Although it was noisy and inefficient and could never have powered a road vehicle, Otto's was the first internal-combustion engine to demonstrate the now-universal four-stroke cycle.

Below and right Karl Benz's pioneering three-wheeler of 1885–6 was the first motor-car designed as an entity; structurally it owed more to the new cycle technology than to that of the horse-drawn carriage. Its rear-mounted water-cooled engine developed about ¾ hp. The vertical crankshaft had a large flywheel located horizontally.

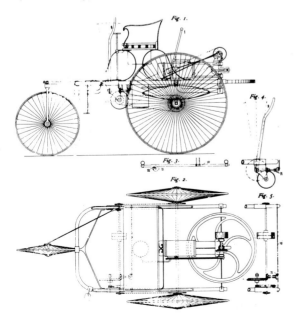

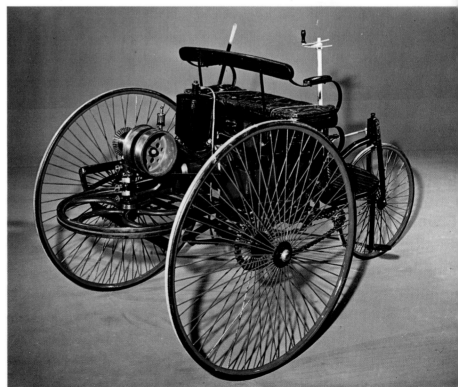

Right Wilhelm Maybach at the tiller of the first *Stahlradwagen* (steel-wheeler) which he designed for Gottlieb Daimler in 1889. It was exhibited that year at the Paris World Fair, where it attracted the interest of René Panhard and Armand Peugeot. Gear-driven, the *Stahlradwagen* was more advanced than the production Daimlers of the next decade.

Below Gottlieb Daimler's experimental workshop at Bad Cannstatt. In the centre is the world's first motor-cycle – Daimler's crude boneshaker of 1885 that he used as a test-bed for the single-cylinder engine he had designed two years before.

petrol car, rather than a converted horse-carriage.

Daimler, on the other hand, saw the petrol engine as a 'universal power source': a horseless carriage was merely one of many applications that he had envisaged for such a power unit. In November 1883 he made experiments with a single-cylinder engine mounted in a 'boneshaker' bicycle frame, and in 1886 he carried out tests with a converted four-seater phaeton built by a firm of coachbuilders who were kept ignorant of the fact that it was to be engine-driven.

Benz, meanwhile, was anxious to promote his motor-carriage commercially. An improved version was put on the market in 1888. It caused much interest but found no buyers in Germany. However, the French agent for the Benz gas engine, Émile Roger, was enthusiastic, and it was through his efforts that one or two of the first Benz cars were sold; one survives today in the Science Museum, London.

All credit is due to Benz for having persisted in his attempt to make a commercial proposition of the motor vehicle. Most of the early inventors were dilettantes who lost interest in their vehicles once they had made them run (or once they became too expensive to persist with). Among the promising designs which failed to be developed further was the little steam car built in 1868 by Joseph Ravel, father of the composer Maurice Ravel. The first steam vehicle to have the boiler heated by petroleum rather than solid fuel, Ravel's machine made a number of successful journeys over several months. (It also became the first car to be fitted with a safety belt. On its long initial test run, Ravel's assistant celebrated the event so enthusiastically that he became drunk and had to be tied to his seat to prevent him from falling out.)

Another inventor, the Austrian Siegfried Marcus, is reported to have fitted a crude atmospheric engine to a wheelbarrow in 1870 as a mobile test bench for a potential airship power unit, but it failed to run more than 180 m (200 yards). In 1888–9, Marcus built a crude motor car that was later falsely claimed to have been built in 1875. There is little doubt that, in terms of successful petrol-driven vehicles, Benz and Daimler made the significant breakthrough.

Right The Daimler-Maybach V-twin engine of 1889 was widely used on both Daimlers and other marques until 1892. Ignition was by platinum tubes that projected into the combustion chambers and were heated by burners. Having no throttle, the engine turned at a more-or-less constant speed (about 700 rpm), but it could be slowed by use of a lever to prevent the exhaust valves from opening.

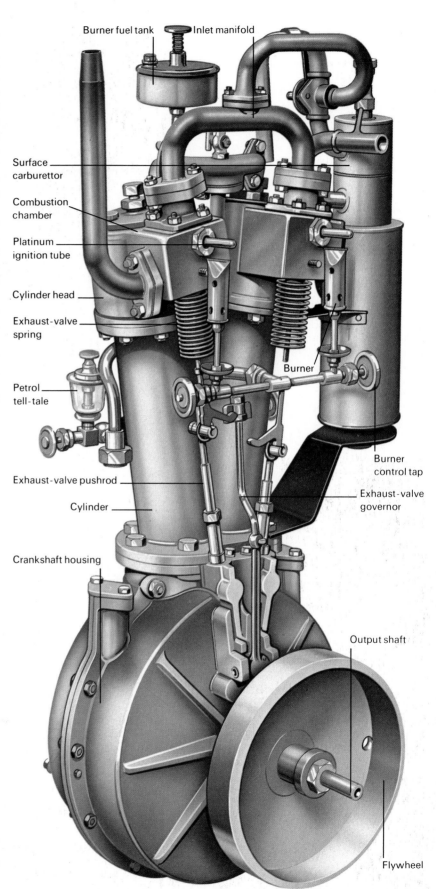

Burner fuel tank · Inlet manifold
Surface carburettor
Combustion chamber
Platinum ignition tube
Cylinder head
Exhaust-valve spring
Burner
Petrol tell-tale
Exhaust-valve pushrod
Cylinder
Crankshaft housing
Burner control tap
Exhaust-valve governor
Output shaft
Flywheel

2 Cars for Sale

Although in hindsight we can see that Benz and Daimler set the pattern for the future with their petrol-driven vehicles of 1885–6, the question of the best type of power unit for cars was not settled until more than a decade later. The most serious rival to the petrol engine was steam, which staged a revival in the last quarter of the century.

One of the most remarkable families in the early history of the motor vehicle was the Bollées of Le Mans. They were renowned bell-founders who had established a factory in the city in 1842. Amédée Bollée, born in 1844, became an enthusiast for the self-propelled carriage in 1867, after a visit to the Paris Exposition. In 1871 he set up a workshop within the family factory and attempted to build a motor vehicle. Working in the evenings, Bollée had by 1873 constructed a vehicle of undoubted originality. He called it *L'Obéissante* (Obedient One). It had independently suspended front wheels mounted in separate forks and steered by chains running over elliptical sprockets to give geometrically correct steering. A separate V-twin steam engine driving each rear wheel eliminated the need for a differential and so allowed more passenger space.

After two years of trials Bollée took *L'Obéissante* to Paris by road. The vehicle caused a great deal of interest but attracted no orders. So Bollée began work on a successor, a machine that would look less unorthodox and perhaps be a more saleable proposition.

In 1878 he unveiled his new design, *La Mancelle* (Girl from Le Mans). It was 15 years ahead of its time, for it established design principles that petrol cars would follow for many years. Its engine was set at the front, under a bonnet, driving the rear wheels through a shaft, bevel gears, and side-chains; the vertical boiler, however, was carried at the rear, on a canopied platform for the *chauffeur* (stoker). Front suspension was again independent, this time by parallel transverse leaf-springs, and the steering was controlled by a pinion operating an arc-shaped rack with a separate track rod to each wheel.

Shown at the 1878 Paris World Exhibition, *La Mancelle* attracted sufficient attention for Bollée to establish a special factory for the manufacture of steam carriages. He appointed a concessionaire who joined forces with a German banker, the intention being to build Bollée buses in a disused railway-engine works. The scheme came to nothing, however, and the company collapsed in 1883.

Bollée received nothing from the venture and so, disenchanted, he abandoned steam-carriage construction. He built only a few

machines after 1880, and these were mostly intended for members of his family. In 1885 his 18-year-old son Amédée *fils* built a well-conceived two-seater steam car; but young Amédée and his brother Léon were to achieve more lasting fame in the early days of the petrol car.

Steam carriages on the market

As Bollée senior bowed out of the infant motor industry, a young French aristocrat, Comte Albert de Dion, took his first steps towards becoming a steam-carriage manufacturer. Renowned as a duellist and gambler, de Dion was also a keen amateur inventor, although his mechanical inclination was regarded with disfavour by his family.

About 1882, intrigued by the workmanship of a model steam engine he saw in a Paris shop window, de Dion backed its makers, two impoverished brothers-in-law, Georges Bouton and Trépardoux, to set up a workshop to build steam-engined carriages. Late in 1883 their first steam quadricycle, belt-driven by a 1 hp engine, appeared on the streets of Paris. It attracted so much publicity that de Dion decided to branch out and took a lease on larger premises at Puteaux (Seine).

In the spring of 1884 de Dion, Bouton, and Trépardoux received their first order, for a steam dog-cart, and thenceforward a succession of light steam vehicles left the Puteaux works. De Dion and Bouton saw the steam engine as a transitional power unit until some more compact prime mover could be found.

Shortly after de Dion had established his factory, a blacksmith's son named Léon Ser-

Amédée Bollée's *L'Obéissante* (Obedient One) of 1873 pioneered independent front suspension, having geometrically correct steering. A separate V-twin steam engine controlled each rear wheel doing away with the need for a differential; the boiler was at the rear. (This carriage, like Cugnot's *fardier*, is preserved in the Conservatoire National des Arts et Métiers in Paris.)

pollet set up a small workshop in Montmartre to build a steam tricycle incorporating his new type of boiler in which the water was instantaneously 'flashed' into steam. This vehicle was completed in 1887, but trial runs were limited in number, for every time he wanted to take the machine on the road Serpollet had to inform the local police. Accordingly, he applied for, and was granted, the first driving licence issued in Paris. This gave him authority to drive his tricycle at a maximum speed of 16 km/h (10 mph) in the city, and without speed restriction on country roads.

There was soon friendly rivalry between the partisans of the Serpollet and De Dion-Bouton steamers, and in 1888 a race was organized in Paris by the journal *Le Vélocipède*. It was almost certainly the first time that two motor cars had ever competed against one another. Unfortunately for Serpollet, his rugged steam tricycle was outclassed by the lighter De Dion.

Armand Peugeot, a cycle manufacturer, became interested in Serpollet's design, and in 1889 a Serpollet steam tricycle was built in Peugeot's factory at Audincourt for exhibition at the 1889 Paris World Fair. All the recent advances in technology could be seen at the fair, notably the latest Benz and Daimler cars.

One enthusiastic passenger in the new Daimler *Stahlradwagen* ('steelwheeler') was René Panhard, a manufacturer of woodworking machinery, whose partner, Émile Levassor, was the fiancé (later the husband) of Louise Sarazin, a young widow whose husband had left her the French rights in the Daimler engine.

Above This crude quadricycle of 1883 was the first of the De Dion-Bouton steamers

Below It was followed two years later by this more substantial De Dion model. Both vehicles had front-wheel drive and rear-wheel steering – a highly unstable combination.

Journeys by motor car

Although the motor car was still a temperamental novelty in the late 1880s, it was already being envisaged as a touring vehicle. Early one August morning in 1888, while Karl Benz was still asleep, his wife Berta and his two teenage sons Eugen and Richard set out to drive the 120 km (75 miles) to Pforzheim from their home at Mannheim. There were surprisingly few troubles on the way. Although the brake block wore out (and had to be refaced with leather by a cobbler), the chains stretched and fell off the sprockets, and a clogged fuel line had to be cleared with Frau Benz's hatpin, mother and sons completed the journey in a day. Although some of the hills on the journey had proved too much for the car's feeble 2 hp engine, valuable lessons had been learnt and a lower gear was subsequently incorporated in the transmission.

Some months later a tour of a very different kind began. After the 1889 Paris Exposition, Léon Serpollet decided with his friend Ernest Archdeacon (later an aviation pioneer) to embark on motor touring, a sport which neither had yet tried. In January 1890, 'with the same precautions and preparations as for making a journey to the North Pole', they set off from Paris bound for Lyons on a steam-powered tricycle built in the Peugeot works.

The trip was eventful. At one point the primitive tiller steering broke, and they had to drive with Archdeacon manipulating the engine regulator and brake while Serpollet lay on the

floor and hung over the front of the machine, hitting the single front wheel with his fist to steer it. The brake broke when they were descending a steep hill; the driving axle snapped near Dijon; and a back wheel fell off. Poor-quality coal (early Serpollets were solid-fuel burners) made it difficult to maintain boiler pressure, and on one stretch the car took four hours to cover 22 km (14 miles). Various parts fell off and were replaced by crudely made components fabricated by local black-smiths; this added considerably to the weight of the machine, whose springs collapsed at Beaune. It took 15 days to cover the 461 km (286 miles) from Paris to Lyons. Under-standably, the car was sent home by train.

Peugeot in business

Incidents like this convinced Armand Peugeot that there was no future in steam, and his association with Serpollet was ended after three Peugeot-Serpollet steam tricars had been built. After a meeting with Levassor and Daimler at which he was shown the 'steel-wheeler' car which Daimler had exhibited at the Paris Exposition, Peugeot began work on a similar machine, using V-twin Daimler engines supplied by Panhard et Levassor.

The first real test of the Peugeot 'motor-quadricycle' came in 1891, when one of the earliest followed the Paris-Brest cycle race, completing the round trip of 2,047 km (1,272 miles) at an average of 15 km/h (9 mph). Like all the early Peugeot cars, it had its engine at the rear of a tubular chassis through which the cooling water was circulated to the frontal radiator. The V-twin engine had hot-tube ignition, in which petrol burners heated platinum tubes projecting into the combustion chambers. In 1891 Peugeot sold five cars to private owners, a figure that was to rise to 29 the following year. The French motor industry was under way.

Meanwhile, Émile Levassor had become determined to make a motor car, and in 1891 he built a prototype with a mid-mounted engine. It was not a great success and so a new layout was adopted, with the engine at the front under a box-like bonnet, driving through a 'brush clutch' to a four-speed gearbox in which the cogs had no casing to keep lubricant in and grit out. Final drive was by twin chains, and the car was steered by a 'cow's tail' tiller with no self-centring action – a defect that was to lead to Levassor's death in 1897 as a result of injuries sustained when his car overturned in the 1896 Paris–Marseilles race. Panhard et Levassor's cars were first offered to the public in 1892, when a four-seat dog-cart sold for the equivalent of £200, a wagonette for £212; solid

Above Panhard et Levassor's first car was this *dos-à-dos* of 1890, with a centrally mounted Daimler V-twin engine (the company soon afterwards adopted a front-engine, rear-wheel-drive layout). In this photograph Émile Levassor is at the tiller, beside his chief engineer; on the left are René Panhard and Mme Levassor.

Right Léon Serpollet was a pioneer of steam-powered road-vehicles between 1887 and 1907 and made important contributions to the design of steam boilers. This poster shows one of his 1903 range of cars.

rubber tyres instead of the standard iron-shod wheels cost another £20.

If Germany had been the birthplace of the automobile, France, with its magnificent network of roads and passion for mechanical novelty, was its cradle.

German production

In Germany Karl Benz enjoyed little commercial success until he switched from building three-wheeled cars to four-wheelers and solved the problem of building 'a steering mechanism . . . with steering circles set on a tangent to the wheels'.

The turning-point came in 1894 when he introduced a new, light, and moderately priced model known as the Velo. That year 67 cars were delivered; in 1895 the figure rose to 135, of which 62 were Velos and the rest an assortment of phaetons, brakes, landaus, and omnibuses. In 1895 no fewer than 49 Benz cars were running in France. Production continued to climb, and by the end of 1899 Benz had built his 2,000th car. Rear-engined and belt-driven, this model was still recognisably descended from the 1886 three-wheeler, and Benz's stubborn refusal to produce a more up-to-date design was to cost his company sales: output peaked at 603 cars in 1900 but tumbled to 385 the following year.

One factor in this slump in demand had been the rise of the Daimler company. At first bedevilled – as Benz had been – by quarrels with his business partners, Daimler established an independent partnership with Wilhelm Maybach in 1893. That same year Daimler took one of his cars to Chicago at the suggestion of his American agent, the piano-maker William Steinway, to display the vehicle at the World's Fair. Although Steinway's death in 1896 and a restrictive patent monopoly on the construction of self-propelled vehicles prevented Daimler from developing his American connection to any great extent, he was nonetheless keen on fostering his export business.

The English scene

In England Daimler engine sales were handled by Frederick R. Simms, who fitted the power units to launches in his workshop beneath the Thames-side arches of Putney Bridge. Simms proposed that he and a number of associates in a group known as the British Motor Syndicate should form a consortium to purchase licences and exploit the Daimler patents throughout the British Empire. Leading the British Motor Syndicate was an astute company promoter named Harry J. Lawson, who had already made a fortune with his bicycle companies and who foresaw the market for the motor vehicle at a

time when cars on British roads were still restricted by law to the speed of a man walking in front of them.

In January 1896 Lawson founded the Daimler Motor Company and set about publicising the 'new locomotion'. He acquired a disused four-storey cotton mill at Coventry and converted it into 'the largest autocar factory in the world . . . for the manufacture of autocars under the

Above This *vis-à-vis* is one of 72 cars sold by Peugeot in 1895. Its rear-mounted engine and handlebar steering are typical of the marque at that time.

Below Karl Benz at the controls of one of his 1890s 4–5 hp phaetons.

Pennington, Daimler, and Bollée systems'. In its early days the 'factory' was little more than a storehouse for imported Daimler and Panhard cars, and when construction eventually began towards the end of 1897 it resulted in markedly inferior copies of the Panhard. Although the main tenants of the factory were Daimler and its sister company, the Motor Manufacturing Company, at various times it also sheltered other dubious members of the Lawson empire: the Great Horseless Carriage Company, the British Motor Syndicate, the Beeston Pneumatic Tyre Company, Humber & Company, and Coventry Motor Company.

Financial manipulation was a way of life with Lawson. The British Motor Syndicate (which does not seem to have made any cars, although it issued handsome leaflets and granted expensive manufacturing licences to would-be autocar builders) acquired the Great Horseless Carriage Company in 1898, and £300,000 of investors' money vanished into the pockets of Lawson and his associates.

Lawson's financial chicanery eventually earned him a year's hard labour, but he was certainly an enthusiastic lobbyist for motoring interests. Using as his mouthpiece the *Autocar* (founded in 1895), Lawson persuaded Parliament to raise the speed restriction on light motor carriages to 19 km/h (12 mph) in the open country. To celebrate the event he organized a motoring run from London to

Above Karl Benz's most popular car, the single-cylinder Velo of 1894.

Below The Hon. Evelyn Ellis, a director of Coventry Daimler, is seen here with one of his company's cars at the summit of Worcester Beacon in 1897.

Brighton on 'Emancipation Day', 14 November 1896. Although at least two of the vehicles entered did not run to Brighton under their own power at all, but arrived there by railway, while the first two cars to arrive were reputedly left out of the results because they had not been built by Lawson's companies, the event signalled the dawn of the British motor industry.

Early American cars

The first two cars to reach Brighton – one of them unfortunately ran over a little girl *en route* – were Duryeas, products of America's first company to open a London office. The United States had been late in developing its own vehicles, and the first native American petrol cars had not appeared until 1891. They were a three-wheeler built by John Lambert of Anderson, Indiana and a four-wheeler constructed by Henry Nadig of Allentown, Pennsylvania. The Duryea brothers, Charles and Frank, built their first car in 1893 and began production in 1896. At first, though, their cars were considered more of a circus attraction than a serious invention, for outside city limits American roads were generally so poor as to make motoring quite impracticable.

Nevertheless other pioneers began building motor vehicles in the early 1890s. Elwood Haynes, who for many years claimed to have built America's first car, made his first trials in July 1894; and in 1896 two experimental cars appeared in Detroit. One, the first self-propelled vehicle to run on the streets of what would become America's 'motor city', was the work of a skilled engineer and designer named Charles Brady King. The other, a belt-driven

buggy known as the Quadricycle, was the work of a young mechanic who had risen to become chief engineer at the Edison Illuminating Company, and who spent what little spare time he had tinkering with this machine, built from scrap metal found on the company's junk pile. He had created America's first private garage, too, when he realized that the completed car was too wide to go through the door of the shed where he had built it, and knocked away the brickwork with a hatchet. The little Quadricycle was the first of a continuing line of over 150 million motor cars to bear the name of its constructor, Henry Ford.

Left Ransom Eli Olds with his 1896 petrol-engined prototype. He built steam- and electricity-powered cars before introducing the epoch-making Oldsmobile Curved Dash runabout of 1902.

Above The Duryea gas buggy of 1895 was the first production car to be made in the United States. The buggy caused a considerable sensation when put on show by Barnum & Bailey's circus.

Below An early production Winton, a two-seat phaeton of 1898; it had a pneumatic throttle control and a laminated-wood frame. Alexander Winton manufactured cars from 1897 to 1924.

3 Industrial Beginnings

During the last decade of the 19th century a variety of cars were produced by hundreds of more or less gifted engineers, enthusiastic amateurs, and cranks, and the names of most of these men are now forgotten. Relatively few models of that time were promising enough, technically or commercially, to encourage further development; fewer still can be regarded as laying the foundations of what was to become a major world industry.

As we have seen, Panhard et Levassor, Peugeot, and others had begun operations in the 1890s. In this decade, too, the brothers Renault, the brothers Opel, and Giovanni Agnelli's Fabbrica Italiana Automobili Torino (FIAT) commenced production – as did such famous but now defunct French marques as Chenard-Walcker, Clément-Bayard, Darracq (later to find expression in the great Lago-Talbot), and De Diétrich.

The two great German pioneers, Karl Benz and Gottlieb Daimler, had relatively brief careers in the early industrial phase of the motor car. Benz was a very conservative designer and he was to contribute little to the technical development of the car after his successful Velo. He sold his interests in the Benz company in the early years of the new century. Daimler, whose central interest was in designing engines – for boats and other vehicles as well as for motor cars – died in March 1900. The great present-day firm of Daimler Benz was created from a merger in 1926.

Daimler's company grew steadily during the 1890s both as a car maker and as a builder or licencer of engines used by other firms. In considering the innovations of Daimler himself, it is difficult to know how much credit is due to him and how much to his brilliant designer Wilhelm Maybach. It is known, for instance, that Maybach was largely responsible for the V-twin engine that was a cornerstone of the company's production in the 1890s and was also used in Panhard, Peugeot, and other cars. Maybach also did much original work on engine components, notably the spray carburettor. The Daimler company's crowning achievement in this period was certainly the work of Maybach alone, for it came to fruition after Gottlieb Daimler's death.

To place this achievement in perspective, we need to know something about the appearance and specification of a typical car of the period. It was commonly high and short (like many horse-carriages of the time), and so was unstable, especially when cornering. Its crude tiller steering could easily be wrenched out of the driver's hand if its hard steel- or solid-rubber-shod wheels hit a large stone. Its feeble brakes consisted of crude brake-shoes pressing

Above An Egg *vis-à-vis* of 1898. Rudolf Egg of Zürich made his first car in 1893 and built three-wheelers in 1896–8. A pioneer of Swiss car manufacture, Egg sold the design of the *vis-à-vis* to his countryman J. Weber.

Left The first De Dion-Bouton *voiturette* (1899) had a 402 cc, water-cooled engine mounted vertically at the rear and a two-speed transmission. About 1,500 of these simple, reliable runabouts were sold within two years.

Above Benz's conservative Landaulet-Coupé of 1899.

Below Tillers or (as here) handlebars began to be replaced by the steering wheel in the late 1890s.

against the rear tyres. Engine cooling was often by a simple tank in which the water boiled away at frequent intervals and had to be replenished. Radiators as such, if fitted at all, commonly took the form of a serpentine coil of pipes underneath the car. In general, then, most cars of this time had a specification that could appeal only to the most dedicated enthusiasts: they were too unreliable to be used confidently as mundane day-to-day transport, and too slow and unstable to offer much pleasure to the sportsman.

Nonetheless, sporting events of many kinds proliferated during the 1890s. One enthusiast who frequently took part in such events was Emil Jellinek, the German Consul-General at Nice. He was a friend of Daimler's and acted as an unofficial agent for his cars on the French Riviera. In 1899 Jellinek entered a Daimler Phönix in a local touring competition. Although he won a prize, Jellinek was critical of the car's height, lack of power, and small wheels. His remarks were relayed to the Cannstatt factory, and Maybach went to work on a new model.

The result was not merely an improvement on the stately Phönix but one of the most significant cars in the history of motoring. Powered by a 5.9-litre, four-cylinder engine developing no less than 35 hp, it had a pressed-steel (rather than a timber) frame, a honeycomb radiator mounted (as on a modern car) at the front of the bonnet, a steering wheel on a raked (rather than vertical) column, a 'gate' change for the gear lever, mechanically operated valves, and a remarkably low centre of gravity. Jellinek was very impressed and ordered 36 of the new cars on the understanding that it was not to be marketed as a Daimler but would take the name of his daughter – Mercédès. At

Nice in 1901 these 35PS cars won almost every race in sight, and they were to influence the design of other marques for years to come.

Maybach continued to develop his new model (Daimler officially adopted the name 'Mercedes' in 1902), and the 1903–6 versions were even finer than the original. But changes on the board of the Daimler company led to increasing friction between Maybach and his employers, and he resigned in 1907; he later became engine designer to Count Ferdinand von Zeppelin, the airship pioneer. (The powerful and highly regarded Maybach cars of the 1920s and 1930s were the work of Wilhelm Maybach's son Karl, who had also worked for Zeppelin before World War I.)

Electric carriages in vogue

During the 1890s many people still believed that self-propelled vehicles should look as much as possible like their horse-drawn counterparts and to have similar performance, and it was to such people that the electric carriage appealed. Outstanding among the makers of electric vehicles was Walter Bersey, who built his first road vehicle in the 1880s. In the mid-1890s his fleet of electric cabs in London achieved favourable publicity.

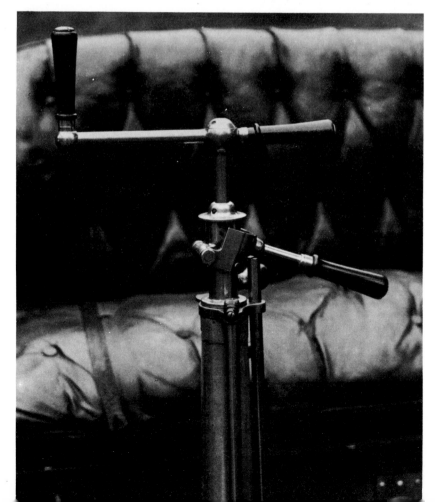

Wrote the *Daily Telegraph*: 'The new cabs will be undoubtedly a vast improvement from every point of view, as compared with those drawn by the insanitary horse. There is no animal more subject to disease, and his presence on the wooden pavements of the City is responsible for most of the disease germs which every breeze sweeps up in myriads from the filth-sodden streets.'

The *Sun* expressed a much more positive response to Bersey's cabs. 'When I got used to the sensation,' commented a writer, 'I discovered it was uncommonly pleasant. The cabs are simply luxurious, easy going, well fitted, and very roomy. Why, in an ordinary cab you and your best girl just fill the whole place; here you could be a sort of Brigham Young, and still find room for your knees. The jolting was of the very mildest, even over the Viaduct, where the roads are awful. And there is no noise at all. I tell you, these electric cabs should catch on.'

But they did not. The electric carriage enjoyed a brief vogue among elegant folk about town, but it had many drawbacks. There was a lack of range; the weight of batteries needed for even a limited area of operation proved too great; and the time and the cost involved in recharging the batteries daily was prohibitive.

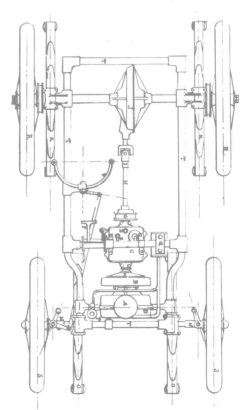

Above Louis Renault at the wheel of his first prototype (centre) in 1899. The car had a 1¾ hp, front-mounted De Dion-Bouton engine and featured shaft drive to a live rear axle (a system Renault falsely claimed to have originated). On the right is Renault's production model of the car. Whereas the prototype had a steering wheel, this version had handlebars; with its three-speed transmission it could carry two people at up to 40 km/h (25 mph). Marcel Renault is in the front seat of the De Dion-Bouton three-wheeler on the left.

Left Original drawing of the chassis and mechanical layout of an early Renault *voiturette*. Note the semi-circular handlebar and steering linkage.

These shortcomings contributed to its early demise.

Nor did steam fare much better. It was an old-established source of motive power, but it needed an engineer to maintain it properly. The petrol engine required no boiler, burner, or complex control system so that the steam engine as a motive source for cars became virtually obsolete once the first Benz and Daimler engines were running successfully.

Both electric and steam vehicles enjoyed some patronage during the first decade of the 20th century – most notably the Locomobile (*see* Chapter 4) and White steamers in the United States – but few of either type survived into the 1920s.

Technical dead-ends

If the internal-combustion engine was clearly the main line of future development, it must be said that many petrol-driven cars of the 1890s were technically inadequate in many ways. Some were the product of mere incompetence, for car technology was still in its infancy. Others, equally unsound, were vigorously promoted by charlatans. One of the most notorious of these inventor/promoters was the American E. J. Pennington. In 1896, after experimenting with flying machines that failed to fly, he came to England, where he sold his vehicle patents to Harry Lawson for £100,000 and set up a production plant at Lawson's Coventry car factory.

Even in those early days there were some generally accepted standards for the design of motor vehicles, and Pennington flouted nearly all of them. The cylinders of his engines were made of thin steel tube and equipped with neither cooling fins nor a water jacket. He advanced absurd claims for his 'oil adjustment' (a screw-controlled needle valve which replaced the carburettor) and for his 'long-mingling spark', which was supposed to enable the engine to run on paraffin. One of Pennington's assistants later exploded the myth of the 'long-mingling spark'. 'What actually happened was that the best petrol was used, and when necessary a densimeter with faked graduations was employed to "prove" that paraffin was being used. . . . On most occasions the ignition failed very quickly and a new spring wiper had to be fitted.'

Pennington's most notorious car was the Raft Victoria, which was driven by the front wheels and steered by the rear. It had an engine with a vertical crankshaft (started by thrusting a handle through a hole in the floor) and retained the 'metering' valve, although a conventional sparking plug now replaced the 'long-mingling spark'. Although the cylinder barrel

Above An 1898 Daimler Taxameter, one of Berlin's first petrol-engined taxis.

Left The first FIAT, a four-seat *vis-à-vis* with a 679 cc, 3½ hp, two-cylinder engine. The driver, Count Roberto Biscaretti Di Ruffia, was one of the FIAT company's founders.

Below A Pennington Torpedo (1896). The long tubes contained the pistons; the 'unpuncturable' tyres burst often.

Above left A formidable array of temperature, pressure, and other gauges faced the driver of this Stanley steamer of Edwardian days. Although steam engines were quiet and reliable, their boilers needed to be replenished with water every 160 km (100 miles) or less.

Above right A Clément *voiturette* of 1900, with rear-mounted 2¼ hp De Dion-Bouton engine. One of these cars came second in the Paris–Rouen–Paris race of that year. Adolphe Clément was a pioneer of the French motor industry, and had been a maker of pneumatic tyres before turning to car production in 1900. His name is now remembered chiefly for the Clément-Bayard marque of 1903–22.

had a water jacket, the head was devoid of any kind of cooling. The drive was taken to the front wheels via a cycle chain running horizontally (and therefore likely to fall off its sprockets) and a twisted rope belt (which broke frequently). Another Pennington model was the equally bizarre Torpedo, whose 'puncture-proof' tyres burst on the Emancipation Run of 1896 and the car was forced to retire from the event. Although Pennington's career as a car maker was short-lived, his factory was something of a showplace – but its output did little to advance the cause of the motor car.

The French industry

By this time French, German, and Italian car manufacturers were beginning to organize for large-scale production. The fortunes of the Renault company began in 1898 when Louis Renault, just 21 years old, took the engine out of a De Dion-Bouton tricycle and installed it in a light four-wheeler of his own design. He drove this home-built car to a Christmas Eve party, where it so impressed the other guests that by the end of the evening Louis had firm orders for no fewer than 12 cars. He at once formed a company, Renault Frères, with his brothers Marcel and Fernand and went into production in 1899. Their early products were mainly two-seat *voiturettes* – light, nippy, and economical little cars. Sound construction, energetic promotion, and many successes in early road races (both Louis and Marcel were skilful drivers) created a steadily increasing demand for Renaults, and within a few years the company had become the largest car manufacturer in Europe.

Meanwhile, by the turn of the century the

Paris factory of Panhard et Levassor had grown into virtually a self-contained town. A visitor wrote in the winter of 1900–1 that from the very first glimpse he was 'impressed with the oneness, the order, and the signs of some great but invisible controlling hand'.

At that period the Panhard works employed some 850 workmen, and there were 350 lathes and polishing and planing machines in the machine shop. Already, scientific test methods were in use, the finished engines being bolted to test benches. But there was little standardization, each car being built as an individual product. The same visitor noted: 'When we were conducted over the shop 43 frames were having their bodies fitted on, and hardly two were quite alike. . . . The selection included such dissimilar vehicles as a twelve horsepower brougham for the King of the Belgians . . . a twenty-four horsepower racing car that may be a starter in the Gordon Bennett race . . . a huge omnibus for military purposes . . . a motor car to run on rails in Algiers.'

When the cars were finished, they were tested for three days before being delivered to their owners. 'During this period of probation the cars stand in a garage, and are taken out one after the other for runs into the country, fourteen expert drivers being employed'.

Early car tests

What sort of hazards were those 'expert drivers' likely to experience? One test driver for Clarkson, an English manufacturer of steam-powered cars in 1899–1902, recorded a typical incident: 'A small tiller-steered Clarkson van was lent to us while our two cars in turn went back to the works for adjustment. My colleague

went out with it on the first day and said that the steering was a bit queer . . . the second day he hit a lamp post. The following day, I went out with it. . . . Of course, the totally different steering wanted a bit of getting used to at first, but it was not too bad, though I was always on the lookout for incidents.

'Going down a slope just beyond Gerrards Cross, the road was a bit bumpy. All of a sudden, the tiller was nearly pulled out of my hand and we shot into the ditch, with the result that a stub axle broke. . . . I took the wheel off, and fastened a crowbar to the main axle, stuck the wheel back on the crowbar, and drove the car up to the pub at the top of the hill, steering with the other wheel, while a man who ran a cycle and motor-cycle repair business in the village ran alongside and kept the wheel from falling off the crowbar. . . . It took us a long time to drive the hundred yards or so up to the pub, for we had to go in reverse all the way.'

Above A Kriéger electric brougham of 1904. Although short-lived (1897–1907), this French company made some of the best electrically powered vehicles of their day. This particular model was briefly pressed into service again during the petrol crisis following the Anglo-French invasion of Suez in 1956.

Right The oldest surviving Mercedes, dating from 1902, this 25/28 hp model is mechanically similar in most respects to the trend-setting 35PS that Wilhelm Maybach had designed for Daimler the year before. In 1909–10 the bodywork of this car, like that of many other early Mercedes, was extensively modernised.

4 Edwardian Days

'The autocar has come to stay,' wrote the *London Magazine* in 1901, 'and it is one of the signs of the times that this fact has had to be admitted in all quarters. Slowly but surely the automobile has grown in public favour, and as the vehicles improve in working and design year by year, they will meet with more than proportionate patronage.'

One of the most influential patrons of motoring was England's new king, Edward VII. Unlike his mother, Queen Victoria, who never rode in a car (though she did buy a pedal tricycle in the 1880s), Edward was an early enthusiast for this novel method of transport. By 1900, while still Prince of Wales, he had ridden in both petrol and steam cars, and in that year he placed orders for a Serpollet steamer and a Daimler petrol car. A year or two later a Columbia Electric Victoria was bought for Queen Alexandra, who used it in the grounds of Sandringham, so that the Royal Family possessed examples of all three rival methods of propulsion.

After the Thousand Miles Trial of 1900, the event which really introduced motoring to the British public, Edward's first car was delivered. The Coventry Daimler company first submitted a car for approval to Lord Knollys, Master of the Horse, in January 1900, six months before delivery. Several features were criticised, such as the shallowness of the seating – the portly Prince valued comfort in his carriages – and the car was rejected.

A 6 hp Mail Phaeton was then driven to Buckingham Palace so that the prince himself could approve the design of the coachwork. Everything was satisfactory and Edward placed his order. Three months later, his partly completed car was taken to Sandringham so that he could check on progress. The Mail Phaeton was built on the latest Parisian Model chassis, with side gear and brake levers as well as a new style of bonnet and a more inclined steering column. The Prince requested minor amendments and the vehicle was returned to the works for completion.

The Hon. John Scott-Montagu, founding editor of *Car Illustrated*, takes the Prince of Wales (later King Edward VII) for a ride in his Coventry Daimler in 1899. This particular car ran the following year in the Thousand Miles Trial, a tour of Britain taking in Bristol, Manchester, Edinburgh, Leeds, Nottingham, and London; today it is a prized exhibit at the National Motor Museum founded by Scott-Montagu's son, Lord Montagu of Beaulieu.

It was eventually delivered to its Royal owner at Ascot in June by Oliver Stanton, the 'motor expert' who had taught Edward to drive and whose advice played a large part in the design of the royal cars. Soon, it seemed, all the British royals and members of the aristocracy were motoring – even the 82-year-old Duke of Cambridge, who was photographed 'enjoying a spin in the country' in the passenger seat of a Bollée *voiturette*.

Where the future king led, society soon followed. By the time Edward succeeded to the throne the list of distinguished motorists read like a page from Debrett. Among the younger set was the Hon. Charles S. Rolls, in those days a motor dealer, who would soon go into business with Henry Royce. All over Europe, this aristocratic patronage of the car followed a similar pattern. In Germany, for instance, Prinz Heinrich of Prussia (a relative of King Edward's) became an enthusiastic competition driver and in 1908 lent his name to what was to become a famous long-distance event – the Prince Henry Trial.

Coping with the law

In Britain, however, the fashionable enthusiasm for motoring came up against an often unreasonable hostility from county councils, which wanted to extend the legal restrictions placed on the use of cars. Some of this hostility, it seems, was fostered by powerful rural interests who depended for their living on horses, and who saw cars as a threat. Police were encouraged to set speed traps for motorists, and fines were often imposed on the strength of inaccurate readings of a half-crown stopwatch. When S. F. Edge, the man who made a commercial success of the Napier car, was 'trapped' by the Sussex police in 1903, however, electrical instruments were used to time his car over a measured length of road.

'Two fully-uniformed policemen suddenly darted out, apparently from a pig-sty,' reported the *Automotor Journal*, 'and stood with arms outstretched blocking the road. This sudden apparition was followed by a sound of men scrambling through the hedge a short distance behind, and two plain-clothes constables hurriedly proceeded to board the car, the one jumping on the step at the back of the tonneau, the other apparently endeavouring to throw himself bodily on to the steering wheel. The breathless four hardly appeared to know exactly what to do, so excited were they at having secured a prey. Mr Edge's name and address having been secured, he was presently solemnly informed that his speed over a furlong was 33 miles per hour [53 km/h] and was notified that a summons would follow'.

Left Motoring at its most basic: this Holsman gas buggy of 1902, with a two-cylinder engine and rope-belt drive, is typical of the high-built, large-wheeled runabouts designed to cope with the dirt roads of rural North America in early Edwardian days. Little more than self-propelled carts, such buggies were made obsolete by the Ford Model T in 1908.

Nor were the fines negligible. Claude Johnson, secretary of the Automobile Club of Great Britain and Ireland, was fined £20 plus costs at Thirsk in 1901 on a 'furious driving' charge. 'The state of things that makes possible such a perversion of justice is indeed deplorable,' thundered the *Daily Express*. The Andover Bench raised £1,000 in a single year on motoring fines, and the notorious Sergeant Jarrett of the Surrey Police caught so many

Below Lillie Hall, the Hon C. S. Rolls's motor-car emporium in west London, in 1903. The cars with the characteristically exposed radiator coil are Panhards (Rolls was Panhard et Levassor's London agent before joining Henry Royce in 1906). The first car on the left is a Mors.

speeding motorists that he was promoted to inspector within 12 months.

There was, of course, another side to this. Cars had become faster, and owners of high-powered cars did undoubtedly extend them to the full. Hoping for some measure of relief from 'persecution', motorists agreed to have their cars numbered for easy identification in exchange for a raising of the speed limit to 32 km/h (20 mph). But the surveillance persisted. *Autocar* continued to publish weekly maps of known speed traps, and the Automobile Association grew out of a road patrol set up to warn motorists of police trapping on the London-to-Brighton road.

Better performance and styling

Development of motor cars in the first years of this century was swift, especially after the success of Maybach's epoch-making Mercedes (*see* Chapter 3). Racing improved the mechanics of the machines. Lessons learned in the marathon road races on the Continent were soon translated into better performance, greater sophistication, and improved reliability. By 1903 lady drivers were to be seen at the wheel of 20 hp cars, where only a couple of years before they would have restricted themselves to light cars of about 4 hp (but they still would have needed a strong-armed coachman to crank-start the vehicle).

Parallel with the development of faster cars for the very rich – the owner of a powerful machine might run up an annual tyre bill of £600 to £1,000 in those days – came the refinement of coachwork. Car makers now began to realize that styling was as important in clinching sales as sound engineering. An important advance came in 1902 when Rothschild of Paris built a handsome four-seat touring body to the order of King Leopold of Belgium. Its comfortable seats, it was said, had been patterned on the armchairs in the boudoir of the king's *petite amie* Cléo de Mérode; but the overall design was the work of a gifted mezzotinter, Ferdinand Charles – who thus became the first car stylist (in the 1930s he would work for Morris). The *Roi-des-Belges* design was widely copied, and brought with it longer chassis to accommodate the side entrance to the rear seats that was an integral part of the concept. It rapidly eliminated the old rear-entrance *tonneau* that had been the most common form of four-seat bodywork since 1899.

Extra power also meant that closed cars became available, although one of the very earliest examples of the type had appeared in 1899 on a Renault *voiturette* of only $1\frac{3}{4}$ hp. For those who could not afford four-figure tyre bills, small cars like the Renault – one of the

first makes to feature shaft drive instead of chains – had much to recommend them. Probably the greatest reason for the success of such vehicles was the development of the $3\frac{1}{2}$ hp De Dion-Bouton engine of 1895, the first and perhaps the best of all the proprietary power units available to car constructors at that period.

Equipped with a reliable electric ignition system, the De Dion-Bouton engine could run at far greater speeds than any other. In production form it was capable of a steady 2,000 rpm; on the test bench it could attain a remarkable 3,500 rpm. It was built in large numbers and at such a rate that any engine which failed to pass its final tests at the factory was dismantled for use as spares – a quicker procedure than searching for the faults and having them remedied.

Mass-production methods

Mass production on the European plan, pioneered by Renault and Panhard et Levassor,

Above A Mercedes-Simplex tourer of 1903–4. Powered by a four-cylinder engine of 5.3 litres, with chain drive to the rear wheels, it could cruise effortlessly at 60 km/h (37 mph).

Below A De Diétrich four-cylinder tourer of 1903. One of the great French marques of pre-World War I days, the De Diétrich enjoyed notable racing success in the first five years of this century. This model, like most others in the range at that time, was based on a design of the Turcat-Méry company.

was based on a large pool of cheap skilled labour. Workmen of the right calibre were easily found, and consequently the cost of hand assembly, fit, and finishing for engines and cars was negligible. In America, however, things were very different. Skilled men had been scarce and a more sophisticated technology had evolved in which unskilled men assembled interchangeable parts that had been made by machines designed by the engineers.

Production of interchangeable parts in quantity went back to 1798, when the United States government gave Eli Whitney, inventor of the cotton gin, a rush order for 10,000 muskets. Whitney built machines that duplicated gun components so precisely that the job of assembling them was made comparatively easy. At a demonstration for the army he placed the component parts of 10 muskets in separate piles, then took parts at random from the piles to assemble a musket quickly. As early as 1783 Oliver Evans had used belt, screw, and bucket conveyors in an automatic grain mill, a technique advanced still further in the 1860s, when Chicago meatpackers used overhead conveyor rails to move pig carcasses through a factory, each worker performing a single operation on a carcass instead of butchering an entire animal at a time. Output per man more than doubled with this method.

With such a background it is hardly surprising that America produced the first truly mass-produced cars. This occurred at the turn of the century with the Locomobile steam car, developed from the original design of the twins F. E. and F. O. Stanley. Cheap and easily produced, the Locomobile accounted for 4,000 of the 8,000 cars running in the United States in 1901. The company's factory at Seaside Park, Bridgeport, Connecticut, was said to be the largest, most modern, and most complete steam-automobile plant in the world and was capable of producing more than 20 vehicles a day.

Locomobiles were made on the interchangeable system, which is a great convenience to the owner of an automobile'. Furthermore, Locomobile supported its production methods with an efficient sales and service network. 'In order to take the best possible care of our customers, we have opened and maintained branch houses in many of the large cities throughout the world, and have contracted with reliable firms to handle our product in other cities, so that our system of stations is very complete and well organized. The Locomobile System is very convenient, because it enables a customer to take extended tours and never be far distant from some station, where his carriage can be replenished with the necessary supplies, or be given such attention

Above Henry Ford's first production car, the Model A of 1903, had an 8 hp flat-twin engine mounted beneath the seats and chain drive. The bodywork is in the *tonneau* style popular at the time, with a 'back' door dividing the rear seat bench.

as it may require. . . . Our six-storey Repository and Salesroom, at Broadway and Seventy-sixth Street, New York, is the largest in the United States. Our London establishment, at 39 Sussex Place, South Kensington, is not only the largest automobile repository in England or on the Continent, but the largest in the world.'

It is ironic that, having so successfully forecast the future pattern of motor manufacture and servicing, Locomobile should in 1903 have abandoned its mass-produced steamers and turned to the manufacture of hand-built, expensive petrol cars designed by A. L. Riker, who had made his name as a builder of electric carriages in the 1890s.

Below One of the best-known American steam cars of the Edwardian period was the White, produced by a Cleveland sewing-machine manufacturer. This 30 hp model of 1907–8 was used by President Theodore Roosevelt (seen here in the back seat); another White served his successor, William Howard Taft.

Herbert Austin's company was just three years old when it produced this smart town carriage in 1909. Its 15 hp, four-cylinder engine was located beneath the driver's seat. The compartment behind was high enough for top-hatted passengers to enter with hardly a stoop. This car is similar to the one used by Emmeline Pankhurst during her around-England tour in the cause of women's suffrage in 1910.

Enter the Oldsmobile

The place of the Locomobile steamer in mass-production methods was taken by the little Oldsmobile Curved Dash, a single-cylinder gas buggy built by Ransom Eli Olds in Detroit, which was now becoming a centre of motor manufacture. Olds recalled the reasoning behind this car: 'My whole idea in building it was to have the operation so simple that anyone could run it and the construction such that it could be repaired at any local shop.' A primitive form of market research proved successful. 'We rushed a few of them out as fast as possible, and they tested out so well that I decided to put them on the market immediately.'

The project, however, almost ended in disaster. The first prototype of the production version had been completed and the blueprints finalized when a workman at the factory pulled his forge fire too close to a gas-filled rubber bag and a terrific explosion occurred. The new factory was gutted by fire within an hour. All the blueprints were destroyed, but a quick-thinking young timekeeper saved the day by pushing the prototype to safety. While another factory was being built at Lansing in Michigan (Olds's home town), the car was taken apart and details recorded so that new blueprints could be drawn.

The little Olds proved an immediate success: 600 were built in 1901, 2,500 in 1902, 4,000 in 1903, and 5,000 in 1904. Then Olds' backers decided to abandon the popular-car field and introduce a high-priced 'European' type of car. Olds sold his interest in the company – but within two months he had found backers to form a new company, which produced the Reo – a name derived from Olds' initials.

It was, however, the Oldsmobile runabout which typified the first successful American cars, for the 'gas buggy' was exactly what people in that vast country wanted. Outside city limits roads were generally poor or non-existent, and few potential car buyers believed that a car would be able to cope with such conditions. The Oldsmobile, however, proved itself fully equal to rural motoring problems when an early production model made a winter trip from Lansing to the New York Motor Show – where a sales contract was signed for a thousand of these runabouts.

Europe viewed early American cars with suspicion. In the bicycle boom of the 1890s large numbers of cheap, shoddy American cycles had been imported, and the motoring public believed American cars must be equally poor. Percival Perry, who helped uncrate the first Ford cars to reach Britain in 1903, and who eventually became the head of Ford operations in Europe, was greatly despondent: 'The motor agent would have none of the car. The public, its opinions fostered by an anti-American press, could not be induced to vacate its position of insular indifference. In externals it conflicted with the accepted canons of motoring form. In internals it was regarded as of string and hoop-iron, and fitting food for the scrap-heap, to which it must certainly go after a few weeks of inglorious life'.

Perry's Central Motor Car Agency sold only a dozen Ford Model As in Britain in a year. This antipathy of the British buyer was not reflected in the United States where the Ford company, after initial worries, proved to be a great success. It began to pay its way within a month of its incorporation in June 1903, and built 1,708 cars in its first year. It was only after Henry Ford introduced his famous 'universal car', the Model T, in October 1908 that American ideas of mass-production would find an enthusiastic response in Europe. But already America was set to take over from France as world leader in car manufacture, and Henry Ford, the 'engineer by instinct' from Dearborn, Michigan, would be the major figure in the growth of the American motor industry.

Motoring in the veteran era

Everywhere, it seemed, the motor car was gaining acceptance as a normal means of transport by those who could afford it, and the number of cars in use rose steadily. By mid-1904 there were 40,000 cars and motorcycles registered in the United Kingdom; in America production rose from 4,200 cars in 1900 to 25,000 in 1905, and would pass 180,000 before the end of the decade.

What is now known as the veteran era of motoring – the period up to 1904 – was the most remarkable in the development of the motor car. Within a decade the maximum speed of the fastest production cars had risen from around 24 km/h (15 mph) to almost 160 km/h (100 mph), and the motor vehicle had become a regular, if not yet everyday, feature of the landscape. Mechanical proficiency would be attained only through the efforts of those enthusiasts who, in the words of Rudyard Kipling (a pioneer motorist himself), 'chased the inchoate idea to fixity up and down the King's Highway with their red right shoulders to the wheel.'

Travelling hopefully, European motorists were already venturing on long continental tours with fair hopes that their vehicles would prove equal to the task. The 'motor logs' that the tourists of those days delighted to keep relate, however, the occasional inconvenience. 'Finding we could get no power out of the car', wrote one traveller, 'we examined the carburettor, and, finding the jet was clear, we were lucky enough to locate the trouble in the inlet valves; these were very sticky, owing, I think, to some new kind of petrol a man had persuaded me to try, and which I never came across again. We discovered afterwards it had a tinge of yellow in it, possibly due to impurities, which may have accounted for the sticky deposit it left in the cylinders. . . .

'We had trouble going up a steep hill. As usual, two of us jumped out to walk up, leaving my uncle to drive the car. The hill, however, proved too steep, and the car started to run backwards. We quickly got out a suitcase from the car and jammed it under a back wheel, then took out all the luggage,

spare oil and petrol, to lighten the car as much as possible, and, with my uncle walking alongside to steer it, the car slowly made its way to the top of the hill, cheered by the onlookers, who had seen few cars at that time. Crowds used to gather round us whenever we stopped in a town or village.'

So the veteran motorist had to be an optimist, mechanic, and athlete, prepared to walk when the car would not run, and hopeful that the next village might have an enterprising cycle agent or hotel-owner with a gallon or two of 'motor spirit' in stock. The prudent tourist always telegraphed his orders for petrol and oil to the dealers *en route* well in advance.

The motorist might even have to spend a night under the stars beside a broken-down vehicle. One of the first lady motorists, Dorothy Levitt, warned that 'if you are going to drive alone in highways and byways it might be advisable to carry a small revolver. I have an automatic Colt and find it very easy to handle as there is practically no recoil.' Motorists in those days had to be prepared for anything.

Above left The 1903 Vauxhall two-seater was one of this marine-engine company's earliest models. It had a single-cylinder engine and chain drive. Its steering tiller, mounted at the side of the body, distinguished it from a similar 1904 model that had a steering wheel.

Above The 8 hp, twin-cylinder Peugeot of 1904 had a pressed-steel chassis, mechanically operated valves, and a honeycomb radiator.

Below A 1909 Thomas Flyer K-6-70, with a massive 72 hp, six-cylinder engine and a chain driving each rear wheel. Although it was a sedate-looking cabriolet, this model was mechanically similar to the car that won the 1908 race from New York to Paris via China and Siberia.

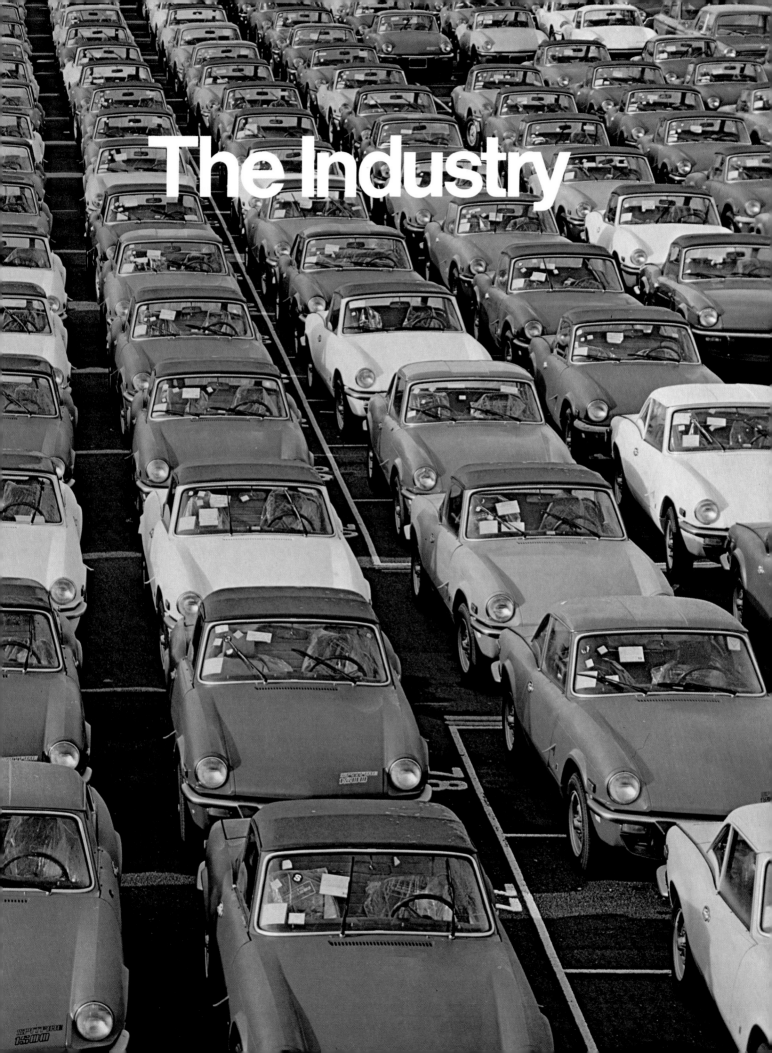

The Industry

5 Rise of a World Industry

From modest beginnings in the closing years of the 19th century, the motor industry has grown to a point where it is dominated by vast corporations operating internationally. In North America, western Europe, and Japan motor-car factories exert a major influence in national economies. The photograph shows an aerial view of the Ford factory at Dagenham, one of the company's 23 plants in western Europe.

Apart from some Coventry Daimlers built under licence by Harry Lawson's British Motor Syndicate, very few cars were made in Britain before the turn of the century. There were pioneers such as Frederick Lanchester and Herbert Austin, who produced some interesting prototypes in 1894 and 1895, but would-be manufacturers were put off by the uncertainty created by Lawson's claims to hold a monopoly of patents for making motor cars. Until this claim was disposed of in the courts there was virtually no British motor industry. Anyone wanting to take up the new pastime of motoring usually bought a French car, for it was in France – even more than in Germany, where the first motor car had been sold to the public in 1887 – that a motor industry worthy of the name had become established.

The French motor industry started in 1892 when the firm of Panhard et Levassor issued its first catalogue of 'carriages powered by petroleum engines on the Daimler system'. As well as producing their own cars, they supplied engines to many early motor manufacturers, including the English Daimler company. The same course was followed by Comte Albert de Dion and his partner Georges Bouton with the engine of their De Dion-Bouton car. More than 30 firms in France started making cars with this engine – enough to constitute an industry in themselves – besides nine in England, six in Italy, and five each in Germany and the United States.

In France the splendid *routes nationales* enabled races to be held from 1894 onwards, thus demonstrating the speed and durability of the new vehicles. In these favourable circumstances French motor firms had produced 1,850 cars by 1898, about 100 of them being exported to Britain. Since racing on public roads was forbidden in the United Kingdom, the Automobile Club of Great Britain and Ireland did the next best thing and organised the Thousand Miles Trial around Britain in 1900 with the object of showing that motor cars were both safe and reliable. As it happened, 23 of the 65 cars completed the course officially – and not one had a serious accident. The trial marked the true beginning of the British motor industry, for the manufacture of cars to meet the resulting public demand at last got under way. By 1906 the number of cars registered in Britain had risen in two years from 8,500 to 23,000.

In spite of their efforts to make up lost ground, British companies still supplied only about 60 per cent of the new cars registered. In 1906 French cars were imported at the rate of 400 a month as against the export of only two British cars a month to France.

The commercial production of cars was carried on in France for nearly a decade before automobiles were made in any quantity in the United States. This slow initial development compared with Europe was largely due to the lack of highways suitable for motor cars outside the cities. Individual American pioneers were early in the field, including Henry Ford, who produced his experimental Quadricycle in 1896. But the manufacture of self-propelled highway vehicles did not appear as a separate industrial classification in the 1900 American census.

It did not take long for the American motor industry to catch up and far outstrip Europe. Within three years 88 firms had joined the 'car rush' and by 1906, when the total number of cars on the road in Britain was 45,000, the registrations of American cars had soared to 142,000. Of greater significance is the fact that the output of cars in the United States that year exceeded that of France for the first time.

Initially the Americans were handicapped by knowing very little about the technical progress in the design of cars being made in Europe. They still thought of the automobile as a horseless buggy with a single- or twin-cylinder engine underneath the seat. It was not until 1904 that they came to accept the European concept of a larger vehicle with a more powerful four-cylinder engine mounted at the front.

The early American industry

Henry Ford, like Ransom Olds (*see* Chapter 4), quarelled with his backers over the type of car to produce. In 1900, after a false start with

the Detroit Automobile Company, he formed the
Henry Ford Company, but was accused by his
backer of being more interested in motor racing
– at which he was quite successful – than in
making cars for sale. So in 1903 Ford left and
formed the Ford Motor Company with a new
financial supporter. They, too, quickly found
themselves at loggerheads, the main investor
and his friends advocating high-priced cars and
Ford hankering after a low-priced model produced in large quantities.

His first effort was the Model A, or Ford-
mobile runabout, a horseless buggy on the
lines of the Oldsmobile with a twin-cylinder
engine under the seat. This was followed by a
similar car but with a four-seater body and the
engine in front.Neither was a success, so Ford
bowed to the wishes of his directors (and to the
current trend towards the European type of
car) by producing the four-cylinder Model B
and the six-cylinder Model K. Eventually Ford
got rid of his troublesome chief shareholder
with the support of his remaining backers and

was at last free to go his own way. A new car,
the Model N, was an immediate success,
netting a profit of $1 million in 1907 and putting
the company alongside Buick and Maxwell as
the front runners of the American industry.

The Model N was only a stop-gap while
Ford perfected the car of his dreams. This was
to be a car for the ordinary man throughout the
United States and, possibly, the world. It was
to be reliable and durable, easy to drive,
maintain, and repair, and able to cope with the
worst roads – or, if need be, no road at all. And
it must not cost more than $500 (the equivalent,
at the time, of about £125).

The famous Model T appeared in 1908 and
superseded all other Ford models. In terms of
sales it seemed likely to supersede all its
competitors as well. In 1909 sales shot up to
12,292 and profit reached $27 million. Three
years later the output was 75,000 cars. But
Ford and his colleagues had set their sights
much higher. At the new factory at Highland
Park, Detroit, which had been completed in

An 1899 Cannstatt Daimler
Phönix. The model was
raced at Nice that year by
Emil Jellinek. Daimler
adopted the marque name
Mercedes for its private cars
in 1902. The Stuttgart firm
of Daimler Benz arose from
the merger of Mercedes and
Benz in 1926.

1910, conveyor systems were installed to bring every component and part to the chassis as it moved along the final assembly line. The system came into operation in 1913, and the next year Ford produced 250,000 cars. By 1916 the price was down to $400. Mass production was not new, but the added benefit of the moving assembly line brought about a technological revolution that put the United States years ahead of the rest of the world.

Henry Ford's concentration on the Model T, with its combination of mass sales and low price, was not the only development that transformed the American motor industry in its formative years. William C. Durant, a successful builder of carts and carriages until he bought a controlling interest in the Buick Motor Company in 1904, set out to market a range of cars that would suit all tastes and purses by amalgamating a number of manufacturers within one group. With Buick as his base, he formed the General Motors Company in 1908 and followed this up by buying every company he could lay his hands on. He acquired not only reputable firms such as Cadillac, Oldsmobile, and Oakland but also a number of manufacturers who had never made much of a mark. He even tried (for the second time) to buy up Ford.

Durant's skill as an entrepreneur was not matched by an equal ability as an administrator, and his hotch-potch of companies, lacking any coordination, soon got into difficulties. In 1910 the bank stepped in to save the company from disaster, on condition that Durant took no further part in its management. Durant was by no means finished, however. Less than 12 months later he started the Chevrolet Motor Company and over the next five years he systematically gained control of the General Motors Company by exchanging five Chevrolet shares for every General Motors share he could obtain. When the bank's control came to an end in 1915, Durant returned to GM as president.

The European scene

Compared with the colossal growth in the United States, the progress made by European motor manufacturers was painfully slow. In 1913, when 483,000 cars were made in the United States, the total output in Britain, for example, was 23,238. Wolseley, the leading British company, made about 3,000 cars that year, just ahead of Humber, followed by Sunbeam, Rover, and Austin. The first Morris left the factory on 28 March, and 352 had been made by the end of the year. Nearly half the 200 companies that had tried making cars had by then dropped by the wayside, but the

survivors included some famous names in the British motor industry. There was Daimler, which had started making cars in 1897, Humber and Sunbeam (1898), Lanchester and Napier (1900), Vauxhall and Standard (1903), and Rolls-Royce (1904).

The situation was healthier in France where Renault, the leading manufacturer, proudly announced in 1913 that it had, for the first time, produced 10,000 cars in one year. The main Italian company, Fiat, made about half that number.

World War I almost halted the production

The firm of De Dion, Bouton, et Trépardoux of Paris produced its first steam-powered tricycle in 1883. Trépardoux resigned when the firm began to manufacture petrol-engined cars in the early 1890s. A major European maker of family cars until 1914, De Dion, Bouton et Cie failed to thrive after World War I; finally ceasing production in 1932.

of cars in Europe, but it made little difference in the United States, which entered the war only in 1917. In that year Ford produced 750,000 cars, six times as many as Chevrolet, which was ahead of Overland and Dodge.

Developments in the 1920s

In 1918 William Durant formed the General Motors Corporation to take over the property of the Chevrolet Motor Company and with it the General Motors Company with its Buick, Cadillac, Oldsmobile, and Oakland subsidiaries. Two years later, faced with the threat of personal insolvency, Durant was rescued by the Dupont company, which bought his stock and settled his obligations in return for his resignation, thereby avoiding a scandal. So Durant left General Motors for the second and last time. By then he had fallen out with two of his colleagues: Alfred P. Sloan, Jr, who reorganized the corporation on decentralized lines that became the pattern for big business all over the world; and Walter P. Chrysler, the head of Buick, who in 1923 formed the Chrysler Motor Corporation to make a new car that was so successful that his corporation would emerge in the late 1930s alongside Ford and General Motors as one of the 'Big Three'. In 1929, just before the slump, America produced 5,337,687 cars; three years later sales had fallen to 1,331,860.

Perhaps the most important trend in the United States in the 1920s was the reversal of the relative positions of Ford and General Motors. Henry Ford's insistence on continuing the ever-popular Model T as his only product caught up with him as the gallant old 'Tin Lizzie' began to lose sales to newer and better cars. The last Model T rolled off the River Rouge line on 28 May 1928, by which time 15 million had been produced. Its successor, a new Model A, saved Henry Ford in the nick of time, but from then on the Ford Motor Company had to yield first place to General Motors.

The 1920s also saw a marked increase in the influence of the United States motor industry in Europe. General Motors, after failing to buy Austin, purchased Vauxhall Motors in 1925. In 1929 Henry Ford, accompanied by his son Edsel and grandson Henry II, laid the foundation stone of an impressive new factory at Dagenham on the Thames, where the first European-made Ford was built in 1931. The two American giants also moved into Germany, Ford starting assembly in Berlin in 1926 and opening a new factory at Cologne in 1931, and General Motors acquiring Opel in 1929.

Some 40 new companies entered the British motor industry within two years of the 1918 armistice, but not all of them survived the

slump of 1920. Austin was put in the hands of the receiver, but recovered by making the famous Austin Seven. National car output was still relatively small. In 1920, when American output exceeded 2 million for the first time, Britain produced 60,000 cars, one quarter of them Ford Model Ts assembled at Manchester; Morris's share was 1,932. The Morris Cowley – and the way it was marketed – was so successful that by 1925 Morris was manufacturing 55,000 cars a year in a total output of 132,000 British cars. William Morris extended his hold on the market by personally acquiring Wolseley Motors from the liquidator in 1927 and selling

Above A 1901–2 Olds Curved Dash, the world's first mass-produced car. Ransom Eli Olds left the company in 1904, and five years later Oldsmobile was acquired by William C. Durant's fast-growing General Motors Company.

Below Henry Ford at the wheel of an early two-seat version of the Model A, which in 1903 became his first production car.

it to Morris Motors in 1935, when that concern also bought the MG Car Company. Three years later Riley Motors was brought into the fold.

Meanwhile a powerful new motor car group appeared when the Rootes brothers, who had started after the war as motor dealers, moved first into distribution and then into manufacture by acquiring Hillman and Humber in 1927, and the Sunbeam and Talbot companies of the Sunbeam-Talbot-Darracq combine which went into liquidation in 1935.

Under the energetic leadership of John Black, the old Standard Motor Company had been lifted to the ranks of Britain's major motor manufacturers before the outbreak of World War II disrupted the production of cars. This had reached a peak of 389,633 in 1937, over 90 per cent of them coming from the factories of the 'Big Six' – Austin, Ford, Morris, Rootes, Standard, and Vauxhall. Of some 100 British car companies that had exhibited at the 1920 Motor Show, only about 20 were still in business.

William Morris and Herbert Austin were both inspired by Ford and General Motors, and so too in France were Louis Renault and André Citroën, the latter starting manufacture in 1919. By 1922 Citroën was producing 100 cars a day, and for the next decade he fought a battle with Louis Renault for leadership of the French motor industry. In the end his reckless financial behaviour proved his undoing, and his debtors forced his resignation when he was on the point of introducing the classic 7CV *traction-avant* (front-wheel drive) that was to vindicate his engineering reputation and assure the future of the company.

Appearance of the multi-nationals

Until 1939 the world export trade had been dominated by American cars, which were strongly made and designed for road conditions that were much the same in many parts of the United States as they were in the rest of the world. When World War II ended, the latest American models were found to be too big, too heavy, and too expensive to run in most countries. The opportunity was seized by the European manufacturers, including the American-owned subsidiaries, to fill the gap with lighter, better designed, and more economical cars that were also sturdy enough to stand up to rough roads. Large numbers were exported to all parts of the world. So acceptable were these small cars (especially the Volkswagen) that towards the end of the 1960s, boosted by the beginning of a flood from Japan, their sales in America actually exceeded those of Chrysler, one of the 'Big Three'.

Once the large American car had lost its

export attraction, the American manufacturers' efforts to supply the world with cars called for a new policy, and so they became multi-national companies.

In the 1950s Ford increased the number of its overseas manufacturing and assembly operations, accelerating the process in the 1960s and 1970s until Ford cars were being manufactured and assembled by 15 separate national companies at 23 locations in western Europe; seven subsidiary companies at 11 locations in the Asia-Pacific area; and six national companies at 15 locations in Latin America and South Africa. In addition there were many dealer-assemblers throughout the world. In 1977 Ford's worldwide factory sales of cars, trucks, and tractors totalled 6.5 million units.

Since the war Ford had gradually developed a policy of co-ordinating the operations of its British and German subsidiaries, culminating in the merging of their separate identities in 1967 into an integrated organization, Ford-Europe. The stage had been reached when the manufacture of one model could be switched from one company (and country) to another, and one model could be made simultaneously in

Above A Wolseley 40/50 limousine of 1910. Wolseley was one of the earliest British marques, its first prototype being designed by Herbert Austin, then the company's manager, in 1896. Wolseley was acquired by Morris in 1927; the last models to bear the name appeared in the mid-1970s.

Right Henry Ford's long-held dominance of the popular-car market in the United States is evident in this street scene in Henderson, Texas, about 1923; almost every car in the picture is a Model T.

Below Louis Chevrolet in his first prototype, a 4.9-litre of 1911. The Chevrolet company became part of General Motors in 1917, and 10 years later its cars outsold Ford's for the first time.

different countries, leading to the ultimate development of a new European car, the Fiesta (*see* Chapter 8), which was designed in the United States and Europe and assembled in three plants in Britain, Germany, and Spain from components made in 12 factories in six European countries. Beginning with sales in 14 European countries (where half-a-million cars were sold in the first 14 months) and with projects for it to be manufactured in Brazil and Australasia and possibly assembled in the United States, the Fiesta had good prospects of becoming Ford's first 'universal' car since the Model T.

General Motors, too, developed its own 'world' model in the form of the T-car, which was master-minded in the United States in liaison with 'satellite' design and engineering teams and resulted in basically similar cars being made under various names (Chevette, Kadett, and Gemini) in the United States, Brazil, Britain, Germany, and Japan. In Europe the two GM subsidiaries remained distinct, but passenger-car engineering was integrated under a single chief engineer at Opel, while a strong design group was stationed at Vauxhall.

In 1977 General Motors sold 5,778,000 cars from its factories in the United States and Canada and 1,313,000 manufactured and assembled overseas, making a global total of 7,090,000 cars – by far the largest output in the world. Cars were manufactured overseas by subsidiary companies in the United Kingdom (Vauxhall), West Germany (Opel), Australia (GM Holden), Brazil (GM), South Africa (GM), Korea (Saehan Motor Company, 50 per cent GM), and Japan, where the Isuzu Motor Company, in which GM had a one-third interest, manufactured the T-car under contract.

Chrysler did not enter Europe as manufacturers until 1958, when it bought Ford's 15 per cent interest in Simca of France. By 1966 it had 76 per cent, and thus had complete control. In 1963 it moved into Spain and bought 40 per cent of the shares of Barreros, increasing this holding to 70 per cent in 1967 and changing the name to Chrysler España in 1970. In 1964 it accepted an invitation to buy a 30 per cent interest in the Rootes Group, which gave it three manufacturing bases in Europe. In 1967 the Rootes Group became Chrysler United Kingdom, a wholly owned subsidiary, but the American parent company had to seek massive financial assistance from the British government in 1975 in order to introduce new British models. In 1977 Chrysler UK lost £21.5 million (which was partly offset by a grant of £10 million from the British government); Chrysler France suffered a setback owing to lower sales and increased costs; while only Chrysler

España, the smallest of the three, improved its earnings.

Faced with the need for heavy capital expenditure at home to meet the new federal standards for exhaust emissions, fuel economy, and safety, and to pay for increased costs of their new model programme, Chrysler Corporation decided in 1978 to sell its European interests to Peugeot-Citroën for £117 million, receiving a 15 per cent share in the new enlarged combine. Although the loss of this European output (estimated to be about 750,000 cars in 1977) would mean a sharp reduction in its world sales, which amounted to 3,068,691 motor vehicles of all types in 1977, Chrysler's main concern was to regain and enlarge its share of the United States market, which had dropped from 15.9 per cent to 14.5 per cent (1,341,014 cars) in 1977.

Even though it was pulling out of Europe, Chrysler was still a worldwide corporation with companies in Australasia, Argentina, Brazil, Colombia, Peru, Mexico, and Venezuela. It also had a 15 per cent holding in the big Mitsubishi company in Japan, which enabled it to sell, and in some cases assemble, Mitsubishi cars as Dodge and Plymouth models in many world markets. In 1977 Chrysler sold 207,428 of the 764,253 cars produced by Mitsubishi.

Mergers in Britain and France

Of the leading native British firms, Austin and Morris closed their ranks in 1952 to form the British Motor Corporation, and seven years later BMC launched the famous Mini. With its transverse engine and front wheel drive the Mini set the pattern for future generations of small cars. In 1966 BMC merged with Jaguar to form British Motor Holdings. Meanwhile the move towards amalgamations had continued in 1961 with the purchase of Standard and its Triumph subsidiary by Leyland, the commercial-vehicle group, followed by the acquisition of Rover in 1967. A year later, under pressure from the government, the two groups were brought together as the British Leyland Motor Corporation. But the conglomeration of companies and widely scattered plants proved unwieldy, and British Leyland was saved from bankruptcy only by being nationalized under the control of the National Enterprise Board. But this was no panacea either, and successive managements were faced with grave difficulties on many fronts. In 1977 British Leyland produced 760,000 cars, compared with 961,000 in 1970. It had 26 wholly or partly owned manufacturing plants abroad, and its cars were being assembled in 44 plants in 33 countries. In the higher-priced categories British Leyland's Jaguar and Rover models

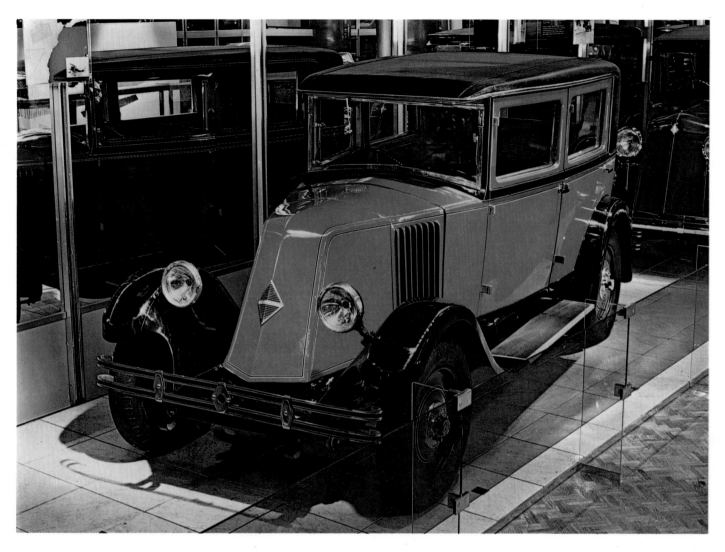

were a match for any of their European or Japanese competitors, while the latest products of the independent Rolls-Royce Motors stood at the pinnacle of the luxury car market throughout the world.

At the end of World War II the Renault company, its Billancourt plant in the western suburbs of Paris devastated by bombs, was made a state-owned concern with a largely autonomous management. Its recovery and subsequent growth was a brilliant feature of the renaissance of France as an international power. Expansion at home was accompanied by even greater expansion abroad, and by 1977 manufacturing plants were operating on a worldwide scale – six in Europe, seven in Africa, six in Central and South America, six in Asia, and two in Australia. Renault cars were also being assembled in 27 foreign countries. The total output in 1977 was 1,737,707 cars. In 1966 Renault signed an agreement with its old rival, Peugeot, to pool their technical resources, the first result being the construction of a co-operative engine factory in which Volvo, of Sweden, became a partner. The first major product of this factory was a V6 engine used in models of all three companies.

Meanwhile, Peugeot had received a signal of distress from Citroën in 1974, to which it responded by taking over Citroën's management as the first step in a complete merger of the two companies – one (Citroën) with a reputation for cars of advanced design, the other for cars of outstanding strength and durability. The new company, Peugeot-Citroën, produced 1,343,389 cars in 1977 and had 11.6 per cent of the European market, with many outlets abroad. The group moved into eastern Europe in 1978 with an agreement to build a £250 million plant in East Germany.

The acquisition of Chrysler France (Simca), Chrysler UK, and Chrysler España has made Peugeot-Citroën (on 1977 figures) the largest car producer in Europe and third largest in the world. From 1979, models of the former Chrysler UK were marketed as Talbots.

A 1927 Renault 3.2-litre saloon. Founded in 1898, Renault had become the largest European car manufacturer before World War I, producing 10,000 cars in 1913 and employing more than 5,000 people at its Billancourt factory in the Paris suburbs. Since 1945 the company has been government-owned, and today its cars are manufactured in 27 plants all over the world.

Italian and German fortunes

State intervention had come to Italy as far back as 1932, when Alfa Romeo was incorporated in the Istituto per la Reconstruzione Industriale (IRI), which was responsible for nationalized industries in Italy. Alfa Romeo is a member of the corporation and directly responsible to it. In the 1960s an ambitious programme was undertaken to enlarge the company's range – and to alleviate unemployment in southern Italy – by establishing a factory at Naples. Production of the small, mass-produced Alfa-sud started there in 1972, but output did not reach the targets set. Alfa Romeo makes all its cars in Italy; there are 14 overseas subsidiary companies, but cars are assembled only in South Africa. The company produced 201,000 cars in 1977.

Since the war the Italian giant, Fiat, has grown even larger at home by the acquisition of Lancia, Autobianchi, and Ferrari. In 1977 Fiat produced 1,275,500 cars of all makes in Italy and 114,200 made by subsidiary companies in Argentina and Brazil. Cars made under licence in Spain, Turkey, Yugoslavia, and Poland totalled 765,800.

The recovery of the German motor industry after its virtual destruction in the war was marked not only by the speed with which it was accomplished but by the emergence of a new state-owned company producing a model,

commissioned by Hitler before the war, known as the 'people's car'. Under the experienced control of Heinz Nordhoff, Volkswagen was soon in the front rank of European manufacturers with a large export trade in carefully selected and prepared markets. By 1977 Volkswagen was producing nearly 2 million cars a year. It was the first non-American company to assemble cars in the United States, where its domination of the import market has been seriously eroded in recent years by the Japanese. There are wholly owned VW subsidiaries in Belgium, Brazil, Mexico, South Africa, and the United States. VWs are also assembled in Yugoslavia and Nigeria.

The German subsidiaries of Ford and General Motors responded to the VW challenge with new models and greatly enlarged output. In the higher-priced field Mercedes-Benz continued its original policy of making cars of very high quality. They in turn were challenged by BMW cars, and both were given increased competition by the larger models produced by Ford and Opel. In all, Germany produced 3.7 million cars in 1977.

Manufacture around the world

Until World War II the manufacture of cars was almost entirely confined to the traditional car-producing countries: the United States, Britain, France, Germany, and Italy. In the post-war years motor manufacture spread in many directions. By far the biggest development, which changed the global picture, occurred in Japan; while the Netherlands, Soviet Union, Sweden, Spain, and Brazil all achieved sizeable motor industries. On a smaller scale the manufacture of cars, usually with the help of American and European companies, was started in eastern Europe, the Near East, Africa, Central and South America, and Asia. Assembly plants proliferated in countless countries.

In Japan both the leading companies, Toyota and Nissan (Datsun), had made cars before the war, but not in large numbers. In 1933 the Toyoda Loom Works, a maker of sewing machines, started a department to develop a motor car. In 1937 it was made an independent business under the name Toyota. After the war the company was reconstructed with the backing of the Bank of Japan and was divided into two separate companies for sales and manufacture. By 1977 Toyota had an output of 1,884,260 cars, of which 968,270 were exported. The cars were all manufactured in Tokyo – there were no overseas manufacturing plants – but 192,000 of the cars exported were assembled in 15 countries. Negotiations were begun to start an assembly plant in the United States, where Toyota was the top importer, and a

An Austin advertisement of the early 1920s. The rapidly escalating price of the Twenty model brought Herbert Austin's 16-year-old company to the edge of bankruptcy in 1922, but its fortunes were to be revived by the famous Seven introduced that year. Austin joined forces with Morris in 1952 to form the British Motor Corporation, and the two marques are now a cornerstone of the nationalized British Leyland.

Where the *Austin* "Twenty" is made.

joint (90 per cent Toyota) company in Australia began making Corolla engines in 1978.

A Datsun version of the original Austin Seven had been made under licence in the 1920s, and after World War II Nissan made Austin cars under licence for a few years. In 1959 entirely new Datsun models were introduced and the company embarked on an enormous expansion of world trade with its own fleet of car-carrying ships. In 1977 Nissan produced 1,615,886 Datsun cars, of which 855,462 were exported. Like Toyota's, Nissan's policy was to manufacture cars, either complete or in completely knocked-down form (CKD), in Japan only. Again like Toyota, it plans to assemble cars in the United States. Most of the companies operating Datsun assembly plants in 21 countries were completely separate from Nissan and were locally owned.

Honda, the motor-cycle firm, produced its first car in 1962. The Civic model, introduced in 1972, had sold 1 million four years later, and was joined by the Accord.

Brazil's motor industry was developed in the first place through the assembly operations of American and European subsidiary companies with CKD kits, working up to 100 per cent local manufacture. Volkswagen was early in the field after the war and became the leading producer, followed in 1977 by General Motors (who sold 66,000 Chevettes) and Ford. In 1976 a new challenger appeared in the shape of Fiat, whose basic product was the Fiat 147, a Brazilian version of the best-selling 127, with a new engine built only in Brazil but exported in large numbers to Europe as a power unit for the Italian-made Fiat 127. The same policy of international use of components was followed by Ford and Volkswagen, who shipped engines from their Brazilian factories for use in Pinto and Passat cars produced in the United States and Germany. Passat parts were also shipped to the VW assembly plant in Nigeria. In 1977 the number of cars sold in Brazil was 715,000.

Only 500 cars were made in Russia before World War II, but in 1947 the Moskvich was made, at first with plant captured from the Germans. In 1966 Fiat was called in to design and equip the gigantic new Togliatti factory to mass-produce the Lada, a Russian version of the Fiat 124. The annual output of the Lada grew to 700,000 in 1977, a large proportion being exported to 75 countries. The 2 millionth Russian car was completed in 1977 and the third millionth was due to appear in 1979.

Another obsolete Fiat model, the 125, also built under licence, enabled Poland to develop its motor industry, which reached an output of 120,000 Polski cars in 1977, 70 per cent being exported to 40 countries. Fiat also contributed

largely to Spain's growth as a motor-manufacturing country through its association with the Seat company, which produced 335,000 Fiat-based cars in 1977. Citroën, Renault, and Chrysler all have Spanish subsidiaries, and a vast new Ford factory was completed at Valencia in 1976 for making body panels and engines and for assembling the Fiesta.

In 1978 the United States still dominated the world motor industry, with about 50 per cent of the total car output compared with Europe's 30 per cent and Japan's 20 per cent. General Motors in first place and Ford in second are the indisputable company leaders.

The future

When, in 1973, the Yom Kippur war between Egypt and Israel led to the main oil-producing countries of the Middle East cutting back their oil exports and raising the price fourfold, the resulting energy crisis severely damaged the economies of western Europe and the United States and left an aftermath of anxiety about the future of the motor car. Whatever the potential reserves of oil yet to be exploited, the finite quantity remaining has made it vital for manufacturers and users alike to do everything possible to prolong the use of the motor car. Steps are being taken to increase the economy and efficiency of the internal-combustion engine, to conserve fuel through reduced consumption, and to investigate alternative sources of fuel and power. The stakes are large in terms of investment, employment, and public amenity, but so too are the financial, technical, and human resources available with which to find solutions.

Part of the overland petroleum pipeline near Fairbanks, Alaska. The first petroleum wells were drilled in the United States and Canada in the 1850s, and today there are about 1,500 oil fields in production around the world. The known reserves of this life-blood of transport and industry are being depleted rapidly, and it is likely that by the middle of the 21st century the very existence of a world motor industry will hinge upon successful development of alternative fuels for cars.

6 Component Manufacturers

Only about 40 per cent of the factory value of a car made in Europe is actually produced by the manufacturers. The rest consists of components bought from outside suppliers. This proportion applies to the cars made by even the largest motor manufacturers with the most extensive production facilities. In the Ford Fiesta, for example, 1,793 of the 3,000 components are bought from 335 outside suppliers and represent 57 per cent of its total value.

That Ford's own contribution amounts to no more than 43 per cent seems to conflict with the policy laid down by Henry Ford I many years ago when he said: 'We should only buy from outside what we cannot economically make ourselves.' In fact, that policy is still followed by Ford today: Ford, Lincoln, and Mercury models made in the United States – in far greater volume than European Fords – contain a much higher proportion of parts made in the company's factories. The electrical equipment, for example, is made in the giant Ford plant at Ypsilanti (west of Detroit). General Motors adopts a similar policy, with electrical components for Chevrolet, Oldsmobile, Pontiac, Buick, and Cadillac models made by GM's AC-Delco division.

In the United Kingdom there are some 2,000 companies that specialize in making particular components, which they are able to produce at low cost because of their experience, their special plant, and the long production runs they can plan, since they supply the requirements of several manufacturers. More than half the total value of the components, however, is attributable to fewer than a dozen big firms. Moreover, several of these British firms have achieved a remarkable level of dominance in the international components industry.

The British giants

The GKN group is one of the largest suppliers of automotive components in Europe, its products ranging from bumpers at front and rear to most of the engine parts. They include crankshafts and connecting rods as well as bearings, gudgeon pins, camshafts, valve rockers, pushrods, gearboxes, overdrive units, propeller shafts, universal joints and constant velocity joints, back axles and drive shafts, road wheels, door locks, numerous cast or forged components, metal pressings of all kinds, and nuts, bolts, and fasteners in wide variety. Well-known component names under the GKN banner are Birfield, Garrington, Sankey, Hardy Spicer, Laycock, Vandervell, Kirkstall, and Salisbury. They supply components to all the British and most of the big European companies. Automotive components of all types accounted for something approaching half of GKN's total

SANS SUSPENSION COMPENSÉE HOUDAILLE

Left Motor manufacturers have depended on an efficient and flexible components industry since the early years of the car. This French poster advertising Houdaille suspension systems dates from the Edwardian period. Houdaille dampers were original equipment in the Ford Model A of 1927.

Below GKN is one of several large British companies that make components for most of the major European and North American car manufacturers. The pressings shown here, including body frames, axles, wheels, bumpers, rocker covers, and brake drums, are made by GKN's subsidiary, Sankey.

turnover of more than £1,600 million in 1977.

GKN has subsidiary companies in West Germany, Sweden, Finland, Denmark, Holland, Belgium, France, Italy, Austria, Canada, and India, and associate companies in India, Spain, and Finland. Its considerable automotive business in the United States, at present supplied by shipments from England, will be supplemented in 1980 by a £25 million plant now being constructed at Sanford, Virginia, for making transmissions for America's new generation of small front-wheel-drive cars. The adoption of this type of car by the United States means that it is becoming universal, and gives GKN the opportunity to extend its dominance in the supply of constant-velocity joints, which are an essential feature of front-wheel drive. It supplies over 95 per cent of the present world market for these components.

Joseph Lucas was already in business supplying lamps for ships and bicycles when the first motor cars appeared in the 1890s and opened a new market for his products. In 1978 Lucas Electrical – one of the companies in Lucas Industries – supplies about three-quarters of the needs of the UK automotive industry for electric and electronic equipment. It provides generators, starter motors, lights, ignition and fuel injection, windscreen-wiper equipment, horns, electrical components and sub-assemblies, plastic and rubber mouldings, and die-castings in zinc and aluminium. It also supplies equipment to Volkswagen, Audi, and Ford of Germany, Fiat, Lancia and Innocenti of Italy, and Saab of Sweden, and it has manufacturing subsidiaries in Australia, South Africa, India, Argentina, and New Zealand. Lucas Electrical is particularly strong in Europe through its joint ownership of Ducellier in France and of Carello in Italy, the leading makers in their own markets.

Lucas Batteries is one of the largest suppliers to the British motor industry, and a greater percentage of its production is sold overseas than that of any other division of the Lucas group. Rist's, another Lucas company, supplies most of the wiring and cables for British cars, and it has a factory near Calais from which it supplies wiring to Renault, Peugeot, and other Continental manufacturers.

Lucas is also very widely involved in the brake business through its Girling subsidiary, which not only supplies braking systems direct to many manufacturers at home and abroad from its own factories in Britain, France, Germany, and Spain and those of its associated companies in Australia, South Africa, and Brazil, but is also responsible for the design and performance standards of braking systems made under licence in many countries, notably

Japan, where Toyota and Datsun cars are equipped with Girling-designed brakes. Girling also has a share in the damper (shock-absorber) market, in which Armstrong and Woodhead are prominent suppliers.

Lucas-CAV, one of the two largest manufacturers of fuel-injection equipment in the world (Bosch of West Germany is the other), is well placed to benefit from the diesel 'explosion' in the car industry likely to result from Volkswagen having shown the potentialities of the diesel engine for small as well as large cars. The VW Golf Diesel has taken the United States by storm, and the big American companies are turning their attention to the diesel engine for its economy and comparative freedom from harmful emissions. Lucas is building a CAV factory in South Carolina for the manufacture of fuel-injection equipment to take advantage of this trend, and it is stepping up promotion of its many products in North America through new headquarters in Detroit. In 1977 Lucas Industries' sales of equipment for all types of vehicles amounted to £738 million.

Although it was formed only 25 years ago, the Associated Engineering Group includes several companies that date back to the early years of the century. Hepworth and Grandage (1907), British Piston Ring (Brico), formed two years later, and Wellworthy (1919) – all makers of piston rings – were brought together in 1947 in Amalgamated Engineering Holdings, which later acquired further engineering companies at home and abroad. Today the group

In addition to individual body and engine parts, the component manufacturers also supply complete units such as starter motors, generators, and pumps. This overdrive unit was made by another GKN company, Laycock, a specialist in this field for many years.

A selection of components made by Robert Bosch GmbH of Stuttgart, whose founder pioneered the development of magnetos around the turn of the century.

is one of the leading suppliers of engine components to the motor industry in Britain and on the Continent, its specialities being pistons, piston rings, cylinder liners, valve-train components, bearings, ferrous and non-ferrous castings, and pressings.

Since the days when it first modified one of its clocks for use in a motor car, Smiths Industries has supplied the growing needs of motor cars for mechanical and electronic instruments, to which it has added sparking plugs, heaters and air-conditioning systems, windscreen-washing equipment, and many other accessories. Much of this equipment is exported, and Smiths' instruments are supplied as original equipment to overseas manufacturers such as Renault, Volvo, Fiat, and Hyaundi (South Korea). The principal Smiths overseas companies concerned with motor-vehicle equipment are in Australia and South Africa, while it has agreements and arrangements for selling know-how and plant for the production of instruments, flexible drives, and sparking plugs throughout the world.

Another company that has played an important part in the British motor-component industry since the early days – it exhibited a chassis at the Richmond Motor Show in 1899 – is Rubery, Owen and Co, which makes chassis sub-frames, fuel tanks, axle housings, sumps, fabrications and assemblies of many kinds, and a range of road wheels.

The British motor-component industry benefited from American technology when Automotive Products was formed in 1920 to make Lockheed brakes and Borg and Beck clutches under licence in the United Kingdom. Today AP is an international company in its own right and has recently set up an American company to make components that are at present shipped from England. In Australia the two big British brake companies, Girling and AP (Lockheed), operate a joint company, Girlock, to supply the Australian motor industry.

The supply of brake linings and pads in Britain is largely in the hands of three companies Ferodo (a subsidiary of Turner & Newall), Don, and Mintex. Ferodo is another British company entering the United States to cater for the new small American cars, for which it has particular expertise to offer, and it has acquired an American brake-lining business as a base. It also has a factory in Italy.

Accessories and mechanisms for car bodies are the speciality of Wilmot Breeden. It produces bumpers in various finishes, door, bonnet, and boot locks, including central locking systems, combined steering and ignition locks, manual and electrical window regulators, and all kinds of arm rests, panels, and facias. For some years Wilmot Breeden has built up a strong business overseas through subsidiary manufacturing companies in France and Australia, and its customers include Citroën, Fiat, Alfa Romeo, Lancia, and Peugeot.

No motor manufacturer makes its own tyres, although a French tyre firm, Michelin, controlled a motor manufacturer, Citroën, for many years. Instead, the manufacturers obtain their tyres from several of the great firms with the specialized resources and equipment required to turn them out in vast quantities. Dunlop (now linked with the Italian Pirelli) supplies other components as well. It seemed logical to supply the wheel on which the tyre was fitted, and Dunlop has become the principal manufacturer of car wheels in Europe, with an output of 15 million wheels a year. More recently, following the same logical progression, the company has become a major manufacturer of suspension systems. Dunlop is also the largest European producer of cushioning foam for car seats, which it sells to all the major motor manufacturers, and is the sole supplier of latex foam.

Among the major producers of other components are Triplex, which supplies most of the glass used in British cars and has been

Above A facia panel with solid-state electronic instruments developed by Smiths Industries.

Below Two main types of glass are used in car windscreens – toughened, in which each surface is specially hardened; and laminated, consisting of a clear plastic skin sandwiched between two sheets of glass. Triplex, a leading British maker has recently developed a variant of the laminated type in which the inward-facing surface of each sheet of glass is toughened.

Above The three elements are assembled in clinically clean conditions.

Below Examining a Triplex windscreen after a simulated head impact at 48 km/h (30 mph).

responsible for important safety developments in this field; Champion, a British subsidiary of an American giant, and the dominant maker of sparking plugs; and Burman, whose steering gear is finding a new market as a result of America's trend towards small cars.

The Continental scene

Although, as we have seen, the major British component manufacturers are firmly entrenched in continental Europe, they face powerful competition in Germany, France, and Italy. In Germany the giant Bosch company makes a wide range of electrical, electronic, mechanical, and hydraulic equipment that is used by car manufacturers all over Europe. Alfred Teves, a subsidiary of the vast American conglomerate ITT, manufactures brakes and clutches. The Sachs group (in which GKN has a 25 per cent holding) makes almost two thirds of all the clutches used in German cars and is also a major manufacturer of dampers. Among other important German component makers, Varta is a big name in batteries; Continental is a notable tyre manufacturer; and ZF specializes in transmissions.

The situation in France is complex, with two of the largest companies being partly owned by foreign capital. Lucas has a 49 per cent interest in Ducellier, the electrical equipment manufacturer. The Ferodo-SEV-Marchal-Cibié group is 70 per cent owned by French Ferodo and 30 per cent by Bosch. Lucas, in addition, wholly owns Roto-Diesel, which makes CAV fuel-injection equipment for Peugeot and Citroën cars. Of the wholly French-owned component manufacturers, probably the best known is Michelin, whose products are used internationally.

Italian motor manufacturers obtain a substantial proportion of their electrical equipment from Marelli (a Fiat subsidiary) and from Carello (40 per cent Lucas-owned), which also supplies lamps to Ford of Germany for Escort models.

Japanese components

In Japan the car makers depend for the supply of components on a strong components industry, but they enforce unusually strict discipline regarding deliveries. They hold almost no stocks themselves and require components to be delivered on specific days – and sometimes at a stipulated hour. Although few Japanese car components are imported, many are made under licence from British firms. Girling-designed brakes, for example, are used by Toyota, Nissan (Datsun), and Honda under Lucas licence, and drive shafts built under a GKN licence are found in the Datsun Cherry.

The charge of monopoly

With the supply of many major items in the hands of a small number of companies, it is inevitable that charges of monopoly, and the practices it can give rise to, are sometimes levelled against the component makers. Some 20 years ago in Britain the supply of electrical equipment for road vehicles was referred to the Monopolies Commission by the Board of Trade, and evidence was taken from four leading companies – Lucas, Chloride Electrical Storage (Exide batteries), Smiths, and Champion – and other interested parties. The commission's report firmly declared: 'We are in no doubt that it is in the public interest that the motor industry, whose exports are so important to the national economy, should have reliable sources of cheap components of good quality. We do not think that these conditions can be fulfilled except by component makers operating on a large scale.'

The commission also commented that Lucas's success in achieving 'a measure of standardization' in the manufacture of components had been to the advantage of the British motor industry and ultimately of the British economy. Before standardization Lucas had been obliged to make 48 types of dynamos, 38 starters, 68 distributors, 12 coils, 18 batteries, 68 windscreen wipers, and 133 headlamps. Now that the production runs of individual cars are often greater than the previous total output of the whole motor industry, the savings in cost by using standardized components are no longer of such significance.

The possibility of strikes preventing vital components reaching the assembly line and thus bringing car production to a standstill has been met to some extent by the growing practice of 'dual sourcing' – obtaining supplies from more than one manufacturer – but there are areas in which this cannot be effective.

In recent years, as we have seen, the British component makers have extended their manufacturing facilities in Europe through subsidiary companies and integration. This provides them with a wider range of customers, who in turn have a better choice of suppliers. Some of the leading European motor manufacturers would like to see an even closer grouping to enable the component makers to enjoy the maximum economies of scale in manufacture, with a consequent reduction in their costs – and prices. Yet moves by the component makers towards the treatment of the European Economic Community as a single market have been frustrated on occasion by the opposition of different governments – opposition that clearly runs counter to the aims of the EEC.

7 Mass Production

When Henry Ford said that customers could have their Model T Fords any colour they liked so long as it was black, he was insisting on producing cars that were suitable for mass-production methods. So all the cars had to be the same, and they were black because at that time it was the only colour of paint available that would dry quickly enough to suit assembly line methods.

It was, of course, the introduction of mass production that made possible the rapid increase in the use of cars in the first half of this century – and so drastic was the reduction in manufacturing costs that people were happy to put up with black cars. An indication of the effects of mass production on costs in the United States can be gauged from the fact that, whereas in 1909 a car cost the equivalent of 22 months industrial wages, by 1914 this had fallen to 11 months, and by 1925 (when mass production had reached a peak and competition was cut-throat) only $2\frac{1}{2}$ months' wages. That really is production for the masses.

But what is meant by mass production, and why was the effect of its introduction so dramatic? The two essentials are that one set of machine tools or one assembly line is devoted continuously to the production of one component or assembly, and that the jobs are broken down into manageable operations. In assembly, for example, the unit is usually mounted on a moving track in front of a row of men. Each man performs a short, simple operation, and then the component passes to the next man. An unskilled man can do such work very quickly, and all the components and the tools he needs are close at hand. The result is greatly reduced labour costs.

Henry Ford introduced these principles to the motor industry in 1913–4. In so doing, he revolutionized car manufacture; and although advances in technology have since taken mass production many steps farther, Ford's manufacturing principles are still the cornerstone of car production.

Now, however, we are entering a new era in which manufacturers attempt to retain the benefits of mass production while giving motorists much more variety and the workers better and more interesting working conditions. The trend is towards what is known as flexible automation.

Early construction methods

In the early days of car manufacture, a firm would start by building one car, and if it sold well and performed successfully it would build a couple more, usually to order. Eventually it would build a batch, but again these would be to special order, since each customer

wanted something different from the others. Until about 1910 it was rare for many cars made by a manufacturer to be identical.

The cars would be built by firms that had machine and assembly shops equipped with standard machinery, and the bodies would be supplied by a bodybuilder, who had probably built up his business making horse-drawn carriages. Highly skilled men would be employed. The machinist, for example, would have to be capable of setting his machine to do any particular job – connecting rods one week, valves the next, probably only a few sets at a time. He would make up his own clamps and fixtures as he went along, which meant that he would spend as much time setting up the jobs as he would actually cutting metal.

In the assembly shop, the men would start by collecting the chassis side-members from the stores and placing them on a pair of trestles. Then they would build up the frame, attach the suspension, and install the engine and transmission.

Meanwhile the panels for the body would be beaten to shape and would be mounted on a frame at the bodybuilders. They would then be painted. Generally there were 20–50 coats of paint, and each coat was allowed 24 hours to dry. As long as cars were being built for a few rich buyers, this laborious and inefficient method was satisfactory.

Ford's revolution

Henry Ford, however, wanted to build a car for Everyman. His Model T was the car that really got the industry going. It was simple and light, largely owing to the combination of a relatively strong alloy steel for the chassis and the use of simple units. For example, whereas it was normal at that time for the engine to have a separate crankcase and cylinder barrel, Ford combined these into a one-piece cylinder block, eliminating costly machining and assembly operations.

Ford's revolutionary methods were based on the use of moving assembly lines, special-purpose machine tools, and careful routing of components during manufacture so that they took the shortest practicable path. The shop where the cylinder blocks were machined demonstrates the advantages of the process well. At that time, it was normal to place lathes in one group, milling machines in another group, drilling machines in another group, and so on. Then the components were taken from group to group as necessary.

In the Ford shop the machines were laid out very close together and in the sequence in which they would be used. Thus the cylinder block went directly from one machine to the

Although the principles of motor-car mass-production were established by Henry Ford before World War I, the techniques involved have steadily advanced in the last seven decades.

Above One of the advances has been in the movement of components from one part of the production line to the next. Here Volkswagen Golf bodies are moved at a precisely determined speed on an overhead conveyor.

Left A Ford plant in 1914, showing early use of moving assembly lines. In this area, radiators travelled down chutes and wheels along conveyors to the point where they were fitted to the car.

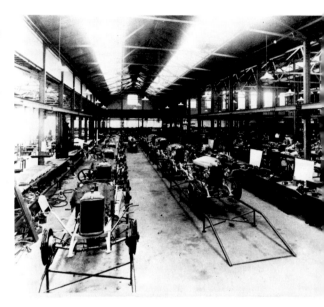

Above Car assembly at Vauxhall Motors' Luton factory in the mid-1920s. Each raised tubular frame was equal in width to the track of the cars, allowing them to be pushed forward on their wheel rims.

Below The body shop at Austin's Longbridge, Birmingham, factory about 1930. At that time, body finishing and installation of interior fittings required a large force of semi-skilled labour.

one next to it, covering only a very short distance between each. Moreover, many of the machines were designed to carry out several operations simultaneously. For example, one machine drilled 15 holes at the same time, and another machined the four cylinder bores simultaneously.

The assembly of the pistons to the connecting rods also shows the advantages of the mass-production technique. The job involved some six operations, and every man was allowed three minutes for each assembly. But after careful study, the foreman found that the men were, on average, spending four hours of their

1. Front and rear underbody frames and floor pan assembled and welded

2. Body side panels and bulkheads assembled and welded

3. Superstructure and underframes brought together and welded

4. Roof panel, wings, and other panels welded to frame

5. Doors, boot lid, bonnet lid bolted to hinges and attached to frame

11. Trim shops: headlamps, horn, and other electrical fittings

12. Under-bonnet parts: battery, radiator, steering column, etc

13. Facia panel, wiring, door casings, standard or de luxe trims

14. Windscreen, windows, handbrake, and other interior fittings.

15. Exterior trim and fittings, door handles, catches, etc

Car assembly. Although different manufacturers vary the order in which some of the components are assembled, the diagram represents the principal stages involved.

nine-hour day walking around collecting parts, or placing finished components in their containers. So the job was split into three operations, each man spending 10 seconds on his part of the assembly, and then passing it on. The whole process was speeded-up by installing a simple chute in the middle of the workbench. When the first man had finished his task he put the assembly in the chute, where it slid to the next man, who picked it up, worked on it, then put it back on the chute where it would travel to the last operator.

When the principles were applied to chassis assembly – involving the building of the chassis frame and fitting the suspension and axles, engine, transmission, and other running gear – the savings in labour cost were dramatic. Previously, each man had assembled a complete chassis on his own in about $12\frac{1}{2}$ hours. In the new system a moving assembly line was installed and men were stationed in teams on each side of the line. The components they needed were stored immediately behind them. The assembly operation was divided into 44 jobs, and because some were more complicated than others the number of men at each station varied from one (at most stations) to three or four. In the preliminary stages the men would assemble the chassis frame itself. Then the engine and transmission would be installed by another group, while one man might fit the radiator, and two men the front wheels. Every job was relatively simple, and the speed of the track was so regulated that if the man did the job in the allotted time, he need not move from his position at all.

Ford installed three of these lines at his Highland Park factory, Detroit, with 72 men on each line. They built 1,000 chassis a day in two shifts, replacing 800 men per shift under the old system. The reduction in labour costs was almost 75 per cent – no wonder Ford was able to pay his men well! By 1915, all Ford cars were being built by mass-production methods.

At that time Europe was at war, and by the time European car manufacturers were able to begin exploiting mass-production techniques, the Americans were producing 1.8 million cars a year. The more open-minded European manufacturers, such as William Morris and Louis Renault, investigated the American methods and set about adapting them to European products and production capacities. André Citroën was also one of the earliest to exploit mass-production techniques, adapting the methods he had used to produce shells during the war.

One of Ford's aims in adopting mass production had been to eliminate the need for highly skilled machinists and mechanics on the shop floor. He realised that tasks requiring great skill took a long time, and that with the production rates he envisaged there would not be sufficient skilled men around. In fact, by 1915 there were 18,000 men working at Highland Park; but as Ford took over some manufacturing operations from suppliers, and as output rose, the number of employees increased to a staggering 60,000-plus by 1923. It would have been impossible to have found a skilled workforce of that size.

Introduction of steel bodies

In the early 1920s the Americans found that bodybuilding and painting were stumbling blocks to increased output and reduced costs. Skilled men were required in both operations, and since the bodies were generally produced by a specialist supplier, a large space was needed to store them at the beginning of the assembly line. The main problem with the paint was the time it took to dry.

So they switched to pressed steel bodies, even although this involved a number of new technologies. Steel pressings were already in

6. Washing, degreasing, and anti-corrosion treatments

7 Primer coats (one red, one grey) applied by hand spray guns

8 Primer coats dried in a gas-fired oven for 40 minutes

9 Three or more top coats applied by mechanically operated spray guns

10 Paint dried in one hour as body passes through steam oven

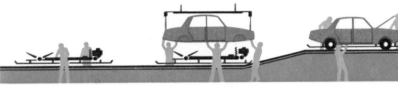

16 Power-train assembly: engine, transmission, suspension, brakes

17 Body on overhead conveyor is lowered for attachment to power train

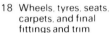

18 Wheels, tyres, seats, carpets, and final fittings and trim

19. Mechanical and electrical testing on rolling-road dynamometer

20 High-pressure water testing, followed by drying and final check

use, but for the body large pressings without blemishes in the surface were needed. It was necessary to evolve a suitably stiff structure from pressings, while welding techniques had to be proved at the high production rates.

In the pressing process a pair of matched dies are placed together so that they leave a space between them that represents the finished shape of the panel. One of the dies is mounted in the bed of the press; the other is carried in the moving part of the press. A flat panel is laid on the stationary die and the moving die is brought down under a heavy force to squeeze and push the panel into the desired shape. The presses operate very quickly – 200 to 1,000 pressings an hour, according to the size – but great care is needed to make sure that there are no blemishes or creases in the panel.

At this time, 'resistance' or 'spot' welding was used to join panels, but it had to be refined and developed to suit mass production. In this technique two panels are held one against the other, and a pair of electrodes on the ends of a pair of jaws squeezes the panels together. Simultaneously a low voltage current of high intensity is passed from one electrode through the two panels to the other electrode. As a result a very small area of metal is heated very quickly, and the surfaces of the panels in contact melt and fuse together. The resulting weld, which is about the size of the diameter of a pencil, is very strong.

With the combination of steel pressings and spot welding the all-steel body was produced, and mass production was taken an important stage further; today the all-steel welded body is still the basis of the motor car.

Although Ford had a relatively quick painting process, with the first primer being sprayed on and subsequent coats being 'flowed on' with a fan-shaped spray under pressure of gravity, a lot of time was needed to dry and 'touch up' the bodies. Ford, in addition, was limited to black, whereas his competitors and many customers wanted other colours. By the end of the 1920s spray painting and quick-drying cellulose paints had been developed and were soon eliminating this bottleneck in car factories. Cellulose dries quickly, but a lot of labour is needed in polishing to obtain the necessarily glossy finish. Some years later the process was further speeded up by the development of stoving enamels. Immediately after the paint has been applied, the body moves along a conveyor through a long stoving oven, where the paint is dried very quickly and acquires a high-gloss finish.

Increasing automation

By the late 1930s the basic stages of car manufacture were similar to those of today. The main differences lie in the steady increase in the use of automation – that is, of machines that do the work of men.

Although Ford had laid out his factories for flow-line production, he was limited by the machinery available at the time. For example, to drill 15 holes simultaneously the operator had to pull on a lever. If he pulled too hard he might break a drill; if he worked too slowly he might hold up the production line. Before long, therefore, drilling, milling, and turning operations were being controlled mechanically, so all the man had to do was press a button and the machine took over.

Then, instead of there being a pile of components on the floor between machines, a simple track of rollers was installed so that the worker took the component from the machine, slid it on to the roller track, and it would then roll along to the next machine. Loading and unloading were thus speeded-up and much less effort was involved. The next stage was to introduce automatic loading and unloading, and to combine these with a system of transfer from the first machine to the last.

With this type of line, which may consist of 30 or 50 synchronized machines, a number of components are placed at the beginning of the line, and one by one they are passed through all the machines. These transfer lines were introduced in the 1920s – one of the earliest was at the Morris engine factory in Coventry.

Post-war developments

Before World War II mass production had reached an advanced stage in many car factories of the United States and Europe. The major components were machined on transfer lines; flow-line principles had been adopted for nearly all operations, and assembly was a rapid sequence, even if it depended on the speed and dexterity of the operators. Although the bodies were spot-welded together, all the welds had to be made by hand, for with so many components and sub-assemblies involved a flow-line welding system was difficult to organize.

Immediately after the war, however, automatic welding machines were developed. Initially these were used for fairly simple spot-welded assemblies. In the case of floor panels, for instance, the men would position a couple of cross members in the fixture and then lower the floor in place. At the press of a button, clamps would lock the panels in place and a battery of welding guns would be started automatically. A few seconds later the clamps would release automatically, and the men would remove the assembly and pass it to the conveyor or stack it ready for the next stage.

It was not long before a row of these multi-welders was formed to provide an automatic welding line. The floor, with the wheel arches, cross members, and dash panel was one of the first assemblies to be welded in this manner.

Generally, the panels other than the main floor would be loaded by hand, but once they were welded to the main panel they would be transferred automatically by a shuttle transfer system to the next station. Up to several hundred welds can now be made at each station.

Volkswagen was quick to exploit automatic welding in a big way during the period 1953–66 in its Beetle factory at Wolfsburg. In some cases the sub-assembly would travel along a line from multiwelder to multiwelder; in others the multiwelders were arranged in a circle, the body travelling around on a carousel from machine to machine. When the VW automated welding shop was complete, only 55 men were needed to build 2,600 cars a day. With the introduction of the more-complex-bodied Golf and Polo models the workforce was increased to 184.

It is an impressive line, with just a few people feeding in minor panels and a few others watching to make sure that nothing goes wrong. Every 30 seconds the line of bodies, or partial bodies, moves swiftly from one multi-welder to the next. There is a bang as the presses come down to lock the panels in position, followed by the hiss of the pneumatic equipment and the spray of sparks as the welders go into action. Then the presses withdraw and the bodies move on again.

The level of automation in a car factory today depends on the production rate and the philosophy of the management. The smaller, specialist factories have little in the way of automation, but transfer lines are used in all the big factories to machine the major components. Japanese manufacturers tend to use automated equipment wherever possible, while Mercedes-Benz, like Volkswagen, uses an automated body-welding line. In contrast, Ford

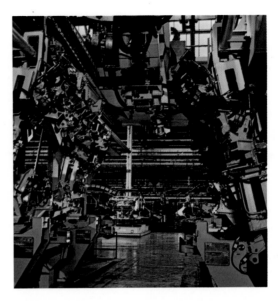

Far left Layout of Fiat's Robogate body-welding line. At the first station the body panels are welded just sufficiently to hold them together; the body then passes from one station to the next until welding is complete. The body is transported from one robot-welder to another on a radio-controlled trolley.

Near left Massive clamps (yellow) grasp the individual body panels, then swing to lock the panels in position at the first welding station.

and the British car manufacturers rely much more on manual welding.

Robot welding

In body welding the trend is to combine multiwelders with robots, a technique adopted by companies such as General Motors in the United States, Nissan and Mitsubishi in Japan, Fiat in Italy, and Saab and Volvo in Sweden. The large multiwelders are used to weld the relatively large, flatter assemblies, such as the floor structure and front end, while the robots are used to make most of the welds when the main sub-assemblies come together to form the bodyshell.

The robot has an arm that sticks out of a turret, and on many there is a wrist-like joint at the end of the arm. The arm is telescopic, and it can move to any position within a prescribed space. The robot is controlled by a computer and it can be programmed to follow a specific path. In a typical application the robot might make 20–30 welds around a door aperture in 50–60 seconds.

In the automated body shop lines of multiwelders build up the major sub-assemblies, which are then transferred by conveyor to the 'framing' area where the body is put together. Here a few men check that all is well, and a multiwelder 'tack welds' the body together. The body then passes along a track between two rows of robots, which make the remaining welds, although there may be a couple of men at the end making a few welds that are inaccessible to the machines.

One advantage of robots is their flexibility: they can be re-programmed to follow different paths and take in extra welds. In principle, once a robot line is installed it is possible to change the body design without altering the welding equipment, at least at the framing stage. Moreover, it should be possible to build two- or four-door cars, estates or coupés, on the same line. Fiat has perhaps got closest to this with the line it installed in two factories in 1978 to build its new small saloon, the Strada (Ritmo). In this system, used in the framing operation, there are no multiwelders, but the robots are arranged on or around massive four-poster structures. These Robogates, as they are called, are arranged in parallel rows and the body is taken from one Robogate to the next by radio-controlled trolleys guided by under-floor cables.

The system is fully automated and two completely different body designs, each with three or five doors, can be passed through the same set of Robogates. This, then, is flexible automation, and when the Strada is replaced by a new design the cost of changing tooling will be minimal.

Painting is another process that has been automated a great deal over the past decade or so, and the paints themselves have been improved as well. Nowadays the rust-inhibiting coat is applied electrostatically as the body passes through a tank of water carrying paint particles. Then primers and colour coats are applied by automatic sprayguns on arms that move up and down along the sides and across and above the body. In most cases these machines cannot reach some of the less accessible areas, which are usually sprayed by hand; underseal is also normally applied manually. But some companies are now using robots to apply underseal and paint to inaccessible areas.

Job satisfaction

Many recent developments in automation have been aimed at improving working conditions.

Robogate: in the foreground are two of the transporter trolleys with control panels exposed; the trolleys are routed from one station to another by means of under-floor cables.

Volvo and Saab have tried different methods of overcoming the boredom of work on the assembly line. In its Kalmar factory Volvo has eliminated the assembly line completely: teams of 10–20 men are responsible for all assembly operations. The body is carried on a radio-controlled trolley similar to the Robocarrier and can move through a number of stations where a team of three to five men may be working. Alternatively, the men can work as one big team at one station; it is up to them to decide how to work.

In the Saab engine factory groups of three operators work on one part of the assembly. Again, they can all work in sequence on the same engines, taking about 10 minutes for each, or they can each work simultaneously on different engines, in which case the process takes 30 minutes.

Renault has adopted a similar system for suspension assemblies, with teams of two men working together quite free of an assembly line, and also in its engine reconditioning plant, where three men work as a team building and testing engines. Although many companies claim that similar experiments have been unsuccessful, Renault have found that team systems improve productivity. The Swedish methods have reduced absenteeism significantly, but perhaps at some expense in productivity.

In the 1980s robots will be used increasingly to take over the tedious jobs in car manufacture and to give a flexible form of automation that can be adapted to a variety of components. They are already being used to handle assemblies between welding fixtures and heavy castings in foundries, and many other similar operations will follow.

Unimation, an American robot manufacturer, has recently introduced a new robot with two arms designed specifically for assembly, and is developing a small assembly robot for General Motors. One of the first applications for these robots is expected to be the assembly of alternators.

Because car manufacture involves so many different processes, it can never be a completely continuous operation but will remain a combination of separate processes knitted neatly together. Nevertheless, automation will increase steadily, first in one shop and then in another, while the combination of robots and computer control seems likely to improve the way everything is brought together, and so remove much of the drudgery associated with machine minding and repetitive assembly. For the motorist, the combination of robots and computer control should result in a greater variety and better quality of cars.

Automatic assembly was once thought to be the answer, but assembly machines are generally so complex that their use is at present regarded as uneconomic. One important exception has been Fiat's Digitron assembly machine that is used to assemble the mechanical units to the body shell, an unpleasant and demanding job if done manually. The body approaches the machine on an overhead conveyor while the mechanical units – engine, transmission, and suspension – are moved into the machine on a radio-controlled trolley. The mechanical units are raised up to the body and all the fasteners are tightened automatically. Other applications of automatic assembly include fitting bearings to shafts and inserting the shafts in housings.

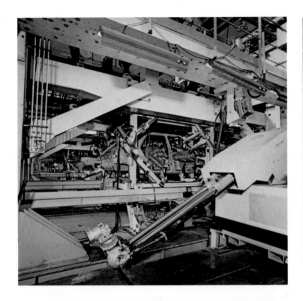

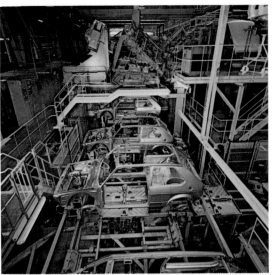

Far left Another type of automatic body-welding equipment. Here the welding gun of the robot is in the 'rest' position.

Near left In modern body plants most of the main components are assembled mechanically. Here the roof is lowered onto the body at the VW Golf plant.

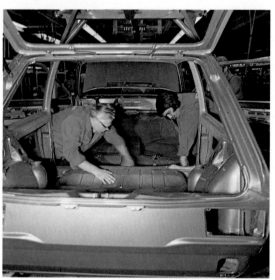

Far left Even in highly automated factories, such as this Golf plant, the less-accessible body parts must still be welded and brazed by hand.

Near left Interior fittings — seats, carpets, and so on — are also installed by hand.

Left The Golf engine and transmission are assembled on a trolley, which then rises up to the body so that the fitters can attach the power train from below. After this the rear axle, wheels, and tyres are fitted and the entire unit is then run on its tyres to the final assembly station.

8 Birth of a Car

Of all the disciplines involved in car design the most implacable are the financial ones. Such is the competitive nature of the car market that the selling price is always set by what the customer is prepared to pay. The design task is therefore to come up with a product which can be manufactured at a cost that allows a profit margin sufficient to justify the enormous investment needed to set up the manufacturing facilities.

Any car maker planning the development of a new model must work within strict cost controls. Every one of the several thousand parts which make up the complete vehicle must be developed within meticulously monitored cost constraints, every penalty being balanced by a reduction elsewhere, and every opportunity for a financial saving being considered against the technical or commercial risks involved.

Planning begins with the identification of the exact slice of the market for which the car will be made and with analysing in detail the potential buyers and their motoring needs. If the new model is a replacement for an existing one, the market may already be 'captive'. There will be comments on the old model in the form of press reports, customer complaints, and dealer reactions, to which can be added detailed comparisons with competitive models of other manufacturers.

From this data and the management's decision on where exactly the new car is to be positioned in the market, the product planners set themselves key objectives long before they set the engineers to work. If a manufacturer is trying to increase his overall share of the market, he may have to look in a new direction – and then the planning process becomes even more important.

In recent years, a notable example of a car planned to capture a new market sector has been the Ford Fiesta. In 1970 world car output reached 22 million, but the North American share had dropped from 85 per cent in 1950 to 41 per cent, as Europe and the Far East developed economically. Ford's share of the world market dropped from 22.4 per cent in 1950 to 16.9 per cent in 1970, so expansion had to come from the growing European market. Once this decision had been made, the market was studied in depth and the decision was taken to make a family car smaller than the Escort.

The car industry divides the market into segments. At the bottom end are the micro-cars such as three-wheelers, bubble-cars, and the tiny Japanese offerings powered by motor-cycle engines. These may be classified as A-class cars. Next up in size are A/B cars, such as

The first sketches of a new car design demonstrate variations on an agreed theme. These two were drawn at an early stage in the evolution of the Ford Fiesta, and were intended to show different treatments of the three-door hatchback concept.

the Fiat 126, Leyland Mini, and Citroën 2CV, followed by B cars (or super-minis) such as the Fiat 127, Datsun Cherry, VW Polo, Renault 5, and Honda Civic. In class C are the Ford Escort, Leyland Allegro, Datsun 1200, Fiat 128 and others; in class C/D are the Ford Cortina, Opel Ascona, Vauxhall Cavalier, Renault 18, and others. And so the categories continue, up to F, the super-luxury or exceptionally powerful sports cars.

Throughout the 1950s and early 1960s, Ford made repeated studies of the A/B-car market, looking to it for the expansion they needed. Each time they analysed the costs involved they came to the same conclusion: they would be unable to sell this kind of a car at a competitive price and still make a profit. So instead of making a mini they developed a new family saloon offering roominess combined with a simple and cheap specification, which was something their research had shown to be more in demand. That car was the Cortina, which virtually created the C/D class, now by far the largest of all the segments.

The thought of moving down the scale into the B class was something the planners never gave up. In the early 1970s they finally found a way to make it work, which was how the Fiesta came to be conceived. Several developments in Europe made a new small Ford feasible. Perhaps most important was the integration of the British and German Ford companies, which eased the way towards economy in manufacturing: high volume in mass production is the key to keeping down unit costs.

Another factor was the emergence of a clearcut and expanding market for this class of car, particularly in southern Europe, where car ownership was on the increase. Several major car makers started to design and build super-minis (as they came to be called) with advanced specification, versatile accommodation, and a higher price than the A/B cars.

Researching the design

No manufacturer can take the risk of working on intuition. New designs are tested on members of the public, who are carefully selected for impartiality but are known to be in the market for a new car of the type being researched. There are many ways their reactions can be sought, but few are as effective as bringing in samples of new designs to a neutral location and asking them to rate specific attributes of the new model against the same attributes of competitive models.

Specialized research firms are used in each country to find recent and prospective buyers and to invite them anonymously to a large conference area where cars can be displayed. Here they appraise every angle and feature of models made to look as similar as possible in all but the vital details. One is usually a prototype and the others competitive cars painted and disguised to make the comparison as fair as possible.

At the time the Fiesta was being planned even the mechanical layout had yet to be decided, so models were made to take front- and rear-wheel drive to demonstrate the difference this made to the passenger accommodation. The options were essentially a cut-down and simplified Escort, a new compact model retaining the Escort drive train, and a front-wheel-drive super-mini with a large tailgate and folding rear seats. Not surprisingly the verdict was overwhelmingly in favour of the super-mini with its many advantages of space, practicality, and stability.

This research, however, went far beyond mechanical specification. It included a study of national preferences all over western Europe; while a second group of research 'clinics' was used to get a clear idea of what the public wanted this small car to look like.

Styling procedures

The first stage in creating a new car shape is usually a set of colour renderings drawn with a broad brush or felt pen. These are known as theme drawings; they are deliberately distorted to emphasize certain features, and are intended to convey more the general impression

of the proposed design than its lines in detail.

From the start of the first paper studies for a new car to production of the first vehicle for sale takes more than five years. (Short cuts may be taken, such as working from the floor plan of an existing model or arranging a facelift to give an ageing model new life.) So it is important to identify certain trends in public taste and interpret them correctly if the proposed design is to stand any chance of success. The team of designers is therefore looking at current influences and trying to predict their effect on the future. Long before any work is started on three-dimensional models, some of these proposed themes are translated into full-size elevations based on the known requirements of the new car package.

Early in the design programme, vital dimensions are fixed; these include the wheelbase, seat positions, and packaging of the main mechanical components. Against full-sized outlines of these established elements, designers 'draw' alternative versions of the bodywork with adhesive tape, which allows alterations to the body shapes to be made quickly.

From these tape drawings and the chosen renderings, clay modellers start building a three-dimensional mock-up. They begin with 1/5 scale models, which are easier to handle and can be used for the first wind-tunnel tests; then they move on to full-size shapes, with the clay applied over wooden frames, but fitted with real wheels and tyres.

The detailed shaping process usually goes

Later in the design programme, full-size line drawings of body profiles are prepared. The profiles are usually drawn with adhesive tape, rather than ink or paint, so that alterations can be made easily. The profiles are especially useful for evaluating the proportion of glass area to sheet metal and the visual effect of side mouldings or feature lines.

Above Skilled modellers build clay reproductions of the proposed facia and interior that are exact in every detail of finish. In production form the Fiesta facia, shown here in clay, was designed as a one-piece plastic moulding.

realistically as possible so that the overall appearance can be assessed.

These fragile clay models are handled as little as possible and, once approved by management, their dimensions are recorded by a special scanning machine. A scan-milling machine can be programmed to reproduce the model from these data, which are also used to manufacture the dies that will produce the body pressings of the production model.

The clay model is used to make a plaster mould, from which glass-fibre shells are produced that are fitted with interior furnishing and made into the first representative styling prototypes. These models are often used in the market-research clinics. In recent years they have also been used in wind-tunnel tests to verify the aerodynamic studies made on the 1/5 scale models in the search to reduce the car's drag and improve its stability when cruising at speed.

The press tools form the steel body panels that are built up into running prototypes for the myriad engineering tests required to prove the durability and safety of the production model.

Engineering development

Meanwhile, many of the mechanical components will have been thoroughly tested in the laboratory and in 'slave' vehicles. Hand-built engines, developed in many cases from single-cylinder prototypes, are mounted on test beds and carefully run to assess their power

on for weeks, alternative features being compared on opposite sides of the same clay model, with thin plastic film applied to the final surface to give the appearance of paint, chrome, trim strips, and glass. At the same time, in open 'bucks', which represent the interior of the new car, clay models of the seats and instrument panels are constructed, every feature being reproduced as accurately and

Above One-fifth-scale clay models of the body are used at an early stage in wind-tunnel tests to determine drag (resistance of the air to the car's motion) and stability at speed. These miniatures are correct in every detail, including the underbody.

Right Full-size models of the car body are moulded in clay over a wooden frame. Special machines make thousands of measurements of the model from which glass-fibre replicas and the press-tool dies for the production-model pressings are made.

output and fuel consumption. At each step in a series of speed increments, the ignition timing and air/petrol ratio are adjusted by hand to achieve the best possible blend of power and economy. The results are recorded and are then used to determine the settings for the distributor and carburettor.

Once the engine has been calibrated to run smoothly, it is tested for strength and durability by continuous running according to a cycle of loads and speeds. During high-speed testing the engines are run at full throttle under full load for 200 hours, which is equivalent to driving at maximum speed for almost 25,000 km (16,000 miles).

General durability is tested according to a special varying cycle which involves a 12-hour test being repeated 24 times. Each sequence includes idling, running at full load at medium revs, at high revs with no load, and running at maximum power for almost 4 hours. The full cycle, which takes 300 hours to complete, is equivalent to over 30,000 km (18,000 miles) of exceptionally hard on-the-road use. Other test engines are used to investigate vibrations, to develop the design of the manifold, and to fine-tune the first calibrations. Exhaust emissions are also measured so that predictions can be made long before the production vehicles are available for testing.

Work on the other components is a combination of empirical measurements taken on the road and special rig tests using road-recorded data. Instrumented test vehicles are driven over all manner of road surfaces, and multi-channel tape recordings are made of the stresses and vibrations undergone by the suspension and body structure. These recordings are then played back to energize special hydraulic activators in the laboratory. By editing out all the small stress readings and repeating the higher levels more frequently, an accelerated test can be devised that reaches the point at which the components fail through metal fatigue much more rapidly than would be possible by testing them on the road.

A manufacturer normally uses one of his existing models to test out new components. When a company develops a totally new type of car, however, there may be no suitable existing model available, so prototype floorpans have to be built. These early prototypes are used to sort out the weaknesses, wherever they exist, by running them over very rough roads in the proving ground until something breaks. A study of the failures shows what needs to be strengthened, where a structure needs to be reshaped, and in some cases where a section can safely be made slightly thinner or lighter to save weight and cost.

Other prototypes are used to study the ride, the handling under extreme conditions, and the performance and fuel economy. As the programme develops, improved prototypes are built incorporating the lessons learnt and using parts closer to those which will eventually be mass produced. As soon as vehicles can be spared, or replacements are complete, they are run into a concrete block to investigate their crash characteristics and the way the energy can be absorbed by the structure to provide protection for the driver and passengers.

In the early years of safety research hundreds of cars were deliberately destroyed in this way, but now behaviour can be predicted accurately by a computer model; tests are used only to verify the predictions. In addition to frontal barrier crashes, mobile barriers are run into the rear end and sides to assess all-round protection.

Prototypes must pass a variety of searching on-the-road examinations before the model is put into production. Here a prototype Fiesta undergoes one of a series of water-splash tests.

Management control

With so much varied and widely dispersed work in progress, strict control is needed of all activities, and there is a system of regular reporting to the top management team. Throughout any programme the most vital aspect is the timing of each action and the

A Fiesta prototype running at speed over a specially built section of exceptionally rough road. Although test rigs can produce the effects of many years of normal use in a few days or hours, prototype on-the-road testing can still reveal unexpected weaknesses. The cars are fitted with special instruments to record the stresses undergone by the body and suspension. Most of the major manufacturers have their own high-security proving grounds that include high-speed sections, rough roads, steep inclines, and water splashes.

phasing together to complete all necessary work before production starts. This can be achieved only by frequent control meetings and strict discipline. Team leaders make their reports to the project supervisors, who in turn feed the information to the board with financial control.

If the key dates are planned efficiently and each target and deadline is met, the work flows smoothly through to the start of production. At various stages there are cross-overs between the separate component areas – it is no use finishing the engine on time if the transmission is running late – and every snag is treated as a risk to the whole programme. As the days run out, the pace quickens and tension rises.

Apart from vehicle weight and cost control and the discipline of keeping to an agreed timing plan, a whole series of other targets are set involving the appearance and character of the finished car. These are usually fixed in relation to a known vehicle, either in the manufacturer's own fleet or in that of its best competitor. They are known as the image ratings and are based on a system of subjective marking out of 10 and a percentage. The system is applied by drawing up a long list of every conceivable feature and deciding how much better than the competition the new model should be. For example, for a new car the target might be to better the quality of gear-shift of the most popular rival make by 10 per cent. Thus if a team of engineers and trained testers gave the competitor an average score of

6.5 points out of 10 for its gear-shift, the makers of the new car would wish for a rating of 7.1.

So the list is worked out, including items as apparently trivial as the effort required to open the door latch or to lift the tailgate, and the more critical aspects of handling, stability, the layout of switches on the facia, and the view of the road ahead.

At regular intervals a management team representing all the interested parties, including those who will eventually be responsible for marketing, takes part in drive appraisals. Prototypes and some of their main competitors are driven under a variety of conditions and rated on a 1 to 10 scale. Any features of the new car which are below the objective are given special attention until the car does exactly what it was planned to do.

There was a time not so long ago when a new model was fully developed before the manufacturing engineers were allowed to be involved; and the service department had to do the best it could when the first examples came into the workshop. Nowadays manufacturing and service engineers are involved from the start, making suggestions on how the car can be improved.

Safety

More and more each year, new vehicles have to comply with legal requirements relating to design. These include all aspects of safety, damageability, exhaust emissions, and noise. Every new model in the UK, for example, must withstand a crash into a barrier at 50 km/h (30 mph) without its steering column penetrating the interior by more than 125 mm (5 in). The permitted levels of unburnt hydrocarbon in the exhaust are controlled, as is the level of carbon monoxide, not just with the engine idling but during a drive cycle meant to represent heavy traffic conditions. In the United States, front bumpers must withstand an 8 km/h (5 mph) impact without damage, and there are limits to how much noise the vehicle can make when on the road.

These conditions would be relatively simple to meet if all countries applied the same regulations, but each has its own ideas on what is acceptable. The formation of the European Economic Community has brought some harmonization, but there is still a long way to go in world terms.

Naming the newcomer

While the prototypes are undergoing their endurance tests and the factories are preparing to get the assembly lines rolling, the marketing team is planning the launch: a marketing strategy is developed, advertising agencies are briefed, and the photographers get to work. Until this stage the car is usually still known by its code name or simply a type number, but now the quest for a name starts in earnest.

A master list is drawn up first, suggestions being pooled from all quarters of the company. The name of a car needs to be short and crisp, easy to read, look good in script, and if possible make sense in several European languages. The first check eliminates those that have been used or registered by other car manufacturers; the second disposes of any which cannot be pronounced easily in other languages.

In the case of Ford's Fiesta, 50 suggestions were quickly reduced to 13; they included Amigo, Bravo, Pony, and Sierra. An inquiry was made to determine what the names on this shortlist meant to people in different countries, but it proved inconclusive. In the end, Fiesta was selected by the man at the top, who liked the way it ran together with his own name, Ford. More often there is a lot of wrangling over names, some trading of registrations between manufacturers, and occasionally threats of legal action. No wonder that some manufacturers take the easy way out and stick to type numbers.

Without modern communications the launch of a new car would be exceedingly difficult. As it is, a big advertising campaign can be linked with the availability of stocks and press coverage. Usually production starts several weeks before the first car goes on sale, so that stocks can be built up and shipped to the

dealers. In some cases there is a 'pre-sell' campaign with selected customers being given a sneak preview so that they can place their orders early. More often members of the press are the only ones allowed to see the car in advance, so that they can prepare their road-test reports.

As soon as any significant reaction becomes available, the planners and analysts get to work again, drawing up long lists of comparisons and examining those aspects of the car that are the subject of praise or criticism. They are already thinking of the time, several years ahead, when the new model will have to be replaced.

Above Prototypes undergo crash tests to demonstrate the degree of protection they offer their occupants. Here a Fiesta is crashed at 50 km/h (31 mph) into a concrete barrier.

Below A Fiesta's exhaust emissions are tested while running the car on a rolling-road dynamometer. European and United States laws require emissions of production vehicles to be certified.

Living with the Car

9 The Car: Boon or Menace?

As late as 1903, when this picture was painted, the presence of a car in an English village was something of an event. In Edwardian days the automobile was a plaything of the wealthy, and in 1908 *The Economist* no doubt reflected the views of its middle-class readers when it referred to motorists as 'the richest class of pleasure-seeker'.

Whatever its other claims on history, 1896 was pre-eminently the year of the car. The *Shell Book of Firsts* has put it all on record: it was the year that a motorist was fined for speeding for the first time in Britain; the year a member of the British royal family first rode in a car; the year of the first car-hire service, the first motor-trade show, the first motoring fatality, the first car theft, the first electric starter, and the first motoring insurance, race-track event, motoring magazine . . . and parking offence.

For Harry Lawson – bicycle manufacturer, dubious entrepreneur, and part-owner of the British rights in the Daimler patents – it was the most eventful year of his life. In May his newly-formed Motor Car Club held a motoring exhibition which was graced by the presence of the Prince of Wales (later Edward VII). Giving a much-needed air of respectability to the noisy, new-fangled invention, royal patronage could not have come at a better time, for Parliament was about to debate a new Bill to repeal the old 'Red Flag Act', which limited all self-propelled vehicles to a walking pace. Lawson's flair for publicity was one of the factors that persuaded the House of Commons that the car might be here to stay.

'It's even possible that these motor cars might become a rival to light railways', suggested one speaker. Although the remark was greeted by laughter, the Bill was passed. From 14 November vehicles would be allowed to run at the breathtaking speed of 19.3 km/h (12 mph). It was a day to celebrate, and that is just what Lawson did. With 32 other drivers he staged the famous Emancipation Day run from London to Brighton.

Plaything of the rich

During most of the Edwardian era, car manufacture was carried on mainly by hundreds of small firms in Europe and the United States. In Europe, especially, it was still too early for manufacturers to gain the advantages of standardization, or to benefit from the economies of large-scale production. The consequence was that up to World War I the car was exclusively a plaything of the rich, and this led to the development of a widespread anti-car feeling that was expressed by just about everyone for whom car ownership could be only a dream. The car became a potent symbol of class.

In America modestly priced cars were available much earlier, so the concept of the car as a class symbol had less strength. Even so, the Automobile Club of America noted that the police were discriminating against the owners of the bigger, more expensive cars. Cheaper cars were allowed through the speed traps even when they were being driven faster or with less care.

It was generally accepted that motorists had consideration for no one. *The Times* coined a new expression to describe them: road hogs. 'MEN OF ENGLAND', ran a hand-bill of 1909, 'Your birthright is being taken from you by reckless motor drivers.' After a diatribe on the killing of women and children, it continued: 'Reckless motorists have compelled one hundred thousand people to withdraw their horses and carriages from the roads. It is estimated that one hundred thousand men have been thrown out of work in consequence.' The car continued to be regarded as socially divisive for some years. In 1911 a British government official saw it as 'the chief cause of labour unrest'; and in 1918, when taxes on luxuries were proposed, cars were included in the same category as precious stones, feather boas, and billiard tables.

The turning point in the more popular acceptance of the car came with the steady fall in prices of models such as the two-seater Morris Cowley: from £465 at the beginning of 1921 to £225 at the end of 1922, the year in which it was joined by the Austin Seven. By the end of that year there was about one car to every 80 people in Britain. The figure had increased to about one for every 15 people at the start of World War II. There were now some 2 million cars in the country and a car was within the grasp of most middle-class families; the better-off working-class man favoured the motor-cycle. Today, when there is on average one car for every two families in Britain, the car as such has shed its class image: but here, as in other countries, there is still plenty of social and snobbish mileage to be got out of the *type* of car one drives. At the same time, the car is now used so widely for so many purposes that we can begin to assess it objectively as a means of personal transport.

Motoring balance sheet

Is it a boon or a menace? Definitely a boon, the average motorist would insist. It is hard to imagine life without it. Statistics show that if you are an average car owner you go to the seaside twice as often as non-motorists; the car helps you spend twice as much time at some sport or physical recreation; you spend four times as much time making excursions as you did before you had a car; you use the car for about three-quarters of your travelling.

Right A face mask and goggles were essential motoring gear during the Edwardian period. Even light and relatively slow vehicles such as this motor-tricycle threw up clouds of dust from the unmetalled roads on a dry day.

Below The London-to-Brighton 'Emancipation Day' run of 1896, master-minded by Harry Lawson, drew large crowds along the route. Here one of the participants leaves a trail of dust and smoke as it passes through Reigate.

And, of course, for millions of people driving is fun, an end in itself.

There is, however, another side to the coin. In 1973 an American writer attempted to put a price on what the car was actually costing the nation. Everything was included: the purchase price of cars, fuel, the roads, pollution, and the estimated cost of accidents. The total bill came to somewhere between £35 billion and £75 billion, one eighth of all the wealth created by Americans that year. It is a grisly formula because it involves putting a price on death.

Such macabre accountancy may provide an interesting exercise for academics; but to thousands of ordinary families, road accidents represent a grim truth. For there are fewer and fewer families that have remained unaffected by some motoring tragedy. In Britain in 1977 there were almost 350,000 road casualties, including some 6,600 people killed and nearly 82,000 seriously injured.

Distressing though these figures are, they are an improvement on the statistics of a decade ago: there were almost 8,000 deaths in 1966. And Britain's road casualties are small com-pared with those of many other countries. Of all the major industrial nations, Britain has one of the lowest casualty rates measured in terms of road deaths per 100,000 of population. The most recently published comparison shows that the United Kingdom has 12 road deaths for every 100,000 people; Norway and Japan both come close at 13 per 100,000. The United States has 21, West Germany 24, France 27, and Austria is top of the list with 33.

Those who maintain that the car is a menace will point out that the car takes too much of its toll from other road users – pedestrians and cyclists. In the latest year for which full figures have been published, the number of pedestrians and cyclists killed exceeds the number of deaths for motorists. Some 1,000 British pedestrians each year are killed or seriously injured at the very places that they are supposed to be safe – on zebra crossings. The cyclist who sets out on a journey is 30 times more likely to become a casualty than the car-driver who sets out on a journey of the same distance.

Cars are not only killers of people: they are

Two bicycle-mounted members of the newly formed Automobile Association on an anti-police-trap patrol in 1905. The AA developed in response to what its founder-members regarded as the persecution of motorists by the Surrey police.

a cause of the destruction of our town and city centres. All over the industrialized world homes, offices, and other buildings are being demolished to make way for more and wider roads, parking areas, and other facilities, without which urban motoring would be an ever greater nightmare than it is already. It seems only appropriate that Detroit, the capital of the world's greatest car industry, should have suffered most. By 1968 the space required for cars had expanded to cover more than two-thirds of the city's centre. One writer, Alisdair Aird, has estimated in his book *The Automotive Nightmare* that if the land occupied by Britain's roads could be concentrated in one place, they would cover the whole of South Wales. Yet in spite of this vast area of concrete and tarmac, Britain's roads are – with the single exception of Hong Kong – the most congested in the world. The British Road Federation announced in 1971 that traffic had doubled since 1958. 'There are now less than three and a half yards of trunk and principal roads, including motorways, for each vehicle in Britain.'

Ten years ago the cost of congestion in the United Kingdom was estimated at over £700 million a year. Much of this congestion must be blamed on the unwillingness of the British motorist to organize 'car pools'. Take a look at any rush-hour traffic jam and count how many cars are occupied by only one person; then imagine the reduction in traffic if each car was full. Some American cities now require cars without passengers to stay in the slow lane on urban freeways. (Ingenious American motorists have already discovered a way round that regulation: inflatable plastic passengers!)

Polluting the atmosphere

One of the undoubted boons of the car is that at the weekend it can take us out into the fresh air of the countryside. The question is: what is the car doing to the air itself? When the first cars appeared, the answer was visible enough. Every car that passed along the country roads created its own cloud of dust. In 1906 Lord Montagu, one of the first motoring enthusiasts, informed a royal commission that dust was overwhelmingly the main cause of the un-popularity of motor cars. The problem was so serious that, on the busy London-to-Portsmouth road, property values had fallen by a third. That problem disappeared as road surfaces improved. But, as the number of cars increased, it was replaced by a more sinister-evil, exhaust pollution.

The car engine throws several poisonous waste products into the atmosphere. In Britain, for instance, some 10 million tonnes of carbon

Above Henry Ford made his fortune by building cheap and simple cars and strenuously promoting the ideal of motoring for Everyman. In this Ford publicity photograph a 1926 Model T roadster is presented as the ideal car for women drivers.

Left In contrast, many manufacturers have based their appeal to the public on the concept of the car as a status symbol. In this Mercedes-Benz poster of 1928 the eight-cylinder Nürburg 460 six-seater is glamorously associated with a luxury liner.

monoxide a year are exhausted into the air by road vehicles. When it enters the bloodstream via the lungs, carbon dioxide reacts with the haemoglobin to form carboxyhaemoglobin. If the level of carboxyhaemoglobin in the blood reaches about 5 per cent it causes a person to become drowsy, and this leads to a dulling of the responses that the motorist relies on to avoid accidents. In an investigation carried out in Switzerland a few years ago, this 5 per cent level (which can also produce serious effects in sufferers from heart disease) was exceeded in two-fifths of the drivers who were given blood tests.

The problem reaches its worst proportions in rush-hour traffic, when carbon monoxide in the atmosphere can reach alarmingly high levels. Some authorities believe that carbon monoxide poisoning of motorists and pedestrians contributes to the urban accident rate. The Paris police have reported that some motorists arrested for drunken driving had not been drinking at all – they were merely showing the effects of inhaling car fumes.

Carbon monoxide is not the only pollutant. Hydrocarbons and oxides of nitrogen can lead to unpleasant consequences if the conditions are right. If the air is still and the sun is shining they can undergo complicated transformations to produce what is known as 'photochemical smog'. Los Angeles is a city blessed by frequent sunshine, little wind, and one of the world's highest levels of car ownership – three factors which in combination make a perfect recipe for photochemical smog. During the 1960s, before California's exhaust-emission laws came into effect, Los Angeles had serious smog for nearly one third of the year. Even in the previous decade, before it had reached its most serious proportions, smog was causing £1.5 million worth of damage a year to crops in the Los Angeles region.

Photochemical smog may not actually kill people but it does cause coughing, headaches, and severe irritation of the eyes and throat. Other cities have also learnt to dread summer

Right For many motorists, the greatest benefit of the car is that it brings freedom of access to the country-side. As a result, the countryside has had to adapt to an automobile invasion, especially at holiday times. Most of the comforts of home can be found at this German *Campingplatz* in Holstein.

Below The car exacts its highest price in cities in the form of traffic congestion and air pollution. This scene in Hong Kong is mirrored daily in hundreds of cities around the world.

smog when the meteorologists announce that stagnant air is about to settle. Tokyo and New York have been particularly affected: during one smog attack, the mayor of New York seriously considered banning the use of all private cars in the city. Photochemical smog has even invaded London, an event that was thought unlikely some years ago in view of the city's low incidence of bright sunlight. The irony is that, as a result of the 1956 Clean Air Act, London has lost its smoky chimneys and now enjoys more clear sunlight, so that there is a greater risk of smog on hot, still days.

Another exhaust pollutant, and perhaps the most worrying of all, is lead. Lead compounds are added to petrol to increase the octane rating. They enable highly-tuned engines to use petrol which is relatively cheap to produce without the engines being affected by 'knocking'. But there is a price to pay, and there is mounting evidence that it is not the motorists nor the petrol companies who are having to pay it. The real cost of leaded petrol, some experts believe, is paid for in brain damage to children living in city centres. In a number of countries recent research has shown a connection between the level of lead in the blood and impaired mental performance; affected children typically show a poor learning ability.

The answer is, of course, to reduce the permitted amount of lead in petrol, and many countries now impose strict limits on lead content. Moscow was one of the first cities to prohibit leaded petrol; the United States, France, Japan, West Germany, and the Soviet Union all set far lower limits than that permitted in Britain. In West Germany, for example, the maximum lead content is 0.15 g/litre (0.02 oz/gal). Britain is aiming for 0.40 g/litre (0.06 oz/gal) in a few years' time.

Is there cause for concern about lead poisoning? Three parents living near the busy Westway motorway in Notting Hill, London, are convinced there is. In the autumn of 1978 they opened legal proceedings against the petrol companies, claiming damages for nuisance, assault, and negligence on the grounds that their children were being poisoned by lead fumes from cars. Government opinion has been more cautiously expressed: 'No cause for special concern', asserted a Department of the Environment report published in 1978 dealing with lead levels in children living near Birmingham's 'Spaghetti Junction' motorway complex. But one of the Birmingham University scientists who took part in the study estimates that one fifth of all the children under 13 years old in the city's inner areas have probably had a disturbance of the central nervous system owing to the high levels of lead in the body.

Above The motor car as destroyer: the eponymous villain stalking its prey in Universal's film *The Car*

Left The car as art: César Baldaccini's *The Yellow Buick* (1961), in the Museum of Modern Art, New York. The sculpture reflects man's ambivalent attitude towards the car, at once asserting and denying the idea of built-in obsolescence.

Accidents, urban blight, and atmospheric pollution are part of the price we pay for living in the age of the car. For some, the price is too high – and certainly a great deal more could be done (and in some countries is being done) to improve the situation. But the benefits of the car are so widespread, so much a part of the fabric of our daily lives, that the perils, the aggravations, and the ever-increasing costs of motoring are accepted, however grudgingly, as part of the deal.

'Keep off our road!' was the outraged cry of British ramblers during a minor controversy aired in the press in the spring of 1978. The pleasures of the Ridge Way were being discovered by motor-cyclists and Land-Rover owners, and the ramblers were concerned that powered vehicles could destroy the fabric of what is one of Europe's oldest roads – a highway that Neolithic tribespeople were treading long before Britain became an island 8,000 years ago.

The Ridge Way, which originally ran from the River Axe on the south coast to the upper Thames, is the best known of the early 'green roads', trackways which were made soon after the retreat of the last Ice Age. The early Briton was a hunter, looking for the best ways to travel in pursuit of game; and because much of lowland Britain was covered by forests and swamps, the easiest routes were along the uplands. So our oldest highways clung to the tops of hills, taking wide detours to avoid river crossings, and had none of the directness of the later Roman roads. They took little account of steep gradients. There was no reason why they should, for there was no wheeled traffic. Along the high chalk downs of the south these early grass tracks can still be traced: they are usually darker than the surrounding grass as a result of generations of

A section of the Ridge Way on the downs between Swindon and Wantage in southern England. One of the Neolithic 'green roads', it is among the oldest highways in Europe.

feet compacting the chalk. Often the tracks are as wide as a modern motorway: when a path became muddy it was simply broadened to make the way easier. And where the contours of the land force a narrow path, the way might in time be worn as much as 6 m (20 ft) below ground level.

When the legions of Rome arrived, the well-developed trackways undoubtedly helped them to conquer the local inhabitants. One of the first tasks of the invaders was to improve the existing roadways, surfacing the most strategic roads with stone and straightening out the kinks. The Romans introduced an element of standardization in the construction of their vast network of European roads. The width of the main roads was dictated by the need to allow military units to march six abreast. Specifications were issued as to the size of stones used in the various layers of the roadway. Almost always, the road was cambered (that is, lower at the edges than at the crown) to allow water to run off.

This camber provides a useful clue for anyone seeking to trace the path of an overgrown Roman road, a pleasant open-air pursuit with the ever-present hope that you might kick over a stone and find a coin dropped by some unlucky legionary.

The Romans departed from Britain in the 5th century. The Angles, Saxons, Picts, Scots, and eventually the Normans all seized their chances and moved in. Over the years the 4,272 km (2,655 miles) of Roman roads were plundered as a useful source of building material.

For 1,000 years little was done to keep the roads in repair. Very occasionally in medieval times a new military road might be constructed, but there was little inducement to maintain the old highways. Local responsibility lay with lords of the manor, who could usually think of better ways of spending their money. By the 16th century, however, the increase in trade – and the consequent wear and tear on the roads – made it clear that stern measures were needed. One attempt to put the English roads in order was the Highways Act of 1551; this stated that each parish must maintain its own roads. Every year the parishioners were required to elect a surveyor of highways and to give six days of their own labour. It was not a great success. The surveyors had no technical skills, and one contemporary observer complained that out of the statutory six days there were 'scarcely two good days' work'. The system changed in 1691, when the parishes were authorized to levy rates in order to hire workmen.

Motorists who criticize juggernaut lorries

for the damage they do to the roads might be surprised to learn that it is nothing new. Several royal proclamations of the 1620s tried to limit the carriage of loads to 1,016 kg (one ton), while an Act of 1662 required that cartwheel rims should measure at least 10 cm (4 in) in width, the view being that narrow wheels created deeper ruts.

While these legal enactments did something to encourage the maintenance of existing roads, they did not promote the construction of new highways. The breakthrough in England came

Above Stone breakers preparing the bed of a turnpike road in Yorkshire in 1813. By the 1830s Britain had more than 35,000 km (22,000 miles) of toll roads.

Below A 19th-century toll gate. The toll system was defeated by the rapidly expanding railway network.

The pioneer road-builders

The technology of road-building was also developing, largely as a result of the efforts of five men. The first was General Wade, who in 1724 was appointed Commander of the Forces in North Britain with instructions to remedy the sorry state of Scotland's communications. Over 12 years Wade built 378 km (235 miles) of roads at a cost of £44 per km (£70 a mile). One of these roads, now derelict, owns the distinction of being the highest public road in Britain, at a height of 765 m (2,510 ft).

The remoteness of Scotland meant that few lessons were learned from Wade's work, and the next laurels go to a remarkable Yorkshireman, 'Blind Jack' Metcalf of Knaresborough. In spite of his blindness, Metcalf supervised the laying of 290 km (180 miles) of well-constructed turnpikes between 1765 and 1797.

In continental Europe, the most influential roadbuilder of this period was Pierre-Marie-Jérôme Trésaguet, an engineer who was appointed France's inspector-general of roads and bridges in 1775. He is notable above all for pioneering the technique of using relatively light surfacing layers over a hard foundation.

Thomas Telford (1757–1834) was the most celebrated of the road-makers. From a humble start as an apprentice stonemason, Telford had gained by the early 19th century an unequalled reputation in many fields of civil engineering. He was the obvious choice in 1810 when the government needed someone to survey a new road to Holyhead. Second in importance only to the Dover Road, the route was in all senses a nightmare. Indeed, when the Post Office had tried to open a mail route between Holyhead and Shrewsbury, no coachman could be persuaded to risk the appalling roads. After unsuccessfully indicting 21 townships for their neglect of the turnpikes, the Postmaster General had attempted to open a sort of Pony Express service. After three horses had broken their legs in a single week, it was time to call in Telford. Taking 10 years to complete, the Holyhead road cost £750,000, a sum that included £26,557 in compensation to a lady who owned the rights to the Menai Ferry, which has been put out of business by Telford's magnificent suspension bridge.

There was only one problem with Telford's roads: they tended to be too expensive for general turnpike use because of his insistence on a heavy cambered foundation for improved drainage. Thus it was to John McAdam that the Bristol Turnpike turned in 1816, for McAdam had maintained that heavy foundations were unnecessary if the road surface was well compacted. So successful were McAdam's roads

Above 'A Quiet Sunday in Our Village' is the caption to this Edwardian cartoon. The weight of traffic is fanciful, if prophetic: in 1909 Brighton, a popular haunt of Britain's week-end motorists, rarely had to cope with more than 100 cars in a day.

Below A quiet morning in Harper's Ferry, West Virginia, about 1906, when dirt roads were the norm in rural North America.

in the late 17th century with the establishment of the first turnpikes (toll roads), the name being derived from the barrier where the tolls were paid. After a few unsuccessful experiments in which the turnpikes were administered by magistrates, a new approach was tried in 1716, when trustees were appointed to develop particular stretches of road. The idea was successful and by the beginning of the 19th century more than 1,600 trusts were in operation. Thirty years later, when the turnpikes were at the peak of their success, the trusts drew an annual toll revenue of £1.5 million from almost 35,000 km (22,000 miles) of roads, about one-fifth of the total road mileage of Britain.

that within seven years he and his sons were supervising more than 100 turnpike trusts.

The railway boom

The opening of the Liverpool-to-Manchester Railway in 1830 was the writing on the wall for the turnpikes. One by one the four-horse teams of the mail coaches were put out to grass as the new iron roads began to cross the country. Losing their revenues from long-distance traffic, the trusts had the choice of bankruptcy or of increasing the number of tollgates – a measure that caused riots in South Wales. It was the unpopularity of this growth of toll charges as much as anything that led to a number of Acts vesting the responsibility for the roads with county and local councils. The last turnpike was dismantled in 1895.

Towards the end of the 1820s steam-powered road carriages set out to compete with the railway train. The odds against them were formidable. The turnpike trusts imposed absurdly high tolls on them and the railway interests put pressure on Parliament to curb the freedom of the road steamer. The Locomotives Act of 1861 imposed speed limits of 8 km/h (5 mph) in towns and 16 km/h (10 mph) in open country. Four years later, in the 'Red Flag Act', these speeds were reduced to 3 km/h (2 mph) and 6 km/h (4 mph) and road locomotives were subjected to a further indignity: they had to be preceded by a man carrying a red flag.

As the railways prospered, the roads went into steady decline. Then two inventions brought the roads back into sudden, unexpected popularity: the safety bicycle in 1885 and Dunlop's pneumatic tyre in 1888. The bicycle became the first-ever national craze. Cyclists discovered that the roads were far from perfect and the two British cycling organizations, the Cyclists' Touring Club and the National Cyclists' Union, formed the Roads Improvement Association to lobby for better highways. Not until this organization became a mouthpiece for motorists was it able to carry much clout, but the two cycling clubs performed sterling work in erecting the first roadside safety signs.

It was not until 1909, however, that the first positive steps were taken to provide a modern road system in Britain. This was the year in which the Budget increased car-licence fees and introduced a tax on petrol. Lloyd George accompanied the announcement of his 'Road Fund' with a promise that all of the money thus raised would be spent on the roads. 'Not one penny of this fund will be touched for Exchequer purposes.' Britain now had the prospect of substantial sums of money to tackle the road problem, and a central body, the Road Board, to administer it.

The first task of the board was to deal with the 'intolerable and injurious nuisance arising from mud and dust'. Luckily, an answer was at hand. A few years earlier a road surveyor, Purnell Hooley, had formulated a hard-wearing mixture of tar and slag which he christened 'tarmac', and for the first few years of its life the board concerned itself almost entirely with applying tarmac to what it referred to as 'road crusts'. Derisory sums were granted for road widening and straightening, such as £12 for improving one curve.

In 1919 the board was replaced by a new body, the Ministry of Transport, which proposed a programme to relieve post-war unem-

Above Collecting toll on a private road in Pennsylvania, about 1909. Thirty years later tolls were used by US state governments to finance new highways.

Below Sightseers gather to watch the construction of a German *Autobahn* in the mid-1930s. By the beginning of World War II Germany had some 3,700 km (2,300 miles) of *Autobahnen* in use.

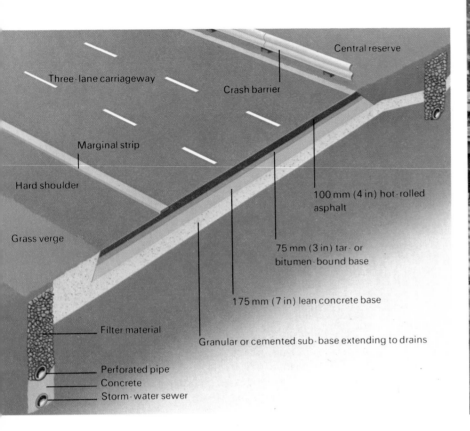

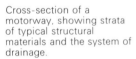

Cross-section of a motorway, showing strata of typical structural materials and the system of drainage.

ployment. Work started in 1920 on the Great West Road. The next year, the first of London's arterial roads was put in hand and work began on the widening of radial roads in other major cities and on the first ring roads and bypasses. Again announced as a means of reducing unemployment, a trunk roads scheme was introduced in 1924 and a year later the ministry was able to claim a number of completed projects, notably the Great West Road and the Croydon Bypass. The 48 km (30 mile) Southend Road seems to have provided the most excitement at the time. 'It's like a trip into the future', exclaimed the *Motor*.

The coming of the motorway

Although Britain was the first country to propose motorways (Arthur Balfour suggested a national network of roads confined to motor traffic in 1900), the first controlled-access road constructed exclusively for motor vehicles was a German development. This was the Avus *Autobahn*, a 10 km (6.25-mile) motorway in Berlin. It was opened in 1921, although it had actually been planned in 1909 and delayed by World War I. A curious feature of this road was a loop at each end, for it was also used as a racetrack and as a vehicle proving ground. Spanned by 10 flyovers, this first *Autobahn* had two 8 m (26 ft) carriageways separated by a central reservation of the same width.

The world's first full-length motorway, the *autostrada* from Milan to Varese, was opened by the king of Italy in 1923. Within a few months it was extended to the Lombardy lakes to become an 87 km (54 mile) route supported by 96 km (60 miles) of link roads and incorporating more than 50 tunnels. The pattern was being created for the future: the *autostrada* had limited access points, was fenced off from its surroundings, and contained no one-level cross-roads. The only significant difference from today's motorways was that there was no central barrier between traffic going in opposite directions. In fact, at some points there were only three traffic lanes.

Italy had some 530 km (330 miles) of *autostrade* by 1932. The road-building effort was then largely transferred to Italy's colonies in North Africa, where a 1,600 km (1,000-mile) highway across Tripoli was opened in 1937.

Just as the construction of the *autostrade* was due in no small part to the vigorous backing of Mussolini, so Adolf Hitler was responsible for the impetus for the building of Germany's inter-city *Autobahnen*. The first of these was the Bonn-Cologne *Autobahn*, which opened in 1932. Hitler had three reasons for the *Autobahn* programme. First, unemployment was high in Germany and the construction work would occupy 250,000 people. Second, it was estimated that improved traffic flow would reduce petrol usage by up to 35 per cent. And third, the new highways, which would allow the very

rapid transport of troops and equipment from one part of the country to another, were vital to his plans for the conquest of Europe. In 1934 he removed the administration of Germany's roads from hundreds of township departments and concentrated them in a single agency, a subsidiary of the state railways. Under the supervision of Dr-Ing. Fritz Todt, the initial scheme called for the construction of 12,200 km (7,500 miles) within 10 years. By the start of World War II in 1939, more than 3,700 km (2,300 miles) were open to traffic. Apart

Motorways, by eliminating bottlenecks, blind corners, same-level crossings, and other hazards, offer faster and usually safer motoring than other types of roads.

Above A multi-lane urban freeway in Los Angeles.

Below Hamble Bridge on the M27 east of Southampton, Hampshire.

from Germany and Italy, only one other European country had developed motorways by this time: this was the Netherlands, which had opened about 115 km (70 miles).

As in Britain, motorways in the United States started with an early dream but little action. The very first resolution passed by the American Automobile Association in 1902 was for a highway from New York to San Francisco. Ten years later the idea was revived by the promoter of the Indianapolis Speedway, who suggested that the highway should be funded by the car manufacturers, who were asked to contribute 30 cents out of every $100 of car sales. The prospect did not appeal to Henry Ford, who was then producing more than half of America's cars. Nevertheless, Ford's rivals persevered to promote the cause of what came to be called the 'Lincoln Highway'. A federal Act of 1921 moved the responsibility for the project from the car manufacturers to the central government.

Four years after the opening of the first German *Autobahn*, the United States had its first road designed exclusively for cars. This was the Bronx River Parkway, a 25 km (15.5-mile) highway with limited access points, running from New York City's Bronx Park to Westchester County. The road was planned in 1914 but was not completed until 1925. Lorries were forbidden. Built with four lanes, it provided an early example of traffic 'tidal flow', for traffic when heavy could be switched to three lanes in one direction.

The success of the Parkway, especially the increase in nearby land prices (and land taxes), led to the adoption of similar schemes. By the start of World War II over 250 km (160 miles) of four-lane and six-lane highways connected New York with surrounding communities.

To finance its inter-city roads in the Depression years, the United States re-introduced the toll principle, bringing the word 'turnpike' back into common speech. The building of the Pennsylvania Turnpike is an astonishing demonstration of what could be done. In June 1937 the first meeting of the Pennsylvania Turnpike Commission was held; on 14 October 1938 tenders were invited for the first section; on 18 October tenders closed and construction started; and on 1 October 1940 257 km (160 miles) of road were open to traffic.

Considering the United States' status as the world's most motorised nation, it seems surprising that it took so long to develop a truly national road system. Not until the Federal Highway Act of 1956 did Congress grant enough money to commence the building of the 67,500 km (42,000 mile) Interstate Highway System, although the system had first been

proposed in a 1939 report to Congress. This vast network looks impressive when drawn on a map of the United States yet it represents only one per cent of the nation's road mileage.

Progress in Britain

With all the pre-war developments elsewhere, what was happening in Britain? Very little to begin with. A government proposal in 1909 for roads without speed limits and exclusively for motorists was rejected by the motoring organizations. Privately built motorways on the toll principle were proposed in 1923 and again in 1924, but the Ministry of Transport blocked the scheme. The toll-road idea came up again in 1937 in a plan for a London-Birmingham motorway. This plan had resulted from a visit by a delegation of 57 Members of Parliament and 167 road surveyors to Germany to inspect the new *Autobahn* system.

The war put a stop to any further developments, although throughout the war various committees drew up plans for the future. At last, in 1949, the Special Roads Act created the legal powers to institute motorways for the exclusive use of motor traffic. Even so, it was still nine years before Britain enjoyed its first taste of motorway driving.

The early 1950s were marked by regular announcements as different sections of motorway were authorised, and on 5 December 1958 the prime minister opened the Preston Bypass – the first section of the M6. A year later 116 km (72 miles) of the M1 from London to Birmingham were opened.

Road signs

Throughout the 20th century as roads have developed it has been a matter of increasing concern to find ways of controlling road-users. The first British traffic signs were introduced in the 1890s by cycling organizations. When the 1903 Motor Car Act directed county councils to erect signs at dangerous corners and crossroads, the Cyclists' Touring Club offered its large stock of signs. The main result of the Act was a proliferation of non-standard signs. It was not until 1930 that Britain had its first uniformly designed signs. (France had them in 1903.) The present range of international signs was agreed in Geneva in 1949.

Britain's first manually-operated traffic lights appeared in 1926. They were not actually the first of such lights, for a gas-lit semaphore system had been erected in 1868 near the Houses of Parliament. When the arms were raised, all traffic had to stop to allow pedestrians – particularly the MPs – to cross the road. It fell into disuse when the Commissioner of Police objected to the cost of the gas. The first vehicle-triggered electric lights operated by rubber pads in the road and using the familiar red, orange, and green colour code were seen on the streets of New York in 1918. They were first used in Britain in 1932.

Parking meters

The United States also had the first parking meters, the invention of a newspaper editor in the 1930s. In Britain a government report in

Above left American motorists trying to make sense of a rustic road sign in 1905. **Above** Modern urban road signs, although using easily understood symbols, can be just as confusing if they are poorly placed. This jumble is in Paris.

Below Parking meters, now common in urban areas throughout the world, were used first in Oklahoma City during the 1930s.

1951 recommended the introduction of meters in towns and suggested that profits from the meters should pay for off-street parking developments. Westminster City Council installed the first meters in London in the summer of 1958. The RAC has complained that the early hopes of meters paying for new car parks have turned out to be a 'disgraceful political swindle'. Local authorities have been allowed to use meter revenues to subsidise public transport. But in most cases, the hope of profits from meters has proved a dream. In 14 years the city of Birmingham lost £139,000 on the installation and policing of meters; Liverpool lost £354,000 in 12 years. The London borough of Lambeth had one of the most disastrous records. Six years after installing 1,000 meters the authority had spent £974,000 and collected only £300,571.

In spite of the motorist's dislike of meters, it has been demonstrated that, by improving the pattern of urban parking, they can lessen journey times by 10 per cent. And, of course, they provide jobs for traffic wardens: it was noted a few years ago that the Scottish city of Perth employed eight wardens to keep an eye on a mere 21 meters!

Keeping roads in repair

The state of many highways is a matter of concern. In the United States, for instance, the 67,500 km (42,000 mile) interstate system is crumbling even before it has been completed. The problem is that better roads attract more traffic, so the roads wear out faster. The cure – money – is not easy to find. The federal government pays nine tenths of interstate costs, but some states cannot even afford their tithe. Moreover, restoration frequently costs more than the original construction. In 1978 it was estimated that to restore America's roads to the condition they were in three years earlier, and to maintain them in that condition until 1990, could cost as much as £160 billion.

The situation in Britain looks even gloomier, according to a report in the AA's *Drive* magazine. During the 1970s local authorities have had to make dramatic cuts in highway maintenance. On average, if present spending is any guide, some minor roads may wait a century before the road gangs get to them. In Cambridgeshire, if cut-backs continued at the present level, some of the county's principal roads would be resurfaced only every 386 years, while many minor roads would have to wait for just over 1,000 years. A spokesman for Northumberland has pointed out that at 1974 spending levels it would have taken 184 years to repair every mile of the district's roads, whereas at the 1978 level of spending the task would take 1,250 years.

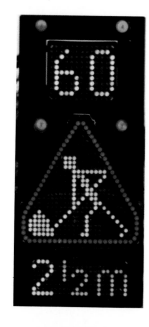

Below A new type of electronic hazard-warning system, developed by Britain's Road Research Laboratory, was introduced on motorways in 1978. The pictorial element in this display can be varied to represent a number of different hazards.

Above Computerized traffic-control centre at Leicester, the first British city to employ a fully integrated system to co-ordinate traffic flow.

Below Fog proves a lethal motorway hazard. Nine people died and scores were injured in this M6 pile up near Warrington in September 1971.

What this means in practical terms is that most authorities will concentrate on major roads while the potholes are allowed to appear in the minor roads. Hertfordshire is considering 'programmed abandonment' of minor roads. Devon county council fears that some rural roads may revert to bridleways unless more money for repairs is made available.

The gloomy prospects, which are by no means confined to the United States and Britain, are due in part to the recession that has affected the world economy since the mid-1970s. But they serve to emphasise the truly frightening costs of keeping our arteries of communication in repair.

11 Traders and Services

Tremendous changes have occurred since the early days of the motor car, when the village blacksmith turned his hand to mending broken parts. (Perhaps this is the reason why the retail motor industry is often referred to as 'a bunch of horse traders'.) The motorists of the 1890s undoubtedly were enthusiasts. They had to be. Few people even saw the new-fangled machines, let alone discovered how they worked, so the owners – or, as was often the case, their chauffeurs – had to be able to carry out repairs and such servicing as was necessary. It is strange how things have come round full circle: 'do-it-yourself' car maintenance now supports a major industry. 'Industry' is written advisedly because the supply of parts (even major components), plus tools and the instruction manuals, has become an industry within an industry. The development of servicing has followed five different routes: the evolution of the retail motor trade, the emergence of the specialists, and the development of three supporting industries – the garage equipment manufacturers, the accessory manufacturers, and the producers of components and spare parts. All five are inextricably linked, but it is simpler to refer to one at a time.

The retail trade

Up to the turn of the century, practically all cars were sold either directly to the public or to the specialist carriage-builders, some of whom are in existence today. There were few motor-car agents as such, but wholesalers had emerged with the success of the cycle industry. As one trade journal stated at the time: 'We quite believe that this system cannot be continued indefinitely. The agent is bound to come, as he did in the cycle trade, and the commission that is now paid to outsiders who introduce customers will find its way into the pockets of men who earn their living from the trade and are therefore vitally concerned in its welfare.'

By 1905 French cars were the most popular in Britain and car owners had difficulty in finding qualified mechanics to service these vehicles satisfactorily. Indeed, there was a dearth of mechanics capable of servicing *any* make of car, and even in those days urgent recommendations were made for the correct training of mechanics.

Companies were rapidly formed to sell motor cars, and by 1907 their numbers in Britain were such that the Society of Motor Manufacturers and Traders, founded in July 1902, attempted to form a special agents' section. This idea was at first viewed with suspicion, but circumstances changed rapidly and the retailers suddenly began to unite. Perhaps one of the

Above An early-20th-century motor-trader's poster. The firm of Eldin et Lagier was the De Dion-Bouton agent in Lyons from the 1890s, and also assembled a few cars in 1898–1901.

Left 'Get out and get under' was the vaudeville anthem of early American motorists. Rural repair stations and breakdown services were almost non-existent in 1909, and these New Jersey travellers had to shift for themselves.

reasons for this was the increasing numbers of complaints about new cars being turned out by the manufacturers in an unsatisfactory state and requiring the agents or owners to put them to rights. The new agents' section gained acceptance and towards the end of 1907 local centres were formed. That really was the foundation of what eventually was to become the Motor Agents' Association.

After World War I and the Depression which followed, there was a period of high-pressure salesmanship for new cars and inflated trade-in prices for second-hand ones. On into the 1930s the accent, virtually worldwide in the motor trade, continued on car sales, with servicing and repairs being regarded as a necessary evil rather than a vital customer service in which reasonable profits could be made. On the spare-parts side, storekeepers were exactly that – they kept the stores and made little or no positive effort to sell them.

The more enlightened retailers, nevertheless, had appreciated that the trade eventually would become a major servicing industry and had erected 'purpose-built' workshops. Although overheads and labour costs were relatively low, it soon became clear that servicing and repairs would be carried out more efficiently and quickly if the mechanics were correctly trained and were provided with specialized equipment.

Petrol, spares, and accessories

While this was happening there were accompanying changes in the distribution of motor spirit, as it was generally called. In Britain, as far back as 1883, 33 organizations or individuals had agreed to supply it to the general public, commonly in two-gallon (9-litre) cans, through bicycle shops, hardware stores, and chemists. By early 1899 demand had increased to such an extent that about 160 agents were in business, supplying petrol in cans and barrels.

One of the earliest references to a petrol pump occurred in 1906, when an example was exhibited in Britain. In 1907 the Berlin Omnibus Authority introduced stations where compressed air was used to force the spirit into car tanks. Then, in 1910, the British Steel Barrel Company offered a wall-mounted semi-rotary 'bilge' pump, the suction pipe for which went into a barrel to raise the fuel into a cylinder mounted high on the garage wall. It then flowed by gravity into the tank of the vehicle below. It was not until 1921, however, that petrol pumps were accepted as safe and accurate and could thus become legal. They were of the type where the fuel was pumped into a glass bowl so that the customer could see the quantity and cleanliness of the fuel.

In 1928 an American company introduced an electric rotary pump. The idea caught on and in the 1930s increasing numbers of companies switched to electricity, although hand-operated pumps continued to be made. Little changed until the 1940s, when 'computer' heads were introduced; the shapes varied according to fashion. Next, as cars became lower, shorter pumps were built with the dials at driver height. Self-service pumps and electronic displays have brought the most recent alteration to petrol forecourts.

It was not until after World War II that the most important changes were made to the

Above This British workshop is typical of garages in the late 1920s. In those days few workshops could boast tools and equipment purpose-designed for cars in general, let alone for particular marques.

Below One of a series of Shell posters of Edwardian days. The two-gallon (9-litre) can was for long ubiquitous in Britain, many cars having a special can-attachment bracket fitted to the running board.

"SHELL"

M O T O R

S P I R I T

IT'S PERFECT PURITY–THAT'S THE POINT.

markets have grown up which incorporate petrol stations and, in some instances, garages where routine servicing can be carried out while motorists do their shopping.

Meanwhile, motor manufacturers saw their own 'after-market' in accessories and shorter-lived spare parts being eroded by the accessory shops in the High Street and the petrol forecourts. British Leyland, closely followed by Ford and Chrysler, embarked on a campaign to counter those of the petrol companies. Not content with recapturing their lost sales, they sought to capture those of their competitors as well. As a result, Leyland, Ford, and Chrysler dealers now carry stocks of high-demand spares for each others' cars as well as those of Vauxhall and many imported makes.

Servicing the car

With the growing demand for first-class servicing and a rapid turnround of cars through repair shops, the major innovation known as flowline servicing caught on with many of the larger garages. By installing the necessary equipment – lifts, testers, lubricating bays, and so on – in a line along the workshops, cars could go through as if on a vehicle production line, with mechanics at each 'station' to carry out the work specified in the vehicle manufacturers' own servicing schedules. The drawbacks to this were that only the make of car handled by that dealer could be serviced effectively, the line had to be full all the time to be cost effective, and any cars requiring major work had to be taken off and handled

retail motor trade; changes that were forced by the almost universal adoption of pressed-steel bodies and the virtual disappearance of the car chassis as a separate entity.

In 1929 there were just under 1 million cars in Britain. This figure grew to 2 million in 1939. By 1959 it was just over 5 million, increasing to 10.5 million in 1967, and about 15 million in 1978. In 1936 there were just over 336,000 goods vehicles; now there are about 2 million. All of them have to be serviced and repaired, but since the 1930s there has been nothing like a proportional increase in the men and the workshop space.

In the years just before and after World War II specialists began to appear in increasing numbers, particularly in the United States. Apathy and shortsightedness caused the British retail trade to lose the lucrative tyre business and later the accessories business. Specialists in these areas quickly came to dominate the market and chains of tyre and accessories shops began to thrive.

To enable their dealers to become more profitable, petrol companies embarked in the 1960s on massive accessory campaigns. They either had products made under their trade name or bought in bulk from the manufacturers with special cartons and display material. On the Continent businessmen were quick to see the possibilities of motorists' shops and, well before Britain, introduced mini-supermarkets into their garages, selling groceries, books, and clothing in addition to car accessories. Now things have gone even further and hyper-

Above In the 1920s traders usually sold many different marques. This firm at Heathfield, Sussex, was an agent for Wolseley, Clyno, Swift, Singer, and Citroën.

Below A filling station and garage in the Netherlands, about 1920. The gravity-feed, hand-operated pump is dispensing Autoline, a Royal Dutch/Shell brand.

separately. This system is still carried on in certain large garages but not on the scale envisaged originally. In many modern garages the system now is to have a row of lifts, with a full range of ancillary tools and equipment alongside, so that each mechanic has his own complete workshop in miniature and has to go outside his area only for specialized testing or checking.

Until recently engine testing and tuning equipment was sold largely as a gimmick to impress customers, but it never became generally accepted in that form. In the early years dozens of colour-coded electrical leads had to be attached to various parts of the engine and the expert concerned twiddled the knobs on a console to get readings relating to the state of engine tune. Later, meters gave way to oscilloscopes, the number of connections was reduced to half a dozen at most, and the readings were obtained more or less automatically. Then came electronics and computers. Now all the testing machine has to 'know' is the make and model of car, and within a few minutes a complete engine diagnosis can be obtained, and the machine will then indicate any corrective action needed.

This system has now advanced to such a stage that certain cars have a built-in diagnostic socket to take the multi-plug from the test equipment; the electronics do the rest and provide a complete print-out. With such equipment, the hit-or-miss element can be removed from engine tuning and analysis.

Specialized services

Changes in vehicle construction have led to the diversion of body and crash-repair work to specialists. While many large traders continue to operate their own body-repair shops, there has developed a large and highly specialized network of crash-repair concerns capable of turning a seemingly written-off car into a safe and well refinished product. In Sweden, in spite of that country's rigid safety standards, a crashed and rebuilt car may fetch a higher price in the second-hand market than an undamaged version of the same age, simply because the purchaser knows that he is acquiring a partially hand-built vehicle, possibly incorporating new panels, that has passed a rigorous safety inspection. The quality of crash-repair work in other countries, however, is not always of such a high standard.

Exhaust-system replacement and fitting shops, which were first seen in the United States, have now spread to Europe. Every car model – and sometimes a higher-powered version of the same basic model – has a different exhaust system. Storing an adequate number of

replacement systems – even of the models of a single manufacturer – would take up an enormous amount of space, and many car dealers and garages have now opted out of the exhaust-replacement service. Moreover the specialists in this field, owing to their expertise and sheer volume of turnover, offer a cheaper and quicker service than a garage could provide.

Another recent but rapidly growing specialization is the sale and fitting of in-car entertainment (although an increasing number of new cars are supplied complete with radio and/or cassette players). In Britain alone there are over 2,000 such establishments.

The trend toward specialization is remorseless. Among the newer areas of activity are underbody protection, engine and automatic gearbox reconditioning, and while-you-wait windscreen replacement. Automatic car washing is a specialist field in some countries, while in others the washers form part of a petrol site or service area. In Britain there are few specialist car-wash operators, but in West Germany, Canada, and other countries car washing and valeting stations have become commonplace. Major improvements in the past 15 years have been made to the brush mountings to give better all-over washing. Wheel washers have been introduced and, particularly useful in countries where the roads are heavily salted in winter, there are high-pressure underbody sprays as well.

So the retail trade has progressed. From the blacksmith who would forge new springs to

Above Car-accessory shops, selling a variety of equipment, including spare parts, for different makes of car, are now abundant in North America and western Europe. Their success reflects an increasingly 'do-it-yourself' attitude in the motoring population.

Below Busy motorway petrol stations have many pump islands protected by open canopies. This one, at Bergstrasse in southern West Germany, is unusual in that it is not 'tied' to a single brand of petrol

Above Electronic equipment is now widely used to indicate an engine's state of tune and to analyse exhaust emissions in the space of a few minutes.

Below The engines of some cars now have a diagnostic socket into which the electronic equipment can simply be plugged.

order there has emerged a professional body of men armed with every possible piece of equipment to maintain, service, and repair cars efficiently and in the minimum time. Repair by replacement, either by new or manufacturers' reconditioned units, is now the order of the day: expensive as car components are, it is usually cheaper to fit a new part than to have the existing one repaired.

Protecting the trade and public

Behind this progress have been the trade associations. In some countries they are little more than trade clubs, but in Britain circumstances now have forced them to offer a worthwhile service.

Typical of a good trade organization is the Motor Agents' Association in Britain (plus its close counterpart in Scotland, the Scottish Motor Trade Association). It sets out to give the car purchaser rights and advantages and it will try to ensure that the customers are treated fairly and honestly by its members. The MAA

and SMTA have a code of conduct which is a condition of membership and, with the Society of Motor Manufacturers and Traders and the Director General of Fair Trading, they have produced a code of practice for the motor industry. This covers new-car sales and such aspects as warranties, replacement parts, accessories and petrol, repairs and servicing, and second-hand car sales. It also defines the action that can be taken by the consumer if he has cause for complaint.

In all the industrialized countries there are organizations that look after the motorist, providing all manner of services – and not always seeing eye to eye with the retail trade. Nevertheless, despite differences, there exists a great deal of cooperation. There has to be. One of the earliest motoring organizations was the Automobile Club of Great Britain and Ireland, founded in 1897, which subsequently became the Royal Automobile Club. The RAC has about 2 million members at present. The rival Automobile Association was formed in 1905 with some 90 members; it now has more than 5 million. The AA began as a result of the appointment of Captain Mowbray Sant as Chief Constable of Surrey in September 1899. He was determined to 'put an end to the nuisance and danger caused by reckless riders and drivers and show them that the warnings were not idle ones'. It was to combat what was regarded as persecution that a group of motoring enthusiasts banded together early in 1905 and organized a trial service of cyclist 'scouts'.

From this grew the idea of forming a more permanent organization to protect the interest of motorists, and so the AA was launched. The new organization had a rough passage during the next few years. Several patrols were prosecuted for 'obstructing the police in the execution of their duties'. The AA's response was brilliantly simple. In 1906 the first AA badge had been introduced, and patrolmen would salute members displaying the badge on their cars. Towards the end of 1909 the salute was given a new significance. The 12,000 members received a notice reading: 'To AA Members. When a Patrol does not salute, stop and ask the reason.' The absence of a salute meant that the patrolman had observed a police trap; but no charge of obstruction could be brought against him if the patrolman gave no active warning.

Both the RAC and the AA, like most of their overseas counterparts, provide members with expert advice and aid such as vehicle examinations, rescue and vehicle recovery, legal representation, insurance, travel and touring services, numerous publications, technical information, and much else. Close contact is

The AA's motor-cycle-and-sidecar road service of the 1930s (below) has given way to a fleet of well-equipped vans (right). The latter are fitted with two-way radio and can often get to the scene of a breakdown in a matter of minutes. The vans carry a considerable range of 'get-you-home' spare parts, but on occasion their driver-mechanics undertake quite extensive roadside repairs. The RAC operates a similar service, as do equivalent clubs in other countries.

maintained with the government and local authorities to try to ensure that the motorists' point of view is considered.

Driving schools existed in several countries long before driving tests came in. The British School of Motoring, for example, was founded in 1910 and has grown into what is claimed to be the world's largest driving school, currently operating over 1,500 vehicles. The larger companies offer tuition from first basic instruction to advanced high-performance driving. In addition there is tuition on heavy goods vehicles, passenger-service vehicles, fork-lift trucks, and industrial equipment. The BSM even teaches drivers how to become instructors.

12 Motorists and the Law

As early as 1900 motorists were worrying about a possible reduction of the 19 km/h (12 mph) speed limit and fulminating over police speed traps. They have been complaining about motoring legislation ever since; or, rather, it is the motoring organizations that have made the denunciations – not always checking to see if their cries reflected the views of their members. Appreciating that speed, or even the mere illusion of it, helps to sell cars, the manufacturers have offered their contributions too. 'The greater menace on the roads today is not the fast driver but the slow driver', the late Lord Nuffield, founder of the Morris company, claimed. It is an argument that begs too many questions to make sense.

The problem facing the law-makers is that they have had to deal with an issue involving the liberties of the individual – and, moreover, have often had to frame regulations on the basis of contradictory evidence. Whether or not you believed, for instance, that speed causes accidents could well depend on whose statistics you had examined. In Providence, Rhode Island, when a 40 km/h (25 mph) limit was strongly enforced in 1925, road deaths fell to 16 in that year, compared with 41 the previous year. The price paid by motorists was low: to get across the town, described as 'the most congested area in the most densely populated state in the USA', took 17 minutes if you drove carefully within the speed limit, or 16 minutes if you speeded and tried to beat the lights. Similarly the introduction of a 48 km/h (30 mph) limit in Britain in 1935 is reported to have halved the number of pedestrian deaths in London. Yet in the same year an analysis of accidents in built-up areas of Oxford showed the new limit to have made no significant difference.

Closer to the present day, a British Road Research Laboratory Report indicated that the imposition of a 112 km/h (70 mph) limit on British roads in December 1965 brought a 20 per cent reduction in casualties, representing 60 lives saved and 500 fewer injured. The report was immediately criticised by the AA, the RAC, and the Society of Motor Manufacturers and Traders. More recently, though, the 1977 British accident statistics showed no notable increase in spite of the fact that non-motorway speed limits had been raised by 16 km/h (10 mph) from a lower figure introduced after the onset of the petrol crisis in 1973. In fact, in relation to the increase in traffic, the fatalities in accidents involving cars went down slightly when the speed limit went up.

The evidence from America is just as puzzling. The accident rate on the Pennsylvania Turnpike was at its highest during the 56 km/h (35 mph) limit in World War II. And in the early 1960s some New York highways with low (and strictly enforced) limits had more accidents than those with higher (and less-strictly enforced) limits. Nebraska, too, found that a relaxation of speed limits was accompanied by fewer accidents.

The simple truth, of course, is that speed on its own does not cause accidents. The average impact speed of accidents is in fact about 32 km/h (20 mph), equivalent to two cars hitting head-on at 16 km/h (10 mph) each. Attention has always been focused on speed limits because they are easy to put into local effect and it is a straightforward matter to police them. It is much more difficult to legislate against carelessness and incompetence.

Above A speed trap, as seen by a *Punch* artist in 1905. The policeman is using a stop-watch to time the car over a measured furlong (201 m). The first British driver to be convicted for speeding was fined one shilling (5p) in January 1898.

Below 'Courtesy cops', whose role was to warn motorists rather than to initiate proceedings against them, were introduced in Lancashire in 1937 and later were used by other police forces. In this 1930s incident members of the Metropolitan Police are having a 'courtesy talk' with an errant motorist.

Drinking and driving

Discussion of motoring laws must include the question of drinking and driving, and especially of the breathalyser test, which was introduced to Britain in 1967. The central issue is whether the limit of 80 mg of alcohol per 100 ml of blood is dangerously high. In some countries the limit is appreciably higher, in others lower, and in Sweden you may not drink at all before driving. Opinion seems to be growing that the British limit is not tough enough: there is now abundant evidence, some dating back to experiments done as long ago as 1938, that the accident rate increases to a serious level at around 30 mg/100 ml.

Possibly the Bill that eventually became law in Britain might have had sharper teeth but for the opposition mounted against it. A Law Society spokesman denounced it as an 'infringement of the liberty of the individual', while the Anti-Breathalyser Campaign referred somewhat hysterically to 'this police-state gimmick, the Deathalyser'. The Transport Minister had included a provision for random breath checks, a suggestion that was withdrawn after spirited protests from bodies such as the AA, and even a senior official of the Metropolitan Police denounced it as 'a terrific attack on personal liberty'. Through all of this the breweries kept quiet. (Perhaps they recalled the outcry some years earlier, when a Birmingham brewery had succeeded in preventing local display of a poster proclaiming 'One for the road may be one for the grave'.)

In France, where 5,000 deaths occur every year from drunken driving, wine growers erect warning signs when there is a road block in their area. That is their angry response to France's breathalyser law, introduced in the summer of 1978 and closely modelled on British rules. Most people who have driven in France shortly after the lunch hour will admit the need to tighten up on the carefree Gallic attitude to drinking and driving – and, for that matter, on the tolerance of French magistrates. In 1976 1 million summonses were issued but only 90,000 licences were confiscated.

A few weeks after the introduction of the new law in France the British magazine *The Economist* reported: 'In a recent check, more than 500 French drivers were given a breath test in the Place de la Concorde in the heart of Paris. Not a single driver was over the limit. Impossible? Not at all. The tests were carried out at 5 pm, which allowed time for the luncheons' intake of wine to be digested. And the time and place for the check were advertised in advance on radio and in the press. . . . Better still, kindly gendarmes turned a blind eye

when male drivers hurriedly swapped places with their wives.' The explanation given by the police is that they were making things easy to start with, to help publicise the new law.

Too many laws?

Undoubtedly one of the difficulties about motoring law is that there is so much of it. There are about 1,000 regulations that can be infringed by the motorist; and they help to fill the 2,000 pages of the *Encyclopaedia of Motoring Law*. It is not even as though this huge body of enactments always has great precision. What exactly is 'driving without due care and attention'? It all depends on the local magistrate.

Many policemen favour placing more controls on the pedestrian. One study showed that over 60 per cent of pedestrians killed in accidents at night had been drinking. In 379 London accidents involving pedestrians, the pedestrians were to blame for 180. Greater control of pedestrians has been tried in New York by fining jaywalkers. The result was 100 lives saved in a year. But pedestrians would protest at the prospect of tougher laws, just

A driver undergoing the breathalyser test, which was introduced into Britain in 1967. The legally permitted concentration of alcohol in the blood varies from country to country; many experts believe that the concentration allowed in Britain is too high. Although the breath test is a fairly accurate indicator, a lively if dubious folklore has evolved of ways in which drunken drivers are alleged to have 'confused' the reactive breathalyser crystals.

Methods of determining the exact speed of a car are steadily improving in accuracy. This highway patrol car of Illinois state police includes radar speed-measuring equipment.

as they did in Britain in 1955, when they reminded the drafters of the Road Traffic Bill that the maximum fine for a disobedient pedestrian was £20 while that for a motorist ignoring a zebra crossing was a mere £5.

Although motorists often feel similarly persecuted, polls have revealed surprising results. A 1970 poll conducted by the Louis Harris Research Organization showed that nearly half of the interviewees approved of tougher penalties for drivers causing accidents; only 1 in 50 recommended lighter penalties. And in flat contradiction of the views expressed on their behalf by so many experts, almost half the motorists in the survey favoured random breath checks. When 10,000 drivers answered a questionnaire published in *The Guardian*, more than half thought the driving test was not severe enough; two-thirds thought drivers should take tests at regular intervals; and three-quarters thought the tests should include a physical examination. Furthermore, more than half admitted that they did not always observe the driving laws.

One of the problems with much new motoring legislation is that it seems to suffer from the law of diminishing returns. When zebra crossings had a novelty value, motorists noticed them and respected them, and there was an immediate 10 per cent fall in pedestrian deaths. Now every day there are fatalities and innumerable near-misses on zebra crossings. Observation of new speed limits shows a similar trend. Only five months after the introduction of the 112 km/h (70 mph) limit in 1965, the percentage of cars breaking the limit was showing a significant increase. Most worrying of all, the number

of detected breathalyser offences has trebled since the introduction of the breath test.

What does encourage the motorist to observe the law is the knowledge that the law is observing *him*. The 'courtesy cops' experiment, introduced in Lancashire in 1937, brought a 40 per cent fall in accidents. Yet, although many motorists maintain that courtesy cops would be effective, a similar experiment failed when it was tried in Buckinghamshire in 1962.

Instant prosecution following detection can be particularly effective. The introduction of roadside courts in France brought a drop in the accident figures. The severity of these French measures may have been a factor: a motorist disqualified as he stood by his car could not necessarily rely on his wife being able to drive him home; in any case, his car might be confiscated as well.

Serious crimes are sometimes punished by what seem quite unrealistic penalties. In *The Criminal on the Road* (1964), T.C. Willet cited the example of a £1 fine imposed on a man convicted of causing death by dangerous driving. A lack of uniformity in penalties also encourages disrespect for the law, and in certain cases even encourages a motorist to compound his offence. Discussing the hit-and-run driver, the Chief Inspector of Greater Manchester Police pointed out that in Britain an intoxicated driver involved in an accident stands to gain if he leaves the scene instead of staying and risking a drinks charge. For being found drunk in a car, an offender loses his licence for a year and may face a £1,000 fine and six months' imprisonment. For failing to stop after an accident, however, he faces a maximum penalty of just £100.

Making the penalty fit the crime might encourage safer driving. Perhaps Britain and the rest of the world should follow the example of some American law-enforcers, who make road offenders spend a few days working in a morgue or a longer period in a hospital casualty department.

Raising safety standards

In the car-safety equation there is another element besides the driver, and that is his car. Unsafe cars so angered the American writer Ralph Nader that in 1965 he launched a fierce attack on manufacturers with his book *Unsafe at Any Speed*. Particularly critical of the handling characteristics of the rear-engined Chevrolet Corvair, Nader pointed out how inherent design faults affected the ability of cars to avoid accidents even when driven by responsible, sober motorists; he went on to describe how cars then failed to protect their occupants when an accident occurred. The furore created by this hard-hitting book led to the passing of the Federal Safety Act in 1967. This specified standard requirements for such features as door locks, collapsible steering columns, safety belts, and seat mountings. Subsequent regulations include one that requires new cars to have a system which prevents the ignition from being turned on until the seat belt has been strapped on by the driver.

The American safety specifications have influenced regulations in other car-producing countries, although there are variations in the standards applied. New British rulings for 1979 require the importers of American cars to change all the glass because it does not bear the British Standards 'kite' mark of approval. As the glass costs about £500 for each car, the importers are upset, and some claim that the American glass is better anyway.

Legislation on car standards did not, of course, begin with Nader. Britain's Road Safety Act of 1956 had established the principle of compulsory annual testing for cars, which became effective in 1960. And at least 10 years before the publication of *Unsafe at Any Speed*, extensive research into accidents and car design was being conducted by Volvo and by institutions such as the Road Research Laboratory in Britain and America's Cornell University. Proposals for built-in safety go back even further. In 1929 the House of Lords debated a Bill which would have compelled the fitting of a mechanical device to all car engines to prevent speed limits from being exceeded. Installed on a voluntary basis, such speed governors were at one time widely used in the United States: 1.5 million vehicles are reported to have had them in 1938. In New Zealand speed offenders were liable to have them fitted compulsorily.

One important pre-Nader requirement was the seat belt. In 1961 the British Minister of Transport announced that a seat-belt law was on its way. It was enacted in 1966. Unlike those in some other countries, the British law does not yet oblige drivers to wear their seat belts.

One of the most fiercely argued controversies in American safety circles concerns the introduction of air bags – passenger-protecting plastic bags that are automatically inflated in an accident by the triggering of sensing devices at the front or rear of the car. The National Highway Traffic Safety Administration has been trying to make the bags compulsory for several years. In the autumn of 1977 the Transportation Secretary announced that all new cars sold after mid-1983 must be equipped with them. Since then car-makers have been told they can offer, as an alternative, seat belts that tighten automatically in a fraction of a second if an accident occurs.

There is considerable opposition in America to air bags, and it is not difficult to see why. They are expensive – about £150 per car, as opposed to £25 for the automatic belts. When they suddenly inflate, the bang and pressure can damage eardrums or lungs (in spite of a pressure-releasing device that simultaneously blows out the rear window), and they can throw children about violently enough to cause serious injury.

Any American legislation affecting car design has a significance for the rest of the world because the United States is such an important market for car exporters. In the near future, American fuel-conservation laws will prevent cars with high petrol consumption from entering the USA. (The American government has, however, agreed to allow the gas-hungry Rolls-Royce in as a special exception.)

Another set of laws that designers have to contend with are those dealing with exhaust and pollution. In 1961 the state of California, concerned by emissions from car engines, passed the first regulations to control exhaust fumes. As a result of campaigns headed by Senator Edmund Muskie, strict pollution rules eventually entered the federal law books. In 1971 President Richard Nixon signed the Clean Air Act, which required the fitting of catalytic converters in car exhaust systems.

In order to meet emission regulations that are becoming increasingly severe, the manufacturers have had to produce engines of greater and greater complexity. Engineers are under instructions to improve fuel economy, but the exhaust catalysts tend to *increase* fuel consumption. Any tinkering by car-owners is likely to put a finely tuned engine outside the regulatory limits, so the Environmental Protection Agency wants carburettors to be made tamper-proof. Bill Taylor, a New York journalist, has predicted that it could lead to 'cars coming from the factory with the bonnet welded shut'.

The Chevrolet Corvair, with its 2.3-litre, air-cooled, flat-six engine mounted at the rear, was introduced in 1960. Its poor handling was one of the focal points of Ralph Nader's polemic, *Unsafe at Any Speed* (1965), which helped to mobilize American public opinion in support of car-safety laws.

Some countries legally enforce the wearing of safety belts, now fitted to all cars. Volvo includes a 'Fasten Seat Belts' warning on the centre consol of this 264 GL and other models. The words are illuminated when the ignition switch is turned on.

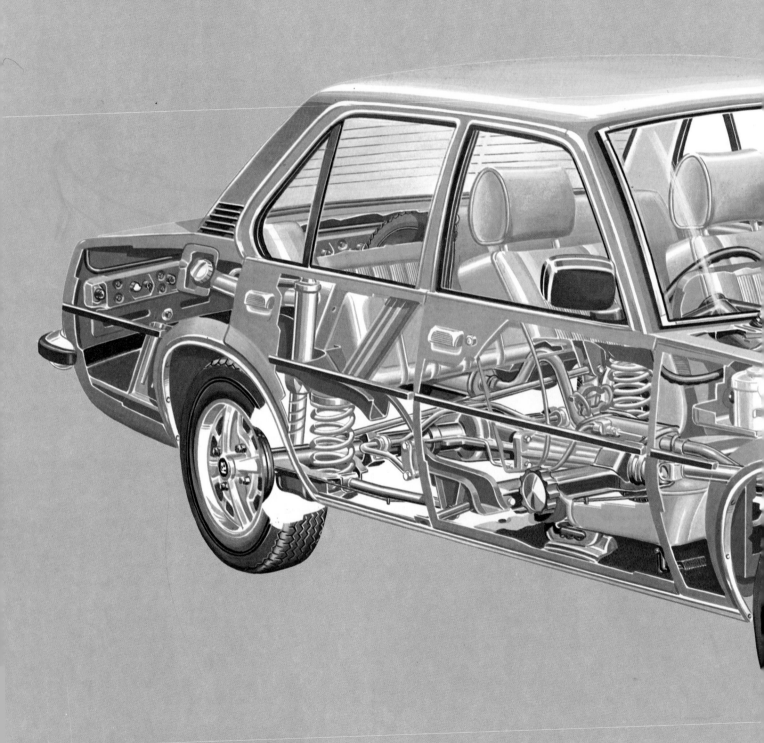

The Works

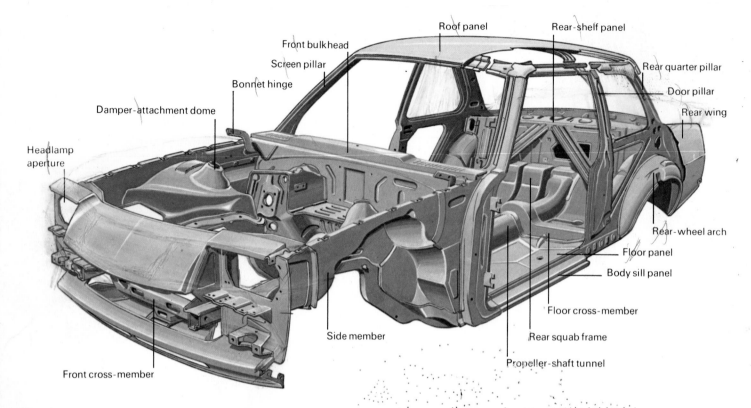

Roof panel
Rear-shelf panel
Front bulkhead
Screen pillar
Bonnet hinge
Rear quarter pillar
Door pillar
Damper-attachment dome
Rear wing
Headlamp aperture
Rear-wheel arch
Floor panel
Body sill panel
Floor cross-member
Side member
Rear squab frame
Propeller-shaft tunnel
Front cross-member

Above The unit-construction, pressed-steel body of the Vauxhall Cavalier L (two-door) model. Every panel, including the roof, wheel arches, front and rear cross-members, and the floor, provides beam and torsional strength. This type of body, with load-bearing panels, has replaced the separate chassis and coachwork found on early cars.

Preceding two pages The Vauxhall Cavalier GL 2-litre saloon (1979), showing structure and mechanical parts.

Below The car as a powered box: a 1926 Austin Seven, with rudimentary frame, rather cramped seating for four, and a 747 cc engine.

A motor car is essentially a powered box for transporting one or more people. The extent to which any car is more than this is a consequence of the engineering problems of producing such boxes, the varying needs and tastes of the people who buy them, and the dictates of laws regarding safety and other matters.

There are a number of features that are essential to even the crudest powered box. The operator must be able to get into and out of it; he must be able to control and steer it; and he must be able to see where he is going. Over the years, of course, the car buyer has come to expect much more than this bare specification

and in some respects the evolution of the car since its earliest days can be seen as the story of how these expectations have been met.

Some of these have to do with the basic role of the car – whence the great variation in size and capacity of different car bodies. Others concern the desire of drivers and passengers to travel in comfort. The modern car, for instance, needs to be fitted not only with comfortable seats but also with adequate storage space for luggage and other goods, and it must protect its occupants from the elements.

The needs of the market also demand that the powered box, however luxurious, is not too expensive for the public to afford. This means that it must be built of the cheapest possible materials consistent with adequate strength and long life. It must be strong and safe, and it must be easy to repair. It must also be attractive in appearance.

As we have seen in previous chapters, car bodies were originally designed and built by the manufacturers of horse-drawn carriages and had massive timber or steel frames to which the coachwork was bolted. Although such bodies were strong they were also heavy and, above all, they could not be produced quickly enough to meet the needs of the expanding motoring public in the years after World War I.

From the 1930s all-steel chassis-less structures were being produced by many manufacturers, and by the end of the 1940s true unit-construction, in which the load-bearing members are fully integrated into the body shell, had become commonplace. It is the type now almost universally used for mass-produced cars. The basic components of the body – the load-bearing panels and the delicately shaped panels forming the 'skin' of the car – are stamped out in their thousands by press tools.

Motor cars with separate frames, however, have not disappeared completely. The advantage of this method of construction is that it enables a manufacturer to offer different body styles on the same frame. It also allows the use of certain lightweight body materials, such as aluminium alloy and glass fibre, that do not lend themselves to unit-construction on a mass scale.

The use of separate frames allows car bodies to be assembled without the complex and enormously expensive jigs employed in a typical mass-production plant, but it involves a great deal of manual labour. For that reason, this method of construction is used nowadays for two particular types of car. The first type is the highly specialized and very expensive sports-car, a typical example being the Ferrari, which is essentially hand-built by skilled craftsmen. The second type is the cars built for 'Third World' countries by General Motors and Ford; they have a relatively simple specification and are assembled in large quantities by cheap local labour.

Body Strength

Whatever its method of construction, a body shell must be strong and rigid enough to withstand the battery of forces that tend to make it bend and twist when the car is in motion. These forces are due to the opposition between, on the one hand, the dead weight of the whole structure, and, on the other hand, the vertical forces generated by uneven road surfaces and horizontal forces generated when cornering and braking. The dead weight includes not just the body itself but also the occupants of the car, the engine and transmission, the fuel tank, the cooling system, the suspension, any luggage in the boot, and much else besides.

If a car body were a simple, six-sided box it would be easy to make it strong and rigid. The trouble is that it is riddled with 'holes' – the door-spaces, the boot-lid space, the apertures for windscreen and other windows, the bonnet-lid space, and other 'cut-outs'. A unit-construction body is nowadays so designed that most of its component parts are capable of bearing loads and stresses. In particular the floor panel, the roof, the door pillars and sills, and (on front-engine/rear-wheel-drive cars)

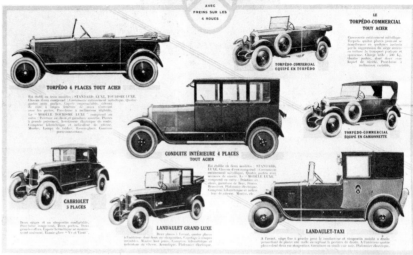

the propeller-shaft tunnel all have a part to play. Torsional strength (resistance to twisting) is provided by cross diaphragms (transverse panels) in the nose, at the scuttle (the bulkhead between engine compartment and facia), behind the rear seats, and at the tail; in an estate car or hatchback, the tail of the body is usually strengthened around the aperture of the rear loading door.

Although the mechanical parts apply considerable stresses to the bodywork (the rotating crankshaft and propeller shaft, for instance, try to twist themselves out of the frame when the engine is running hard), the biggest forces of all are fed in from the suspension and its linkages. On an uneven road surface, the wheels are constantly rising and falling. Modern tyres help to even out the ride, and most of the shocks occasioned by bumps and potholes are absorbed by the suspension (*see* Chapter 17), but the body structure still undergoes considerable jolting. It is usual, therefore, for suspension-attachment points to be as widely spaced as possible

Above Before the advent of unit-construction, car-makers frequently offered a variety of quite different bodies on a single chassis/power-train design. This poster advertises variants of a Citroën 10 hp model of the 1920s.

Below Unit-construction imposes restraints on variation of a basic body design; usually all variants have the same floor pan, engine, suspension, transmission, and front end. The Vauxhall Chevette versions shown here are the hatchback, four-door saloon, and estate; the range also includes a two-door saloon and a commercial light van.

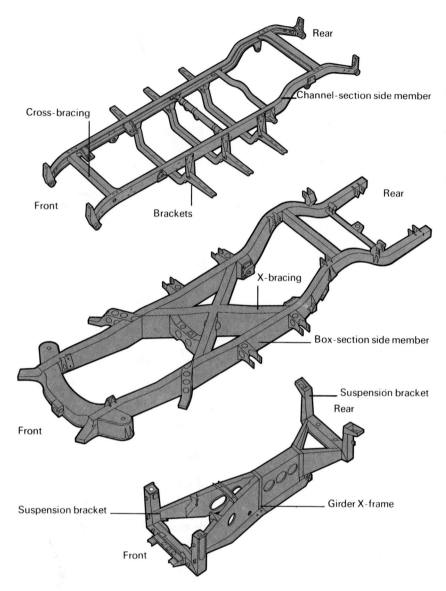

Cross-bracing

Front

Brackets

Rear

Channel-section side member

X-bracing

Front

Box-section side member

Rear

Suspension bracket

Rear

Suspension bracket

Front

Girder X-frame

Above Three typical chassis forms: a simple ladder-type frame, a cruciform frame, and a backbone girder frame; the last provides a massive, rigid foundation for the glass-fibre bodies of Lotus sports cars.

Right A Rover 3500 body enters the paint plant. Mild-steel bodies are prone to rust and require anti-corrosion treatments and primer paint coats before the customer-specified top-coats are applied.

to allow those loads to be dispersed over as large an area of the structure as possible. A typical family car such as the Ford Cortina has its rear-axle suspended on two coil springs, which are controlled by two dampers and accurately located by four steel links; all these components take some of the loads imposed by cornering and road undulations.

In the past decade much of the drive toward strengthening body structures has been in the cause of safety. In particular, laws passed in many countries have required designers to tackle the problem of protecting the occupants involved in crashes. In some countries, for instance, cars must be able to withstand a head-on collision at 50 km/h (30 mph) without serious distortion of their structure, and without the steering wheel being pushed significantly back towards the driver's chest. They must also be able to roll over at speed without the roof being crushed, and to survive a serious impact from the side without the doors being pushed onto the passengers.

As a result of these and other regulations, the passenger compartment of most modern cars is now a very strong box (or 'safety cage', as some manufacturers call it), and the front and rear ends of the car are so designed that they crush in a 'controlled' manner in the event of a serious collision. Front-mounted engines, for instance, are attached to the body in such a way that they are pushed under the toeboard, rather than through the scuttle, in a head-on crash. Fuel tanks, which are an ever-present fire hazard, are now usually located under the rear seats instead of within or below the luggage compartment. (The practice hitherto of putting the fuel tank of rear-engined cars at the front has had to be abandoned in view of the 50 km/h [30 mph] head-on crash regulations.) Front and rear bumpers, which from the 1930s onwards had little more than a decorative function, have become more massive in recent years, and in some countries must be able to withstand an 8 km/h (5 mph) crash without impinging on the bodywork behind them.

None of the new safety laws, nor the improvements they have enforced in the strength of body shells, has led to any fundamental changes in structural design, although several variations in approach have been tried. One is the 'base unit' in which all the load-bearing components are concentrated in an inner structure to which all external panels, doors, and other service covers are bolted. The Citroën DS (1955) and the Rover 2000 (1963) series were examples of this approach. Another approach is the platform or 'punt-type' structure, consisting of a strong lower shell to which the rest of the body is welded.

A choice of body styles

The prodigious increase in size of the market for cars since World War II has posed two conflicting problems for the motor manufacturers. One of the problems – the sheer numbers of customers clamouring for cars – has been dealt with by steady advances in mass-production methods. The other problem is that the car-buying public has become not merely larger but more diverse in its needs and tastes. As we have already mentioned, the car maker who builds cars with separate frames can offer a variety of quite different body styles based on a single frame. With unit-construction cars, however, this would be prohibitively expensive.

The only alternative for the mass-manufacturer is to offer not radically different bodies but variations on the same body shell. In practice, such variations will all have the same basic floor pan, front end, and facia panel, and the differences will be concentrated behind and above the front seats. Thus basically the same car can appear as a four-door saloon, a two-door coupé, a three-door hatchback, or a five-door estate car. Further variations may take the form of a choice of engines of different sizes and various options such as more expensive 'trim' – special body colours and decoration, more opulently furnished interiors, and so on.

The estate car (known also as the station wagon and shooting brake) evolved in the 1930s from the original 'utility' models, which were themselves developed from light vans. It found a small but steady market among motorists who, for one reason or another, needed a car with a greater or more flexible carrying capacity than a saloon. The only disadvantage of estate cars was that, being regarded as strictly practical forms of transports, they tended to look sturdy rather than stylish. This workaday image has been dispelled by two variations on the estate-car theme. First was the hatchback saloon pioneered by the Renault 16, introduced in 1965, which combined the comfort and performance of a better-than-average saloon with a large loading door at the rear; it was followed in 1969 by the equally versatile Austin Maxi. Most of the recent generation of 'super-minis' – the Renault 5, VW Polo, Ford Fiesta, Chrysler Sunbeam, and others – are also hatchbacks, although with three doors rather than five. In such small cars, however, the need for an opening rear door, rather than a boot lid, seems to owe more to styling fashion than to practicality.

The second variation is the sporting estate,

a concept invented by Reliant in 1968 for the Scimitar GTE, taken up by Ford for the Capri II and by Opel and Vauxhall in the hatchback versions of the Manta and Cavalier coupés, and also adopted by other manufacturers in Europe, the United States, and Japan. It came about as a compromise between sporty styling and performance and the need for accommodation of bulky objects. Hatchbacks and sporting estates all have large rear-loading doors and rear seats that can be folded away to increase carrying capacity. For such cars a front-mounted engine seems imperative, otherwise the loading deck would be unacceptably high off the ground.

It is now usual to refer to a car with two doors and a loading hatch as a 'three-door', and to one with four doors and a loading hatch as a 'five-door'. Although it is technically quite feasible, no car with two doors on one side and a single door on the other has ever been marketed commercially. A few cars used for special purposes are so large that they can have three or even four doors on each side. The

Above The Mazda 1400 Estate typifies the recent trend among major car manufacturers to offer estate-car or hatchback versions of saloon models. On some recent hatchbacks the rear bench-seat is divided into two, allowing either or both seats to be folded away to improve luggage-carrying capacity.

Below Another recent development is the emergence of the expensive, high-performance hatchback, exemplified by this 1979 Vauxhall Royale Coupé. The type has its origins in the Reliant Scimitar GTE of 1968.

Reinforced glass-fibre bodywork is used in some high-performance cars made in small numbers because it is strong, light in weight, will not corrode and does not involve the use of enormously expensive press tools. This Lotus Elite has a steel backbone chassis, and some steel reinforcement of the body itself.

The Volkswagen company uses this wind tunnel to test the aerodynamic properties of scale models and prototypes. Bodywork with low wind resistance helps to lower a car's petrol consumption and may improve its handling.

Mercedes-Benz 600 Pullman is an example of the 'ceremonial' six-door car, and the Checker Aerocar (commonly used as a 'courtesy' taxi or as a personnel carrier) may have an eight-door body shell – or nine doors if fitted with a rear hatch. The structural principles of such vehicles, however, are essentially the same as in the bodies of ordinary cars.

The convertible – that is, a car with a fold-away roof – is now a dying breed. The very first cars had no roof at all, like the horse-drawn carriages on which their body designs were based. The fold-away roof, made of canvas or other suitable material stretched over an articulated wood or metal frame, became very popular on touring and sports cars in the 1920s and 1930s. There are two main reasons for its decline, apart from the fact that the special bodywork cannot be produced and assembled on the same production line as a saloon. The first reason is that a unit-construction body derives much of its strength, and in particular its rigidity, from the roof: a convertible is rather like a box lacking one of its sides. The second reason has to do with safety. If a convertible turns over, its soft (or folded-away) roof offers no protection to the occupants. The trend is for sports cars with convertible pretensions to be fitted with a strong roll-over hoop behind the front seats, as in the Porsche 911 Targa and Triumph Stag. But most of the fastest sports cars nowadays are fully enclosed.

An attractive compromise is a roof panel that can be slid open. Panels of this kind were introduced on saloons in the 1930s, but after a few years they tended to develop leaks even when closed. In recent years, the sealing problems have been solved and factory-built 'sun roofs' are now an option on many cars. The Porsche Targa and a few other sports cars represent probably the best compromise between the sliding panel and a fully convertible body: on these the entire roof section between the top of the windscreen and the roll-over bar can be removed and stowed away.

Departures from conventional design structures are rare: even the Rolls-Royce is nowadays a unit-construction car. Among the most interesting variations in recent years have been the multi-tube frame of the Mercedes-Benz 300SL 'gull-wing' sports car of 1952, the combined tubular and unit-construction body of the Jaguar E Type (1961), and the pressed-steel backbone chassis of the present Lotus road cars. But all these cars are (or were) built in small quantities, and their structural designs have little if any relevance to the problems of mass-production.

Bodywork materials

Almost all unit-construction bodies are made of mild steel. In some respects mild steel is one of the least-suitable materials for this purpose. In particular – as every car-owner knows only too well – it is prone to rust, which is not only unsightly but eats away the metal and so critically weakens the structure. Mild steel rusts in the presence of oxygen, so rust-prevention depends on the efficiency with which the metal is sealed off from the atmosphere and from rainwater. This is the real reason (apart from appearances) why the bodywork is painted. Much has been done in recent years to improve the quality of car-body paints and of the various chemical 'pre-treatments' of the steel that help the paint to adhere to the metal. Another recent improvement has been the use of 'underseals' – thick coatings of a bituminous or other compound applied to the underside of the body and to the wheel arches. Much can also be done by designers to avoid purely decorative bodywork details that tend to trap water.

Although light-alloy pressings are widely used for skin panels such as doors, and are more corrosion-resistant than mild steel, they are not as strong as steel panels, are much more difficult to weld, and cost several times as much. Glass-fibre bodies have found favour among low-volume car producers such as Lotus, but they do not lend themselves to mass-production runs owing to the time needed for the newly built shells to be 'cured' after the glass fibre and resin are brought together in the moulds. Glass fibre is rather brittle and so will not bend, like steel, in a minor accident (although holes can be effectively, if expensively, 'patched'); on the other hand, it will not corrode.

Moulded plastic has occasionally been tried for exterior body panels, but it, too, is brittle and unyielding. Although the plastic itself is cheap, the tools needed to form it are even more costly than those for stamping out pressed-steel or aluminium-alloy panels. Moulded plastics are, however, used widely in the car's interior, notably in the facia and instrument panels, in the central console over the transmission tunnel, and for decorative trim.

The shape and construction of car-body panels are governed by the task for which they are designed. Flat panels are cheapest and easiest to produce, but they lack strength and rigidity. In contrast, skin panels of intricate shape may be very strong, but they require more expensive tools to stamp them out. The design and production of these tools is a technology in itself, and manufacturing the dies takes a long time. For the largest or most intricate panels, such as the inner door skins or the floor-panel pressings, work on shaping the production press dies usually begins more than two years before the new model is due to go into production.

Even today, when production techniques have reached a high degree of general uniformity among the major manufacturers, there are detail differences in methods of assembly. As we saw in Chapter 7, automatic or semi-automatic welding techniques are almost universally used in assembling the main body shell. But some companies still bolt (rather than weld) the wings and door hinges to the shell. This is a decided advantage to the car owner, since bolt-on parts such as wing panels are much easier (and therefore cheaper) to replace in the event of accidents.

Body furnishing

After the shell has been assembled it is furnished. Apart from the painting and trimming, this includes adding all the glass, the carpets, the sealing around the doors, and the seats. All the systems which in earlier days were attached to the chassis – fuel lines, brake lines, connections between front and rear suspensions, and electrical wiring – have to be plumbed into the structure of a unit-construction car after it has been assembled.

One of the most important features contributing to the comfort of a modern car is ventilation. Passengers must be warmed in cold weather, cooled in hot weather, and given draughtless, moving air even when the windows are closed. This is done by the heating/air-conditioning system which is usually installed behind the facia panel; the more elaborate systems have ducts to the rear compartment and even, sometimes, to the side windows. It is no use getting fresh air into the car if stale air cannot be let out, so most modern cars now have ducts (usually behind the rear side windows) which not only extract the stale air but prevent exhaust fumes from entering the passenger compartment.

All doors have wind-down windows (and some also have swivelling ventilators) and can be locked. An important safety feature on some cars is rear doors that can be arranged to open freely from outside while remaining locked on the inside. This prevents child passengers from opening the doors when the car is moving. Nowadays all side doors are hinged at the front, so that they will tend to stay closed when the car is in motion. On some of the more expensive modern cars the windows open or shut at the press of a button, and all the doors can be locked by an electronic mechanism controlled by the driver.

Safety legislation in the United States and elsewhere requires convertibles or open-topped cars to be fitted with a protective roll-over bar. On this Porsche 911 Targa the bar is neatly incorporated into the body shape rearward of the doors; the steel roof panel and the rear window can be removed to give open-air motoring.

In the United States car bumpers are required to withstand an 8 km/h (5 mph) impact without transmitting damage to the bodywork. The Volvo 244 GL's massive rear bumper is typical of those conforming to the new legislation.

14 Engines

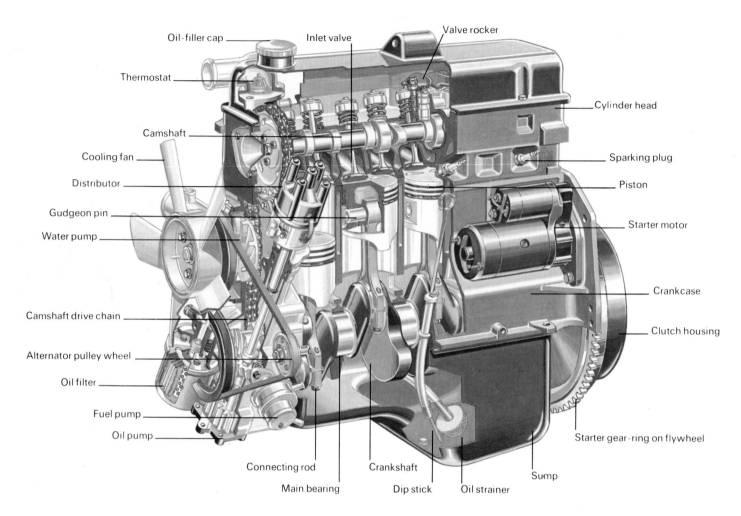

Oil-filler cap — Inlet valve — Valve rocker

Thermostat

Cylinder head

Camshaft

Cooling fan

Sparking plug

Distributor

Piston

Gudgeon pin

Starter motor

Water pump

Crankcase

Camshaft drive chain

Clutch housing

Alternator pulley wheel

Oil filter

Fuel pump

Oil pump

Starter gear-ring on flywheel

Connecting rod — Crankshaft — Sump

Main bearing — Dip stick — Oil strainer

The Vauxhall/Opel 2-litre engine introduced in 1978 has four cylinders, a five-bearing crankshaft, two valves per cylinder, and a camshaft mounted in the cylinder head alongside the valves. The camshaft, chain-driven by the crankshaft pulley, opens the valves, which are closed by powerful coil springs. The distributor and oil pump are driven by the crankshaft skew gear. The cast-iron cylinder block is water-cooled, and the flow of air through the radiator is assisted by an engine-driven cooling fan.

If the body shell can be said to be the skeleton of a car, the engine is its heart. Without its engine a car is effectively dead; moreover, a troublesome engine often leads to other problems, for the engine actuates, directly or indirectly, a variety of systems on which an efficiently functioning car depends.

Basically, the engine exists to provide power. An engine develops power by tapping the energy stored in its fuel. There are several different types of fuel that, potentially at any rate, are suitable for use in motor-car engines. The choice of a fuel depends not only on the amount of energy it stores but, even more, on how easily, cheaply, and efficiently the energy can be converted into usable power.

In the early days of the motor car, and for some years afterwards, petrol, steam, and electricity were all used as power sources. Electricity proved unacceptable because, in cars, it has to be stored in large, heavy batteries that must be recharged frequently and so greatly reduce the range of a vehicle. Steam engines, fired by coal or oil, develop a good deal of power but have a high fuel consumption and are usually too heavy for an ordinary car.

If fired by coal, the amount of storage space required for the fuel is unacceptably large. On the other hand, if oil is to be the fuel, it might as well be used directly, as in a diesel engine, rather than being burnt to boil water in order to produce steam. Steam-powered cars had quite a long run, the last practical road vehicles being built in the early 1930s.

The shortcomings of electricity and steam cleared the way for petroleum (in the form of either petrol or diesel oil) and the piston engine – a combination that has dominated the motoring world since the last few years of the 19th century. Until the 1970s the general pattern was for petrol engines to be used mainly in motor cars and diesel engines in commercial vehicles, especially the larger trucks and buses. Recently, however, many of the major European manufacturers have been offering a diesel-engine option on medium-sized and small cars. Mercedes-Benz has been a pioneer in this field. Peugeot introduced a 2.3-litre turbocharged diesel for its top-of-the-range 604 in 1978. For smaller cars, the 1.5-litre diesel in the VW Golf has proved outstandingly successful, especially in the United States.

Converting fuel into power

To convert the energy locked in petroleum fuels into usable power it is necessary to burn them in the presence of oxygen. The gases produced by combustion expand rapidly and so build up high pressure in the engine's combustion chamber (the top end of the cylinder). It is this pressure that provides the power to turn the engine. In petrol engines the fuel is mixed with air before being fed into the combustion chamber, and is then compressed before being ignited; in a diesel engine the fuel oil is injected after the air has been heated by compression. After combustion, the spent gases are removed, and the process begins again. In a petrol engine the fuel is ignited by a spark from a sparking plug; in a diesel engine the fuel, entering the combustion chamber when the air is already highly compressed (and therefore very hot), ignites spontaneously. In both cases, the moment at which the fuel ignites must be timed exactly if the engines are to operate efficiently.

A piston engine can be designed to work on either a four-stroke or a two-stroke cycle – a 'stroke' being the movement of the piston from one end of the cylinder to the other. In a four-stroke engine the cycle of movements is as follows: induction (downward movement), in which the fuel/air mixture is drawn into the cylinder; compression (upward movement), in which the mixture is compressed by the piston progressively reducing the effective volume of the cylinder; power (downward movement), in which the fuel is ignited by the sparking plug (or, in a diesel engine, ignites spontaneously); and exhaust (upward movement), in which the spent gases are expelled from the cylinder. The fuel enters, and the exhaust gases leave, via separate valves at the top of the cylinder.

The two-stroke cycle is simpler but more difficult to describe. Two-stroke engines do not have valves but ports (holes) in the cylinder walls that, at certain points in each stroke, are uncovered by the piston. On the first (upward) stroke the fuel/air mixture in the cylinder is compressed by the piston and is then ignited, while at the same time fresh fuel is drawn into the air-tight crank chamber *below* the piston. On the second stroke, the ignited fuel reverses the direction of movement of the piston. Near the bottom of this stroke, the exhaust gases are expelled, while the fresh mixture is transferred from the crank chamber to the cylinder. Most modern cars have four-stroke engines; two-stroke engines, at one time widely used in motor-cycles, have lost favour in recent years because their exhaust gases generally contain an unacceptably high proportion of unburnt toxic substances.

The fuel/air mixture is carefully metered into the cylinder by means of a carburettor or an injection system (*see* Chapter 15). In most engines, whether fueled by diesel oil or petrol, the air is sucked into the cylinder by the downward movement of the piston, a movement which enlarges the effective volume of the cylinder. On the equivalent, but opposite, principle the exhaust gases are expelled by upward movement of the piston. But greater power will be generated if, on the induction stroke, a greater amount of air is forced under pressure into the cylinder by means of a pump.

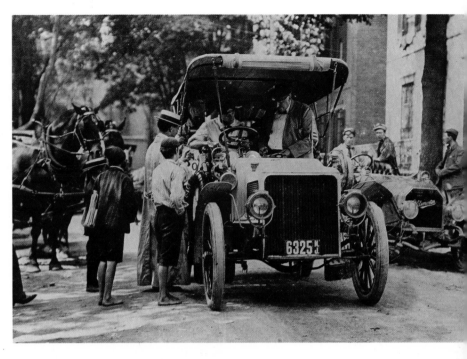

Above A White steam-powered car of 1904–5. Although steam engines are quiet and powerful, they require several minutes to raise a head of steam from cold and must be frequently replenished with water – disadvantages that proved decisive in steam's rivalry with petrol-engines.

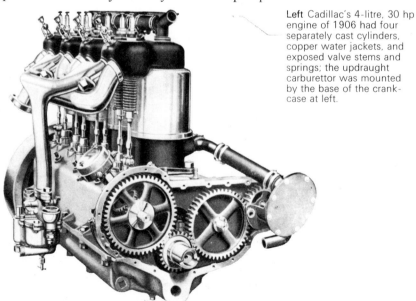

Left Cadillac's 4-litre, 30 hp engine of 1906 had four separately cast cylinders, copper water jackets, and exposed valve stems and springs; the updraught carburettor was mounted by the base of the crank-case at left.

Such a pump is called a supercharger, and it is driven by the engine. An alternative system uses a turbine in which the turbine blades are driven by the engine's exhaust gases. This system, called a turbocharger, is more efficient than a supercharger because it does not cream off any of the usable power developed by the engine.

The four- and two-stroke cycles produce power in the form of *linear* motion – that is, the up-and-down movements of the piston within its cylinder. But these movements must be converted into *rotary* motion, as of a wheel or shaft turning, before it can be used to propel the car. This is achieved by linking the piston to a crankshaft, the connecting rod between the two having a linear motion at its top (piston) end and a 'winding' (rotary) motion at its bottom end. The crankshaft is linked, via the transmission system, to the road wheels.

Admitting the air and fuel into, and allowing exhaust gases out of, the engine is the job of the inlet ports, the valves, and the camshaft which operates these valves. Most four-stroke engines have valves in the 'head' (the top end of the cylinder). In some engines the valves are opened and closed by cams on a shaft mounted in the head; in others they are operated by rods pushed by a camshaft mounted at the side of the engine. Most cars have two valves per cylinder, but some high-performance engines use four, which increases the gas flow considerably.

Most modern petrol engines operate on a fuel mixture that is somewhat richer (that is, contains a higher proportion of petrol) than is strictly necessary. This maximises the power output, but it results in exhaust gases having a high concentration of carbon monoxide, unburnt hydrocarbons, and other pollutants. Recently the Japanese, in response to the stringent exhaust-emission laws passed in their own country and in the United States, have tackled this problem by developing what are known as stratified-charge engines. These have a 'pre-chamber', fitted with a single inlet valve, in which a rich 'core' of fuel is ignited, and this in turn ignites a much weaker mixture surrounding the core. By this means a higher proportion of the fuel is actually burnt. Among production models using this type of engine is the version of the Honda Civic marketed in the United States.

Petrol or diesel engines?

There is a good deal of controversy about the relative merits of the two types of piston engine. Diesel engines are more expensive to produce because they have to compress their fuel/air mixture to about twice the pressure of that in a petrol engine and so require a more robust structure; but, by the same token, they tend to last longer. Moreover, they use less fuel: the 1,500 cc engine of the VW Golf diesel has only about three quarters of the fuel consumption of the Golf's 1,100 cc petrol engine. On the other hand, petrol engines develop more power: in the VW example quoted above, both engines have an output of 50 bhp, although the petrol engine has only 70 per cent of the diesel's cubic capacity. At present, petrol engines are the more refined in operation, especially at low speeds, when diesels emit a characteristic 'chatter'. For the motorist, then, each type has certain advantages over the other. The further expansion of the diesel engine in the private-car

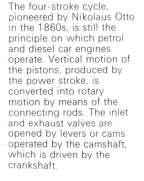

The four-stroke cycle, pioneered by Nikolaus Otto in the 1860s, is still the principle on which petrol and diesel car engines operate. Vertical motion of the pistons, produced by the power stroke, is converted into rotary motion by means of the connecting rods. The inlet and exhaust valves are opened by levers or cams operated by the camshaft, which is driven by the crankshaft.

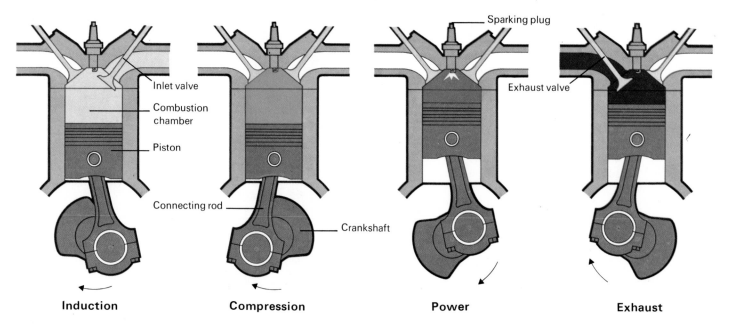

Induction **Compression** **Power** **Exhaust**

Sparking plug

Inlet valve

Combustion chamber

Piston

Connecting rod

Crankshaft

Exhaust valve

market is likely to depend as much on national taxation policies as on technical criteria. In continental Europe, for example, diesel fuel is usually cheaper than four-star petrol, whereas in Britain it is at present considerably more expensive.

The cooling system

The internal-combustion engine – whether in a Rolls-Royce limousine, a Formula 1 racing car, or a single-cylinder moped – is an inherently inefficient source of power. A typical motor car engine is capable of transforming only about 25 per cent of the energy of its fuel into *usable* power on the road; most of the remainder goes to waste in the form of heat or exhaust gases. The heat must be dissipated, otherwise the engine parts would quickly seize up. All motor-car engines are cooled by air, either directly or through the medium of air-cooled water that circulates in a water jacket within the engine block.

Even very powerful engines can be kept cool by forced draughts of air (as the exceptionally fast Porsche 917 sports-racing cars have proved), and suitable ducting and efficient fans can keep any normal engine's temperature within acceptable limits. The two major problems of air-cooled car engines are keeping the engine reasonably quiet (a water jacket is a very efficient sound absorber) and heating and ventilating the passenger compartment (where the heat source is normally hot water tapped from the cooling circuits).

Although both these problems are of minor importance in strictly engineering terms, they have been sufficient to persuade the overwhelming majority of manufacturers to use water-cooled engines, in which the combustion chambers and cylinder blocks are wrapped in water jackets that extract surplus heat. When the engine is running, the water continuously passes into and out of the engine on a closed circuit, and its temperature is kept in check by air passing through a cooling radiator, usually mounted in the nose of the car. The water is circulated by a water pump driven by the engine. Additional cooling of the radiator, especially important when the car is standing motionless with the engine running, is provided by a fan driven by the engine or (in some recent models) by an electric motor.

Engine configurations

The design of an engine, and especially the number and layout of its cylinders, are at least partly determined by where, within the bodywork, the engine is to be located. In most cars the engine is at the front, which seems to offer designers the most scope for making the

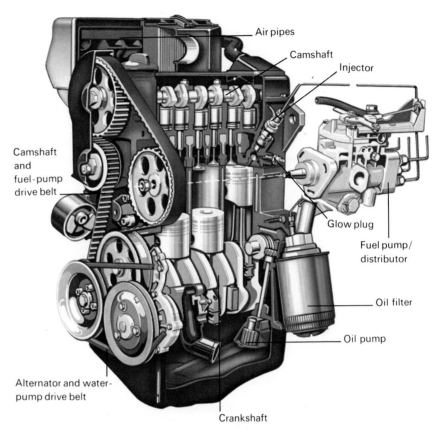

Air pipes

Camshaft

Injector

Camshaft and fuel-pump drive belt

Glow plug

Fuel pump/ distributor

Oil filter

Oil pump

Alternator and water-pump drive belt

Crankshaft

best use of the total space available. Some cars (most notably the VW Beetle) have their engines mounted at the back. A few two-seater sports cars are 'mid-engined', with the unit behind the seats but ahead of the rear wheels. This represents a rather prodigal use of the total space, but designers believe it improves a car's high-speed handling.

To run with what the modern car buyer would consider to be acceptable smoothness, an engine needs a minimum of two cylinders, and preferably at least four. The engine's cubic capacity and the number of cylinders specified depend largely on the power required. In broad terms, modern mass-produced engines produce about 50 bhp/litre, about twice the power developed by engines in the early 1930s. A small family saloon needs about 40 to 50 bhp to give it an acceptable performance, which explains why there are so many small cars with engines of between 800 and 1,000 cc.

In recent years several models have reflected the growing conviction that an engine that is somewhat larger but less highly tuned than those used hitherto will have not only a longer life but better fuel consumption. The point has been well made in the Renault 5 range, which includes a 956 cc unit producing 44 bhp and a 1,289 cc unit that develops 2 bhp *less* and uses up to 20 per cent less fuel.

The VW Golf 1,500 cc diesel engine is based on the design of a petrol engine of similar capacity used in another version of the model. In this and other diesel engines, air is drawn into the cylinders and compressed, which makes it hot. At the point of maximum compression, diesel fuel is squirted into the combustion chamber by an injector and ignites spontaneously, thus doing away with the need for sparking plugs. The fuel is delivered to each injector, at the exact moment and in the exact quantity required, by the fuel pump/ distributor. The glow plug is used for starting the engine from cold.

Left Since the idea was pioneered in Alec Issigonis's Mini of 1959, many four-cylinder front-wheel-drive cars have had their engines mounted transversely (known colloquially as an 'east-west' layout). This permits the design of shorter engine compartments and, hence, a saving on a car's overall length. The example shown is the 1,700 cc 'O' Series engine of the 1979 Leyland Princess.

Below The transverse layout can also be applied to cars with mid-mounted or rear-mounted engines. The mid-engined Fiat X1/9 rear-wheel-drive sports car is seen here from above with its earlier 1,290 cc engine. In the Fiat 128 CL saloon the same engine is front-mounted transversely, driving the front wheels.

The layout of an engine – the way the cylinders are positioned – depends on many factors, including the traditions and experience of the manufacturer concerned. In Europe, for instance, the four-cylinder in-line engine is the most popular for the family saloon; in North America the majority of cars (which are generally much larger) have V8 engines, with two banks, each of four cylinders, inclined at 90 degrees to each other. Volkswagen, which began building Beetles with air-cooled, horizontally opposed, four-cylinder units in the 1930s, persisted in this layout through several models into the 1970s. Horizontally opposed engines are, as it were, flattened-out V engines, with the two banks inclined at 180 degrees. The Beetle-type unit is commonly called a 'flat-four'.

The in-line four- or six-cylinder unit has a long, slim engine block, and this has resulted in some such units being mounted transversely – a position pioneered in the Leyland Mini, introduced in 1959, and adopted subsequently by other manufacturers of small and medium-sized cars.

Most of the major manufacturers build a wide range of models, and they can save a great deal of money, in terms of machine tools

and production time, if they design 'families' of engines, each with identical cylinder dimensions, to cover all or most of their model ranges. Thus there are families of in-line fours and sixes, or V4s and V6s; or an in-line four can be double-banked to make a V8.

A V-formation engine, whether with four, six, or eight cylinders, has several advantages. A V6 unit, for example, with two banks of three cylinders is probably not as long as an in-line four, but it may have 50 per cent greater cubic capacity and power for very little extra weight. Its compact shape, moreover, fits neatly into the more or less cube-shaped engine compartments of modern cars.

In the 1920s and 1930s in the United States there was a vogue for in-line eight-cylinder engines, which were both powerful and very smooth-running. As a result, enormously long engine bonnets became something of a fad, seen at their best, perhaps, in the classic Duesenbergs of that era. Even the largest present-day American V8 engines, which are smoother and even more powerful, occupy significantly less space although they are wider than the old 'straight-eights'.

Where price is little or no object, very powerful cars are sometimes provided with 12-cylinder engines, the two most notable present-day examples being the V12 of the Jaguar XJ 5.3 and XJS and the horizontally opposed 12 of the Ferrari 512. Twelve cylinders are justified by the need to keep each cylinder quite small, the rotating masses low, and the revving capabilities of the engine high. A 12-cylinder engine does not have to have a large cubic capacity: in 1946, for instance, Gioacchino Colombo designed for Ferrari a highly successful V12 of only 1.5 litres. But, small or large, engines with such a multiplicity of cylinders are marvellously smooth-running, effortlessly powerful – and extremely thirsty.

Although four-, six-, and eight-cylinder units, whether of in-line, V, or horizontally opposed layout, are the most popular, there is no theoretical need for in-line engines to have an even number of cylinders. Audi's well-established 100 series of four-cylinder saloons has recently been joined by a model with a five-cylinder in-line unit, which the company claims to be as smooth-running as an in-line six. In-line fives have been used in trucks and buses for a long time.

Rotary engines

Two other types of internal-combustion engines have application – actual or potential – as power units for cars: the rotating-combustion engine, of which the best-known example is the Wankel, and the gas turbine. The first

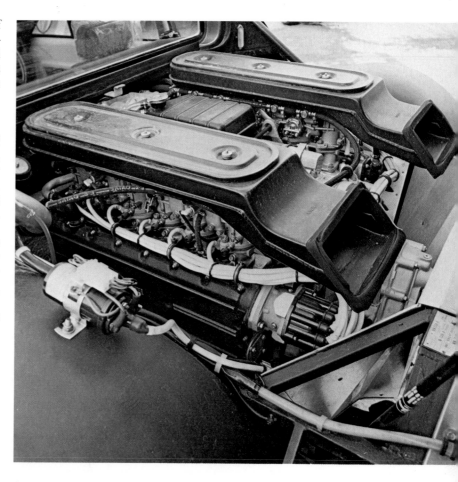

The 5-litre flat-12 engine of the Ferrari 512 Boxer coupé, a classic example of an ultra-fast sports car with mid-mounted engine. The cylinder layout produces a more or less cube-shaped engine, so that transverse mounting would have saved little space. The mid-mounted location differs from a rear-mounted one in that the centre of the engine mass is forward of the line of the rear wheels.

Wankel-engined production car was the German NSU Spider, introduced in 1964; today Mazda of Japan is the most prolific manufacturer. The Wankel engine has a normal four-stroke cycle, but instead of pistons it has a rotor, a structure that in plan view resembles what might be called a convex-sided triangle. This structure rotates within a chamber shaped rather like two intersecting circles – a shape that enables each lobe (corner) of the rotor to maintain contact with the chamber wall throughout each revolution. The fuel is ignited by one or two sparking plugs placed at the appropriate point in the revolutionary cycle. Wankel engines usually have at least two rotors.

At first sight rotating-combustion engines of this type have considerable advantages over conventional reciprocating (piston-and-cylinder) engines. The rotor is directly connected to the transmission, so the Wankel does not have to convert linear motion into rotary motion, as must a conventional engine. This means it needs considerably fewer moving parts – only the rotor on its shaft, compared with the normal arrangement of pistons and connecting rods, together with valves, valve gears, and camshaft. But at its present stage of development the Wankel has several important

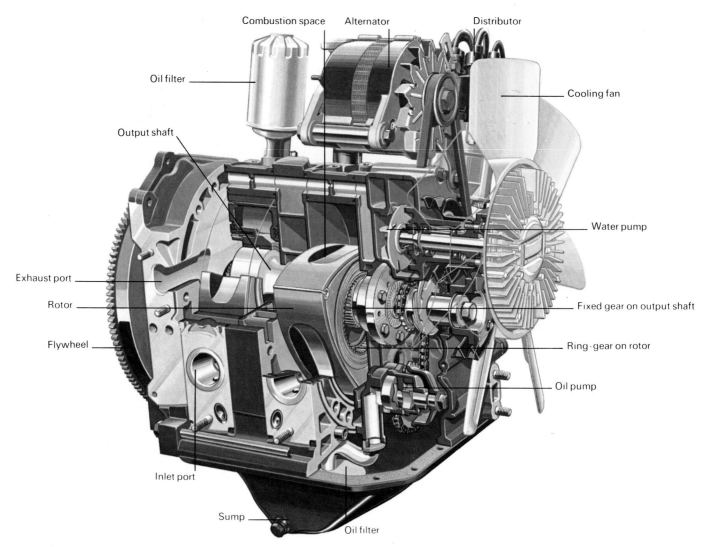

Combustion space   Alternator   Distributor

Oil filter

Output shaft

Cooling fan

Exhaust port

Rotor

Flywheel

Water pump

Fixed gear on output shaft

Ring-gear on rotor

Oil pump

Inlet port

Sump

Oil filter

A twin-rotor Wankel engine. The basically triangular rotors have a combustion space cast into each of their three sides. Each rotor chamber has a single sparking plug (or sometimes two mounted close together), so that there are three power (combustion) 'strokes' for every revolution of each rotor. When one of the combustion spaces is in the combustion position, the other two spaces are in the exhaust, induction, or compression phase of the rotary cycle.

drawbacks. It is relatively expensive to manufacture; there has been persistent difficulty in contriving efficient, durable gas-tight seals between the rotor lobes and the chamber walls; and the design sets up severe temperature gradients in the chamber casing. Moreover, Wankel engines have a higher petrol consumption than piston engines of similar power. All these factors have discouraged manufacturers from using rotating-combustion engines, although research on the type continues in Europe, Japan, and the United States.

The gas-turbine engine, developed for aviation purposes in the 1930s by A.A. Griffith and Frank Whittle in Britain and by Pabst von Ohain in Germany, is potentially, at least, an excellent source of power for a motor car. It is comparatively simple – and therefore reliable – and can develop formidable power in a very compact package. Broadly speaking it works as follows: air is drawn into a compressor, where its pressure is raised, and then passes into a combustion chamber. Here fuel is

injected and burnt to produce a high-velocity gas. This is directed against the blades of a turbine, which is connected to the compressor by a shaft. The rotating turbine extracts a small proportion of the energy in the gas to drive the compressor; the rest of the energy can be tapped as power to drive the car by linking the turbine shaft to the transmission.

The technical viability of this type of engine for cars has already been established: a Rover fitted with a specially developed gas-turbine engine developing 200 hp ran successfully in 1950; Fiat experimented with a gas-turbine-powered coupé in 1955, as did Renault the following year; and considerable experimental work has been carried out on gas turbines for heavy goods vehicles, notably by British Leyland. The main deterrent to their use in road vehicles is the cost of both materials and production. The turbine blades and the compressor have to work at very high temperatures, and they require the use of special alloys that must be machined to exceptionally fine tolerances. At present, the price of the alloys and of the machine tools needed to shape them makes the gas-turbine engine uneconomic for use in cars.

Engine speed and power output

While it is true that very fast cars invariably have powerful engines, the horse-power rating of an engine is not the only guide to the car's performance. In fact, a better idea of an engine's capabilities is often given by its torque rating – the twisting effort, measured in metre-kilograms or pounds-feet, that indicates the usable power available at the crankshaft. The reason for this is that, in different engines of equal horse-power, maximum torque may be available at quite different engine speeds, and this in turn determines the way in which the engine and, in particular, the gearbox must be used to obtain maximum performance. (Of course, the torque rating is limited by the engine's horse-power; it is simply the engine speed at which the maximum torque is available that can be varied by the designer according to the needs of a particular model.)

The technically minded person can get a pretty clear idea of an engine's road performance by examining graphs of its power and torque curves. If maximum torque is recorded at a relatively low engine speed – say 3,500 rpm (revolutions per minute) or less – and the curve is not too steep, it indicates that the engine will be a good low-rpm slogger and that in town, for instance, the driver will not constantly have to use the lower gears to keep the engine pulling smoothly. (High torque at relatively low engine speed, incidentally, is the best recipe for an automatic gearbox.) If, on the contrary, the torque curve is steep and the maximum is reached at a high rpm, it indicates a highly tuned engine that will deliver maximum performance (especially acceleration) by frequent use of the gearbox. Most sports-car engines are of this type.

The Future

The thermal efficiency of car engines is undoubtedly capable of improvement. But the characteristics of engines in the future are likely to be influenced as much by external factors – especially the problems of fuel conservation and atmospheric pollution – as by the technical ingenuity of designers. During the past decade the United States and Japan have applied a number of restrictions on the gases that car engines are permitted to exhaust into the atmosphere. It is probable that many of these restrictions will be introduced into Europe and elsewhere before long. This has resulted in the development of complex equipment,

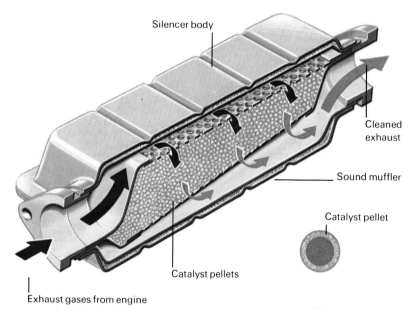

Silencer body

Cleaned exhaust

Sound muffler

Catalyst pellet

Catalyst pellets

Exhaust gases from engine

such as catalytic converters, that are built into the exhaust systems and render harmless (or, at least, less harmful) the toxic substances contained in exhaust gases. Such systems inevitably make car engines less efficient and more thirsty, and this, of course, runs counter to the world need to use less, not more, fuel.

It is possible that fuels other than petrol and diesel will be developed for piston engines. Potentially one of the most promising is liquefied petroleum gas (LPG), which consists of propane or a mixture of propane and butane. At present, however, the world production of these gases is already earmarked for vital industrial applications; in any case, LPG, too, is derived from our dwindling reserves of crude oil. Other possibilities include syncrude (synthetic crude oil), which is extracted from coal and is already in use in South Africa; methanol, which can be produced from waste matter, and liquid hydrogen, which is extremely expensive to produce and dangerous to store.

Research into electric engines continues. The problem is to find an alternative to the conventional bulky and extremely heavy lead/acid battery, which offers a very short range. Nickel/iron and sodium/sulphur types are likely to offer improvements, but it is doubtful if battery engines are going to power anything except urban delivery vehicles for many years to come. Even if more efficient batteries are developed and are widely used on other types of vehicle, it will not help us to conserve our reserves of petroleum. The batteries will still need to be recharged at fairly frequent intervals, and this of course will consume large quantities of electricity that, in most of the world's power stations, is generated by burning petroleum oil.

A catalytic converter is now required in the exhaust systems of many cars sold in North America, Japan, and Scandinavia. The converter neutralizes most of the toxic by-products formed when petrol engines burn fuel. This converter is a chamber packed with pellets, each consisting of a core of ceramic material in honeycomb form enclosed within a layer of a precious metal such as palladium, platinum, or rhodium. The metal acts as a catalyst, initiating the chemical conversion of the toxic substances into less harmful forms, which are then absorbed by the ceramic core. The 'clean' gases then pass through the car's exhaust system in the usual way.

15 Engine Accessories

Mechanical fuel pumps are actuated by a cam on the engine's camshaft. When the cam pushes the pump lever the right-hand spring-loaded valve in the upper drawing opens, allowing fuel from the petrol tank to be drawn into the pump chamber. As the cam rotates and allows the lever to return to the 'off' position (lower drawing), the left-hand valve opens and the fuel passes along the pump's outlet pipe to the carburettor.

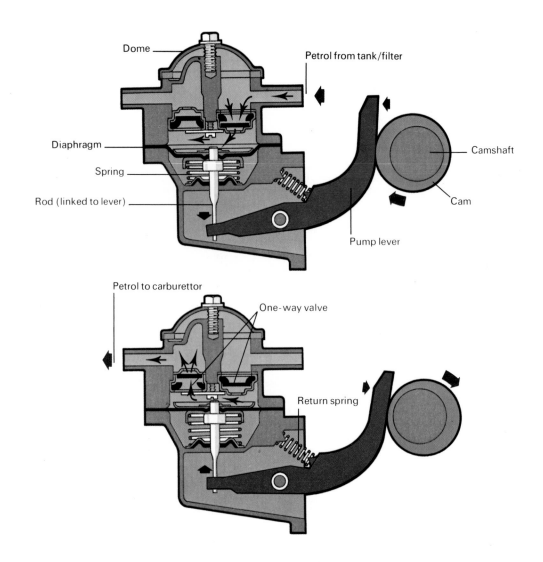

A look around the engine compartment of a modern car, particularly one of the more expensive models, and of an equivalent car of the 1920s would show striking differences. Yet very little of the extra complexity of a 1970s installation is due to new engine concepts. The differences are due to the fact that the modern engine has many tasks to perform in addition to propelling the car.

Carburation

Fuel used to be fed to primitive carburettors by the force of gravity, which meant that many fuel tanks were installed on the bulkhead behind the engine and updraught carburettors were mounted low down beside the engine. Today fuel is delivered to the carburettor by engine-driven mechanical pumps or electric lift pumps, whose efficiency has greatly improved in the past 20 years.

Most fuel systems today have a fuel tank mounted remotely from the engine bay; for safety reasons tanks in front-engined cars are now being mounted under the back seats rather than under or within the boot. The tank must be fitted with a 'breathing' system so that air can be drawn in as fuel is fed to the engine.

The fuel passes from the tank to the engine through small-bore metal or plastic pipes, which are usually clipped to the underside of the body; the pump may be in the tank, alongside it, or in the engine compartment. The fuel is filtered very finely to make sure dirt and water do not get into the carburettor.

Preparing the fuel for the engine is done by one or more carburettors or (in the case of diesel engines and some high-performance petrol engines) by fuel injection. A carburettor is a complex instrument in which the required fuel mixture is produced by passing air over jets of vapourized petrol. An injection system squirts small and very precisely metered jets of fuel into the passing air stream. In a diesel engine the oil is injected directly into the

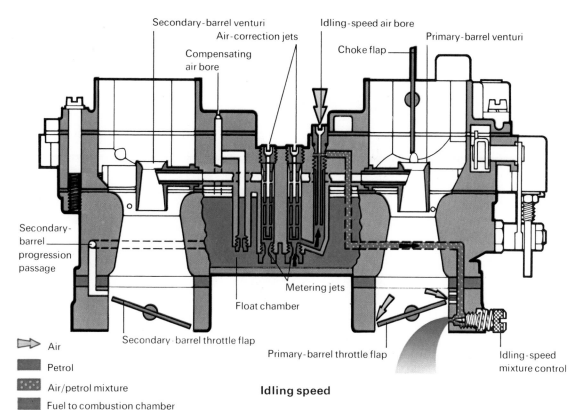

Secondary-barrel venturi
Air-correction jets
Idling-speed air bore
Primary-barrel venturi
Compensating air bore
Choke flap
Secondary-barrel progression passage
Metering jets
Float chamber
Air
Petrol
Air/petrol mixture
Fuel to combustion chamber
Secondary-barrel throttle flap
Primary-barrel throttle flap
Idling-speed mixture control

Idling speed

Left The carburettor's job is to mix the air and petrol in the correct proportions and deliver it in precisely metered quantities to each combustion chamber in turn. The metering is done by an adjustable choke. Many small cars use a simple single-choke carburettor, but more powerful engines may be fitted with a twin-barrel (two-choke) unit, such as this one used in the Vauxhall Cavalier 2-litre. The drawings show the carburettor operation at various engine speeds. At idling speed (large drawing) only one choke needs to be open to deliver sufficient fuel to the combustion chambers. At intermediate speed (lower left), as when the car is accelerating slowly, the primary choke is fully open while the secondary choke is partly open. At full throttle (lower right), used for maximum acceleration, both chokes are fully open. Progressive opening of the chokes is provided by a geared linkage on the carburettor body that is connected to the accelerator pedal.

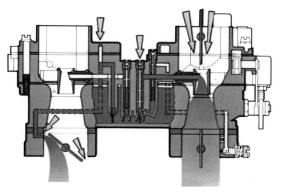

Half throttle

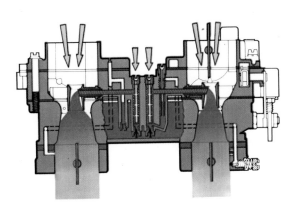

Full throttle

combustion chamber at the precise moment when the air has been compressed to its smallest volume. At such pressures the air is hot enough to ignite the oil.

Starting from cold needs much richer mixtures than normal, and these are provided by the choke, which employs a system of flaps and levers to allow less air to get into the engine than normally. As the engine warms up its fuel needs return to normal and the knob of a manually operated choke must progressively be pushed back to the closed position. Many cars have a temperature-sensitive 'automatic'

choke built into the carburettor or fuel-injection system. One stab on the throttle pedal pre-sets the control, after which it can be allowed to regulate itself.

Ignition

A petrol engine needs a reliable system to ignite the fuel/air mixture in the cylinders. The ignition circuitry accounts for much of the complex wiring in the engine compartment. Ignition involves four basic functions: electricity generation, amplification of the voltage, distribution of the electrical current to each of the combustion chambers, and discharge in the form of sparks. These functions are carried out, respectively, by the generator, the coil, the distributor, and the sparking plugs.

The generator is engine-driven by a belt connected to the crankshaft. It pushes out direct-current electricity at a pressure of between 12 and 15 volts. The coil is an electrically simple component that induces very high voltage electricity from the indirect flow of normal supplies, which are periodically cut off and restored by a device called a contact breaker fitted into the base of the distributor. The distributor itself is shaft driven from the engine, either from the crankshaft or from a camshaft, and serves to direct the high-tension electricity from the coil to each cylinder at the appropriate instant. Sparking plugs are simple ceramic-clad components that provide a spark powerful enough to ignite the fuel/air mixture in the cylinders (*see* Chapter 18).

Cooling

Another space-consuming sub-system in the engine compartment is that which keeps the engine cool and the passengers warm. When engines are running they produce frictional heat. The engine's operating temperature has to be kept in check by a cooling system. In a water-cooled engine the water transfers the heat from the engine to a point where it can be dispersed. The engine castings have water circulating inside them. Many years ago this circulation relied on the property of hot water to rise above cold, but all modern cars have water pumps driven from the engine's crankshaft. The water is pushed out to the cooling radiator.

In very cold weather an engine may tend to become over-cooled, and ways have to be devised to keep the temperature of the water sufficiently high to prevent this happening. This is done by fitting a valve called a thermostat in the cooling system. Unless the water temperature is above a pre-set level, the valve stays closed; the water is thereby prevented from passing to and from the radiator system and is by-passed back into the engine. The valve also allows the engine to warm up quickly from cold.

Water expands when it heats up, and so there has to be provision for overspill to escape from the system. In the simplest of all systems the water is allowed to escape through an open-ended small-bore pipe. Nowadays, however, on many cars this overspill pipe is led into a small auxiliary container, so that when the engine cools down the water can be drawn back into the system. Such a layout is known as a sealed system, and it never needs topping up

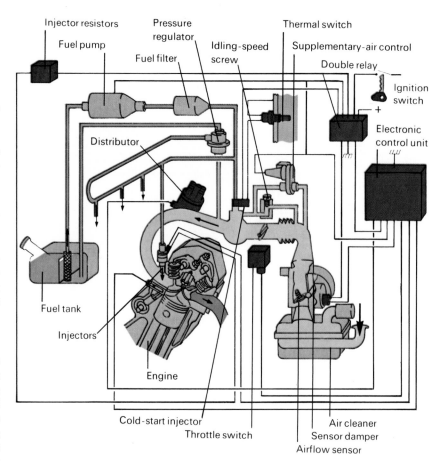

with fresh supplies unless it develops a leak.

The modern car also uses the power of its engine to operate several other subsidiary systems, such as power-assisted mechanisms for steering and braking, pumps to power the suspension hydraulics, and pumps to circulate the fluids in an air-conditioning and refrigeration unit. In countries such as the United States, where there are laws governing the emission of exhaust gases, cars may be fitted with a pump to inject air into the exhaust system. All these mechanisms and pumps are driven by the engine. Indeed, one of the most striking aspects of the modern car is the steadily dwindling proportion of its output of power that can be devoted to the basic job of turning the road wheels.

Emission-control systems

Entire departments in motor-car companies are nowadays devoted exclusively to developing methods of reducing or neutralizing the poisons emitted in engine exhaust gases. There are three main areas of development at present. The first is carburation. It is important for efficient combustion that the quantity and proportions of the fuel/air mixture fed into the combustion chamber are metered with great accuracy. Many manufacturers now seal their

Electronically controlled fuel injection is a sophisticated alternative to the carburettor. Although it is considerably more complex and expensive, it meters the air-and-petrol mixture with greater precision by means of electronic sensors that respond to throttle opening, engine speed, and the pressure of air entering the inlet manifold. The drawing represents in diagrammatic form the system used in the Citroën CX 2400GTi.

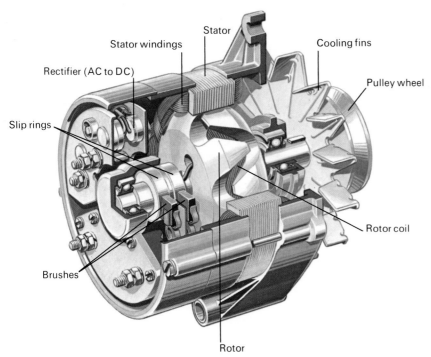

Stator windings

Stator

Rectifier (AC to DC)

Cooling fins

Slip rings

Pulley wheel

Brushes

Rotor coil

Rotor

Above An alternator produces alternating current (AC) when driven by the car's engine, but this is rectified — converted to direct current (DC) — before being supplied to the car's electrical system.

carburettors and injection equipment so that they cannot be tampered with. The second area is the combustion chamber itself. Much work has been done in recent years to improve the shape of the chamber in order to achieve complete combustion. The stratified-charge engine (*see* Chapter 14) is a notable example of this. The third area is the exhaust system. Every internal-combustion engine, however efficient, exhausts a small residue of unburnt or partly burnt gases containing toxic gases. These must be burnt before they are exhausted through the tail pipe. One method is to inject air into the exhaust system, as mentioned above; another is to feed a proportion of the gases back into the inlet pipes and thence into the combustion chamber again. A third method (now required by law in North America) is to feed the exhaust gases into a device called a catalytic converter, in which a rare metal in lattice frames acts as a catalyst in the chemical transformation of some of the toxic gases.

Electronic diagnosis

The engine bay also accommodates other systems, notably the power house of the electrical storage and supply activities, which are described in detail in Chapter 18. It is worth noting here, however, that some cars now have what is called a diagnostic socket included in the electrical wiring. This allows electronic machinery installed at service garages to be plugged in to the car's systems while the engine is running so as to monitor the circuits.

Right Most car engines are cooled by water, which is circulated continuously by means of a pump and cooled by the passage of cold air through the radiator. After passing through the engine the water is routed through the heater system to provide warmth for the car's occupants. The greatest engine heat is generated around the combustion chambers; the detail sketch at extreme right shows the plumbing in that area.

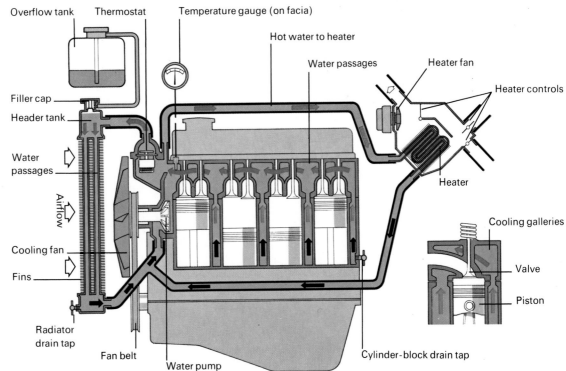

Overflow tank

Thermostat

Temperature gauge (on facia)

Hot water to heater

Water passages

Heater fan

Heater controls

Filler cap

Header tank

Water passages

Airflow

Heater

Cooling fan

Fins

Cooling galleries

Valve

Piston

Radiator drain tap

Fan belt

Water pump

Cylinder-block drain tap

16 Transmission

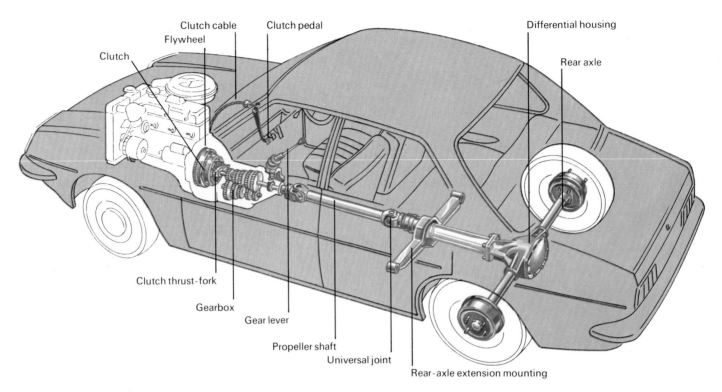

Clutch cable · Clutch pedal · Differential housing
Flywheel · Rear axle
Clutch
Clutch thrust-fork
Gearbox
Gear lever
Propeller shaft
Universal joint
Rear-axle extension mounting

The engine and transmission layout of the Vauxhall Cavalier, which is typical of most conventional, medium-sized cars. The front-mounted engine has a manual gearbox in unit with it, a propeller shaft linking gearbox and differential, and a 'live' axle for transmitting the drive to the rear wheels.

No conventional motor-car engine has sufficient torque throughout its speed range to propel the vehicle efficiently without the help of a transmission system. No matter what type of vehicle is involved – whether a small family runabout or a big articulated truck – this system has three essential functions to perform. The first is to allow the engine's full power to be available at different road speeds. This is the job of the gears, which provide a link between the engine's crankshaft and the driven road wheels. The gearbox contains gears of different ratios (usually four or five forward gears with manual transmissions, and three gears in the case of 'automatics') to enable the car to cope with a variety of situations: starting from rest, accelerating slowly or quickly, performing adequately whether lightly or heavily loaded, climbing steep hills, and cruising at high speeds on level roads. And, since the crankshaft always rotates in the same direction, the gearbox must include an extra gear to allow the car to be driven backwards.

The second function is to apply the power of the engine, once the appropriate gear has been engaged, directly to the driven road wheels. This is the job of the differential, or final drive, which has to take into account the fact that the road wheels are often turning at slightly different speeds, especially when the car is going around a corner.

The third function is made necessary by the first. When a driver changes gear there is a sudden alteration in the relative rotational speeds of the crankshaft and the shaft that drives the road wheels. If the gears and crankshaft tried to mesh at different speeds the gearbox would be severely damaged. So a means must be found of, first, cushioning the impact of shaft and gears and, second, locking the entire system together once the gear has been engaged. This is the job of the clutch or (in the case of an automatic gearbox) of the torque converter or fluid coupling.

In the past 50 years the transmission layout has changed only in detail. The gearbox is almost invariably bolted directly to the engine block instead of being separated from it. The most notable exceptions to the single-package engine/transmission system are models made by Alfa Romeo and Porsche, in which the gearbox is bolted directly to the rear-axle casing, with the drive shaft linking it to the front-mounted engine. The object is to improve the weight distribution (and therefore the handling) of these high-performance cars.

Four-wheel-drive transmissions are provided for vehicles where the ultimate in traction is required, as with cross-country machines which must often struggle for grip in slippery conditions. The basic transmission system is modified in that there are two drive shafts from the main gearbox, one linking in the normal way with the rear axle and the other with the front axle. Usually it is possible to disconnect the front-wheel drive by mechanical means, so that conventional rear-wheel drive can be used on ordinary roads.

The Clutch

In a manual transmission the clutch is actuated by movement of the driver's left-hand pedal. The principal component of a clutch is a thin, steel disc, called the driven plate, which is attached to the input shaft of the gearbox. Both faces of the driven plate are covered with a friction material called the lining. When a car is in gear, the driven plate is clamped firmly against the flywheel (which is bolted to the crankshaft) by the powerful springs of the gearbox-mounted pressure plate. To change gear, the driver depresses the clutch pedal. This causes the pressure plate to withdraw, allowing the flywheel and driven plate to rotate independently of each other. Then, when another gear has been selected, the driver releases the clutch pedal. As the driven plate comes up against the flywheel again, the friction lining allows the two surfaces to skid against each other for a moment until they are both rotating at the same speed. Then the power of the pressure-plate springs locks the driven plate and flywheel together so that the crankshaft and gearbox input shaft turn at exactly the same speed.

A very few high-performance cars with enormously powerful engines need multi-plate clutches to transmit the power, but most cars use a single-plate design. Between the wars there was a vogue for 'wet' clutches that operated in a bath of oil and used a particular type of lining material, but all modern designs are 'dry' and must be kept so to prevent the fully engaged driven plate from slipping.

Above The 'chain-gang' Frazer Nash (this model is from about 1930) was so called because chains rather than a propeller shaft were used to transmit the drive to the rear axle.

Manual gearboxes

On a modern car the manually operated gearbox contains sets of gear wheels of different sizes mounted on two parallel shafts – the output shaft and the layshaft. Each of the gear wheels on one shaft is meshed at all times with its opposite number on the other shaft, with the exception of the wheels for reverse gear. Now, if every gear wheel was permanently locked to its shaft, no movement would be possible since

Left Front-wheel-drive cars have engine, gearbox, and final drive in unit in the nose of the car. The constant-velocity joints permit angular movement of the drive shafts when the front wheels are steered.

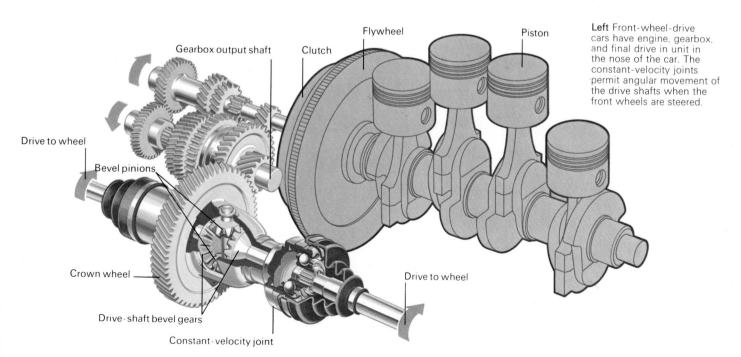

Gearbox output shaft   Clutch   Flywheel   Piston

Drive to wheel

Bevel pinions

Crown wheel

Drive to wheel

Drive-shaft bevel gears

Constant-velocity joint

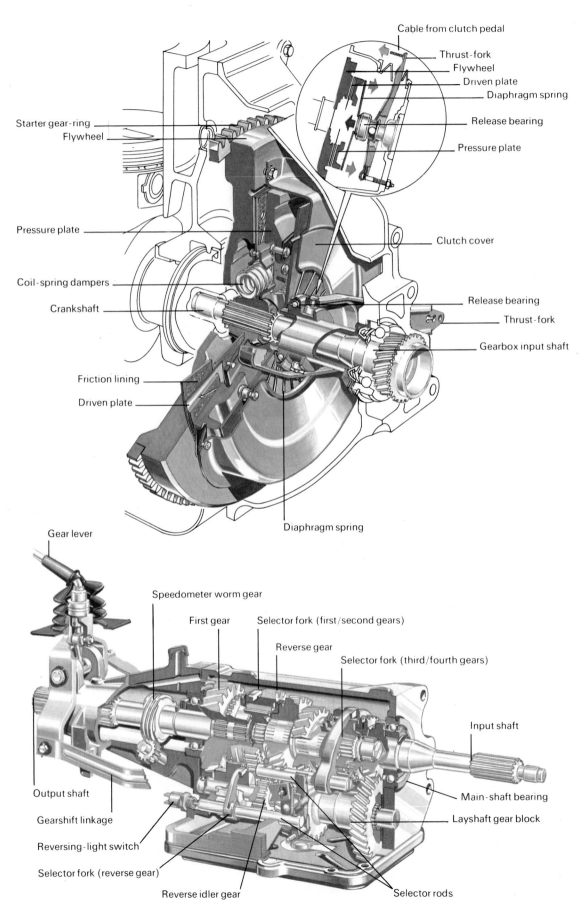

Cable from clutch pedal

Thrust-fork

Flywheel

Driven plate

Diaphragm spring

Release bearing

Pressure plate

Left The clutch is a shock-free method of taking up the drive from engine to transmission, and it provides a solid drive line when the clutch pedal is lifted. The coil springs around the shaft help to cushion the action of the driven plate, which has friction material on both faces. The diaphragm spring clamps the driven plate to the flywheel face when the pedal is released.

Starter gear-ring

Flywheel

Pressure plate

Coil-spring dampers

Crankshaft

Friction lining

Driven plate

Clutch cover

Release bearing

Thrust-fork

Gearbox input shaft

Diaphragm spring

Gear lever

Speedometer worm gear

First gear

Selector fork (first/second gears)

Reverse gear

Selector fork (third/fourth gears)

Left Most popular cars now have manually operated four- or five-speed, all-synchromesh gear-boxes in their standard specification. This four-speed box is in the Vauxhall Cavalier GL.

Input shaft

Output shaft

Main-shaft bearing

Gearshift linkage

Layshaft gear block

Reversing-light switch

Selector fork (reverse gear)

Reverse idler gear

Selector rods

all the gears would be simultaneously engaged. To get around this problem, all the gear wheels on the gearbox output shaft can spin independently of the shaft's rotation until a gear ratio is selected by the driver. Movement of the driver's gear lever locks one of the gear wheels onto the output shaft, so that the two shafts rotate together, but in opposite directions. The wheel on one shaft is of a different size from that on the other shaft, the difference in each case corresponding to the gear ratio.

The locking of gear wheels to the output shaft is done by collars that are placed between each of the gear wheels. The collars are locked in to the turning motion of the shaft but can slide along it. The side faces of each collar have rings of projections called dogs; each of the gear wheels on the output shaft has similar dogs on one of its sides, so that when the collar is clamped against the gear wheel the dogs mesh and turn as one unit. The collar for each gear is moved by a system of forks and rods actuated by the driver's gear lever. Reverse gear involves much the same process, except that a third gear wheel is interposed between those on the output shaft and layshaft in order to make the system turn in the opposite direction.

Now, before a gear is engaged, the collar locked to the output shaft is likely to be rotating at a speed different from that of the free-running gear wheel with which it is going to mesh. This made for noisy and potentially damaging gear changes until the development of the synchromesh system (first used by General Motors in 1928 and now universally employed). In simple terms, synchromesh consists of a conical recess on the side of the collar and a conical projection of matching size on the side of the gear wheel. The two cones come into frictional contact, and so synchronize the speeds of collar and gear wheel, before the two sets of dogs mesh. A refinement of the synchromesh system employs a baulking mechanism that prevents engagement of a gear until the collar and gear-wheel speeds are exactly the same.

Most manual gearboxes have four forward gears and one reverse gear, but an increasing number are now being provided with five forward speeds. Cars with a normal four-speed gearbox may alternatively be equipped with a device known as an overdrive. This is a separate sub-assembly, usually bolted to the back of the gearbox casing and often sharing the same transmission oils. Overdrive gears up the transmission even more than a direct fourth gear, and so offers high-speed cruising at low rpm. Usually overdrive can be engaged or disengaged by means of an electrical switch mounted on top of the gear-lever knob. Cone clutches and a train of epicyclic (sun-and-planet) gears enable this change to be made without use of the ordinary gearbox clutch. Some overdrives can operate on third as well as top gear, giving the driver six forward ratios.

Automatic transmissions

Almost all North American cars, and a growing proportion of those built in Europe and Japan, are equipped with automatic transmission. Although they vary in detail, almost all such systems are built to the same general design. In automatics, the clutch is replaced by a fluid coupling or, more usually, by a torque converter. Basically, a fluid coupling consists of two bowl-shaped moving parts with their rims facing each other but not quite touching; each bowl is lined with 20 or more radial partitions (vanes). The first bowl, called the impeller, is driven by the crankshaft; the second, called the turbine, drives the gearbox input shaft. At engine idling speed, oil is flung by the impeller into the turbine, but not with sufficient force to make it rotate. When the driver puts his foot on the accelerator to increase engine (and impeller) speed, the force exerted by the oil increases, the turbine begins to turn, and the car is set in motion. As engine speed increases, the speed of the turbine gets closer and closer to that of the impeller until, at full throttle, their rates of rotation are almost identical.

The fact that the turbine speed can never exceed that of the impeller means that it cannot produce greater torque (turning effort) than that delivered by the crankshaft. It is in this respect that the torque converter is superior to the fluid coupling. The designs of the two systems are very similar, except that in the torque converter a small vaned wheel (rather like a paddle wheel) is located between the impeller and the turbine. At normal cruising speeds this vaned wheel, called the reactor (or stator), is turned by the oil at the same speed as the turbine. When extra power is needed, however, as when accelerating from rest, the reactor is locked motionless and its vanes direct the oil back from the turbine into the impeller in a much more efficient way than is possible in a fluid coupling. By this means, the impeller effectively doubles the crankshaft torque at engine speeds of up to about 3,000 rpm.

The automatic gearbox is designed to select gears in response to the speed and torque of the input shaft attached to the turbine. The gearbox, which may have two, three, or four ratios (but usually three), is a complex system of epicyclic gear trains, dog clutches, brake bands, relays, and hydraulic clutches. The heart of the system is the linked epicyclic gears. Each of these

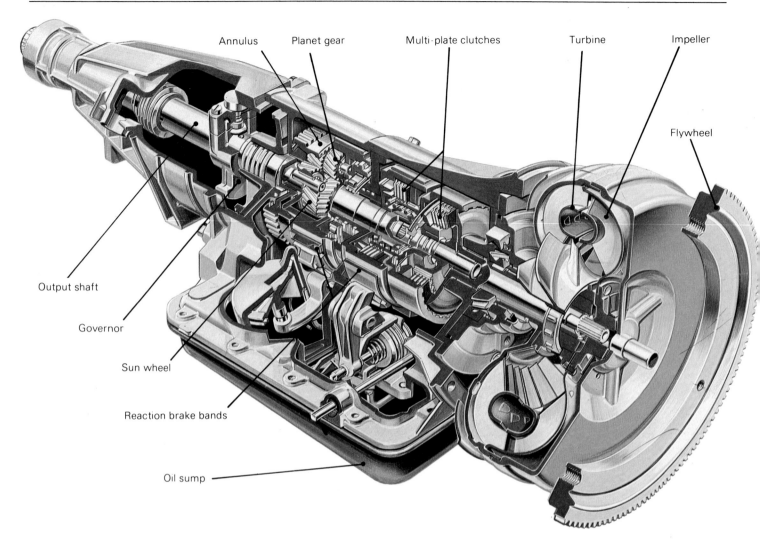

Annulus   Planet gear   Multi-plate clutches   Turbine   Impeller

Flywheel

Output shaft

Governor

Sun wheel

Reaction brake bands

Oil sump

An automatic transmission is a complex but effective way of making driving easy. A fluid-drive torque converter replaces the conventional clutch, and most systems have three forward speeds provided by a combination of epicyclic (sun-and-planet) gears. A sensitive hydraulic-control system, which responds to engine speed, road speed, and movement of the accelerator pedal, selects appropriate gear ratios independently of the driver when the selector lever is in 'Drive' position.

consists of a geared sun wheel, which meshes with two planet wheels that orbit around it. The planet wheels also mesh with the teeth on the inner circumference of a flat, ring-like structure called the annulus. The usual arrangement is to have two epicyclic gears with an elongated sun wheel common to both. The system is designed so that each of the main components – sun wheel, either set of planet wheels, or either annulus – can be braked while the others combine to turn the output shaft. The gear ratio selected at any given moment depends on which component is braked. The appropriate selection is determined by sensors that respond to the speed of the output shaft and the turning effort delivered by the torque converter or fluid coupling. The sensors operate a hydraulic system which in turn activates clutches and brake bands.

The Daf-Volvo transmission system is unique in that it provides continuously variable ratios between the high (cruising) ratio and the low (starting or hill-climbing) ratio. This is done by having two sets of vee-pulleys, one at the engine end of the transmission and the other connected to the driven rear wheels; the pulley sets are linked by belts. Sensors change the shape of the vee-pulleys relative to the belt,

and therefore change their effective operating diameters. The result is that the car's engine operates at a steady speed during acceleration, and the transmission modifies its effective ratios to deliver the correct torque. In such a layout a separate dry-disc clutch is needed, which is bolted to the engine in the conventional way.

Propeller shaft and differential

On conventional front-engine/rear-drive cars, the drive passes from the output shaft of the gearbox to the back axle along a rotating propeller shaft. Usually this is exposed to view, but on some cars it is enclosed in a chassis-mounted torque tube, which is also used to locate the rear axle for suspension purposes. At the axle it is necessary to split the drive and turn it through 90 degrees so that power can be fed to each side of the car; the principle is the same whether a beam axle or a form of independent suspension is specified.

When going around corners, or hopping about on bumpy surfaces, the rear wheels rotate at different speeds. This means that a device must be built into the final drive unit not only to change the direction of the drive but also to allow the speed of the two drive

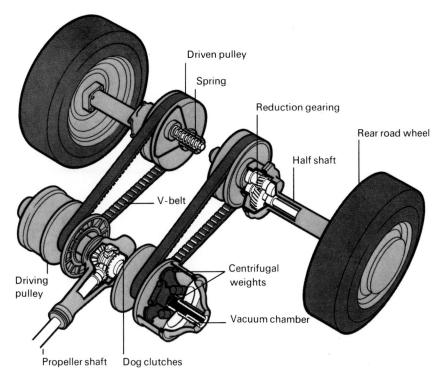

Driven pulley
Spring
Reduction gearing
Rear road wheel
Half shaft
V-belt
Centrifugal weights
Driving pulley
Vacuum chamber
Propeller shaft   Dog clutches

shafts to the wheels to be varied. This device, the differential, consists of two basic units. The first is the ring-shaped crown wheel, which is driven by the propeller shaft. Attached to a 'cage' fixed to the crown wheel are two bevel pinions, each with an axis at right angles to that of the crown wheel; they orbit in unit with the crown wheel, but each can also spin freely about its own axis. The second unit consists of the half shafts that drive the road wheels; at the inner end of each shaft is a bevel gear that meshes with both of the bevel pinions. When the road wheels rotate at the same speed, both the units rotate as one, so that the crown wheel, bevel pinions, and bevel gears are stationary relative to each other. When the road wheels rotate at different speeds, the crown wheel rotates at the *average* of their two speeds; the compensatory effect is achieved by the bevel pinions being made to turn about their own axes by the faster-rotating of the two half shafts.

This is satisfactory unless one tyre loses some or all of its grip, when it begins to spin help-lessly and the differential gear cannot cope. In some very powerful cars, in all racing cars, and in rally cars that have to drive fast over loose surfaces, a device called a limited-slip differential is employed. This uses a complex arrange-ment of friction discs between one side of the cage and the other in order to limit the speed difference between the two.

Four-wheel-drive machines use the same transmission principle, except that the drive has first to be split between front and rear

Above Daf-Volvo models use a belt-drive automatic transmission. Gear ratios are continuously variable between upper and lower limits. This is achieved by altering the effective diameter of the vee-profile drive pulleys.

Below Rear-wheel-drive differential, which splits the torque from the engine, turns the direction of drive through 90 degrees, and allows the half shafts (and hence the rear wheels) to turn at different speeds.

wheels behind the gearbox, and then split again to left and right at each differential. Well-engineered four-wheel-drive vehicles therefore employ a central differential to make this fore and aft torque split smooth.

If operating height and refinement were not problems, the simplest form of differential gearing would be straight bevel gears on the small propeller-shaft pinion and the large crown wheel. For smooth and quiet operation, however, it is desirable that tooth profiles should 'wipe' progressively into and out of mesh rather than clash solidly into mesh all along their length; for this reason the bevel gears have teeth cut in a spiral form.

Standardized components

Axle units and gearbox assemblies are the basic building blocks of a transmission system, and considerable savings can be achieved by using a single design of each in more than one car model. The same basic Leyland rear axle, for example, is used in the Morris Marina, Triumph Dolomite, and Triumph TR7 models. Gearboxes of one type are used in Ford Escort RS models, Ford Capri, Ford Cortina, and even in the large Ford Granada. Most of the major manufacturers have adopted this component-swapping approach, most notably in the United States.

To accommodate different needs, the ratio inside the back axle will vary from one model range to another, and even from differently powered variants within the same range. Gear-boxes generally have at least two internal sets of ratios available, and several companies, including Fiat and Leyland, manufacture gear-boxes which may have four or five forward speeds according to the needs of the market.

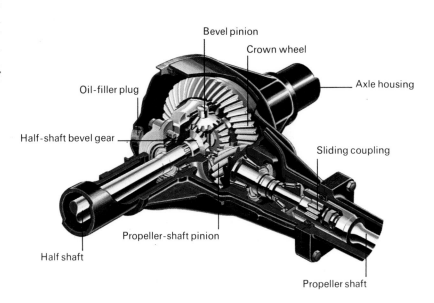

Bevel pinion
Crown wheel
Oil-filler plug
Axle housing
Half-shaft bevel gear
Sliding coupling
Propeller-shaft pinion
Half shaft
Propeller shaft

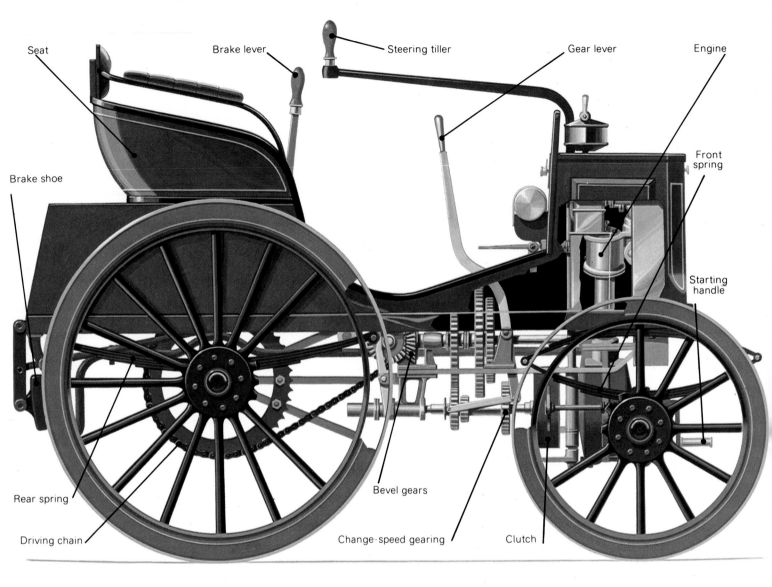

Seat

Brake lever

Steering tiller

Gear lever

Engine

Brake shoe

Front spring

Starting handle

Rear spring

Driving chain

Bevel gears

Change-speed gearing

Clutch

This Panhard-Levassor of 1894 had the classic layout of front-mounted engine and rear-wheel drive. Front and rear suspension were by simple leaf springs similar to those of contemporary horse-drawn carriages. Tiller steering with a vertical steering column was normal for cars of the period, and a hand-brake lever operated crude, quickly wearing 'shoes' that clamped onto the rims of the rear wheels.

In this chapter we consider two aspects of a car that make motoring comfortable and safe: the suspension and steering, which influence a car's dynamic behaviour on the road, and the brakes, which convert a car's dynamic energy into heat. The first cars had crude suspension and derisory brakes; it was only in the 1890s, when motor cars had become capable – at least potentially – of transporting people over long distances at reasonable speed, that much thought was devoted to these aspects of the car.

It is easy to imagine the discomfort of riding in a car in the early years of motoring, when poorly surfaced roads and rigid suspension systems must have made it difficult for passengers even to keep to their seats, let alone enjoy their journey. What is not so obvious is that today even the surface of a newly constructed motorway may look perfectly smooth but is, in fact, full of undulations and irregularities that

provide a searching test for the most sophisticated suspension systems.

The job of a suspension system is in effect to iron out the surface features of a road so that, whatever may be happening at the points where the wheels make contact with the road, the body of the car provides its passengers with a smooth and level ride. To achieve this each wheel must be able to move up and down in a controlled manner in relation to the rest of the structure. At the front end of the car the problem is complicated by the fact that the wheels must not only be capable of vertical movement but must also be steerable to left and to right.

Designing suspension systems involves difficult problems in the science of physics because the surface features of any road – and therefore the nature of the job tackled by the suspension – alter constantly and unpredictably. For this

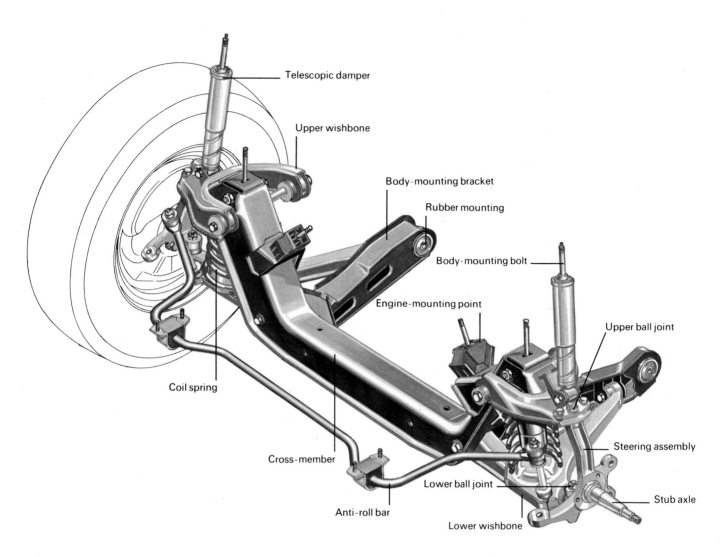

- Telescopic damper
- Upper wishbone
- Body-mounting bracket
- Rubber mounting
- Body-mounting bolt
- Engine-mounting point
- Upper ball joint
- Coil spring
- Steering assembly
- Cross-member
- Lower ball joint
- Stub axle
- Anti-roll bar
- Lower wishbone

reason, not only must each road wheel be efficiently suspended but the entire system has to be carefully matched, from one side of the car to the other, and from the front wheels to rear wheels. Only if the designer can achieve this will the car prove stable at all speeds and over different types of road surface.

When a car wheel goes over an irregularity in the road the impact is absorbed by the springs, which impart a bouncing motion to the car. If left to themselves, the springs would continue to bounce, in a slowly diminishing way, for several seconds after the car had passed over the irregularity. Since a road surface is not perfectly flat but consists almost entirely of irregularities, large and small, a car equipped only with springs would bob along a road like a cork in rough water. In order to prevent this happening, the suspension must also include dampers (often called shock absorbers), which absorb the energy that is compressing or stretching the springs.

The designer of a car's suspension and steering systems faces a variety of problems

that are the more difficult because the answer to one may contradict the answer to another or may conflict with the design needs of other aspects of the car. For instance, he would like the suspension to allow considerable vertical movement of the wheels, but this might require too much space, especially in a small car. Technically, it is desirable to have a rather soft suspension, but this may cause the car to lean excessively when cornering. In any case, it is difficult to define the terms 'soft' or 'hard' unless a car is going to carry a more or less constant load. A suspension that is pleasantly soft when the car has four occupants and their luggage may be uncomfortably hard when only the driver is on board.

Front suspension

At one time front and rear road wheels were suspended from heavy beam axles. As the power and performance of cars increased, however, it became apparent that the system was inadequate to cope with the front-end problems of steering and road-holding. This

The Vauxhall Cavalier has a double-wishbone independent front suspension – a compact and effective system found on many cars. The system is mounted on a pressed-steel cross-member bolted to the body shell. On this model the dampers, with upper ends attached to strengthened 'domes' in the engine compartment, act on the upper wishbones; in other double-wishbone layouts, and in the MacPherson strut system, the dampers are mounted within the coil springs.

led to the development of independent suspensions for the front wheels. (The term 'independent' is in fact misleading, since the front wheels must be connected by the steering system, and there is often some form of indirect linkage between the springs.)

There are several basic types of independent front suspension. These differ in the way links are arranged between the wheel carriers and the pivots on the body structure. Some cars have transverse links (sometimes called 'wishbones'), some have leading or trailing links, some use spring and damper bodies as locating members, and some use combinations of these features. Two types of conventional spring, however, predominate: the double wishbone and the MacPherson strut.

The double-wishbone system has two sets of transverse links connecting the top and bottom extremities of individual wheel carriers to the structure. The exact position of their pivot points has been frequently changed over the years in order to improve the vertical movement of the wheel and tyre and to minimize shocks through the steering system. In many examples the suspension spring is a steel coil clamped between the car's body structure at one end and one of the wishbone members at the other. In addition there will be a telescopic hydraulic damper which is very resistant to large, abrupt movements but quite compliant to small, slow ones.

In the MacPherson strut system, coil spring and damper tube are combined in one big, near-vertical member fixed to the wheel hub at the bottom and by a flexible mounting to the body structure at the top; the system is completed at the bottom end by a lower wishbone to resist horizontal braking and acceleration forces. Apart from being cheap to manufacture and install, the MacPherson strut spreads shock loads widely around the structure, making for a quiet and refined suspension system.

There are several variations on these two basic suspension linkages, the most important being the nature of the springs. Whatever its form may be, a spring acts as a store of energy, which it absorbs by being flexed or twisted. Coil springs, which are compact in shape, are much the most popular nowadays. Another type of spring is the torsion bar, a rod of square, circular, or flat section, which absorbs energy by being twisted along its length; it is sometimes used instead of a coil spring on double-wishbone layouts. Rubber in compression is a good if unrefined substitute for coil springs, and almost every car uses rubber 'bump stops' to cushion the approach of a suspension linkage to the limits of its movement.

In recent years, radically different forms of suspension have been used on some cars. They have replaced steel springs with various forms using high-pressure gases, high-pressure air and fluid separated by diaphragms, and other substances. These systems are either completely sealed or are operated by engine-driven hydraulic or mechanical pumps. Typical of hydraulically operated systems is the Hydrolastic suspension of some Leyland cars, while the complex hydro-pneumatic suspension of the larger Citroën cars is an example of a very advanced mechanically operated system.

It is difficult to provide a car with front suspension soft enough to give an acceptable ride at low speeds yet firm enough to control the sideways roll which develops when a car corners at speed. Some designers, in fact, advocate firmness at the expense of comfort, but the commonest solution to this problem is to fit an anti-roll bar, which in essence is a torsion bar mounted across the structure and fixed to a suspension member (wishbone or strut) at each side of the car. The bar has no effect if both front wheels rise and fall by the same amount. But when a car corners at speed, its rolling motion forces the outer wheel to rise and the inner wheel to fall relative to the body. These movements twist the anti-roll bar, which responds by exerting a counter-force to restore it to its normal, unstressed condition.

Rear suspension

While the job of the front suspension is quite clear, at the rear it is complex. Many cars have adopted independent rear suspension in order to obtain the least possible unsprung weight and the best possible road behaviour, but many others remain faithful to a big and heavy 'live' or beam axle – that is, a single unit made up of the half shafts and differential, enclosed in a rigid housing, and the wheel hubs.

In its simplest form, a beam axle is located by what is known as the Hotchkiss drive layout. Two longitudinal leaf springs (which nowadays are almost flat but are known as semi-elliptics because in the early days of motoring they had a pronounced curve) serve to suspend the axle and locate it to the body, and to transmit the driving forces to the structure. Telescopic dampers also link the axle beam to the structure, and in some cases anti-roll bars are fitted.

One stage more advanced than this is the beam axle whose position relative to the structure is controlled by a series of radius arms or transverse links (the latter usually known as Panhard rods) that are attached to the axle at one end and to the body at the other; the radius arms trail backwards from the body, while Panhard rods are mounted transversely. The

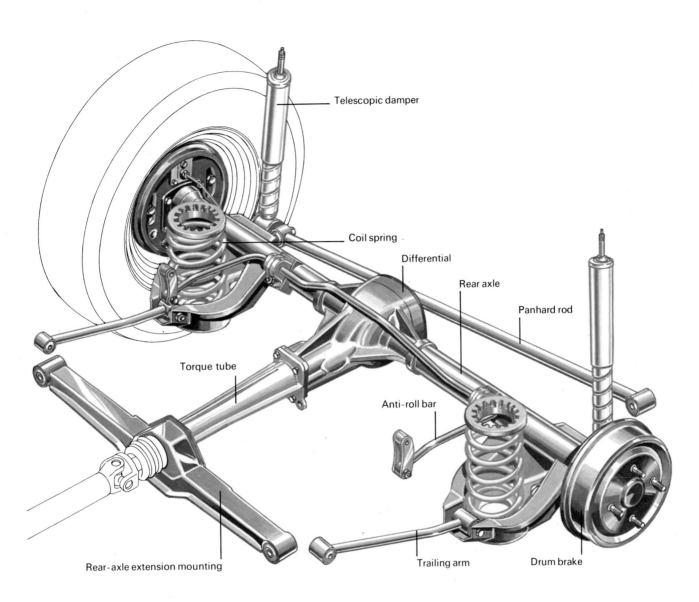

Telescopic damper

Coil spring

Differential

Rear axle

Panhard rod

Torque tube

Anti-roll bar

Rear-axle extension mounting

Trailing arm

Drum brake

springs may be leaf or coil type, and the suspension is completed by telescopic dampers.

In both the above types the half shafts are totally enclosed in the axle tubes. If, however, the differential or final drive is fixed to the structure or the car has a rear-mounted engine in which the shafts are exposed and articulated, an independent suspension is required. In some cases a variation of the MacPherson strut system is chosen, but many cars use a trailing or semi-trailing arm suspension. Trailing-arm types have two arms, each of which is attached to the body by two pivots at right angles to the car's longitudinal axis and ahead of the rear wheels. The other end of the arms is attached to the wheel-hub carriers. The system prevents sideways movement of the wheels but allows vertical movement, which is controlled by coil springs and dampers. Semi-trailing arms are similar except that the pivots are attached at an oblique angle to the longitudinal axis. This

allows a certain amount of camber in the wheels as well as vertical movement.

Trailing-arm systems are very widely used, many in conjunction with transverse torsion bars. In some Renault models the torsion bars are packed closely together and in such a way that one of the rear wheels is positioned slightly farther back than the other.

The De Dion system is a half-way house between live axle and independent rear suspensions. In this system the two wheel hubs are attached to the ends of an axle beam but the differential and exposed drive to the wheels are mounted separately, and the system can use coil or other types of spring. The main advantage of this system is that it reduces the unsprung weight of the car, but it is somewhat wasteful of space.

The simplest of all independent rear suspensions is the swinging half-axle layout, in which only the inner ends of the drive shafts are

The Vauxhall Cavalier's rear suspension has a 'live' axle and torque tube. The live axle contains the differential, half shafts, and wheel-hub mountings in a rigid housing and is cushioned by coil springs and dampers. The whole system is attached to the car body by trailing radius arms; transverse movement is damped by a Panhard rod. The torque tube, which helps to 'locate' the live axle, encloses part of the propeller shaft and is attached to the body at its front end by the rear-axle extension mounting.

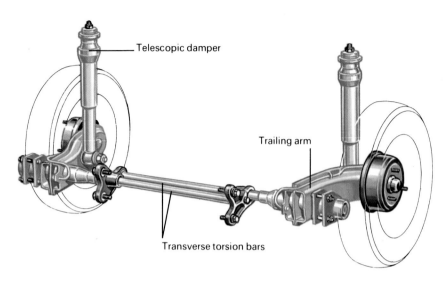

Telescopic damper

Trailing arm

Transverse torsion bars

The Renault 14 has an independent rear suspension that uses two transverse torsion bars instead of coil springs. The bars are linked to the wheels and body by trailing arms, and to keep the layout compact one bar is installed behind the other. As a result the left rear wheel (on the right in the drawing) is mounted slightly farther back than the other rear wheel.

articulated. Although it is relatively cheap to make, it allows a considerable change in wheel camber when a car is cornering at speed. This reduces the capacity of tyres to grip the road at moments when maximum adhesion is vital.

In many cars there is a very wide discrepancy between the weights when empty and when fully laden, and between the loadings on the front and rear suspensions. To counteract the adverse effects on handling caused by these factors, some cars have self-levelling systems fitted to their suspensions. This enables the cars to be set up at the right attitude whether lightly, heavily, or unevenly loaded. The simplest form of self-levelling, by mechanical means, is seen on the Citroën 2CV and Ami models. More sophisticated self-powered levelling devices are installed in the rear-suspension struts of the Range Rover and many Mercedes models. The most complex systems, hydraulically operated, are found on the Rolls-Royce and the Citroën CX range.

Steering

Although it is technically possible to fit a steering system to the rear wheels or to all four wheels of a car, even the earliest car makers realised that front-wheel steering is the safest and simplest method. Anyone who drives a car quickly in reverse around a series of sharp corners will soon discover that rear-steered wheels can cause serious problems in stability. (Some specialized devices such as dump-trucks do have steered rear wheels, but they usually have very low operating speeds.)

The steering mechanism must deal with three problems if it is to be acceptable to the modern motorist: it must be accurate in opera-

tion even if the front suspension is being violently disturbed by a rough road surface; it must be so designed that the steering wheel requires little effort to turn it even when the car is travelling slowly; and it must not transmit suspension shocks to the steering wheel.

The road wheels are steered by a system of rods and pivots that pull or push the wheel hubs from side to side. The simplest and most popular form is the rack-and-pinion system. In this a pinion (a spiral gear wheel), mounted on the bottom end of the steering-column shaft, engages on a transversely mounted toothed rack. Thus, when the steering wheel is turned, the rotating pinion moves the rack to left or right. The rack is connected at each end to a road wheel via ball joints, which allow the wheels to rise and fall on the suspension. This simple system takes up little space, is cheap to manufacture, and is highly efficient.

Where engine masses intrude between the line of the wheels, a more complex linkage may be needed to thread the steering system around them. The linkage can take a variety of forms, depending on the space available, but all have what is known as a steering box, where the rotation of the steering column is converted into a motion that swings a short lever called the steering drop arm in an arc; the arm is connected, via links, to the wheels.

However efficient the linkage of its steering system, a heavy car may require an unacceptably large effort to steer it. In such cases, power assistance is provided in the form of hydraulic pressure applied to the rack or the drop arm. The power comes from pressurizing hydraulic fluid in an engine-driven pump. Some systems offer graduated assistance through a sequence of valves and sensors that monitor the turning effort required.

The steered road wheels are rarely exactly parallel to each other. When in the straight-ahead position, for instance, the wheels on many cars in fact point very slightly inwards; this is intentional because the small but unavoidable amount of play in the steering linkage would otherwise cause the wheels to point slightly outwards when the car was in motion. If the steering linkage tends to make the wheels point slightly inwards, the initial wheel setting will be outward-pointing. These alternative settings or alignments are known respectively as toe-in and toe-out.

When a car is cornering, however, the front wheels are out of parallel for a quite different reason: the inner wheel is following a tighter curve than that of the outer wheel, and so it must be turned through a greater angle. If the angle was the same, the outer wheel, which takes the greater share of the cornering forces,

Rack-and-pinion steering is a simple and efficient system widely used on modern cars. When the steering wheel is turned, a pinion (spiral gear) at the bottom of the column makes the toothed steering rack move transversely, causing links at each end of the rack to deflect the front wheels to left or right. The drawing also shows the safety steering column installed on the Vauxhall Cavalier. A section of the column has a mesh-like structure that will collapse progressively in a severe head-on collision. This prevents the steering wheel from being violently thrust backwards against the driver's chest.

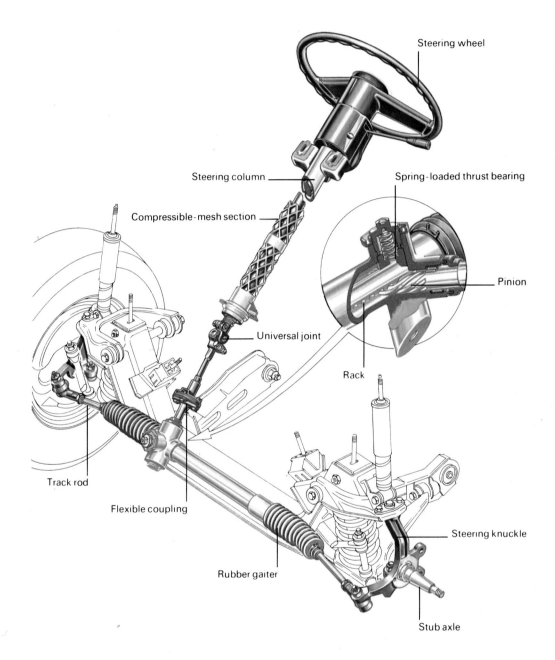

Steering wheel

Steering column

Compressible-mesh section

Spring-loaded thrust bearing

Pinion

Universal joint

Rack

Track rod

Flexible coupling

Rubber gaiter

Steering knuckle

Stub axle

would 'scrub' the road and cause tyre wear.

Experienced drivers know that there are considerable variations in the cornering characteristics of cars. A car that corners in a way that exactly reflects the amount of turn the driver has applied to the steering wheel is said to have neutral steering. A car that always seems to take a slightly wider arc than the driver intends, so that the front of the car tends to drift towards the outside of the bend, is said to understeer. Conversely a car which tucks tightly into the apex of a bend, with the tail tending to drift outwards, is said to oversteer.

These characteristics are due partly to a car's steering and suspension, and partly to tyre design and pressures, wheel camber, weight distribution, and various other factors. Most expert drivers are of the opinion that the best steering systems understeer slightly at low cornering stresses but self-correct towards neutral behaviour as roll and cornering forces increase.

For safety reasons, modern cars usually have steering columns built in such a way that they will collapse progressively in the event of an accident which pushes against the steering linkage. They may also have well-padded steering wheels that are designed to spread the loads if the driver's chest comes into contact with the wheel. Collapsibility may be achieved by putting sturdy mesh sections in the column, or by including joints which physically part company when they are subject to an end force of great magnitude.

A typical hydraulic-braking layout on a car having front-wheel disc brakes and rear-wheel drum brakes. Split hydraulic circuits separate the front and rear systems, and a vacuum servo (which lessens the effort the driver has to exert on the brake pedal) is in unit with the brake master-cylinder. Hand-brake operation is by cable to the rear brakes.

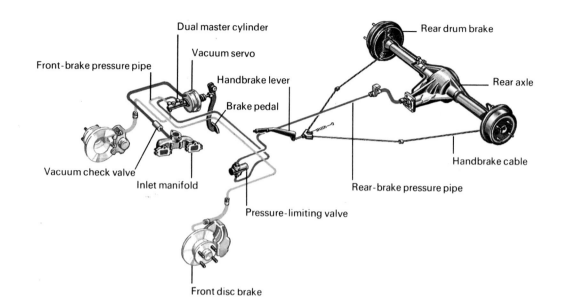

Braking systems

While the engine is a complex machine that produces power to drive the car and all its systems, the brakes are relatively simple mechanisms whose sole purpose is to dissipate the energy represented by the car's motion by converting it into heat. This is simple in principle but complicated in practice because brakes will work efficiently only if the heat is dispersed quickly.

There are two different types of brakes: the drum brake and the disc brake. The former type has been used since the earliest days of the motor car. The drum itself rotates with the wheel or the axle shaft and is braked when a 'shoe' lined with friction material is pressed onto its inside face by hydraulic or mechanical means. The disc also rotates with the wheel or axle, but is slowed down when friction pads are clamped onto both its faces.

The disc brake has great advantages because the disc, being open to the elements, can dissipate the heat generated by friction much more quickly than can the enclosed drum brake; for this reason it is less likely to 'fade' (temporarily lose its retarding efficiency) when used repeatedly – as when a car is descending a long, winding hill. It can also be smaller, simpler, and more economical to manufacture. Disc brakes were blooded on high-performance cars. The Jaguar C Type was the first racing sports car to adopt disc brakes, using them when winning the Le Mans 24-hour race in 1953. Two years later the Citroën DS19 became the first saloon car to fit them.

Braking systems operate when the driver depresses his pedal, which causes hydraulic fluid stored in a master cylinder to flow into smaller cylinders sited at each brake. Pressure built up by the fluid actuates the pads or shoes. Hand brakes are usually actuated mechanically by means of cables and rods; in some countries, indeed, it is illegal to have both systems operated by hydraulic circuits. Nowadays most brakes adjust automatically as the friction materials are gradually worn down.

On an increasing number of cars part of the effort that the driver needs to exert on the pedal is now taken on by a mechanical system. The brake servo, as it is called, exploits the partial vacuum in the engine's inlet manifold to act on a diaphragm, which helps to push the hydraulic fluid to the brake cylinders. More sophisticated systems build up the hydraulic pressure by means of engine-driven pumps.

For safety reasons pedal-operated braking systems are often split into two (or even more) separate circuits, each drawing fluid from its own master cylinder. The duplicated circuits may each work all four service brakes, but a simple circuit split (front to rear, sometimes diagonally, so that one front and one rear brake share the same circuit) is more usual.

Even the cheaper family cars may now have braking systems that are sensitive to changing loads. If a car is braked hard a much heavier load is thrown on the front brakes than on the rear. The nose of the car dips and the tail of the car rises, and in these circumstances the rear wheels are likely to lose adhesion and lock. Locked wheels have a much lower braking efficiency than wheels that are progressively slowed down (and they also wear away tyre treads). To deal with this problem, devices are included in hydraulic braking systems to limit the amount of braking effort which can be applied to the rear wheels. These can take the form of either pre-set hydraulic pressure-

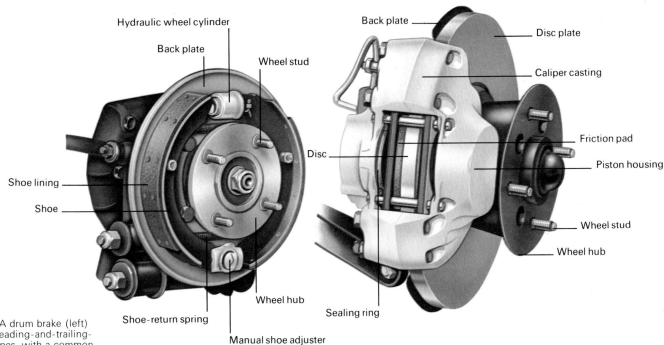

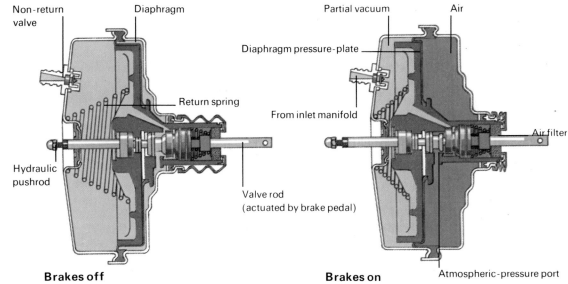

Brakes off

Brakes on

Above A drum brake (left) of the leading-and-trailing-shoe types, with a common shoe pivot at the bottom of the installation, and a wheel cylinder (which receives hydraulic fluid from the master-cylinder) at the top. When the brake operates, hydraulic pressure forces the shoes outwards against the inner surface of the drum (not shown). A disc brake (right) operates when the friction pads are clamped to each side of the disc, which rotates with the wheel.

Right Many brake systems now have vacuum-servo assistance. The servo unit works by exploiting the partial vacuum that develops in the inlet manifold when the engine is running. When the brake pedal is depressed, a valve allows air to enter the servo unit, forcing a spring-loaded piston to boost pressure on the hydraulic fluid in the brake master-cylinder.

limiting valves (which have the drawback of taking no account of the rear-wheel loading) or self-adjusting valves actuated by links that measure spring deflection, and therefore the load, on the rear wheels.

As we have mentioned already, brakes convert the energy of motion into heat, and this heat must be dispersed as quickly as possible. Dispersion is by conduction through the hubs and wheels and by radiation from the discs or drums. Both of these are potentially dangerous because they tend to pass heat to the hydraulic fluids. Brake fading is due directly to the inability of the system to disperse the heat efficiently, and it is usually caused by a temporary altera-

tion in the physical properties of the friction materials or by vaporization of the hydraulic fluid.

One important improvement in brake design, which is now used widely in aircraft and in commercial vehicles but is not yet common on cars, is anti-lock braking, which ensures that road wheels do not lock and skid no matter how much force is applied to the pedal. Anti-lock devices work by sensing when a wheel is tending to lock up and immediately relaxing the hydraulic pressure. A system designed by Dunlop was installed in the four-wheel-drive Jensen FF in 1967, and another version has been refined experimentally by Mercedes-Benz.

18 Electrics

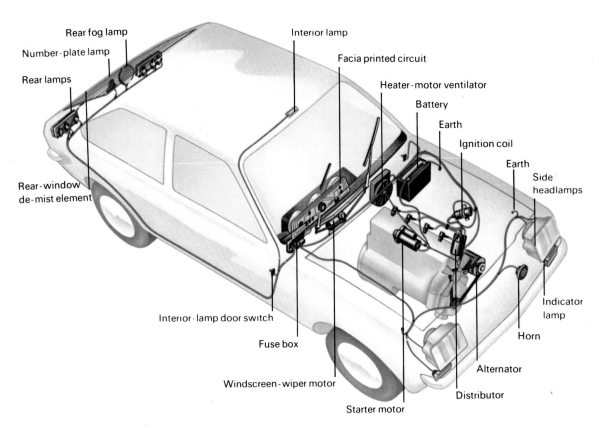

Rear fog lamp

Number-plate lamp

Rear lamps

Rear-window de-mist element

Interior-lamp door switch

Fuse box

Windscreen-wiper motor

Starter motor

Interior lamp

Facia printed circuit

Heater-motor ventilator

Battery

Earth

Ignition coil

Earth

Side headlamps

Indicator lamp

Horn

Alternator

Distributor

A car's electrical system relies on the 'earth-return' properties of a metallic body shell or frame to complete all of its circuits. Wires are usually grouped together in a neatly wrapped main harness. The main supply is from the storage battery, which is continuously being 'topped-up' by the generator when the engine is running.

A car gets its electricity from two sources: from the storage battery, and from the engine-driven generator. Without fresh charge, of course, the battery would soon be exhausted, so the generator is used to charge the battery as well as to supply a variety of other electrical services.

Almost every car built today works on the 12-volt system, although there are hundreds of thousands of cars still on the road in which the older 6-volt system is used. There is no special significance in the choice of 6 or 12 volts. When electrical equipment was first being installed in cars the reliable two-volt lead-acid cell was readily available, and it could be made up conveniently into banks of three or six cells.

The earthing system

Unlike household wiring, with its positive, negative, and earth wires in standard identifying colours, wiring systems in cars use what is called the earth-return method.

One of the battery's two terminals is wired to the car's structure. Electricity is taken, via single wires, from the other terminal to each component — headlamp, heater motor, radio, or whatever — which then provides a return path, to complete the circuit, through the metal to which it is bolted and thence, via the bodywork and the first terminal, to the battery. This is an extremely effective and economical method of carrying electric current, and it works well as

long as there is a good, clean connection between the component and the body structure — in motoring jargon, a 'good earth'. It follows that the structure must be a good conductor of electricity, which for all practical purposes means that it must be made of ferrous metal — iron, steel, or their alloys — or of non-ferrous metals such as aluminium. The earth-return system cannot be used with glass-fibre bodywork; nor can electricity be expected to flow across rubber or plastic fixings.

For many years there was much argument about the direction the current flow should take around the car. Some cars were wired with the battery's positive terminal directly linked to the structure (a 'positive-earth' system), and others with the negative terminal linked to it (a 'negative-earth' system). Notwithstanding a theory that corrosion can be reduced by using a positive earth, there appeared to be no real advantage or disadvantage to either system. However, the use of positive earth in some cars and negative earth in others began to cause great confusion in the motor industry and, particularly, in the retail trade, because many electrical instruments and accessories had to be made in two different forms. By fitting a battery the wrong way round in a car, for instance, it was possible to damage some of the electrical equipment. Accordingly in the 1960s car makers throughout the world agreed to adopt the negative-earth wiring system.

The battery

All car batteries are of the lead-acid type, which is cheap to manufacture but quite heavy. Batteries have not changed much in the last 50 years except that they have been progressively reduced in size, and recently transparent cases have been introduced. The storage capacity of a battery is expressed in ampère-hours, a measure of the amount of current that can be extracted from the battery for a given period of time before it is exhausted.

A modern car battery nominally provides a 12-volt supply (two volts from each of its six cells), but in practice a healthy unit pushes out a good 14 volts or more. Every electrical component of the car is designed to take account of this bonus and operates best when the supply is at that level. Some of the more expensive cars include a volt meter among the facia-panel instruments; it commonly has a band of from 11 to 15 volts, and if the battery is sound the indicator usually settles near the top of the band when the car is in motion.

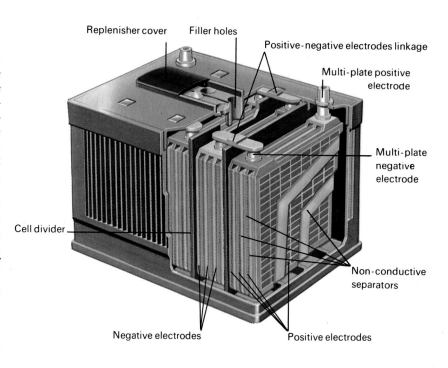

Replenisher cover Filler holes
Positive-negative electrodes linkage
Multi-plate positive electrode
Multi-plate negative electrode
Cell divider
Non-conductive separators
Negative electrodes
Positive electrodes

The generator

Electrical supplies need to be replenished all the time a car is in use, and particuraly at night when headlamps make heavy demands on the battery. This is done by the generator, which is belt-driven by a pulley on the crankshaft. At one time the generators were dynamos, which produce direct current, but now alternators, producing alternating current, have largely replaced them.

The battle between dynamos and alternators was joined at the end of the 1950s and finally resolved in favour of alternators by the beginning of the 1970s. Dynamos are simple and cheap to make, but they produce little power at low engine speeds, such as when a car is crawling in heavy traffic. Alternators are more complex, more expensive to make, often larger than a dynamo, and have to have their alternating current supply rectified (converted to direct current) before it can be used to recharge the battery. Their big advantage is that they produce more power than a dynamo at low speeds and can therefore cope better with modern traffic conditions and with the considerable increase in the amount of electrical equipment fitted to cars over the past decade.

The starter motor

Although a car makes many demands on its electrical system, the biggest single task of the battery is to supply current to spin the engine's starter motor. Because the engine is not running when this load is needed, the alternator cannot help. A lot of energy is needed to spin a cold engine fast enough to fill its cylinders and start the combustion process. Several hundred amps (ampères) may be needed for a very short period until the engine first fires. It is easy to see why the load taken by the starter motor has to be fed to it directly through unusually thick, and preferably short, cables. If, for any reason, an engine is reluctant to fire, continuous use of the starter motor can exhaust a battery in a few minutes.

Wiring

Apart from the starter circuit, the car's electrics are powered by circuits originating from the ignition/starter switch. In some cars the entire electrical system is immobilized when the ignition key is removed from its slot; in most, however, items such as the lamps can be used independently.

The more expensive modern cars have a formidable array of equipment that is operated electrically, rather than manually as on more workaday models. Examples already in wide use are electrically powered window winders, sliding sunshine roof, radio aerials, air-conditioning systems, remote door and boot locks, and seat adjusters. These have created a need for larger and more robust batteries than those of 20 or 30 years ago.

At one time whole groups of wires were channelled in the same direction along the body or chassis and bound neatly for protection and stowage. This meant that wires had to be readily identifiable for maintenance and re-

In almost 100 years of motoring, no viable alternative has been found to the lead-acid battery, or accumulator. The positive and negative electrodes are made of lead, and the liquid electrolyte is a dilute solution of sulphuric acid in distilled water. Most batteries are nominally rated at 12 volts, but they produce more than 14 volts when fully charged.

The basic elements of an engine's ignition circuit. The high-voltage electricity required by the circuit is generated in the coil. The low-tension (12-volt) supply from the battery or engine-driven generator is continuously interrupted (at frequencies determined by engine speed) by the contact breaker in the base of the distributor. This induces high-tension current in the coil circuit, which is fed to the distributor, and then (via the rotor arm) to each of the sparking plugs in turn.

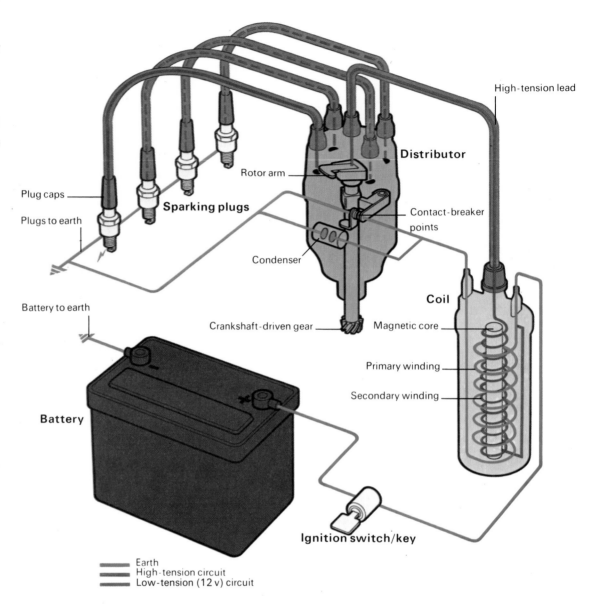

High-tension lead

Distributor

Rotor arm

Plug caps

Sparking plugs

Plugs to earth

Contact-breaker points

Condenser

Battery to earth

Coil

Crankshaft-driven gear

Magnetic core

Primary winding

Secondary winding

Battery

Ignition switch/key

Earth
High-tension circuit
Low-tension (12 v) circuit

pairs, a problem that car manufacturers solved by having different colours for different wires. Colour coding is now being largely standardized throughout the industry, so that the same colour or combination of colours for a given function (wires leading to indicator bulbs, for instance) is found on many competing makes of car. Much has also been done to rationalize the enormous variety of fixings that were previously used to attach wires to electrical components. Speed in initial assembly and in major servicing operations has been greatly increased by feeding the wiring at major obstacles, such as the scuttle (front bulkhead), into connecting blocks from multi-connectors on each side.

Headlamps

Good headlamps are vital to safe motoring at high speed in the dark, and continuous research in this field since World War II has led to the development of remarkably powerful lamps, most notably those using quartz-halogen bulbs. Ten years ago it looked as if most headlamps for mass-produced cars would eventually be built on the sealed-beam principle, in which the bulb filament, the reflector, and the glass were sealed together after assembly, so that the entire unit was effectively one large bulb. This trend now appears to have been reversed; it was unpopular with motorists because of the high cost of replacing a complete unit.

In spite of the use of headlamps of complex external shapes to blend with the lines of cars, the circular headlamp with parabolic reflector bowl is still the most efficient of all, and in the United States no car may now be sold without circular-section headlamps, although the outer frames may be of various shapes.

Recent trends

Loads in some parts of the circuitry of modern cars are such that normal switching operations are not possible for fear of overloading the system. To overcome this problem, simple relays are now being increasingly used, and these are now commonly found in overdrive-operating devices, for putting groups of headlamps on full beam, and (in competition cars, for instance) for bringing several auxiliary lamps into or out of use.

Electrical sensing devices or small electric motors are now being used for many functions that used to be powered mechanically. Few cars now have mechanically driven tachometers (revolution-counters), and many use electrical fuel pumps and windscreen-washer pumps. Most cars have reversing lamps that are switched on by the movement of the gearlever to engage reverse gear.

Different cars use electricity for different purposes. A good many use cooling fans driven by electric motors (instead of by a belt from the crankshaft), which allows them to be switched off unless the engine temperature rises above a pre-set level.

The number of dials on a car's instrument panel has tended to decrease in recent years (except in the case of the more expensive sports cars), but they have been replaced by simple warning lights. One found in all cars is the ignition light, which comes on when the ignition switch is turned on but goes out as soon as the engine is running and the generator has taken over the supply of current from the battery. (If it continues to light up, it indicates that the generator is not functioning correctly and that current is still being drawn from the battery.)

Other warning lights may indicate low oil pressure in the engine, headlamps on main beam (rather than dipped), and operation of the direction flashers. More comprehensive systems include lights that warn of a low level of brake fluid, worn brake pads, and the fact that seat belts have not been fastened; in some cars the seat belts are connected to the ignition circuit, so that the engine cannot be started unless the driver has fastened his belt.

The dials and warning lights on modern cars can give rise to a bewildering tangle of wires behind the instrument panel. Some manufacturers have simplified the system, and saved considerable space, by using printed circuits. These are made by bonding a sheet of copper to a small, flat, rigid board of insulating material. The required circuit is then printed on the copper in acid-resistant ink, and the rest of the copper sheet is removed by acid.

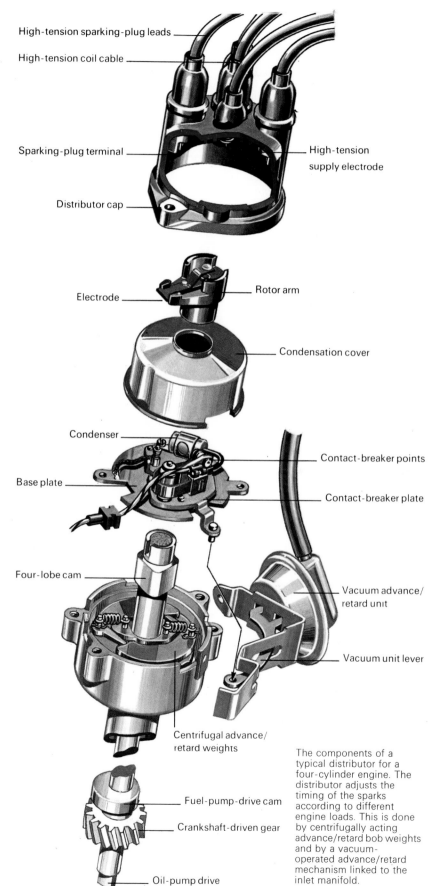

High-tension sparking-plug leads

High-tension coil cable

Sparking-plug terminal

High-tension supply electrode

Distributor cap

Electrode

Rotor arm

Condensation cover

Condenser

Contact-breaker points

Base plate

Contact-breaker plate

Four-lobe cam

Vacuum advance/retard unit

Centrifugal advance/retard weights

Vacuum unit lever

Fuel-pump-drive cam

Crankshaft-driven gear

Oil-pump drive

The components of a typical distributor for a four-cylinder engine. The distributor adjusts the timing of the sparks according to different engine loads. This is done by centrifugally acting advance/retard bob weights and by a vacuum-operated advance/retard mechanism linked to the inlet manifold.

Car Types

19 Cars for Everyman

Preceding two pages The Lotus S2 Esprit, a striking example of a two-seat, mid-engined sports car in the Italianate body style. Fast and with exceptional road-holding and handling, the car is powered by an engine of less than 2 litres.

Below The Morris Oxford two-seater of 1913 was the first production model of William Morris, at that time a cycle and motor-car dealer. It had a 10 hp 1-litre engine and cost £175. About 1,000 were sold in the first year of production — a remarkable number by British standards of the time, although it did not represent mass-production on the scale then operated by Henry Ford. The 'Bullnose' Morrises — the Oxford and the larger Cowley (1915 onward) — helped to make Morris the leading British car maker by the mid-1920s.

In its earliest days, and indeed until well into the 20th century, the motor car was a rich man's toy. Much had to happen before the car could become truly popular. The car itself had to develop; but, even more important, economic and social conditions had to change drastically. The existence of a mass market for cars depends equally on high average incomes in a population at large and on the use of production methods that brings the price of cars within reach of that population. Even today, widespread ownership of private cars is found only in the industrialized countries of the world.

It is no accident that the car first achieved genuine popularity in the United States, where by the turn of the present century the shortage of skilled craftsmen in a rapidly expanding population had enforced the spread of mass-production methods into almost every branch of industry. In that vast country, where public transport outside the major cities was primitive or non-existent, the car had only to prove that it was cheap and reliable in order to tap a huge and growing market. Henry Ford proved that quicker and more successfully than his rivals. He owed his success not only to mass-production methods but to his insistence on sticking for no less than 15 years to what was basically a single model and, as sales soared, to progressively cutting its price.

Ford Model T

In many respects Ford's first major success, the Model T introduced in October 1908, is the most important car in history, for it pioneered production techniques that have been followed by major car makers ever since. What sort of a car was it? For the customer it was above all three things: cheap, reliable, and easy to drive. It was not small by any means. The wheelbase was 2.5 m (99 in) — about the same as that of many modern family cars — but the wheels themselves were much larger. This had several practical advantages, the most important of which was the ground clearance they afforded for travelling rural American roads, most of which were still unpaved. The Model T stood 2.1 m (7 ft) high with its roof up, and could manage about 72 km/h (45 mph) and about 40 km (25 miles) per gallon. Its 2.9-litre, four-cylinder engine drove through an epicyclic transmission that made gear-changing simple.

While Ford brought his prices down to ever lower levels and concentrated exclusively on the Model T, other firms were growing up in Detroit. They were run by men who were willing to learn from Ford's success and waiting for a chance to gain a slice of his apparently captive market. The Model T continued in production until 1927, by which time over 15

The Ford Model T (1908–27) sold by the million and was the world's first truly popular car. Strong, simple, and easy to drive, the Model T was made in many different body styles, of which this touring version of 1915 is typical. Note the generous ground clearance and large wheels, which enabled it to cope with the rough dirt roads of rural America.

million had been sold. Meanwhile, the lead in the American market had passed to General Motors, whose Chevrolet has since the late 1920s maintained its position as America's most popular marque.

Throughout this period, the American public has retained a taste for large, powerful cars. The most popular models (like the more expensive ones) have rarely weighed less than 2,030 kg (2 tons) or had a wheelbase of less than 2.8 m (9 ft) – with their total length increased by considerable overhang at front and rear; engines have usually been in-line sixes or, since World War II especially, V8s. In spite of their size, however, these monsters have been consistently cheaper than many of the much smaller popular cars in Europe; and running costs have been kept low by the relative cheapness of American petrol. The attempt by manufacturers in the 1960s to interest the American public in 'compact' cars (which were still, in fact, larger than most European models) met with limited success. It is only in the last year or two, when the need for fuel conservation has begun to loom larger than ever before, that there has been a definite trend towards the production of what, in Europe, would be called medium-sized cars.

The European scene

The popular car did not appear in Europe until after World War I. Until then economic conditions – not only average earnings but also national taxation policies, the price of petrol,

and the relatively small scale on which most Europe car makers operated – had made car ownership a serious possibility only for the well-to-do.

There was undoubtedly a demand for private transport that was more comfortable than the motor-cycle – hence the emergence in the period immediately after the war of the cyclecar. This was a contraption with bicycle wheels, a tiny engine, and cramped accommodation (often in tandem) for two. It combined the worst features of a car and a motorbike, and the idea never caught on. The problem was to produce a car that would sell for less than £150. The difficulty of achieving this target can be seen in the fact that the Rover Eight, which was scarcely more than a well-appointed cyclecar, cost about £300 in 1920.

The breakthrough came in 1922 when Herbert Austin launched his legendary Seven. It was something of a gamble, for nothing quite like it had been seen before, and only two years previously Austin's company had been in the hands of the official receiver. However, although it was not greeted with great enthusiasm when it first appeared, it eventually achieved phenomenal success and became one of the best-loved cars ever made in Britain. Although tiny, it could seat two adults and two children in reasonable comfort, had four-wheel brakes, and its sturdy little 747 cc engine developed a respectable 13 bhp. The specification effectively killed the cyclecar stone dead. Modified

Left The Austin Seven, launched in 1922 (this tourer is of 1925 vintage), was perhaps the first British 'people's car'. Known affectionately as the 'bathtub on wheels', it could seat four and was quick and agile for its day.

Severs were successfully raced in supercharged form, and one of them won the 500 Mile Race at Brooklands in 1930. More significantly, it was built under licence by car manufacturers all over the world, notably by BMW in Germany, by Rosengart in France, by Datsun in Japan, and by Bantam in the United States.

Other small popular cars of the 1920s included the Morris Eight (1929), which sold for £125, and the shortlived Clyno Nine in Britain, the Citro''n 856 cc 5CV (1922) and Renault KJ-type (1923) in France, and the Opel Laubfrosch (almost identical to the Citroën 5CV) in Germany. The smallest cars Fiat produced in quantity during this decade were those of the 509 series with 990 cc engines.

Below The Opel 4/12PS, introduced in 1924, had a 951 cc, four-cylinder engine, and was almost identical to the contemporary Citroën 5CV. It was called the Laubfrosch (tree frog) owing to its vivid green colour; most of the 5CVs were bright yellow.

The 1930s

As the industrialized countries began to emerge from the Depression it became apparent that the motoring public in Europe was looking for cars offering a little more room, performance, and luxury than the Baby Austin and Citroën 5CV. In Britain an excellent example of the way things went was the 1932 Hillman Minx, a 1,185 cc saloon priced at £159. It was an instant success and was hastily followed by rivals of similar specification: Austin Ten, Morris Ten, Standard Ten, and (in 1935) the Ford Ten. Almost overnight the baby cars were eclipsed in popularity, although they continued in production right up to the war (and in 1935 Ford successfully marketed a two-door Eight for exactly £100).

All these models and most of their rivals on the Continent were simple, reliable cars offering comfortable motoring, but they were unadventurous in specification and performance. But revolutionary developments were on their way. In the early 1930s André Citroën asked his designers to produce a car that could carry four people at more than 96 km/h (60 mph), and manage 10.5 km/litre (30 mpg) with a 1.3-litre engine.

The result was the 7CV *traction-avant* (front-wheel-drive), unit-construction model, in some respects the most significant European car of the 1930s. It was a resounding success; its

front-wheel drive (and the fact that all four wheels were placed firmly at each corner of the bodywork) gave the car remarkable handling and stability. The *traction-avant*, in various engine sizes, became the standard car of the French police. The bodywork remained little altered from its introduction in 1934 until the range was discontinued in 1955.

The 7CV seems an especially striking car when one looks at other popular models of the 1930s. Many of the important standard features on even the cheapest cars – four-wheel hydraulic brakes, independent front suspension, synchromesh gears – had been introduced in the previous decade. Styling was unadventurous: popular saloons were almost invariably of the upright 'two-box' design with, occasionally, a built-in boot at the rear. Perhaps the best of the small saloons of the mid-1930s, apart from the Citroën, was Fiat's Millecento (1,100 cc) of 1937, which was nippy and economical.

Of even greater significance, however, was the Millecento's smaller brother, the tiny Topolino (Little Mouse) introduced the year before. In some respects the Topolino seemed almost to hark back to the cyclecar era. It was strictly a two-seater, and it had an engine of

Above Billy (later Lord William) Rootes test-drove many of his firm's new vehicles in the inter-war years. Here he leans on the 1931 prototype of the first Hillman Minx, near the Great St Bernard Pass on the Swiss/Italian frontier. Note the car's sliding sunshine-roof panel.

Right The Citroën *traction-avant* unit-construction range was launched in 1934. One of the greatest designs of the 1930s, the *traction-avant* was available with various engine and body sizes, although all the saloon models were similar in style. This version is the 11CV of 1935, with a 1.9-litre engine.

Below The Fiat Topolino, launched in 1936, proved popular in Europe because, although tiny, it was practical, economical, and fun to drive.

Below Ferdinand Porsche's prototype Volkswagen of 1936. The basically similar post-war Beetle, the best-selling European car for more than a decade, succeeded partly because of its practicality and partly because of VW's remarkably efficient international servicing and spare-parts organization.

only 570 cc. Despite the disasters that might have been predicted for it, the Topolino sold well not only in Italy but throughout Europe (in Britain it cost only £120). It succeeded because it was a 'proper' car in miniature, was great fun to drive, and returned no less than 88 km (55 miles) per gallon. Above all, it had advanced styling which gave it a cheeky character: smoothly rounded lines with an eager, sloping front end, and none of the ponderous bulges of some of the more earnest aerodynamic designs tried during this decade.

Post-war cars

After the war, engineers and designers sought new solutions to car-design problems. In Germany manufacture of the Volkswagen (People's Car) for public sale began in 1949. The same year saw the introduction of the spartan-looking but remarkably comfortable Citroën 2CV (at first with a tiny engine of 395 cc), a model that continues in production today. The other staple of the French industry was the small but very agile Renault 4CV with a 760 cc rear-mounted engine; it was built also in London and, under licence, in Japan. In Italy the Topolino continued in production for a few years until it was replaced by a new family of rear-engined small cars, the 500 and 600.

The situation in Britain was different; most car firms had survived the war in some form and many of them simply put their pre-war cars back into production. The trouble was that they were trying to sell to a different world. The war had left everyone poorer, and petrol had not only become very expensive but was rationed. What was needed was a latter-day Austin Seven, and it arrived in 1948 in the form of the new Morris Minor, designed by Alec Issigonis. At first sight the Minor was not as technically interesting as some of its overseas rivals. For one thing, its somewhat old-fashioned side-valve engine of 803 cc was at the front, at a time when many experts insisted that the best place for a small-car engine was at the back. But its rack-and-pinion steering and torsion-bar independent front suspension gave it excellent handling for its day, it was economical, it carried four people in comfort, and

Right Alec Issigonis's first post-war production car was this Morris Minor of 1948. Of excellent if conventional design, the Minor's rack-and-pinion steering and torsion-bar independent front suspension gave it better handling and roadholding than most of its rivals.

Below American popular cars have for long been much larger than equivalent European models: compare this 1951 Chevrolet coupé with the Morris Minor. Bigger engines and motorists' tastes led to the widespread use of automatic transmissions much earlier in the United States than in Europe. Chevrolet offered a two-speed automatic gearbox on its 1950 range of cars; today all but a few American models are 'automatics'.

it was fun to drive. Above all, like the Austin Seven of the 1920s, it had that indefinable quality, an appealing character. Over the years, its engine capacity increased to 1,098 cc (1968) and the car continued in production until 1970.

Following the merger of Morris and Austin in 1952 there appeared the British Motor Corporation's Austin A30, replaced later by the uprated A35. But the main British small-car rival of the Minor was the Ford 100E Anglia of 1953; and by now Ford had also launched its long and successful attempt to dominate the market for the medium-size car with the first of its Consul and Zephyr ranges.

In Germany Volkswagen was making great strides with its rear-engined Beetle, as it came to be called. The design was already old: it dated from three prototypes built by Ferdinand Porsche in 1936. But it became the most successful of all the popular cars built in Europe in the first two decades after the war, passing the five million mark in 1961. The car's virtues were strength, reliability, comfort (it had all-independent suspension), and a capacity to be driven flat out all day without complaint, owing to its relatively large (1,192 cc), unstressed engine and high gearing. It was neither very fast nor very economical, and its handling was not good in the wet. But, like the Morris Minor, it undoubtedly had a character all its own. Volkswagen was lucky because, in its early

years, the Beetle had little domestic competition, since Opel and German Ford were mainly building larger cars. But the company also made its own luck by brilliantly aggressive marketing, especially in the United States, where it was almost entirely responsible for creating what developed into a very significant American taste for small exotic saloons.

Meanwhile in Europe the next generation of popular cars was in the making. The crucial years were 1956–9, which saw the launching of the new Ford 105E Anglia, the rear-engined Renault Dauphine (the first French model to sell more than two million), and the BMC Mini.

In designing the Mini, Issigonis wisely ignored the fad for rear-mounted engines: both the Beetle and the Dauphine can now be seen to have derived few of their virtues and most of their faults from this engine layout. Instead he started from scratch, looking for a design that would offer space for four people in the smallest possible box. Front-wheel drive, with the engine mounted transversely and the gearbox placed in the sump, was Issigonis's triumphant solution. The car became a best seller. In Mini-Cooper versions it notched up an astonishing record of success in production-car races and rallies. Above all, it has profoundly influenced the design of European small saloons ever since its introduction in 1959.

In the meantime Citroën had concentrated on

It takes an expert eye to spot the outward differences between a first-series Mini, shown here, and a 1979 Mini 850. It is a tribute to Issigonis's design that so few mechanical or styling changes have been necessary. The Mini's use of front-wheel-drive and transversely mounted engine was adopted, more than a decade later, for the 'super-mini' models of Europe and Japan.

the 2CV on the one hand and the big and very advanced DS series (1955) on the other. Its lack of any model in between meant that Renault overtook it in the French market. Renault reverted decisively to front-wheel drive, first with the all-independently sprung 4, a utility/estate car (1962), and then with the 16 (1965), which introduced the concept of the five-door hatchback.

By the beginning of the 1970s the small-car revolution set in motion by Issigonis had begun to find expression in the design departments of the major European manufacturers. The new generation of 'super-minis' began with the Fiat 127 (1971), which was followed by the Renault 5 (1972) and Peugeot 104 (1973). From the resurgent Japanese industry came the Datsun Cherry (1973) and a little later the Honda Civic. Volkswagen, by now losing the market leadership long held by the venerable Beetle, executed a major *tour-de-force* by replacing it with a new front-wheel-drive, transverse-engined model, the Polo, in an astonishingly short time. Finally, Ford adopted the same layout for its Fiesta. It remained only for General Motors, in the form of Opel and Vauxhall, to take the plunge.

If the 'super-mini' battle seems to be the most fiercely fought in the European market, that is not to say that the smallest saloons are always the biggest sellers. There is, for instance, a very important market for slightly larger cars, typified by the Ford Escort, VW Golf, Opel Kadett, Vauxhall Chevette, Renault 14, and others. But even more significant is the intensely fierce contest to capture the market for

medium-sized saloons in the 1.5 to 2-litre range – a market in which sales can be enormously swelled by the orders of the commercial-fleet operators. During the last two decades one of the most important European cars in this category has been the Ford Cortina and its German equivalent. For long, these models dominated this sector of the market, although during the 1970s the other major European and Japanese manufacturers had at last begun to compete in a very big way.

Above The Chrysler Horizon (1978) typifies cars in the fiercely competitive European small-saloon market.

Below The Renault 5 range for 1979 included five models, perhaps most notably this 1.3-litre version with an automatic gearbox — a rarity on 'super-mini' cars, but undoubtedly a pointer to the future.

20 Cars for the Rich

As we saw in the previous chapter, in the earliest days of motoring all cars were luxury cars, for only the rich could afford them. They were also exclusive, since at that time car bodies were custom-built to the specification of the individual buyer. Henry Ford was to prove conclusively that the biggest profits lay in the mass-production of a limited range of cheap cars. Yet throughout the history of motoring there have always been car makers who have insisted on building only what they conceived to be the very best, regardless of expense, and customers who would accept nothing less.

Several of today's producers of luxury vehicles date back to the turn of the century. Mercedes-Benz, of course, is the direct descendant of the two earliest firms of all – Gottlieb Daimler and Karl Benz -- and began trading as Mercedes in 1902. Rolls-Royce emerged in 1906 when Henry Royce, a crane maker, joined forces with the Hon C. S. Rolls, a motoring enthusiast and Panhard's London agent. There were also many other marques, almost equally famous at the time: Bugatti, Cottin-Desgouttes, and Delaunay-Belleville of France, Hispano-Suiza of Spain and France, Excelsior and Minerva of Belgium, Austro-Daimler and Gräf und Stift of Austria, Horch of Germany, Isotta-Fraschini of Italy, and Napier of England all built some cars of superb quality and all were founded before 1910; none has survived. The

United States is a special case. Each of the big corporations has long had its luxury car division – Cadillac (1903) of General Motors, Lincoln (1920) of Ford, Imperial (1926) of Chrysler – which makes models of high quality; but they are built in far greater quantities than the truly luxurious European cars. Yet the American tradition of genuine luxury also has a long pedigree in names such as Cunningham (1907–36), Crane-Simplex (1915–24), Daniels (1915–24), Duesenberg (1920–37), Lafayette (1920–4), Lozier (1905–17), Peerless (1900–31), Pierce-Arrow (1901–38), ReVere (1917–26), Stearns-Knight (1899–1930), and Wills Sainte Claire (1921–7) – all marques that included models which could compete in specification with the super-luxury cars of Europe.

From the very beginning, buyers of luxury cars have been of two kinds: those with sporting instincts who drive themselves, and those who employ chauffeurs to do the driving. The most magnificent luxury cars in the first 30 years of this century were aimed at the latter kind. It was for them that coachbuilders developed the famous *coupé-de-ville* style, with the passengers in a closed cabin but the driver out in the cold. Such a style could be comfortably achieved only on a very long wheelbase, and so the super-luxury cars of those days were exceptionally large and heavy.

Such cars needed very big engines to give

The Rolls-Royce name has been synonymous with super-luxury cars since the launching of the Silver Ghost in 1906 (the one shown here dates from the following year). The model was powered by a 40/50 hp, six-cylinder engine of 7 litres that continued with minor modifications until 1925. The Silver Ghost's reputation for mechanical excellence was established by a remarkably successful 24,000 km (15,000 mile) RAC-observed test in 1907.

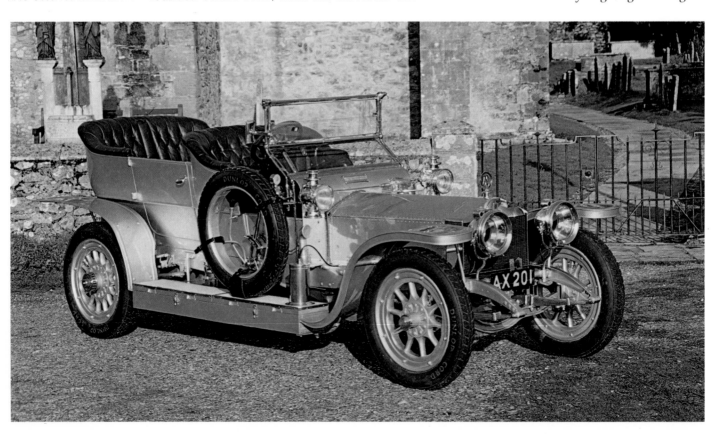

them a reasonable performance. Very large four-cylinder engines are never smooth, and by the end of the Edwardian period six-cylinder units had become standard in luxury cars. In Britain, Rolls-Royce and Napier were the first pre-eminent examples. Rolls-Royce, indeed, having experimented unsuccessfully with a V8 unit in 1906, persisted with engines of no more than six cylinders until 1935.

Elsewhere, the trend towards more cylinders gathered pace, most of all in America. Two pioneers in this respect were the V8 launched by Cadillac in 1915 and the V12 which powered the top Packard models of the following year. In spite of Cadillac's example, however, most manufacturers of luxury cars after World War I favoured the straight-eight engine, with all eight cylinders in line: the attendant problems of crankshaft stiffness and mixture distribution were not great enough to overcome the attraction of a long, fast-looking bonnet.

Heyday of the luxury car

Notwithstanding the Depression, the greatest years of the luxury car were the late 1920s and early 1930s. In the United States, the bulk of the luxury market was served by Cadillac and Lincoln, followed at some distance by Packard, whose top-of-the-range 1932 model was a highly regarded V12 of 7 litres. But finest of all the super-luxury American cars of this period, and indeed one of the greatest models ever produced in the United States, was the 1928 Duesenberg Model J.

Two years before, Fred Duesenberg's firm had been bought out by Erret Lobban Cord, who also owned Auburn and Lycoming, the aero-engine firm, and who demanded something exceptional for the first wholly new Duesenberg to be launched under his aegis. The Model J was longer, more complex, and more expensive than any other American car of its day. The chassis alone cost $8,500; with bodywork by Murphy or Le Baron, the finest coachbuilders in the United States, the price was near $18,000. The car was powered by a 6.9-litre straight-eight Lycoming engine; with twin overhead camshafts and four valves per cylinder, it developed 265 bhp. Four years later, for any owner who might think the car a little sluggish, the Model SJ was available: it had the same engine, but supercharged; developing 320 bhp, it could accelerate from rest to 160 km/h (100 mph) in 17 seconds, and had a top speed of about 208 km/h (129 mph).

In Britain, Napier, one of the great Edwardian marques, had given up making cars in the early 1920s to concentrate on aero-engine manufacture. By the middle of this decade Rolls-Royce's great rival in the British market was

Daimler, whose status as a luxury car maker was greatly enhanced by royal patronage. The most impressive Daimler of the inter-war years was the Double Six of 1927, which in King George V's version had a 4.1 m (13½ ft) wheelbase and was powered by a 12-cylinder engine of 7.1 litres.

In Europe there was a host of splendid super-luxury cars. The Italian Isotta-Fraschinis were especially coveted by wealthy patrons in the United States, and from 1932 their big straight-eight-engined limousines were fitted with pre-selector gearboxes. Minerva, the pride of the Belgian motor industry, was to cease production before World War II, but in the late 1920s it introduced its superb 6-litre AK series on a 3.8 m (12½ ft) wheelbase, followed later by the enormous 6.6-litre AL, which was available with *coupé-de-ville* coachwork. The Austrians were well to the fore in the Gräf und Stift SP-8 6-litre limousine, with its distinctive silver lion mascot on the radiator cap, and the magnificent Austro-Daimler ADR series, of which the

Above An early royal Mercedes: Kaiser Wilhelm of Germany rides with King Edward VII and Queen Alexandra in a 39/80, one of Wilhelm Maybach's last designs for Daimler. The massive vehicle had a 10.2-litre engine and was developed from the 120 hp racing Mercedes.

Below During the 1920s car owners in the United States, as in Europe, could choose their own body designs on the more expensive models. That they did not always choose wisely is evident in this custom-built Lincoln of 1927, which is powered by a 5.8-litre V8 engine. Lincoln was bought by Henry Ford in 1922, and it continues today as Ford's top-quality marque.

Above Hispano-Suiza's legendary H6 engine, with its aluminium block and overhead camshaft, was based on aero-engine technology. The one shown here is the H6C of 1924–9.

Right The Hispano-Suiza Type 68 of 1935 had a V12 engine of 11.3 litres. This drophead coupé version, with coachwork by Saoutchik, is one of the most expensive cars ever made.

ADR6 Bergmeister of 1929 and the ADR8 4.5-litre drophead coupé of 1932 were perhaps the finest. Mercedes-Benz introduced its Grosser Mercedes in 1930, an enormous car powered by an eight-cylinder engine of 7.7 litres.

Of all the great European super-luxury marques of the 1920s and early 1930s, however, perhaps none had quite the cachet of Hispano-Suiza. Although the company was founded in Spain in 1904, it achieved its greatest fame as a Paris-based company after 1919 under the guidance of Marc Birkigt, a Swiss engineer who had designed some notable aero-engines in World War I. The post-war fortunes of the marque were launched in 1919 with the H6 based on a superb all-aluminium 6.6-litre, six-cylinder engine; the cars offered a combination of luxury and high performance unique in their day. The largest of all the Hispanos, the Type 68, was introduced in 1931 based on a 9.4-litre (later 11.3-litre) V12 engine and with a variety of open and closed coachwork designs.

The V12 engine layout of the Hispano was by no means unique. Indeed, during the 1930s 12-cylinder engines became quite common on luxury cars. In Europe they appeared, for instance, in the Horch 600 and 670 range, the latter including a superb drophead coupé in 1931; in the Tatra Type 80 from Czechoslovakia in 1935; and, following the company's success in developing the Type R engine for the Schneider Trophy air races, in the Rolls-Royce Phantom III of 1935. In the United States Cadillac, having launched a V16 model in 1930, added a V12 range the following year; Lincoln introduced its V12 KA and KB types in 1932–3; and in 1933 Pierce-Arrow introduced several

V12-engined models, including the sensational, but short-lived, Silver Arrow.

It is remarkable how few manufacturers down the years have succeeded in building authentic sports cars as well as super-luxury cars. Although nowadays Bentleys are luxury vehicles, in the 1920s W.O. Bentley concentrated almost entirely on fast tourers and sports cars; and while the great short-chassis Hispano-Suiza H6 Boulogne achieved important sporting successes in the 1920s, this was essentially a very fast tourer rather than a genuine sports car. The most significant exception to the rule is the great firm of Mercedes-Benz, which has built classic examples of both types almost throughout its long history.

Of many manufacturers of sports cars who

Below The Duesenberg Model J, introduced in 1928, was arguably the finest American car of its time. Its sophisticated 6.9-litre straight-eight engine had twin overhead camshafts, four valves per cylinder, and developed more power than that of any other contemporary luxury car.

tried their hand at the production of super-luxury models, the greatest was Ettore Bugatti. His most celebrated venture into the super-luxury field was the Type 41 Royale of 1929, which he intended to be the car of kings (he planned to build only 25 examples). The Royale had a vast chassis on which was mounted an eight-cylinder engine of no less than 12.7 litres; the coachwork would, of course, be to the customer's own specification. Unfortunately, the Depression put paid to this gigantic marvel: only six were built, and of these only three were sold. Bugatti had more success with a sort of mini-Royale, the Type 46 (1930) of 5.3-litres.

During the late 1930s the aftermath of the Depression proved too much for many of the smaller builders of luxury cars. In the United States, Cadillac, Lincoln, and the Chrysler Imperial offered superb specifications at prices which left the hand-crafted Duesenberg, Cunningham, Pierce-Arrow, and their like out in the cold. In Europe, Minerva, Excelsior, Gräf und Stift, Austro-Daimler, Horch, Isotta-Fraschini, and many others effectively ceased production before World War II.

Trends since 1945

When the war was over many more of the famous old names had gone, including Hispano-Suiza. Daimler was still going, although drawn on an inexorable course towards merger with Jaguar and thus, ultimately, with Leyland. In the meantime it produced some good post-war cars, of which the excellent Majestic Major (1960), with its 4.6-litre V8 engine, was as renowned for its handling as for its comfort and performance. Leyland still builds its successors, the V12-powered Daimler Limousine and the Double Six, both with Jaguar mechanical parts. Indeed, the Double Six and its Jaguar equivalent are widely considered to be the finest luxury saloons in the world.

Rolls-Royce, meanwhile, has gone from strength to strength. With the introduction of the Silver Shadow in 1965, it shocked some purists by going over to unit-construction for the first time in its 60-year history. The model also included self-levelling all-independent suspension and a braking system with three separate circuits. While other companies have feared to make their cars too expensive, Rolls-Royce has had no such qualms. After the Silver Shadow it launched the two-door Corniche (1971), followed by the £50,000 Camargue. The biggest Rolls of all is the Phantom limousine. In all cases, power is now provided by a V8 engine of 6.9 litres.

The pre-eminence of Rolls-Royce in the super-luxury field since World War II has been

seriously challenged only by Mercedes-Benz. Inevitably the German company was slow to mount its challenge while reconstruction was in progress. In 1964, however, it was able to offer the 600, a logical successor to the pre-war Grosser Mercedes. The new model put the German company firmly back into the business of supplying transport to heads of state, and in its various forms – including the Pullman, which has a total length of 6.3 m (20.5 ft) – it is still available to special order.

Cars such as the Rolls-Royce Phantom, the Mercedes 600, and the 'Presidential' Lincolns in America are at the very top of the luxury-car ladder. It would be rare indeed to find their owners driving them. Yet the firms that build them derive enormous prestige from their use,

Above During the 1930s Horch (acquired by Auto Union in 1932) vied with Mercedes in producing large, luxurious cars for German VIPs. Typical of its 1939 range was this Horch 855 with a 5-litre straight-eight engine.

Below The top-of-the-range Jaguar and Daimler are now the only prestige saloons in series production powered by V12 engines. The model shown is the Daimler Double Six Series III, introduced in 1979.

and the reputation rubs off on their smaller stable-mates. In many cases, the next car down the line – built as it inevitably is in larger numbers – is technically more advanced. The Rolls-Royce Camargue, not the Phantom, was the first Rolls to have the company's fully automatic air-conditioning system, for example, while the Mercedes-Benz 450SEL 6.9 had a superior suspension to that of the 600.

In luxury cars, as in most other types, the glory of the huge-capacity pre-war engines has departed, probably for ever. Even the big Jaguar/Daimler engine – one of the few V12s to be found in present-day saloons – has a capacity of 'only' 5.3 litres. The customary power unit for today's luxury cars is a V8 of around 7 litres, tending – for the sake of refinement – to be mildly tuned. Performance, when it is needed, comes from the excellent torque that goes with a large-capacity engine.

In the United States, Cadillac, Lincoln, and Imperial all continue to serve the needs of the White House, the Capitol, and the captains of industry. Cadillac caused a stir in 1968 by launching the Eldorado, a front-wheel-drive car based on the Oldsmobile Toronado. As though to protect its position, Cadillac continued with its conventional Fleetwood models as well. This adventure apart, there is no sign of any luxury manufacturer departing from the established formula of front engine and rear-wheel drive. There is, however, scope for technical innovation in these most expensive of cars. Active-ride control (to ensure constant ride height and to eliminate roll when cornering) and anti-skid brakes are two obvious possibilities. Such developments are much easier to justify if expense is virtually no object. Sadly, recent developments have tended away from engineering innovation and towards even more items of interior equipment: two-way radios, refrigerators, stereos, and air conditioning.

Since World War II few other companies (either existing ones or new enterprises) have attempted to enter the market for the luxury limousine. The trend has rather been towards luxurious vehicles for the wealthy enthusiast who likes to drive himself. For this reason there is now a considerable overlap between the super-luxury car and the true sports car. Even allowing for this blurring of types, it is still possible to identify some exceptionally fast cars that fall into the super-luxury category. Typical of these were the two-door, four-seat coupés produced by Facel Vega (1954–64) in France, Gordon-Keeble (1964–7) and Jensen (founded in 1936) in Britain, and the Swiss firm Monteverdi, founded in 1967, all of which used powerful American V8 engines. The great Italian sports-car marques have also produced genuinely four-seat expresses from time to time. Notable examples have been the Maserati Quattroporte (four-door) saloon of 1964, with a double-overhead camshaft V8 of 4.1 litres, and the beautiful Lamborghini Espada coupé of 1968 with a V12 engine.

In Germany the might of Mercedes has been seriously challenged by BMW, although the Munich-based firm has not yet built anything approaching the class and size of the Mercedes 600, nor has it used anything larger than a six-cylinder engine. BMW, indeed, has concentrated mainly on establishing a solid reputation with its small and medium-sized high-performance saloons.

In Britain, while Rolls-Royce has remained supreme in the big-car super-luxury class, there has been a number of interesting developments. One of the most enduring of the car firms to be formed since the war is Bristol, founded in 1947 as an offshoot of the Bristol Aeroplane Company. Its first cars were closely based on the excellent pre-war BMW 2-litre tourers, but since then successive models have steadily increased in size. The current 411 model with a 6.3-litre American V8 engine clothed in rather

Left The Fleetwood has for long been Cadillac's top model. US petrol-economy regulations have enforced the production of less-powerful engines for the largest American cars, and this 1979 Fleetwood Brougham d'Elégance's 7-litre V8 engine develops a modest 183 bhp.

Below Shape of the future? The graceful Aston Martin Lagonda, with a powerful 5.3-litre, V8 engine.

ponderously modern two-door coupé body-work, is a luxuriously appointed car offering effortless cruising at high speed.

Another approach – an unabashed attempt to recapture the glory and the sheer presence of the great limousines of the early 1930s – has been tried with some success by a small company, Panther West Wind. Its Panther De Ville, a very large limousine with more than a passing resemblance to the Bugatti Royale, is powered by the Jaguar 4.2-litre engine. As an exercise in nostalgia it is certainly interesting; but perhaps a more likely indication of future trends is to be seen in the latest model of an old marque, Lagonda. Founded in 1906, the company made its name in the years between the

wars with fast tourers and drophead coupés. In 1947 Lagonda was taken over by Aston Martin and in 1961 the impressive but short-lived Lagonda Rapide, a four-door aluminium-bodied saloon capable of 201 km/h (125 mph), was introduced. Thereafter the marque was more or less dormant for more than a decade, but in 1977 the company launched an entirely new super-luxury car, an immensely long, low, four-door model of strikingly futuristic design. Powered by the very potent V8 engine of the Aston Martin DBS sports car, the new Lagonda bristles with electronic gadgetry. Whether there is a steady market for an entirely new car as ambitious in scale and specification as this one remains to be seen.

21 Sports Cars

Any discussion of sports cars needs to begin with a definition of the type. This is not as easy to do as one might think. For instance, in the 1920s and 1930s most sports cars could be recognized, apart from their mechanical specification and performance, by their open bodywork. But nowadays virtually all the ultrahigh-performance sports cars are enclosed. Again, high top speed and acceleration are no longer the exclusive properties of sports cars: there is a considerable number of luxurious, high-speed coupés on the market that would be better described as *gran-turismo* cars, if that term had not become so debased by indiscriminate use. Perhaps the best definition is that the sports car is a car that, in comparison with a saloon of a similar price, makes some sacrifices in room, comfort, and convenience for the sake of superior performance and handling.

The sporting instincts of motoring enthusiasts became apparent in the first decade of the car, and it found expression in a whole series of inter-city races in France and elsewhere during the 1890s.

The distressing tendency of the cars of those days to fall over rather than go round corners was soon associated with a high centre of gravity and a narrow track. Cars were therefore built with wider tracks and with the engine and seats installed between the chassis frames rather than above them.

Until a few years before World War I most cars were open, although some offered a wood- or metal-framed canopy that could be raised over part or all of the passenger compartment. With the coming of the great trials events (*see* Chapter 26) in the Edwardian period, the demand for greater power and speed led to the development of fast 'touring' cars. It was from the tourer that the authentic sports car, both for private use and for competitions, evolved.

Many famous companies laid the foundations of their success in competitive events – none more so than Mercedes with its 1903 60PS (hp) and its successors, which grew into monsters with engines of 12 litres and more. Other companies to take an active interest in early competitions included Panhard et Levassor, Renault, Fiat, and even Vauxhall, whose 3-litre Prince Henry of 1910 evolved into one of the earliest British sports-car classics, the Type E 30/98 that appeared in 1919.

Even before World War I, many designers had begun to doubt the supposed advantages of very big engines. The problem was that, in the still backward state of car technology, large engines could not deliver all the power of which they were theoretically capable because they could be run only at extremely low speeds – about 2,000 rpm was a typical maximum figure. They were also extremely heavy, and so sacrificed a lot of the performance they were meant to gain, while demonstrating the effect of poor weight distribution on handling.

The French responded by designing smaller cars with much more efficient engines. The classic pre-war design was that of Peugeot's 1912 *grand-prix* car, whose engine was inspired by that of the lively Hispano-Suiza Alfonso of 1911. It was a strikingly modern, four-cylinder unit of 'only' 7.6 litres fitted with twin overhead camshafts and four valves per cylinder. This car profoundly influenced the thinking of all designers immediately after World War I.

The 1920s

In the period after the war there was still much to be learnt from racing. More to the point, it was possible to buy sports cars which enthusiasts could race as well as use for domestic purposes. In the United States this tradition had, indeed, been established even before the war with the sporty Stutz Bearcat of 1914 and the Mercer Raceabout, and both these marques were to make successful, if rare, forays into European competitions. In Europe, meanwhile, the sports-car enthusiast had a choice of two distinct types. The French were building light, handy, efficient cars, very much in the mould of the *grand-prix* Peugeot and the *voiturettes* of the previous era. The British were making a much heavier kind of car, typified by the Bentley. When the Germans – meaning, above all, Mercedes – restored their industry to health their sports cars were built more on British lines than French.

There was no doubt that the French had gone the right way to take the main share of the popular end of the market, even in Britain. Perhaps the best of their light sports cars was the Amilcar, which developed from the Type CC of 1921 through to the respected CGSS, all with four-cylinder engines of about 1 litre and considerable technical merit. The Amilcars' main rival was the 1.1-litre, twin-cam Salmson, while Darracq offered the DS, Delage the 2.1-litre DI, and the short-lived firm of BNC the sporty 1.1-litre Monza.

The British answer to this challenge took some time to make itself felt. Firms such as AC and Aston Martin were thinking along the lines of an efficient, 1.5-litre sports car. But during the 1920s the most prestigious British sports cars were the increasingly powerful Bentleys. It is ironic that in the year of the marque's fifth and final win at Le Mans (1930), W.O. Bentley's company was on the verge of collapse; the following year it passed into the hands of Rolls-Royce, and its days as producer of true sports cars were over.

Below The Hispano-Suiza Alfonso (named after the king of Spain) was the most famous car produced by the firm's Barcelona factory. It was based on a successful racing voiturette of 1910, and a number of versions were built. This 1912 model, with a T-head engine of 3.6 litres, was capable of about 130 km/h (80 mph).

Right The Stutz Bearcat was (with its rival, the Mercer Raceabout) the best-loved American sports car of its day. This 1916 model has a four-cylinder, 6.3-litre engine of 60 hp and sparse bodywork. Its three-speed gearbox is in unit with the rear axle — a layout recently revived by Alfa Romeo and Porsche to improve weight distribution.

For Frenchmen who wanted something altogether more potent than the small-engined sports cars – and for many other wealthy enthusiasts all over the world – the marque that stood for the very highest expression of sports-car design was Bugatti. Although he started his own business in 1909, when he was 28 years old, Ettore Bugatti made his reputation with the cars he produced in the 1920s and 1930s. Their appeal lies in their unique combination of technical merit and aesthetic flair. Bugatti was a firm believer in lightweight sports cars. Indeed, his first models in the pre-1914 period were mostly small cars of 1.3-litre capacity. In the 1920s, he continued to produce sports cars of modest size, but he began to instal engines of progressively greater capacity and power. In 1919 he produced the Type 13, powered by a 16-valve 1.4-litre engine; the short-chassis version of this model became famous as the Brescia. In 1922 came the Type 30, Bugatti's first eight-cylinder car, with a capacity of 2 litres, and this led in 1926 to the Type 35C, perhaps the finest and most handsome sports car of the 1920s. Bugatti's greatest sports cars were so fast and handled so superbly that some of them were successfully used as *grand-prix* racers. The Type 35, for example, won the world championship in 1926. (The pattern was to be repeated in the 1930s, when Bugatti produced a roadster version of his twin-overhead-camshaft, eight-cylinder Type 51 racer – the legendary Type 55.)

Meanwhile, at a more modest level, the British challenge to the French small sports car came not from the ACs or Aston Martins but from MG. It was the practice in the 1920s for almost every manufacturer to sell some kind of two-seat version of his current saloon car. Few of these were genuinely sporting, although for many people the look of the thing was enough. But Cecil Kimber, who ran Morris Garages (William Morris's Oxford agents) made an altogether more successful and thorough job of it.

The first MGs were not small, for they had to use the 1.8-litre Morris engines from the saloon range of 1924. In 1928 Kimber also created the MG 18/80, using Morris's new 2.5-litre six-cylinder engine. However, the most famous MG emerged as a riposte to the success of Herbert Austin's little Seven in its two-seater form. MG took the Morris Minor (itself a reply to the standard Austin Seven) and evolved, in 1928, the MG Midget. This car, the M-Type, was an immediate success and eclipsed the Austin Seven Sports in sales, although the more

Above The Amilcar CGSS of 1926 was the final development in a line of small sports cars that handled well and drew a good performance from their modest 1074 cc, side-valve engines.

Below The immortal Bugatti Type 35C was powered by a super-charged straight-eight engine of 2 litres – a racing car in road-going form. This 1927 model shows to good effect the famous 'horse-shoe' radiator and alloy wheels.

specialized Austins continued to do very well on the track. Part of the secret of MG's success was its continuous development, through the J-Type to the PA and finally the T series, which was to continue until well after World War II.

As already mentioned, W.O. Bentley's philosophy of building massive, big-engined sports cars was adopted by Mercedes in the early 1920s under the aegis of the great designer Ferdinand Porsche. The basis of a range of large and progressively more powerful models was the supercharged 6-litre 24/100/140 PS of 1922. This led directly to the famous Model K, with a supercharged 6.25-litre engine – the fastest touring car in the world – in 1925 and to the ferociously powerful SSK, with supercharged 7.1-litre engine, which was introduced in 1928.

The 1930s

In Britain the 1930s are remembered as the heyday of small, modestly priced sports cars: the MGs, the Wolseley Hornet Special (1932), the Singer Le Mans (1936), and, above all, the twin-

cam Rileys – the Nine (1929), Imp (1934), and the 1.5-litre Sprite (1936). The next steps up the ladder were the AC 2-litre (1933), the 1.5-litre Aston Martin (1934), the 1.5-litre overhead-camshaft Frazer Nash (1934), and the 1.5-litre Lea-Francis (1938).

Good as some of these British cars were, the truly classic sports cars of the early 1930s came from Alfa Romeo. Although this company had had sporting ambitions almost since its foundation in 1910, its first great period of sports-car manufacture began soon after the arrival of Vittorio Jano as chief designer in 1924. Jano's first model had a twin-overhead-camshaft six-cylinder engine of 1,500 cc (later bored out to 1,750 cc); in supercharged form, these models were almost invincible in major sports-car events between 1928 and 1930. Jano's next great design, the 8C, with a supercharged straight-eight engine of 2,300 cc developing 142 bhp, won innumerable sports-car events, including the Le Mans 24-hour race four years running (1931–4); it was then re-

W.O. Bentley built massive, reliable, and finely engineered sports cars throughout the 1920s. Most of them were four-cylinder, 3-litre cars, of which this four-seat Speed Model of about 1925 is typical. The cars' height was due partly to the long stroke of the pistons. In the last years before the firm was acquired by Rolls-Royce in 1931, the range included 4.5-litre fours and 6.5- and 8-litre sixes.

placed by the six-cylinder 2300 model, whose engine formed the basis of most Alfa sports models until World War II.

These superb Alfas, like the great Bugattis of the 1920s, relied for their performance on relatively small but powerful engines in light-weight bodies. Whereas part of the appeal of the Bugattis was their highly individual, some-what exotic appearance, the Alfas had the slim, uncluttered lines of the thoroughbred. The beauty, moreover, was more than skin deep: they were among the first cars in which the finer details of chassis design were developed to improve road-holding and handling. For the wealthy enthusiast, an added attraction was that the normal road cars were essentially the same as the machines that had proved so dominant in the Le Mans, the Targa Florio, and the Mille Miglia (see Chapter 26). Of other sports car's of the 1930s with engines of less than 2.5 litres, perhaps the best was the BMW 328 – a very attractive model, with a 1,971 cc engine developing 80 bhp, which had notable success in rallies and sports-car races from 1938 onwards.

Mercedes-Benz continued to dominate among the large sports cars. The K, SS, SSK, and the SSKL (the last an outright sports-racing car) remained in production until the early 1930s. But for ordinary road use they were replaced by the technically more advanced, if not so sensa-tionally fast, 500 and 540K models, the latter

with a 5.4-litre engine. Of other large sports cars in the years immediately before World War II, perhaps the most striking were the Delage D8-120 of 4.7-litres, the Lago-Talbot Type 150-SS with a 140 hp 4-litre engine, and the Lagonda LG6 with a 180 hp V12 engine designed by W.O. Bentley; by now the elegant Invicta 4.5-litre, very fast but with suspect road-holding qualities, had gone out of production.

In the United States the sports-car market was dominated in this decade by Auburn and Cord, which with the great Duesenberg formed Erret Lobban Cord's remarkable triumvirate. The mid-1930s Auburn, with a supercharged 150 hp engine, was distinguished by pointed-tail bodywork and formidable acceleration. The Cord sports cars pioneered front-wheel drive in America, beginning with the Model L-29 of 1929–32. Perhaps the finest Cord was the 810 of 1935, powered by a 4,730 cc V8 Lycoming engine; its futuristic body style in-cluded retractable headlamps – a feature widely adopted on European sports cars of the 1970s. Both the Auburn and the Cord ceased produc-tion in 1937.

The 1930s saw a decisive break between sports cars and racing cars. By 1935 the special-ized grand-prix Mercedes-Benz and Auto Unions, which were soon to develop over 600 bhp, were more than a match for the smaller-capacity Alfa Romeo and Bugatti racers, which had been developed from sports cars, or for

The Vauxhall Type E, better known as the 30/98, was designed for competition work in 1913 and went into production six years later; this 1927 model was one of the last of the line. From 1922 onwards the 30/98, with a 4.2-litre engine developing 120 hp, was probably the finest fast tourer made in Britain, its performance marred only by feeble brakes. The fluted bonnet remained a feature of Vauxhall cars until the 1950s.

Above The supercharged 7.1-litre Mercedes-Benz SSK (this is a 1929 version) developed 225 bhp and was one of the fastest road-going sports cars of its time. This model and its competition variant, the 300 hp SSKL, evolved from earlier supercharged sports tourers designed by Gottlieb Daimler's son Paul, who in 1922 was succeeded as Mercedes' chief designer by Ferdinand Porsche.

racing *voiturettes* such as ERA. The two types have remained distinct ever since, even though the so-called 'sports cars' that now contest the Le Mans 24-hour race are quite as fast as, and in some respects are technically more advanced than, the present Formula 1 racers.

The post-war sports car

In the years immediately after World War II there was a distinct pause in the evolution of the sports car. General shortages and petrol rationing in Europe ensured that production concentrated on sterner, more utilitarian vehicles than high-performance cars; in general, those that were produced were based on pre-war models. It was in this context that the United States discovered the small European sports car – in particular the MG 1.25-litre TC, which was almost identical to the TB of 1939 except that it had a synchromesh gearbox. Thus began a long-sustained North American love affair with British two-seater sports cars that had a profound effect on the commercial viability of this type of car. The MG's traditional appearance was to continue, via the TD, to the 1.5-litre TF (1953); this was succeeded by the aerodynamically more efficient MGA in 1956, which included a high-performance twin-cam version.

Perhaps fortunately for Britain, the Italians did not make as much of the potential market for small, lightweight sports cars as they could have done. Alfa Romeo seems for a time to have become more interested in glamorous bodywork than in technical excellence, while the newcomers to the scene, Ferrari and Maserati (the latter had been in existence since 1926, but previously only as a racing-car builder) chose to make superb but extremely expensive cars of very high performance. That left only a tangle of small builders trying to make something out of the Fiat 1100S. Fiat had done well – like other major manufacturers – with sporting versions of its touring cars before the war, and the 1100S was a promising platform on which to work. Some of the designs, such as the Cisitalia coupé of 1948, were extremely beautiful, but none achieved lasting success.

In Britain, meanwhile, the MG was joined by two other sporting marques, Triumph and Jaguar. Triumph had always had a decently sporting reputation – from the supercharged Super 7 of 1929 to the Gloria and Dolomite of the 1930s – and built on it by developing the four-cylinder, 2-litre TR2 (1953), using a lot of standard components to best advantage in a striking modern body shell. The first car broke several class speed records and that, together with its low price, ensured success. The TR2 was developed through a whole range of versions from the TR3 to the TR6 (1969), which

Below The SS Jaguar 100 of 1938, with a 3.5-litre, overhead-valve engine producing 125 hp, was the last and best of a series of inexpensive sports cars made by William Lyons' company in the 1930s. Attractively styled, and offering a 160 km/h (100 mph) performance, it was a fitting prelude to Lyons' superb Jaguar sports cars of the post-war years.

Vittorio Jano's Alfa Romeo 6C-1750 (i.e. six cylinders, 1,750 cc) of 1928–30, with a body designed by Zagato, was one of the greatest sports cars of all time. Its supercharged version, the 102 hp 1750SS, allied a good (if not exceptional) top speed of 170 km/h (105 mph) to superlative roadholding and outstanding reliability. Its virtues were reflected in a remarkable record of victories: in 1929 the Mille Miglia (driven by Giuseppe Campari), the Spa 24-hour race (Attilio Marinoni), and the Irish Grand Prix (Boris Ivanowski); and in 1930 the Mille Miglia (Tazio Nuvolari), the Tourist Trophy (Nuvolari), and the Spa 24-hour race (Marinoni).

had a 2.5-litre six-cylinder engine with fuel-injection, a revised body shape, and independent rear suspension. The line continues with the TR7 coupé, powered by the Triumph Dolomite Sprint's lively 16-valve, four-cylinder engine.

Jaguar was the successor to the pre-war SS company of William Lyons, who had started by building motorcycle sidecars in 1922, moved on to special-bodied Austin Sevens, and ended up by making a series of long, low, fast, and remarkably cheap sports cars. In the late 1940s Jaguar unveiled its successor to the SS100 two-seater of 1939. This was the XK120, a totally new sports car with a streamlined modern body enclosing a powerful six-cylinder, 3.4-litre, twin-cam engine. It was a classic virtually from the moment it left the drawing board.

This model was steadily developed through the XK140 and 150, while at the same time Jaguar launched competition versions in the form of the even more advanced C-Type and D-Type. These cars won the Le Mans 24-hour race in 1951, 1953, 1955, 1956, and 1957 and numerous other major events during this period, the 1953 C-Types pioneering the use of disc brakes on sports cars. In 1961 the XK150 gave way to the E-Type. This model, with its futuristic styling, remarkable performance and handling, and (compared with its Italian and German rivals) extraordinarily low price, was one of the greatest sports cars of its time. In 1971 it became available with a new 272 hp, double-overhead-camshaft, V12 engine for a price of £3,123.

Of other British sports cars of the 1950s and 1960s, the Austin-Healey 100 (1955) and its six-

cylinder successor the 3000 (1960) deserve mention, as does its smaller brother, the 948 cc (later 1.3-litre) Sprite (1958–71), which was mechanically identical to the MG Midget. Among the small, specialist marques founded during this period perhaps the most notable were Marcos and TVR, who began by selling their models in kit form and who achieved important successes in sports-car events.

The Italians, meanwhile, had abandoned open bodywork in their fastest sports cars in favour of more comfortable and aerodynamically more efficient closed cockpits. They also pioneered the practice – already established in racing cars – of putting the engine behind the driver but ahead of the rear wheels. By the late 1950s Ferrari (with a series of superb V12-engined models) and Maserati were dominating the super-luxury sports-car market in Europe and North America, but they were soon to be joined by several other Italian firms – De Tomaso from 1959, Iso from 1962, and Lamborghini from 1963 – all of whom proved that there is a small but steady market for beautifully designed, ultra-high-performance, and very expensive sports cars. In particular Ferrari, with its remarkable post-war *grand-prix* record, established a reputation as the supreme builder of sports cars for the lucky few who can afford them. At a much lower price level Lancia (which since the early 1920s has given so much technical inspiration to sports-car design without ever making a truly high-speed classic of its own) has produced a steady succession of excellent small coupés, from the Aurelia (designed by Jano) of 1950, via the Fulvia of 1964, to the Beta Monte Carlo of the 1970s. Present-generation Alfa Romeo sports cars include the 2-litre GTV and the similar but smaller-engined Alfasud Sprint, both among the best in the medium-price range.

Mercedes began its post-war sports-car programme in 1952 with the 3-litre, six-cylinder, 215 bhp 300SL with fuel injection. A remarkably fine car by any criterion, the 300SL was the more notable for its 'gull-wing' (upward-opening) doors on the fixed-head coupé version. A more specialized sports-racing version, the 300SLR, had an eight-cylinder 3-litre engine developing 300 bhp. It proved formidable in major sports-car events, but it was involved in the disastrous Le Mans crash of 1955, in which 100 people died and which caused Mercedes to abandon racing. Since then the company has moved steadily in the direction of the *gran turismo* rather than the true sports car, developing its SL series through the 280 (1968) to the 350 (1971), with V8 fuel-injected engine, and later to the 450 of 4.5 litres.

Alongside Mercedes – almost literally, since

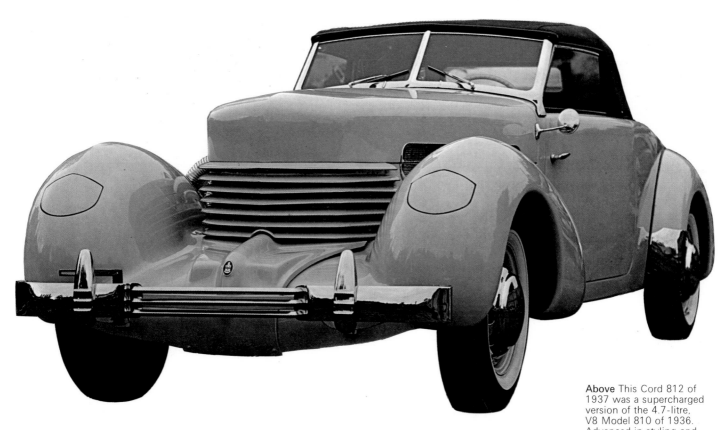

they both have factories in Stuttgart – Porsche began building sports cars based on the Volkswagen Beetle in 1950. In many ways it was a poor starting point, since the Beetle's handling drawbacks were greatly magnified once it was given any kind of sporting performance. Porsche, however, persisted with development and with racing, which it used as an alternative to conventional advertising. In 1964 it replaced the Beetle-based Series 356 with the 911 – still rear-engined, but with a 1,991 cc flat-six unit developing 130 bhp. The model has been continuously developed over the years, with a number of competition versions and with steadily increasing engine capacity and power (in the mid-1970s boosted by turbochargers). In recent years Porsche has enjoyed unparalleled success in competitions with its 911- and 917-based cars. During the late 1970s the company broke away from its long-established tradition by introducing two front-engined cars: the relatively cheap 924, with a 1,985 cc engine (which nonetheless costs well over £8,000), and the remarkable 928 of 4.5 litres, one of the finest designs of the past decade.

In Britain the long tradition of very-high-performance sports cars is carried on mainly by two firms – long-established Aston Martin and post-war Lotus. Since World War II Aston Martin has had a chequered career – from winning the Sports Car Constructors' Champion-

ship (including Le Mans) in 1959 to temporary insolvency in the 1970s. Through it all the firm has continued to build high-performance sports cars of great quality, beginning in 1950 with the DB2 powered by a 2.6-litre six-cylinder engine designed by W.O. Bentley. The series culminated in 1979 in the Volante drop-head coupé and the formidable Vantage, both powered by a four-cam V8 engine of 5.3 litres.

Lotus was founded in 1952 by Colin Chapman, whose subsequent record of success in *grand-prix* racing is challenged in the post-war

Above The Mercedes 300SL coupé caused a sensation when it appeared in 1955, owing partly to its 'gull-wing' doors and partly to the top speed of 232 km/h (144 mph) available from its 3-litre, six-cylinder engine – one of the first to use petrol injection.

Below If one sports-car marque had to be selected as the greatest in the world, the prize nowadays would probably go to Ferrari for the race-bred strength, mechanical excellence, road-holding, handling, styling, and sheer performance of its cars. This 308GTB, with an engine of only 2.9 litres, is capable of 250 km/h (155 mph).

period only by the great Enzo Ferrari. In the sports-car field, Chapman has built his formidable reputation on relatively lightweight cars with small, highly tuned engines. The Mark 14 Elite (1959), with glass-fibre body and a 1.2-litre Coventry-Climax engine, was followed in 1962 by the 1.5-litre Elan, which swiftly gained a reputation for the finest road-holding of any sports car of its day. In 1966 came the Europa coupé, the first British 'mid-engined' sports car. This configuration continues today in the beautifully Italianate design of the Esprit, powered by an advanced 1,973 cc engine.

There could scarcely be a greater contrast to the Lotus philosophy than that of Morgan, a firm that made its name with three-wheelers and produced its first four-wheel sports car, the 4/4, in 1936. The outward form of Morgan cars has changed little since then: even its most

recent model, the formidably fast Plus 8 two-seater powered by the Rover 3.5-litre V8 engine, has bodywork that harks back in style to the 1930s.

Sports cars in the 1970s

Today, with maximum speed restrictions on motorways throughout Europe (except in West Germany) and North America, it might seem that there ought to be little demand for ultra-high-performance sports cars. Yet quite a number of sports cars, including the Lamborghini Countach, the Maserati Bora, the Aston Martin Vantage, the Porsche 911 Turbo, the De Tomaso Pantera, the BMW MI, and at least four Ferrari models are capable of over 240 km/h (150 mph) and will accelerate from 0 to 100 km/h (62 mph) in under seven seconds. Several of the Italian models are mid-engined, while marginally less-fast cars of the same marques have conventional front-mounted engines. The theory is that the mid-engine posi-

WPJ 930S

tion gives better handling at ultra-high speeds. But where can the drivers of such machinery find public roads to put such a theory to the test? Evidently the attraction of these cars lies in what they are capable of doing rather than what the law allows them to do.

The principle world market for these exotic machines is the United States. It is curious that the Americans themselves have in recent years produced only one really high-performance sports car, the Chevrolet Corvette, introduced with glass-fibre bodywork in 1953 and extensively developed and re-styled since then. Powered by a massive V8 engine developing over 350 bhp, the Corvette has formidable acceleration and a high top speed, but its handling is inferior to that of the best European sports cars. While Porsche has been the most

successful exporter of luxury sports cars to the United States, the market there for less-expensive sporting machinery – for long dominated by MG and Triumph – has been taken over by the Japanese. The most dominant of all in this field have been the Datsun 240Z and its successor, the fuel-injected 280Z. Their sales in American – and indeed in Europe, too – are likely to be threatened by the Wankel-engined Mazda RX7 introduced in 1978.

As we enter the 1980s, exhaust-emission restrictions and fuel-conservation laws may conspire with the motorway speed limits to consign the great sports cars to oblivion. Meanwhile the specialist manufacturers continue, endearingly if shortsightedly, to develop faster, more powerful, and more expensive masterpieces than ever.

Above Starting in 1950 on the umpromising basis of the VW Beetle, Porsche has built an ever-improving series of sports cars. The 928 model, introduced in 1978, although not as sensationally fast as the turbocharged 911, is a grand-touring car of the highest quality. Like the smaller 924, the 4.5-litre V8 928 breaks new ground for Porsche in having a front-mounted, water cooled engine. Its gearbox is in unit with the final drive to the rear wheels.

Left The Japanese Mazda company is a world leader in the development of rotating-combustion engines for cars, having installed Wankel units in several production saloons during the 1970s. The Mazda RX7, launched in 1978, is the world's first Wankel-engined sports car and has become a best-seller in the United States.

22 Cross-Country Cars

The different types of cars we considered in the previous three chapters are all designed to carry people and a limited amount of luggage on normal roads. In this chapter we look at vehicles that are built to operate over more difficult terrain and to carry a variety of different loads but that are still in the category of private car.

The first cars, of course, often had to run on rutted dirt roads, and so they were usually built with good ground clearance and large wheels to cope with the difficult surfaces. One of the first cars to demonstrate an ability to deal with atrocious off-road conditions over long distances was the 7.4-litre, four-cylinder Itala that won the famous 16,000 km (10,000 miles) Pekin-to-Paris race in 1907. The car was a specially prepared open two-seater with a large, open luggage boot at the back. In spite of many near disasters the car, driven by Prince Scipione Borghese accompanied by a special correspondent of the *Daily Telegraph*, completed the journey in 60 days (see page 167).

After World War I most ordinary cars were built lower to improve their handling on metalled roads, and the average family vehicle was a fully enclosed saloon with four seats. It was now that many motorists, notably farmers or estate managers in rural areas, began to feel a need for cars with a more flexible carrying capacity that could be used for transporting either passengers or bulky loads. At this time

many popular cars were still constructed with a chassis separate from the bodywork, and firms of coachbuilders soon began to offer purpose-built bodies, basically van-like in shape (but with side windows) and including large loading doors at the back. The uses to which these vehicles were put is evident in their names: in Britain they became known as estate cars or shooting brakes; in the United States they were called station wagons (they were often used to collect goods from the local railhead in country areas). The Americans also gave them the more informal name of 'woody' – a reference to the fact that the special bodies usually had visible timber frames (and sometimes timber panels as well).

During the years between the wars the demand for this type of vehicle was too small to interest the major European manufacturers. It is only during the post-war period that estate cars have made significant inroads into the family-car market. Today even small mass-produced cars are often built with saloon and estate-car bodies as alternative options; the current vogue for 'hatchbacks' reflects the popularity of the type. Moreover, the extra space available in the larger versions is sometimes used to boost their passenger-carrying capacity by the fitting of an extra bench seat behind the normal rear seats – as in variants of the Peugeot 504 and Citroën CX 2400 estates and several large American station wagons.

The French pioneered the development of off-road vehicles in the 1920s. This 13.9 hp Renault 'Routier du Desert' (1923) was intended to establish a route across the Sahara between French Algeria and Mali. The Renault used six twinned wheels, with drive to the four rear pairs.

Such vehicles are specialized only in terms of their capacity and load flexibility: they are normally intended for use only on metalled roads, since in most cases they differ mechanically from their saloon-car equivalents only in their more robust rear suspension. In an altogether different category are vehicles specifically designed for cross-country use. There is a surprisingly long history of cars built for this purpose. Among the first in the field was Citroën, which in 1922 built a car with 'caterpillar' half-tracks instead of rear wheels. This car became the first powered vehicle to cross the Sahara Desert. Similar Citroëns later made two epic journeys: the first, in 1925, from Morocco, across the Sahara, through the Congo basin, to the east coast of Africa; the second, in 1931, from the Mediterranean coast to Pekin via the Himalayas and the Gobi Desert. Renault, Citroën's chief competitor in France, also built off-road vehicles in the 1920s – 13.9-hp, six-wheel cars (with double tyres on the two front and four rear wheels), in one of which a husband-and-wife team motored the length of Africa from Morocco to Cape Town in 1925.

Both these models were remarkably successful for their day. But each of them illuminated in a different way the essential dilemma facing designers of vehicles of this type. The half-tracked Citroën could travel over the most hostile terrain, but it was noisy, bumpy, and very slow on normal roads; the Renault, on the other hand, could be driven in comfort on metalled roads but, with drive transmitted only to the two sets of rear wheels, it swiftly became bogged down or unsteerable in mud or sand. The answer to these problems was large, knobbly tyres instead of half tracks, and transmission to the front as well as to the rear wheels.

Four-wheel-drive cars

Series production of a car with both front- and rear-wheel drive had to await the development in 1940 of the Jeep – the result of a US Army specification for a small, nippy staff car with cross-country ability. The first successful prototype was a four-cylinder model built by Bantam, a firm that had previously been making Austin Sevens under licence in America. The bulk of the massive wartime order for Jeeps, however, went to Willys-Overland and Ford. The secret of the Jeep's extraordinary success was a big engine driving four large wheels under a very light, simple body. Its six forward and two reverse gears were sufficient to get it out of the stickiest situations. Jeep variants included an amphibious version and a special 'double-decker' for carrying stretchers. The only World War II car to rival the Jeep was

the aptly named Kübelwagen (bucket car) based on Ferdinand Porsche's VW prototype, but this had four-wheel drive only in the amphibious version.

After the war, Willys-Overland found there was a ready market for Jeeps, and the firm and its successor, the Kaiser-Jeep Corporation, has continued to build them in a variety of two- and four-wheel-drive versions and body styles ever since. The world demand for such vehicles persuaded Rover to develop a somewhat larger variation on the theme, and the Land-Rover was introduced in 1948. The car has undergone steady development over three decades; diesel- and petrol-engine options have been available to power literally scores of variants on standard and long-wheelbase chassis; ingenious gearing, using a transfer box to provide eight forward speeds, enables the car to keep going over the most hostile terrain.

The prodigious success of the Jeep and Land-Rover encouraged other manufacturers to enter the field in the 1960s. In the United States, General Motors and the truckmaker

Above A Citroën B2 half-track in the Himalayan foothills. This was one of 14 such vehicles used on the *Croisière Jaune* (Yellow Cruise), a journey from Europe to Pekin, in 1931.

Below The original Jeep, produced in its thousands for the American armed forces during and after World War II, was the first successful four-wheel-drive vehicle. Its remarkable off-road performance was enhanced by use of a large-capacity engine and a lightweight body.

Above The Land-Rover, introduced in 1948 and continuously improved since then, is an immensely strong vehicle capable of tackling the most difficult off-road conditions.

Right The Land-Rover is complemented, rather than rivalled, by the Range Rover (1970), which has excellent cross-country performance but is also a comfortable, high-speed road car.

Variations on the theme

Although it is generally agreed that four-wheel drive is necessary for vehicles that must negotiate the worst conditions of mud and swamp, many people believe that good cross-country performance is still possible without the complexity and expense of that form of transmission so long as most of the weight is over the driven wheels and the right kind of tyres are used. This was the thinking that produced the Beach Buggy – a form of fun car that became a craze in California in the late 1960s. The definitive Buggy used a VW Beetle floor pan, engine, and suspension linkages and clothed them in a light, open shell made of glass-reinforced plastic. The shell had very large rear-wheel arches to accommodate extremely wide tyres operating at low pressure.

Although the Beach Buggy was exhilarating to drive, at least over dry ground, it had many disadvantages at more mundane levels. It had barely enough space for four people, and virtually none for luggage; it offered no protection from the weather. As a consequence, many Americans – again, first of all in California – turned to the pick-up truck, an idea pioneered for non-commercial vehicles by the Japanese firms of Datsun and Mazda. With their strong, separate chassis and high ground clearance, their car-sized pick-ups proved to be lively performers over moderately difficult terrain even without four-wheel drive. United States manufacturers soon followed the Japanese lead.

In Europe the need for smaller and cheaper cross-country vehicles than the Land-Rover led from the mid-1950s onwards to some interesting models based on production saloons. One of the first and most interesting of these was the Citroën Sahara, derived from the agile little 425 cc 2CV but with an engine at both front and rear, giving four-wheel drive. About the same time Fiat introduced its excellent little four-wheel-drive, Jeep-like Campagnola based on the 1400 model.

The 1960s and early 1970s saw many more of these small saloon-derived cars. In Britain the Mini-Moke, a tiny, angular, four-wheel-drive vehicle based on the ubiquitous Leyland Mini, proved immensely popular (it is still made in Australia). In France, Citroën's successor to the ingenious Sahara was the Méhari, based on the 2CV's up-market sister, the Dyane. In 1970 Volkswagen introduced its VW 181, a cross-country vehicle based on the Beetle and built in civil and military versions. Renault followed in 1972 with the Rodeo, derived from the popular 747 cc, front-wheel-drive R4.

All these cars had the virtue of cheapness while offering off-road performance superior to

International Harvester (with its four-wheel-drive Scout and Travelall) were prominent; in Britain, however, Austin's interesting Gipsy and Rolls-Royce-engined Champ (the latter developed for the army) were dropped after Rover merged with Leyland in 1966. By now the rapidly expanding Japanese motor industry was also taking an interest, and the Nissan (Datsun) Patrol and Toyota Land-Cruiser (the latter, in various styles and wheelbases, powered by a 4.2-litre, six-cylinder truck engine) were introduced in the mid-1960s.

The Land-Rover, meanwhile, continued to lead the field in all-round excellence and quality of construction (today, more than 30 years after its introduction, Leyland could probably sell at least twice as many as it can produce). The attributes the car lacked were a high level of comfort, refinement, and speed when used as a road car. This led to the introduction in 1970 of the four-wheel-drive Range Rover. Although the car superficially resembles the Land-Rover, the two models are quite different both in design and in purpose. The Range Rover's suspension is much softer, allowing the wheels much greater vertical movement. This enables the car to negotiate cross-country terrain in remarkable comfort, although it does not have the Land-Rover's performance in extreme conditions. The Range Rover is fitted with disc brakes on all four wheels and is luxuriously furnished.

the saloons on which they were based. None of them, however, could be said to be genuine cross-country vehicles in the terms defined by the Jeep, the Land-Rover, or even the Range Rover. Much the same is true of the Matra-Simca Rancho – rugged-looking, but with only two-wheel drive – introduced in the late 1970s.

The way ahead

The 1970s have, however, seen a steady increase in the number of genuine cross-country vehicles introduced in response to a fast-growing demand all over the world. In the United States Kaiser-Jeep continues to extend its range of four-wheel-drive models; both the Cherokee and the Wagoneer are available with a 4.2-litre six or a 5.9-litre V8 engine. International Harvester has recently introduced its four-wheel-drive Traveller and the similar but shorter-wheelbase Scout. The Japanese have concentrated on small vehicles. The tiny Daihatsu Taft, the smallest of the current crop of four-wheel-drive cars, with a 958 cc engine, looks very much like a scaled-down Jeep; the Suburu Estate, with a 1.6-litre engine, resembles an ordinary road-going car; the Mitsubishi 'Jeep' is available with a petrol engine of 2 or 2.4 litres or a diesel of 2.7 litres.

Two interesting four-wheel-drive cars have recently been developed in the Soviet Union. The Jeep-like Tundra, with a 2.4-litre engine, is at present only for domestic use. The Lada Niva, however, is now being exported, and with its high ground clearance and sturdy 1.6-litre engine driving large road wheels, it has demonstrated a performance under extreme conditions that is comparable with that of the Land-Rover.

One of the most significant cross-country vehicles to be introduced in the last decade is the Mercedes-Benz Geländewagen series, which is likely to be a powerful contender in the higher-price end of the market at present dominated by the Rovers. The car is available with a choice of four engines – including a 3-litre, five-cylinder diesel and a 2.8-litre, six-cylinder petrol engine with fuel injection – and a considerable range of transmission options and bodywork styles.

The choice of genuine cross-country vehicles available is now wider than ever before. In price they range from the smallest Japanese models, costing about £4,000 in 1979, to built-to-order machines such as the Range Rover-like Safari made by Monteverdi (hitherto a builder known mainly for its super-luxury *gran-turismo* cars) costing three times as much or more. Manufacturers all over the world are now following the lead of the Americans in offering a multiple choice of engine capacities and

petrol/diesel options. In the future one of the most important areas of improvement is likely to be in suspension systems. At present the manufacturers have to strike a compromise between the relatively soft ride required for cruising at speed on roads and the stiff suspension needed for stability over rough ground.

Another important development will be an increasing use of automatic transmissions to take some of the strain out of what can be a very arduous task for the driver under extreme conditions. Automatics are already available as options on several four-wheel-drive American models, notably the Chevrolet Blazer and the Plymouth Trail Duster (and mechanically identical Dodge Ramcharger). It is inevitable that such options will be offered on the larger-engined European and Japanese models.

The Mercedes-Benz Geländewagen range, launched in 1979, is likely to offer fierce competition in the sector of the market for long dominated by the Land-Rover. Shown here are models with different wheelbases and body styles; diesel- and petrol-engined versions are made.

Below The Chevrolet Blazer is one of several American four-wheel-drive vehicles with automatic transmission – a refinement that allows rough-road drivers to keep both hands on the steering wheel.

Motor Sport

When personal mechanical transport in the form of the bicycle appeared in the 19th century, racing very quickly became popular; and when the bicycle industry spawned the motor car and the motor cycle, it was quite natural that man should match those mechanically propelled vehicles against each other too. The close association between cycles and cars was shown by the earliest competition for motor cars, which was organized by a member of the French magazine *Le Vélocipède* in 1887 Although there were several successful steam-powered road vehicles in France at the time there were very few petrol-engined cars. Comte Albert de Dion, with one of Georges Bouton's steamers, turned out to be the sole contestant.

Six years passed before petrol-engined vehicles, propelled by motors of the Benz or Daimler type, existed in sufficient numbers, along with steam cars, to inspire Pierre Giffard of *Le Petit Journal* to propose a competition for horseless carriages in July 1894 between Paris and Rouen. There was no lack of response, and on 22 July 19 cars and two steam delivery vehicles assembled at the Porte Maillot ready for an 8 am start. After lunch at Mantes the entrants were timed over the final stage to Rouen. De Dion in his steamer covered the 127 km (79 miles) in 6 hours 48 minutes, $3\frac{1}{2}$ minutes less than that taken by Lemaître in a $3\frac{1}{2}$ hp Peugeot petrol car. Of the 21 entrants, 17 finished the course. The petrol cars were adjudged to be more efficient and first prize was awarded jointly to Panhard et Levassor and the Peugeot company, both of whose cars were propelled by Daimler engines. Second prize went to De Dion, Bouton, et Cie for its steam tractor and carriage.

From Paris to Bordeaux and back

The following year the first real motor race was contested, the historic Paris–Bordeaux–Paris event. A Panhard-Levassor driven by Émile Levassor was the first machine to return to Paris. Levassor drove the entire journey single handed in 48 hours 42 minutes. (He had arranged for a relief driver at Ruffec, south of Poitiers, but was so far ahead of schedule that the man was still in bed when Levassor passed through the town.) His average speed was 24 km/h (15 mph).

Of the 15 petrol-engined cars, six steamers, and one electric car which started, eight petrol vehicles and one steam car, a Bollée, finished. The race established beyond doubt the superiority of the petrol car: the Bollée arrived in Paris two days behind Levassor. The brothers André and Marcel Michelin completed the course on a Peugeot fitted with their pneumatic

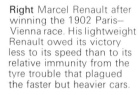

tyres after a daunting series of punctures and breakdowns. Another technical advance was seen in the winning Panhard-Levassor, one of the first French vehicles to break away from the Daimler influence. It was powered by a side-by-side, twin-cylinder Phénix engine of Panhard design and manufacture. An important outcome of this event was the formation by the organizing committee of the Automobile Club de France (ACF).

The idea of racing motor cars was not lost on the Americans. In the same year as the Paris–Bordeaux–Paris race the *Chicago Times-Herald* organized an event similar to the 1894 Paris–Rouen concourse. Two contestants, a Duryea and a Benz, raced over a 151 km (94-mile) course. The Benz won in a time of 8 hours 44 minutes. A second race was held later among six contestants over a course reduced to 87 km (54 miles) because of slushy snow. This time it was the turn of a Duryea to win, with a Benz the only other car to finish.

Spurred on by the success of the Paris–Bordeaux–Paris event the Commission Sportive of the ACF announced a contest from Paris to Marseilles and back to be run in 1896 in 10 daily stages to avoid racing at night on public roads. For the first time a set of rules was agreed, with classes for two-seat and four-seat cars and for motor cycles with and without pedals. These 'motor cycles' consisted of tricycles and the new Bollée fore-car. An elimination race was held for these, and four De Dion-Boutons and one Bollée qualified. On the day of the race proper, 24 petrol-engined vehicles, three steam-ers, and five tricycles assembled at the starting point in the Place d'Armes at Versailles.

At first the Bollée steamer, running on Michelin pneumatic tyres, passed through Melun well ahead of the others. But the Bollée's weight proved too much for *les pneumatiques* and it had to abandon the race through lack of spares.

As the competitors rested that night, storms swept across the country, blew down trees, and flooded the roads. Next day the wind was so strong it brought some cars to a standstill and blew others off the road. A fallen tree caused the demise of Amédée Bollée's petrol car. The car driven by Bollée's brother was charged by a bull and damaged beyond repair. Émile Levassor, leading the race, ran over a dog near Orange, causing his car to overturn. Badly hurt, Levassor drove on to Avignon (where his co-driver took over); but he was to die a year later from the injuries he had suffered. The eventual winner was an 8 hp Panhard.

What was a 'racing car' of this era like? The typical Panhard of the 1895 Paris–Bordeaux-winning type still bore most of the hallmarks of its horse-carriage ancestry. The vertical twin-cylinder engine was mounted at the front end of a suitably reinforced wooden chassis and drove a countershaft, from which the power to the rear wheels was transmitted by chains through an open gearbox. The wheelbase was only about twice the diameter of the huge, wood-spoked driving wheels. The front wheels were relatively small, a relic of carriage days when front wheels on a swivelling axle had to pass under the frame. On contemporary cars, however, the front axle was fixed, the wheels swivelling on king-pins and being controlled by an Ackermann linkage; they were steered by a tiller rather than a wheel.

Engines in those days were governed to run at about 800 rpm; speed variation by use of a throttle had not been invented. Cruising speed would have been about 29 km/h (18 mph) with the possibility of increasing this by disengaging the clutch when running downhill or by disengaging the governor.

In the two years between the Paris–Bordeaux and the opening of the 1897 season a number of cars were specially built for racing. Panhard et Levassor still dominated the scene, their cars having progressed to four cylinders and a capacity of 2.4 litres. The gears were now enclosed in an aluminium casing and the cars were soon to have geared steering, steering wheels, and castor angle for self-centring the front wheels.

The fascination of motor racing encouraged the Automobile Club of the Côte d'Azur to organize a three-day Marseilles–Nice–La Turbie

The Nice Race Week of 1901 saw the first sporting success of Wilhelm Maybach's epoch-making 35PS – the first Daimler model formally to bear the name Mercedes. The picture shows Wilhelm Werner's car after winning the Nice–Salon–Nice race.

race early in 1897. This event included a hill climb, and for the first and last time a steam car won a major race. The vehicle was an 18 hp De Dion-Bouton steam brake driven by Comte Gaston de Chasseloup-Laubat, who the following year was to establish a world speed record in an electric-powered car.

The final proceedings were enlivened by Bruninghaus in a 6 hp Panhard when the brakes failed on the way down from La Turbie to Monte Carlo, causing the car to run away and force an entry into the Café de Paris near the Casino.

Early international events

The highlight of 1898 was the first of the great international races, from Paris to Amsterdam and back. In addition there were the Marseilles–Nice and Bordeaux–Agens events. The importance of the Paris–Amsterdam–Paris was that it was also intended to show how reliable and safe self-propelled vehicles could be, for they had still not been fully accepted by the public. The total distance was 1,430 km (889 miles), and there was a touring class for motorists who did not want to cover the ground too quickly.

Once again Panhard dominated the speed event, with Fernand Charron averaging 43.2 km/h (26.9 mph). Second was Léonce Girardot in the latest Panhard with the new steering wheel that was beginning to replace the tiller on racing cars. Charron's nominally 8 hp Panhard had an Equilibré four-cylinder engine of 2.4 litres and a crude form of streamlining. With wheel steering, pneumatic tyres, castor

angle in the front-wheel geometry, new Crouvelle et Arquembourg grill-radiators, and four cylinders, the Panhards were beginning to look something like the motor cars of the Edwardian era. In contrast, Peugeot stuck to two cylinders and located the engine under the seat, but its tubular-steel chassis was more advanced than Panhard's.

An interesting preliminary event was a meeting at Achères, on the outskirts of Paris, organized by Paul Meyan of *La France Automobile*, to establish speed records. Four cars took part, two Bollées, a De Dion tricycle, and a Jeanteaud electric car. Electricity triumphed with a maximum speed of 63.3 km/h (39.2 mph).

The increasing speed and reliability of the motor car was demonstrated in the big event of 1899, a race around France over a total distance of 2,217 km (1,378 miles). But the public was becoming hostile toward the spectacle of long columns of cars tearing through the countryside, scattering and killing livestock, and knocking over the occasional farmer. Matters came to a head in a Paris–Roubaix race when two cars collided at a bend and crashed into the crowd. One of the injured was Madame Bos, the wife of a Deputy. For weeks the fate of motor racing in France was in the balance. Even before this, race organizers had begun to realize the need for tighter organization and control of crowds. The first-ever circuit race took place in 1900 over a 72 km (45 mile) circuit based on Melun, south of Paris. (One of the cars at Melun was a prototype of Wilhelm Maybach's epoch-making design that, as we saw in Chapter 4, Emil Jellinek was to promote as the first Mercedes.)

The Gordon Bennett Cup

The first Gordon Bennett race (named after an American newspaper magnate) was run between Paris and Lyons in June 1900 – but only after dissension among the French about the choice of drivers and indecision about whether the race would be held at all after the disastrous Paris–Rubaix event of the year before. The only foreign challenge came from the United States in the form of a single-cylinder Winton with tiller steering. The Gordon Bennett Cup was a race between representatives of national clubs represented by teams of three cars which had to be wholly manufactured (tyres included) in the country of the clubs' origin. The German-made tyres on the Benz were not up to a full-speed dash over the chosen 568 km (353 mile) route. The five entrants – René de Knyff, Fernand Charron, and Léonce Girardot from France, all in Panhards, Camille Jenatzy from Belgium in a Bolide tourer, and Alexander Winton in his 'one-lunger' – were sent off in a bunch from

Montretout, between Paris and Versailles. A mere dozen spectators greeted the survivors, Charron and Girardot, at the finish in Lyons.

Purpose-built racing cars

The racing car emerged as a type distinct from the touring car in 1901. The French firm of Darracq had a 50 hp racer, while in England Napier was constructing 70 hp racers for the Gordon Bennett Cup. To take account of these developments the Grand Prix de Pau of 1901 was contested in three weight classes: heavy cars weighing more than 650 kg but less than 1,000 kg (1,430–2,200 lb); light cars weighing between 400 and 650 kg (880 and 1,430 lb); and *voiturettes* weighing less than 400 kg.

In spite of a poor showing in the Grand Prix de Pau, Maybach's new 35PS Mercedes clearly showed the way forward in the design of racing cars as well as of tourers. Its most notable features in this respect were improvements for controlling the speed of the engine and the choice of gears. Hitherto all cars had

had fixed-speed engines and quadrant gear shifts with a neutral between each gear. Maybach abandoned the engine-speed governor and, by fitting mechanically operated inlet valves with variable lift, he was able to control the speed of the engine with a pedal or lever which gave instant and variable throttle response. Moreover, he endowed the car with a gatechange gear shift, similar in principle to the modern type, which automatically found neutral every time he changed gear.

Most racing cars of this period were lumbering monsters whose weight took a heavy toll of the rather crude tyres available. A most notable exception was the little Renault single-cylinder racer, which weighed only 395 kg (869 lb). In the big event of 1901, the Paris–Berlin race, one of these cars finished eighth overall, averaging 59.3 km/h (36.8 mph).

The significance of weight was recognized in 1902, when a limit of 1,000 kg (2,200 lb) was imposed on the big cars. It was an ineffective restriction in the long run because engineering

Louis Renault at the wheel of his car before the start of the catastrophic Paris–Madrid race of 1903. He is talking to Ferenc Szisz, Louis' mechanic who rode with him. Szisz himself was a skilful driver, his greatest victory being the French Grand Prix of 1906; he died as recently as 1970 at the age of 97.

Right The first transcontinental 'race' in the
United States was a 1905
publicity stunt to prove the
strength and reliability of
the Olds Curved Dash on
country dirt roads. These
two runabouts completed
the journey in 44 days.

Below The Gordon Bennett
Cup, an annual event
staged from 1900 to 1905,
was the forerunner of the
grand prix. Probably the
greatest of the series was
the 1904 event in the
Taunus mountains north-
west of Frankfurt. In this
event Camille Jenatzy in a
90 hp Mercedes (seen
here passing the richly
decorated stands in Bad
Homburg) came second to
Léon Théry in an 80 hp
Richard-Brasier. This was
the first major race to be
run on tarred roads.

techniques and materials were improving rapidly and the end result was cars that were too
light for the power available and were dangerous and difficult to handle. 1902 was the year
that Peugeot produced its first four-cylinder
racer, an 11.3-litre machine, for the Paris–
Toulouse event. Marcel Renault caused the sensation of that year, however, by winning the
Paris–Vienna race with his four-cylinder machine of 3.3 litres. It weighed 650 kg (1,430 lb),
but used far fewer tyres than the heavy cars.
Panhard had 13.7-litre and Mors 9.2-litre engines of 70 and 60 hp respectively, while the
new 40 hp Mercedes sported 6.5-litre, four-
cylinder, T-head units.

The Gordon Bennett Cup was contested at the
same time and was scheduled to finish at Inns-
bruck, in Austria. Herbert Austin in a Wolseley
of his own design and S. F. Edge in a Napier
represented Britain, and Girardot, Henri Four-

nier, and Knyff represented France. Girardot and Fournier retired before they reached Switzerland; the engine of Fournier's Mors blew up after he had averaged more than 96 km/h (60 mph) from Paris to Troyes; Knyff's Panhard was going well until his differential casing cracked. Edge won the cup, and Britain had the right to stage the race the following year. In the event it was held not in England, where road racing was prohibited, but in Ireland on a figure-of-eight course between Dublin and Kildare. It was the first motor race to be staged in the British Isles. The winner was Camille Jenatzy, the 'Red Devil', in one of the superb new Mercedes 60PS racers.

The 1903 Paris–Madrid

In spite of growing public and official opposition, the Automobile Club de France persisted with the organization of its favourite race over the N10 highway from Paris to Bordeaux. For 1903, however, the club wanted to extend the route to Madrid. The French authorities were against this, but when the king of Spain gave permission for the club to use the Irún–Madrid section the French government relented.

The Paris–Madrid was one of the most tragic events in motor-racing history. In spite of the weight limit, the cars were more powerful than ever. The Paris–Bordeaux section was run on a Sunday, 24 May, and crowds lined the road for hundreds of miles. Some say there were 3 million spectators but a more likely figure is 700,000. Many people stood on the road itself, leaving the narrowest of channels for the cars to go through. Speeds were remarkably high: Louis Renault, the leader, was said to have covered the 32 km (20-mile) straight between Chartres and Bonneval at an average of almost 145 km/h (90 mph).

A Mercedes in a practice run before a Vanderbilt Cup race on Long Island, about 1908–9. The picture was probably specially posed, since in the race itself the car would have had a number painted on the front. However, it shows clearly the nature of the road surface and the lack of public-safety precautions typical of American races at this time.

The first disaster occurred at Couhé-Vehac, south of Poitiers. Marcel Renault pulled out to overtake Léon Théry's Richard-Brasier, but his car hit a drain and overturned. His mechanic was killed instantly, and Renault died soon after. The leaders then came to the winding section over the low hills to the north of Bordeaux, where the road crosses the Dordogne river. Lorraine Barrow swerved to avoid a dog and hit a tree at 128 km/h (80 mph); both he and his mechanic were killed. Then Stead's and Salleron's cars touched; Stead's De Diétrich hit a pile of stones, overturned, and crushed the driver.

As the cars filtered into Bordeaux, terrible stories began to circulate. Leslie Porter's Wolseley had failed to take a corner and hit a house, killing his mechanic. Another car had swerved into the crowd and killed several spectators. The road from Paris was littered with smashed cars and dead and injured drivers and onlookers. The authorities quickly decided to stop the race and the cars were returned to Paris by train. It was the end of the great city-to-city races.

The classic events evolve

The year 1903 marks a watershed in motor sport. Henceforward racing was gradually to proliferate into a number of quite different types of event. The scale of the Paris–Madrid catastrophe almost ended motor racing in France, so greatly did it outrage public opinion at large. Indeed, in its preparations for the 1904 Gordon Bennett Cup (held in Germany), the ACF felt obliged to hold its trials almost in secret on an out-of-the-way circuit near the Belgian frontier; and no major road race was run in France that year.

Nonetheless, France was still the most important motoring country in terms of both car production and numbers of sporting enthusi-

asts, and racing events were bound to return. The existing pattern of events, however, was clearly unsatisfactory. Inter-city races were banned. The Gordon Bennett Cup, moreover, was leading to friction among the car makers. The rules of this event required that each national team consist of three cars. But by 1905 there were at least 10 French manufacturers whose racing cars were good enough to participate, so the ACF's task of selection had become invidious, to say the least. Although the French staged the cup that year, the ACF announced its intention of mounting its own international event in 1906 – an event that would be open to all manufacturers of racing cars. Thus was born the first *grand prix* – the classic race (*see* Chapter 24) that was to become the most prestigious event in the sporting calendar.

Grands prix were intended from the beginning for out-and-out racing cars. But all over

Europe an enthusiasm was developing for sporting events designed for touring cars – ordinary high-performance production cars that could be bought by the public. For safety's sake, such races (like the *grands prix*) were run on circuits – that is, on more or less circular systems of public roads that were closed to non-competitive traffic for the duration of the race. The pioneering events of this type were the Tourist Trophy, which was first run in 1905 on the Isle of Man (road races being prohibited elsewhere in Britain), and the great Targa Florio inaugurated the following year in the mountains of Sicily (*see* Chapter 26).

Motor racing had now firmly established the pattern for the future, with events designed to cater for the increasing variety of cars that an expanding automobile technology was beginning to make possible. In the following chapters we shall see how motor sport has developed since those pioneering days.

Most famous of the ultra-long-distance races staged during the Edwardian era was the Pekin-to-Paris of 1907. It was won by a 7.4-litre, four-cylinder Itala, seen here taking advantage of the straight and firm track of the Trans-Siberian railway. The driver was Prince Scipione Borghese (in pith helmet); his companion was Luigi Barzini, a journalist whose reports of the race appeared in the *Daily Telegraph*.

24 Grands Prix

As we have seen, there had been motor racing of one sort or another for more than 10 years before the French introduced the idea of a *grand prix* ('great prize') in 1906. Since then it has become the most prestigious form of motor sport – although it is by no means obvious why this should be so. After all, it has not always been the fastest form of racing, nor invariably the most technically distinguished. Since 1950 it has carried the *cachet* of the world championship, yet it has never been truly world-wide in the sense, say, of the Olympic Games. *Grand-prix* racing has become wealthy, yet it is not the world's richest racing.

One reason for its pre-eminence may be connected with the motives of the participants, which have traditionally transcended sport. Technical development on behalf of the motor industry as a whole is sometimes claimed as justification; in fact, the notion that the racing cars of today are the production cars of tomorrow has always been difficult to justify, more so now than ever. Racing has often provided an incentive for inventiveness but, for every worthwhile development, fortunes have been lost in innovations that did not work. In short, motor racing is not a cost-effective means of research.

Grand-prix racing drew sustenance from its potential for sales promotion in the period up to World War I and from the pursuit of excitement by wealthy sportsmen in the 1920s. In the 1930s it prospered as a result of being used as a vehicle for the strident nationalism of Germany and Italy. Today, as never before, *grand-prix* cars resemble mobile advertisement hoardings: the sport depends crucially on sponsorship by industrial and commercial organizations, many of whose products or services have little or no connection with cars or sport. So long as *grand-prix* racing, now a mixture of sport and show-business, continues to attract large crowds and the attention of the press and television, it will generate money and appeal to the entrepreneurial instincts of many participants (not all drivers) in search of profit.

The first GP

The idea of racing a number of cars simply to see which was the fastest was something of a novelty when the Automobile Club de France announced the first *grand prix*. Until then racing had been essentially a contest to see how quickly competitors could get from place to place, such as Paris to Bordeaux or Paris to Vienna. Even the idea of a single outright winner was something of a departure, since the Gordon Bennett Cup – the most widely supported event until then – had been awarded to national three-car teams.

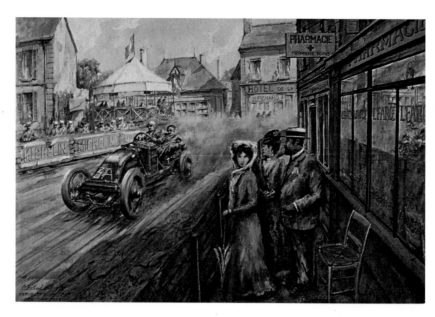

Above An artist's impression of the 13-litre, 90 hp Renault in which Ferenc Szisz won the first *grand-prix* – the French race near Le Mans in 1906.

Below One of the Renaults (foreground) in the 1906 French Grand Prix makes a stop in the pit road; the term 'pits' was first used in the 1908 event at Dieppe.

The French proposal was for a race over six laps of a 103 km (64-mile) circuit of public roads near Le Mans on 25 June 1906, to be followed by a further six laps the next day. The rules were simple. The cars had to weigh not more than 1,000 kg (2,200 lb) and would start at 90-second intervals over roads that, in spite of rolling and tar-sealing, were to remain a worrisome feature throughout. Eleven of the 32 starters completed the course, which most agreed was too long at 1,237 km (769 miles). The winner was Ferenc Szisz in a Renault with an average speed of 101.17 km/h (62.88 mph). The 'grand prize' cost the organizers the equivalent of £250,000 at today's prices – about the same as a modern *grand prix*.

That first race produced one major technical advance. Detachable wheel rims with replacement tyres already mounted reduced the time for changes from 15 minutes to as little as four minutes for the fortunate Renault, Fiat, and Clément-Bayard teams. It was an important development in a field composed mainly of huge cars with four-cylinder engines of between 12 and 18 litres.

More important still was the acceptance of a formally laid-out course, with spectators in enclosures. The *grand prix* had great attraction because it tested cars on ordinary roads as opposed to an artificially constructed track (Hugh Fortescue Locke-King was at that moment building the great banked oval on his Surrey estate at Brooklands).

Even though mass starts were not to come until 1922, the pattern of the *grand prix* was set. Courses would change, and also the cars, but the closed-circuit trial of speed solely for racing cars had arrived.

Rules of the race

In 1907 an international committee was formed and began to thrash out the rules of *grand-prix* racing. One outcome of its first deliberations at Ostend was that a fuel-consumption limit equivalent to 3.3 km/l (9.4 mpg) was imposed. A minimum weight was later introduced, plus a limitation on the diameter of the cylinders in an attempt to make the cars less 'freakish'. A maximum body width was also tried, and in 1913 another fuel-consumption limit was introduced, requiring 5 km/l (14.1 mpg). Not until 1914 was the straightforward solution of engine cylinder capacity agreed.

The 1914 French Grand Prix at Lyons for cars of 4.5 litres and 1,100 kg (2,425 lb) had turned out to be a rehearsal for the *grand-prix* races of nearly 25 years later. The technical superiority of the Mercedes team vanquished the hitherto successful Georges Boillot, who had won the race for Peugeot in 1912 and 1913. In spite of an

engine which now could turn at 3,000 rpm, and brakes on all four wheels, Boillot lost over the 753 km (468 mile) circuit to the well-prepared German cars of Christian Laütenschlager, Louis Wagner, and Otto Salzer, the first 1-2-3 victory in *grand-prix* racing.

As circuits became shorter, with the cars passing the stands more often, *grand-prix* racing improved as a spectacle, even though wheel-to-wheel races were still a long way off. By 1922 an international body, the Commission Sportive

Left A poster advertising the 1912 Grand Prix de l'Automobile Club de France – the formal title of the French Grand Prix. One section of the Dieppe circuit ran parallel to the coast, as the picture jokily confirms. The race, totalling 1,539 km (956 miles), was run over two days. The winner was Georges Boillot, who averaged 110.2 km/h (68.3 mph) in his Peugeot.

Below Leader of the 1912 Dieppe race after the first day, the American driver David Bruce-Brown donned foul-weather clothes before the start on the second day. He stands by his massive 14.1-litre Fiat, which was disqualified when he refuelled it away from the pits. Behind him is his compatriot Ralph DePalma.

Internationale (CSI), had been formed to organize the rules, although uniformity was not achieved until 1945. Generally the races which had become the most important (the so-called *grandes épreuves*, the national *grands prix* of each European country) came to be run under the combination of engine-capacity and weight limits that have characterized *grand-prix* racing ever since. These formulas were intended to encourage the fastest cars that could be built within the rules, leaving as much as possible to the skill and ingenuity of the designers.

Some racing traditions were already well established when the first *grand prix* was run. National colours such as green for the United Kingdom, blue for France, and yellow for Belgium, had been allotted in the Gordon Bennett races; with later additions – notably red for Italy – they were used until recent years. Nowadays they have largely been replaced by the colours and logotypes of the commercial sponsors of the racing marques.

Pits for repairs and replenishment appeared in 1908 for the French Grand Prix at Dieppe, where a divided trench with a counter just above ground level was provided. Subsequent installations have invariably been above the ground, but the term 'pit' has stuck. Riding mechanics were dispensed with in 1924, although the second car seat was retained for several more years.

The 1920s

Many of the cars that took part in the *grand-prix* races of the 1920s and early 1930s sometimes doubled as sports cars – notably the pointed-tailed, eight-cylinder Type 35 Bugatti, which was the epitome of most people's idea of the racing car from 1924. It was rarely among the winners until the major manufacturers withdrew their support in the Depression of the late 1920s; yet its elegant lines and fine proportions stamped it as a classic.

With the 1.5-litre Delage, the Bugatti was the last of the classic two-seaters, descendants of the huge Fiats and Renaults that were themselves derived from the city-to-city cars of the opening years of the century, with their tall engines and sketchy bodies. An important early racer was the 1912 Peugeot designed by

One of the greatest *grands prix* before World War I was the 1914 event – 20 laps of the 37.6 km (23.3 mile) circuit of Lyons-Givors, in which the carefully planned tactics of the Mercedes team destroyed the challenge of Georges Boillot (Peugeot) on lap 17. Here the winner, Christian Laütenschlager in his 4.5-litre, 110 bhp Mercedes, descends the bends known as the Piège de la Mort (Deathtrap), he was followed home by two more Mercedes in a German triumph that was greeted with hostile disbelief by a French crowd of 300,000.

the Swiss, Ernest Henri, who was first to employ the cylinder-head layout of twin-overhead camshafts working inclined valves in hemispherical combustion chambers. Henri used them with four valves per cylinder.

The Mercedes that was eventually to vanquish Henri's Peugeots in 1914 was lower-built and remained competitive after the war; it was equipped with four-wheel brakes. It won the Targa Florio, the great Sicilian road race, in 1922 and went on to form the basis of a long line of successful Mercedes sports cars.

Hydraulic brakes were a development of Duesenberg, which won the 1921 French Grand Prix; and the 1924 Sunbeam 2-litre, another Henri design, marked an important stage in the evolution of the supercharger in Europe. But the car that dominated the closing years of the 2-litre rules, from 1922 to 1925, was the Alfa Romeo P2. Designed by Vittorio Jano, it had a supercharged, eight-cylinder engine, and it continued winning when most race organizers chose to ignore the formula that followed (for 1.5 litres) from 1928 to 1930.

The 1930s

With the world in the grip of economic crisis there was a shortage of racing cars, and following the change in the formula some of the big names such as Fiat dropped out of competition, leaving Delage and Sunbeam to compete against privately entered Alfa Romeos and Bugattis in a racing free-for-all. Agreed rules went by the board, with individual organizers making up

their own, depending on the cars available. Because the owners had less cash than before they sought new means of defraying their costs.

Race organizers found themselves faced with demands for assistance, and owners sought sponsorship from oil and tyre companies, who stood to benefit from advertising. Races were promoted as entertainment as well as sport, and instead of dying out, as had seemed possible, *grand-prix* racing began a remarkable rise in popularity which has continued almost without interruption to the present day.

Attendances improved, but there were to be important consequences of this new-found popularity. The 1932 rules called for races of between five and 10 hours, new cars began making their appearance, and attention became focused more closely on the drivers. Hitler and Mussolini began to see motor racing as a medium of propaganda.

Mussolini decided to re-establish Italian supremacy through Alfa Romeo, which responded with a magnificent new car, the P3 Monoposto ('single-seater') designed by Jano. With its eight-cylinder engine and twin superchargers it could do 241 km/h (150 mph). It went from victory to victory, its only real adversary being the 3-litre Maserati 8CM, for which hydraulic brakes were 're-invented' a decade after the Duesenberg. Drivers of the P3 Monoposto included the incomparable Tazio Nuvolari, who later turned to Maserati after he fell out with Alfa's team manager, Enzo Ferrari – the man who was to enjoy the longest

The French were also denied victory in the next *grand prix*, held in 1921 on the Circuit de la Sarthe, which approximated to the present Le Mans circuit. Victory went to Jimmy Murphy in a Duesenberg straight-eight – the only American car ever to win the French Grand Prix. The picture shows Louis Wagner, who took seventh place in this eight-cylinder Ballot, at La Maison Neuve – near Virage d'Arnage on the present circuit (see map on page 226). The breaking up of the unsealed road surface caused a great deal of tyre trouble during the race, prompting Joe Boyer (another Duesenberg driver) to describe it as 'a damn rock-hewing contest'.

Above The Bugatti Type 35B (seen here in a Vintage Sports Car Club event) was the most successful racing car in the free-formula *grands prix* of 1928–30. A 'production' model, it was often raced by private owners.

Below Vittorio Jano's classic *grand-prix* car, the Alfa Romeo Type B Monoposto (single-seater), better known as the P3. With an eight-cylinder, 2,654 cc engine developing 215 bhp, it won the very first race in which it was entered, the Italian Grand Prix of 1932.

his regime. His chosen instruments were the newly formed group of Auto Union and the established Mercedes, since 1926 allied with Benz to form Mercedes-Benz.

Auto Union took over from Ferdinand Porsche the design of a revolutionary 16-cylinder rear-engined car with independent suspension on all four wheels, while Mercedes-Benz produced the W25, a more orthodox car but one which, like the Auto Union, was built regardless of expense by design teams and engineers numbered in hundreds. By 1937, when the 750 kg formula came to an end, the Mercedes-Benz W125 had a 5.7-litre engine of 646 hp and could reach 325 km/h (200 mph).

The success of the German cars was not immediate. In 1934, for example, the Mercedes-Benz won only four races – two *grandes épreuves* and two secondary events. They suffered particularly humiliating defeats in the French Grand Prix at Montlhéry (as did Auto Union), and also in the Swiss Grand Prix at Berne. But in 1935 they were beaten only four times, and even when the formula changed in 1938 to provide for a maximum engine capacity of 3 litres supercharged and 4.5 litres unsupercharged, they continued to dominate.

Bugatti made a half-hearted attempt to overtake the Germans with a straight-eight racer in 1938; but the French were eclipsed, the British had virtually no cars at all, and only the Italians

association of anyone with *grand-prix* racing.

Grand-prix racing became better organized in 1934 with the introduction of a weight limit of 750 kg (1,650 lb). About the same time Hitler, a keen enthusiast of motor racing, decided that Germany must reach the forefront of the sport, which he considered a fine advertisement for

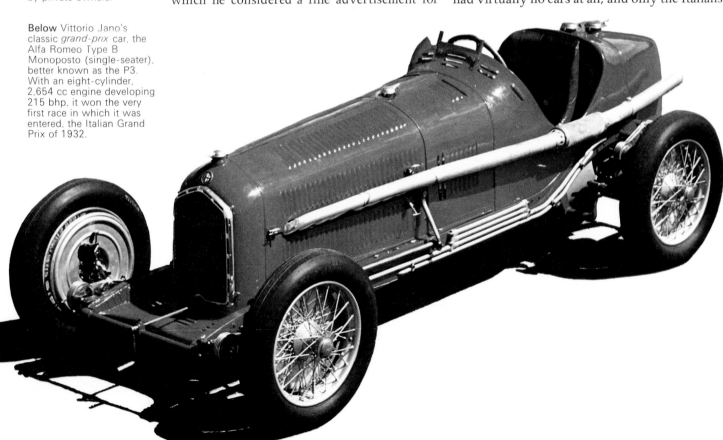

fielded anything that could hope to take advantage of a lapse by the silvery white racers.

By the 1930s, many of the great tracks were well established, such as the Nürburgring, the dramatic 28.2 km (17.5 miles) of track in the heart of the Eifel mountains. Monaco's famous round-the-houses circuit was established in 1927, while the French Grand Prix saw a variety of venues after the inaugural Le Mans race, including Dieppe (1907–12), the Circuit de Picardie at Amiens (1913), Lyons (1914 and 1924), Strasbourg (1922), Tours (1923), Montlhéry (1925, 1927, 1931, 1933–7), Miramas (1926), Pau (1930), and Reims (1932 and 1938–9).

In England Donington Park saw the two great Auto Union victories of 1937 and 1938 in races known as the Donington Grand Prix (the British Grand Prix was not yet established owing largely to the lack of a suitable track). Donington was not really up to the international standard of the rest of Europe, where public roads could be closed for racing.

By the end of the 1930s a regular calendar had been established, with the principal *grandes épreuves* run by the Germans, French, Italians (at Monza), Swiss (at Bremgarten, near Berne), and Belgians (at Spa).

Post-war developments

After World War II enthusiasm for motor racing was undiminished, and it was not long before the CSI drew up its Formula A rules to take account of the cars available.

Before the war a subsidiary formula had been established for what were known as *voiturettes* – slightly smaller, less powerful, and less expensive cars than the big *grand-prix* racers. The intention had been to revive a form of racing which would be free from the domination of the German and Italian works teams. This turned out to be a vain hope, for Alfa Romeo promptly produced a scaled-down version of its *grand-prix* cars that was more than a match for the British ERAs, the surviving Delage 1.5 litres from 1926–7, the Bugattis, and the Maseratis. The Germans got in on the act briefly in the Tripoli Grand Prix of 1939, astonishing the Italians with the Mercedes W163 model, a beautifully made V8 which scored a convincing win.

These *voiturette* races meant that after the war there was a supply of cars which encouraged the CSI to frame the rules around single seaters of 1.5 litres supercharged and 4.5 litres unsupercharged, and Formula A was to last from 1948 to 1953. It also saw the introduction of one of the most important developments in *grand-prix* racing, the establishment in 1950 of the drivers' world championship.

Above Mercedes-Benz and Auto Union dominated *grand-prix* racing in the late 1930s. The picture shows them at the start of the Donington Grand Prix of 1937. Front row, from left: number 4 Richard Seaman (Mercedes-Benz), 2 Hermann Lang (Mercedes-Benz), 5 Bernd Rosemeyer (Auto Union, the winner), and 3 Manfred von Brauchitsch (Mercedes-Benz); Rudolf Caracciola (Mercedes-Benz) is in 1 in the second row.

Left Pre-war Alfa Romeo Type 158s came into their own in the late 1940s when the *voiturette* formula was adopted for *grand-prix* racing. The car brought Juan Manuel Fangio his first world championship in 1951.

There had been a European championship in the 1930s, but the new contest was more formal. Points were awarded for performances in the *grandes épreuves*, which in 1950 comprized the British (at Silverstone, Northants), Monaco, Swiss, Belgian, French, and Italian *grands prix*. The world title had been established, but four years would pass before a *grand prix* was held outside Europe, and the best part of a decade before the championship events

Above Fangio, seen here finishing third in the Spanish Grand Prix of 1954, won his second world championship that year in this Mercedes-Benz W196.

Right Tony Brooks in a Vanwall in the British Grand Prix at Aintree, 1957. Later in the race Brooks handed over to Stirling Moss, who took the car to victory.

Below Graham Hill at Oulton Park in 1960 with the rear-engined BRM prototype, at that time being prepared for the 1.5-litre *grand-prix* formula.

really took hold in the rest of the world. Drivers from any country were eligible.

Grand-prix racing gained great impetus from the drivers' championship, and also from the manufacturers' championship, instituted in 1958. New races were continually added to the calendar. These included the Dutch Grand Prix (at Zandvoort) and the Argentinian Grand Prix in 1953, the United States Grand Prix in 1959, the South African in 1962, the Mexican in 1963, and the Canadian in 1967. Some, like the Portuguese and Moroccan, came and went. New circuits emerged: Brands Hatch and Aintree for the British Grand Prix, and Rouen, Ricard-Castellet, and Clermont-Ferrand for the French were notable examples.

The organization of teams altered. One of the last major car manufacturers to take part in *grand-prix* racing was Alfa Romeo with its 1.5-litre, eight-cylinder Type 158 *voiturette*, designed before the war by Gioacchino Colombo, which dominated the early races. Alfa supremacy was overthrown in 1951 by Enzo Ferrari, now established as a manufacturer of sports and racing cars in his own right.

Mercedes-Benz came back for two momentous seasons in 1954 and 1955 and its eight-cylinder, 2.5-litre racer, driven by the great Juan Manuel Fangio, proved almost unbeatable. Lancia appeared briefly at about the same time, but it was another 20 years before a major car-maker was to field a *grand-prix* team, despite the advertising opportunities that were being taken up by tyre and accessory manufacturers, fuel companies, and firms quite unconnected with the motor industry.

Racing-car construction now became the province of small, specialised firms such as Lotus, Cooper, and the re-formed BRM (which had started as a co-operative venture subsidized by the British motor industry as a whole). Ferrari and BRM made their own engines, but most of the newer teams bought theirs in from firms such as Coventry-Climax and later Cosworth Engineering, forming the nucleus of a new British industry that built, raced, and sold racing cars.

For a while Ferrari kept the British from dominating the sport entirely, but as the 1950s merged into the 1960s and the formula changed once again to 3 litres, Ferrari found it more and more difficult to compete. When John Surtees won the drivers' title in 1964, it proved to be Ferrari's last championship for nearly 10 years.

The technological initiative was now firmly with the British. Cooper succeeded with the engine behind the driver in 1959 and 1960, when Jack Brabham won the world championship. These cars were, strictly speaking, mid-engined rather than rear-engined. The greatest influence of all during the last two decades has been Colin Chapman, whose Lotus cars have pioneered most of the significant developments in chassis and suspension design, reduction in frontal area, and aerodynamics that have shaped the racing car of the 1970s.

A big-business sport

The *grand-prix* circus is now a tightly knit community, deriving its income from race purses approaching £250,000 for each *grand prix*, plus lucrative contracts for commercial sponsorship. The Formula 1 Constructors' Association has effective control of *grand-prix* racing with the CSI in danger of being reduced to a mere cypher. Finance, safety, and even the regulations are now effectively in the hands of the men who own the cars.

Above Ferrari successfully adopted rear engines for its 1961 *grand-prix* car, the V6 Type 156 with its characteristic 'nostrils.. In the hands of Giancarlo Baghetti (seen here), Wolfgang von Trips, and Phil Hill it took the manufacturers' title that year, Hill becoming the first American to win the drivers' championship.

Left Monaco circuit is unique among European *grand-prix* venues in the serpentine route it takes through city streets. In this view the cars are sweeping down to the seafront, then turning right at the Virage Portier before the tunnel (see map on page 227).

A scene at the McLaren pits during the 1976 Japanese Grand Prix. James Hunt is in the McLaren's driving seat; Alistair Caldwell, the team manager, stands on the left; leaning over Hunt is Gordon Coppuck, the car's designer; seated with back to camera is Teddy Hayer, managing director of the McLaren company.

The drivers are not simply highly paid competitors, the focus of attention at the race track. They have to interpret handling characteristics and communicate these to the engineers charged with matching the cars to each of the 16 or so tracks on which the world championship is contested. Long test sessions are held on private tracks, such as Ferrari's at Fiorano, south of Modena, where the performance of the cars is recorded electronically and monitored by closed-circuit television. Racing has become so competitive, with cars winning by fractions of a second, that the designers must build in fine adjustments to the springing, or the gearing, or the profiles of the wings. In effect, a different car can be produced for each circuit.

Technology dominates *grand-prix* racing today – and this marks the decisive difference between the sport now and 20 years ago. When Fangio won his five world championships in the 1950s he more or less climbed into his cars and drove. It was a matter of feel, of visual acuity, of balance to get the very best out of the car – and he did it supremely well. Between 1950 and 1958 he won 24 *grand-prix* races for Alfa Romeo, Maserati, Mercedes-Benz, and

Ferrari. Fangio was one of the greatest racing drivers in the first three post-war decades. Another was Jim Clark, who scored one more victory than the legendary Fangio. Clark's career ended tragically in a minor race at Hockenheim in 1968, after he had won two world championships. His total of *grand-prix* victories has been eclipsed only by a fellow Scot, Jackie Stewart.

Jack Brabham, Stewart, and Niki Lauda, who followed in the mid-1970s, represent stages in the evolution of the technologist-drivers. Brabham was a pioneer in the art of chassis-tuning,

Coil springs and dampers

Front spoiler

Adjustable spoiler mounting

Torsion bar

Disc brake

Rear-view mirror

Engine-oil cooler

Roll-over bar

Ground-effect spoiler

Torsion bar

Fuel tank

Steering arm

Gear lever

Cooling water radiator

Throttle cable

Drive shaft

Coil springs and dampers

Rear spoiler

Battery

Gearbox-oil cooler

Brake light

Gearbox

Fire extinguisher

Differential

Inboard disc brake

Dry-weather slick tyre

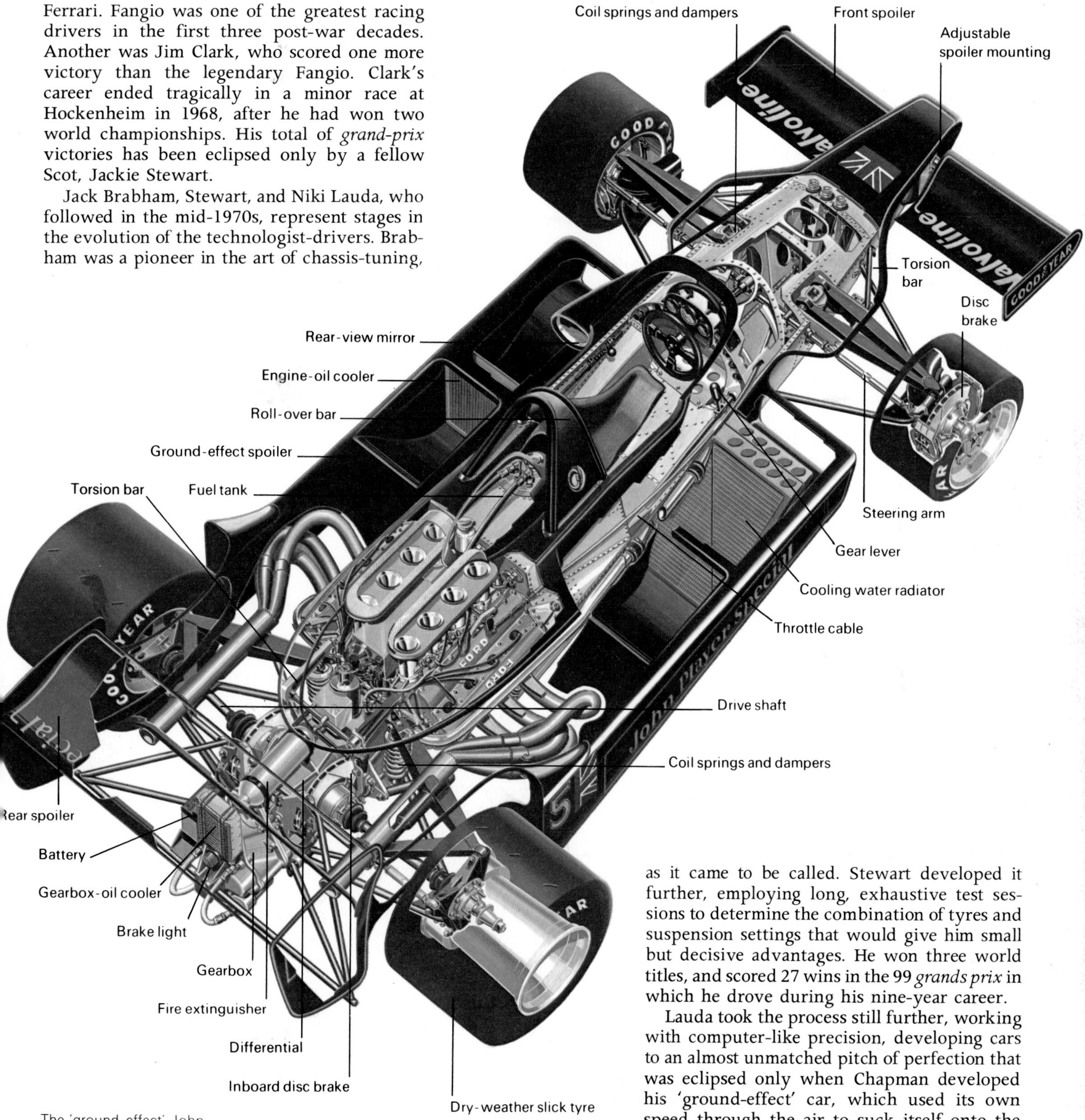

The 'ground-effect' John Player-Lotus that captured the world title in 1978.

as it came to be called. Stewart developed it further, employing long, exhaustive test sessions to determine the combination of tyres and suspension settings that would give him small but decisive advantages. He won three world titles, and scored 27 wins in the 99 *grands prix* in which he drove during his nine-year career.

Lauda took the process still further, working with computer-like precision, developing cars to an almost unmatched pitch of perfection that was eclipsed only when Chapman developed his 'ground-effect' car, which used its own speed through the air to suck itself onto the ground and aid roadholding through corners. This was the car, the John Player-Lotus, in which Mario Andretti in 1978 became the first American to win the drivers' world championship since Phil Hill's success in 1961.

25 Formula Racing

While *grand-prix* racing was firmly establishing its pre-eminence in the 1920s, there arose a demand for less-extravagant forms of circuit motor racing. Even in the pioneer days not all the best drivers had wanted to compete in the *grand-prix* field. Furthermore, not every driver wanted to race professionally: some saw motor racing as a week-end activity or a recreation, particularly in the 1920s and 1930s, when professional drivers neither had the status nor could hope to achieve the earnings of their more recent counterparts.

Racing in those days was often regarded as only part of the fun. What many competitors enjoyed even more was tuning, tinkering, and inventing means of making their cars go faster. This kind of do-it-yourself attitude, however, was by now becoming a thing of the past in the increasingly professional, factory-dominated, and very expensive world of *grand-prix* racing. Thus it was that the junior classes of circuit racing emerged.

The secondary class of the 1920s saw official recognition accorded the spidery cyclecars that were a product of the economic rigours of the time. In the late 1920s and 1930s many promising young drivers served their apprenticeship on second-hand Austin and MG 750 cc racers. Works participation on the scale mounted by Alfa Romeo in the *voiturette* formula of 1938–9 was an aberration; most junior-category racing of the period was dominated by amateur drivers or, at most, by small, budget-conscious teams each with perhaps one full-time mechanic.

When the new Formula A (for *grand-prix* cars) came into being in 1948 the demand for a Formula B arose immediately; and it was laid

down for engines of 2 litres, or 500 cc supercharged. The cars it led to were either purpose-built single seaters or sometimes stripped-down sports cars, but the very internationalism of the category in the early 1950s meant that it remained fairly specialized and still expensive. Indeed it resembled Formula A, or Formula 1, so closely that, when a shortage of competitive cars occurred in 1952–3, *grand-prix* organizers turned to the nominally lesser category and promoted it to world championship status until the new Formula 1 was ready in 1954, with plenty of 2.5-litre cars to compete.

Half-litre events

That still left the field open to the development of new classes. For 30 years hill climbs had provided the opportunity for 'special' builders – often young men with ideas making cars in their own backyards. In the late 1940s one of them, Colin Strang, built a tiny single-seater with a 500 cc motor-cycle engine driving the rear wheels through a chain. The design was successful and attractive; replicas soon followed, and eventually numbers were sufficient for them to race – at first unofficially, and then under national rules guaranteed by the RAC.

Half-litre racing became more sophisticated as time passed, but even when it had gained an international reputation, if not international recognition in the form of an overseas circuit, it never lost sight of its origins as a modest-budget affair for young, keen drivers. Stirling Moss and Peter Collins were only two of many great drivers who came up through 500 cc racing.

Formula Junior

If 500 cc racing established the principle, it was Formula Junior which set the pattern for all

Right above Typical of club-racing cars of about 1950 was this Healey Silverstone, with a 104 hp Riley 2.4-litre engine. The car also had notable class victories in European rallies and sports-car races.

Left Club racing, mainly by amateur drivers, was popular all over Europe during the 1930s. Here two MG Midgets sandwich an Austin Seven at the start of a handicap race at Donington Park in 1935.

Right below During the 1960s formula racing became highly professional with the cars resembling their *grand-prix* counterparts. Here Peter Gethin, in a McLaren-Chevrolet, takes Druid's Corner at Brands Hatch during a 1969 Formula 5000 event.

subsequent variations of national and international single-seater racing classes. Initially an Italian national category, Formula Junior was largely the invention of Count 'Johnny' Lurani Cernuschi. The guiding principle for him was not so much a standardized chassis or a tight framework of rules as the use of easily available production-car engines.

Nearly all the sub-formulas have followed this in essence ever since. Formula Junior soon became Formula 3, and when Formula 2 was revised in due course it, too, employed engines with production-car cylinder blocks. There have been variations. Some regulations have required production engines only as a basis, with a wide range of alterations permitted. Others have forbidden modifications that would involve removing any metal from the standard units, or have allowed changes but instituted a throttling flange to restrict the intake of air.

Formula 2 became established with its own

European championship, and both Formula 2 and 3 produced their quotas of new drivers and even of new teams. Tyrrell, for example, was founded as an amateur group to run the Cooper-BMC team, with the promising Jackie Stewart among its early recruits.

Even so, there remained room for something other than the international formulas, and this led in the 1960s to the adoption of Volkswagen engines in a new type of basic single-seater racing called Formula Vee. Formula Ford followed with Cortina 1.6-litre engines; it was soon joined by Formula Renault in France, Formula SEAT in Spain, and so on. The object was invariably the same: highly competitive racing, and a ready supply of cheap components based on mass-produced road cars.

Technically the cars have produced few innovations, although the use of standard road tyres has sometimes lent interest to the lightweight suspension systems devised. Car manufacturers have inevitably been keen to learn how their engines behave under conditions of high stress, but it is doubtful if this type of racing has helped engineers significantly apart from providing them with data on the production tolerances which make some engines fit together well and others badly.

A more tangible result of the various formulas has been the burgeoning racing-car industry, which by the 1970s had a turnover of some £20 million a year in Britain alone. It employed 1,500 people directly and many more indirectly, making complete racing cars, engines and gear-boxes, and bodywork for customers all over the world but most notably for the United States, where amateur and semi-professional racing of all sorts is a major recreational activity.

Right The start of the 1978 Formula 2 race at Thruxton, Hampshire. The winner and 1978 European champion, Bruno Giacomelli (March-BMW) is already ahead, out of camera frame. In pursuit, in the centre of the picture, is the Irish driver Derek Daly (Chevron-Hart), who finished sixth. The red March-Hart on the right — aided, seemingly, by a superhuman sponsor — is driven by the Brazilian Alex Ribiero, who came fifteenth.

Below Formula 3 events are invariably hotly contested by young drivers making their way up the motor-racing ladder. The cars are powered by 2-litre, four-cylinder units based on production engines, notably Ford (as in this early 1970s event) or, more recently, the Toyota Celica.

The sports car, as a distinct category of motor vehicle, owes its origins to the increasing sophistication of automobile technology in the mid-Edwardian era. Until then, as we saw in Chapter 23, a big motor race, although it might be divided into various weight categories, was open to almost every kind of motor car that had, at least potentially, some prospect of getting among the prizes. But by 1905, when the Automobile Club de France announced its intention of staging the first *grand prix* the following year, racing cars were already a distinct breed. Moreover, the ACF's regulations for the *grand prix* made it certain that, henceforward, major events for racing cars would be dominated by manufacturers' works teams.

There was clearly a need for a type of event that was open to the individual enthusiast driving his own touring car. A decisive step in the evolution of this category of event came in 1905, when the Automobile Club of Great Britain and Ireland organized the first Tourist Trophy race on the Isle of Man. The meeting proved popular not only with the drivers but also with the manufacturers, who were anxious to create favourable publicity with the small but growing public of car buyers. The first TT race was won by the Scot J. S. Napier in an Arrol-Johnston he had designed himself. The car had a 3.7-litre, horizontally opposed twin-cylinder engine, each piston having two connecting rods with a rocking lever between

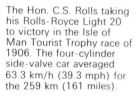

The Hon. C.S. Rolls taking his Rolls-Royce Light 20 to victory in the Isle of Man Tourist Trophy race of 1906. The four-cylinder side-valve car averaged 63.3 km/h (39.3 mph) for the 259 km (161 miles).

them. Captain Percy Northey was second in the new 'lightweight' Rolls-Royce 20. The following year the Rolls Light 20 won the race in the capable hands of the Hon. C. S. Rolls, Henry Royce's partner in the young English company. The Light 20 illustrated the technical progress being made in touring-car design. It had a 'vertical' four-cylinder engine with dual ignition (magneto and coil, and two sparking plugs per cylinder), mechanically driven overhead-inlet and side-exhaust valves, an engine-driven water pump, and a four-speed gearbox in which top gear was indirect to provide an 'overdrive'.

The TT spawned other events for touring cars all over Europe, including tough reliability trials. Gradually, specialization in car design evolved to cater to the needs of the growing breed of competitive touring-car drivers.

The Prince Henry Trials

It is widely agreed that the greatest single impetus in the evolution of the sports car was given by the gruelling series of reliability trials sponsored by Prinz Heinrich of Prussia from 1908 onwards. The Prince Henry Trials, as they came to be known in Britain, were for touring cars of limited engine capacity. The formidable route, starting in Berlin, usually ran south-eastward through Breslau (now Wroclaw, in Poland), then south-eastward again to the Hungarian capital, Budapest. From there it turned westward, through Austria, to Salzburg, and

W. O. Bentley had exhibited his 3-litre, overhead-camshaft, four-valves-per-cylinder, dual-ignition, 128 km/h (80 mph) sports tourer. The marque was to scale prodigious heights in sports-car racing, notching up no less than five victories in the prestigious Le Mans 24-hour race between 1924 and 1930.

The Bentley represented one aspect of sports-car design – a massive, immensely strong body that relied for its sporting characteristics on a large, powerful engine (Ettore Bugatti, the brilliant Italian-born designer, called the Bentley 'the fastest lorry in the world'). But other types of sports cars, of simpler specification, relied for success on light weight and agile handling. Bugatti himself produced sports cars that, in a sense, reflected both philosophies. Like Bentley, he had been involved in aero-engine design during World War I. He went on to produce a long succession of small cars in which lightness and agility were allied to great (if sometimes eccentric) mechanical sophistication. His finest sports cars, indeed, were so good that they were often used, with little modification, as out-and-out racing cars.

The early 1920s also saw the emergence in the sports-car field of another great marque, Alfa Romeo. Founded in 1910, the company was making racing cars soon after World War I, but in 1923 a 3-litre, six-cylinder Alfa Romeo 22/90 sports tourer took second place in the Targa Florio, the gruelling Sicilian road race.

finished in Munich. Year by year the competition for Prince Henry's cup grew fiercer and fiercer, the emphasis switching from reliability to speed as the pace hotted up. So great was the event's importance that it inspired manufacturers to produce cars that, although they complied with the letter of the regulations, were to all intents and purposes racing cars in tourer form.

The 1910 trials illustrated the way things were going, for Ferdinand Porsche, the brilliant Austrian designer, arrived with a team of Austro-Daimler 22/80PS models with four-cylinder, overhead-camshaft engines developing no less than 95 bhp. The German Benz team cars featured four inclined valves per cylinder; but the victorious Austro-Daimlers had five – one inlet and four exhaust. The British entries, Vauxhall Prince Henry tourers, had much less sophisticated side-valve engines of 60 bhp, but in spite of their unadventurous specification the pointed-tail Vauxhalls proved reliable and achieved reasonable success.

The 1920s

During World War I the development of warplanes brought about a rapid improvement in the design of petrol engines, and these improvements were soon applied to motor cars in the post-war years. The 1920s also saw the tourer and the racing car achieve completely separate identities. The former was becoming heavier and heavier, with increasing emphasis on comfort, while the latter was becoming impractical for normal road use. The gap between the two types gave rise to the sports car.

It was around 1919 that English motoring journals started using the term, by which time

Above Count Masetti (Mercedes) won on the rough roads and multiple corners of the Targa Florio in 1922.

Below John Duff and F.C. Clement's 3-litre Bentley roars down Mulsanne Straight in 1924 on its way to the first of the marque's five victories in the Le Mans 24-hour race.

Right The great Tazio Nuvolari (with co-driver Guidotti) on a gruelling section of the 1930 Mille Miglia. He won the race that year and in 1933. The car is a Zagato-bodied Alfa Romeo Type 6C-1750, with a supercharged six-cylinder, twin-overhead-camshaft engine. Alfas won 10 of the 12 Mille Miglias held in 1927–38.

Below Map of the 1957 Mille Miglia, the final year of this classic endurance race. The route, starting and finishing at Brescia, was substantially the same for most of the race's 30-year history.

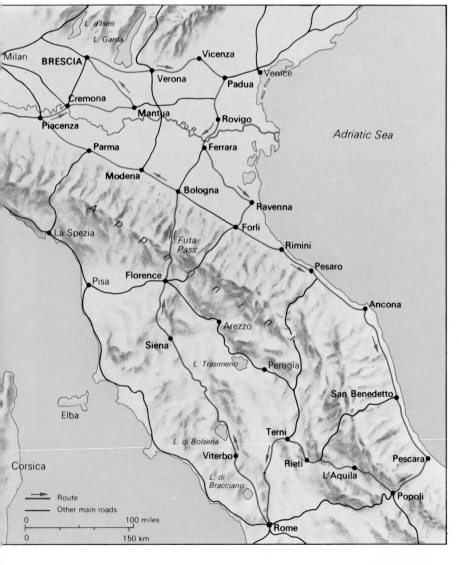

Le Mans and Mille Miglia

In those years immediately after the war motor manufacturers were hungry for sales. Some of the bigger (or more optimistic) entered the expensive field of *grand-prix* racing in order to demonstrate their technological and engineering prowess. But other manufacturers believed that the public was more likely to be impressed by success in events for cars that had at least some resemblance to the products available in the High Street showroom. For such manufacturers, long-distance sports-car events were ideal. So when plans were announced in 1923 for a 24-hour race on the roads south of the ancient French city of Le Mans, the manufacturers responded with enthusiasm. This first Le Mans race was judged an enormous success, particularly by the French who won on their home ground with a victory by A. Lagache and R. Léonard in a 3-litre Chenard-Walcker. Apart from two Belgian Excelsiors and a single British Bentley 3-litre, all the 32 entries were French marques.

By 1927 the Italians, not to be outdone, had inaugurated the exciting Mille Miglia ('1,000 Miles'), an open-road race for sports cars. The route, taking in much of the northern half of Italy, began and finished at Brescia (west of Lake Garda) and included Ancona (on the Adriatic coast), Rome, Florence, the difficult Futa and Raticosa passes in the Appennini mountains, and Bologna. To the surprise of many, the first race resulted in a 1-2-3 victory for modestly powered Italian OM sports tourers with 2-litre, side-valve engines.

The Mille Miglia was almost a unique event at that time. Whereas the Le Mans race took place on a circuit using public roads that were temporarily closed to normal traffic, the Italian marathon was run on open roads which, although policed, were apt to be littered in rural areas by peasant farmers, mules, and carts. The Targa Florio in Sicily was run under similar circumstances. The other main sports-car event, the British Tourist Trophy series, had resumed in 1922 in the Isle of Man, but then lapsed until 1928, when it was run on the triangular Ards circuit in Northern Ireland, continuing there for another eight years.

Le Mans and the Mille Miglia accelerated the development of the sports car. In terms of engines, the Le Mans-winning Bentleys of 1927–30 were a notable example of progressively increasing capacity and power. The 1927 car (based closely on Bentley's original model of 1919) was of 3 litres and developed about 70 bhp; in 1928 the capacity was increased to 4.5 litres, offering 100 bhp; in 1929 and 1930 came the Speed Six, with a 6.5-litre, six-cylinder engine developing 180 bhp. These later models weighed about 2,000 kg (two tons) and, with a large frontal area (their height was due in part to the depth of the long-stroke engine) they certainly needed all the power their designer could build into them.

The Bentley's main rival in many Le Mans and TT races was the Mercedes-Benz, which had pioneered supercharging in Europe, offering production four- and six-cylinder 'blown' cars in 1925. During this inter-war period Mercedes used a unique supercharging system in which the Roots-type blower forced air into the intake of the carburettor. The driver could run his car in unsupercharged form by using the accelerator pedal normally; when he wanted maximum power he slammed it to the floor, the blower was engaged, and the car shot forward with a characteristic howl.

By the late 1920s the Mercedes K series, with supercharged six-cylinder engines of 6.8 and, later, 7.1 litres, were among the fastest and most powerful sports cars in the world, gaining numerous victories – the Ulster TT in 1929 and the Mille Miglia of 1931 being the most important; but they never won the Le Mans. In contrast the Bentley, so successful at Le Mans, won neither the Mille Miglia nor a TT.

The 1930s

In the early 1930s dominance in sports-car racing passed decisively to Italy, in the shape of a series of superb Alfa Romeo models designed by Vittorio Jano. Following various supercharged 1,500 and 1,750 cc six-cylinder models, Jano unveiled his classic 2.3-litre supercharged straight-eight with twin overhead camshafts. Unlike the Mercedes-Benz and Bentleys, the Alfas were light in weight; since they were modelled closely on the company's successful *grand-prix* cars, they were also extremely fast and had great stamina. They won Le Mans four years in succession (1931–4), the Mille Miglia in 1929, 1930, and 1932–8, the Tourist Trophy in 1930, and the Targa Florio in the five races held between 1930 and 1935 (the event was not staged in 1932). The mechanical similarity between the Alfa sports cars and racing cars recalled the days before World War I and set the pattern for the future. But there are often exceptions to the rule in motor sport. In the 1930s the most striking example of this was the victory of Lagonda at Le Mans in 1935. In design principles this car harked back to the old Bentleys. It was a big, heavy tourer propelled by a pushrod-overhead-valve, six-cylinder engine of 4.5 litres which had originally been produced (by Meadows) for commercial vehicles! (In fairness it must be added that it was a very adaptable, reliable engine; installed in a

Above Peter Whitehead (whose co-driver was Peter Walker) in the winning Jaguar C-Type at Le Mans, 1951. Here he accelerates away from Mulsanne Corner followed by the Rolt/Hamilton Nash-Healey which came fourth. Jaguars repeated this victory in 1953, 1955, 1956, and 1957.

Left Stirling Moss, with navigator Denis Jenkinson, takes a corner in Ravenna on his way to victory in the 1955 Mille Miglia. His average speed in the formidable Mercedes-Benz 300SLR was 157.6 km/h (97.9 mph) – an all-time record. It was one of Moss's supreme performances on road or track.

Speed Model Invicta it had won the 1931 Monte Carlo Rally.)

The years immediately before World War II saw something of a technical mix at Le Mans. The 1937 race was won by Bugatti's remarkable 3.3-litre Type 57 with unsupercharged twin-overhead-camshaft, straight-eight engine. The following year the race was won by a French car of completely different character – a Delahaye with a conventional six-cylinder, pushrod-overhead-valve engine derived from the company's lorry unit. The last Le Mans before the war saw another victory for Bugatti, this time with a supercharged version of the 1937 car. And so ended an era of racing when merit was decided on outright wins, index-of-performance awards, and class wins. The idea of a world sports-car championship had to wait until after World War II.

Early post-war racing

Sports-car racing in the first decade after the war was notable for the absence of super-chargers. The outstanding engines of this period were Enzo Ferrari's marvellous V12s of modest capacity but astonishing power. The motors, designed by Gioacchino Colombo, were essentially *grand-prix* units and were very similar to those of slightly smaller capacity used in Ferrari's supercharged single-seat racing cars. Ferrari's 2-litre V12s won the 1948 and 1949 Mille Miglia and Targa Florio races, and also the first post-war Le Mans in 1949.

Then the scene was invaded by the higher-class volume manufacturers, who saw the need to boost post-war sales through racing success and world-wide publicity. Jaguar won Le Mans in 1951 with the C-type, a sports-racing two-seater with multi-tube steel frame and the 3.4-litre, twin-overhead-camshaft, six-cylinder engine from the production Jaguar XK120 sports car. The following year Mercedes-Benz came back to Le Mans and won with its 300SL 'gull-wing' coupé, powered by an efficient 3-litre, single-overhead-camshaft, six-cylinder engine, later to have petrol-injection in production form but at that stage equipped with three carburettors. It was Jaguar's turn in 1953, again with the C-type.

The world championships

The year 1953 was the first in which the World Sports Car Championship was held. Events counting in that initial series were the 1,000 km of Buenos Aires (Argentina); the Sebring 12-hours (USA); the Mille Miglia (Italy); the Le Mans 24-hours (France); the Spa-Francorchamps 24-hours (Belgium); the Nürburgring 1,000 km (West Germany); the TT (Britain); and the Pan-America road race (Mexico).

The new series put excitement into sports-car racing and spurred technical development. Mercedes contributed desmodromic valve-gear (valves opened and closed by mechanical means) as well as petrol injection, and Jaguar pioneered the highly effective disc brake.

Speeds went up and up, the main Sports Car Championship contestants being Jaguar, Ferrari, Ferrari, Mercedes, and Aston Martin. By 1958 the FIA (Fédération Internationale de l'Automobile, the governing body of the sport) had introduced a 3-litre limit in an endeavour to contain speeds. Jaguar, as a factory, pulled-out of racing (Mercedes had already withdrawn after the tragic disaster at Le Mans in 1955, when more than 100 people were killed), and Aston Martin won the 1959 championship with a six-cylinder, twin-overhead-camshaft car with rear-mounted five-speed gearbox.

One of the features of the post-war championship races was the admission of 'sports prototypes', a class which enabled constructors to enter near-racing cars which bore some resemblance to production models. For about six years Ferrari dominated the category with its front-engined, and later rear-engined, 12-cylinder masterpieces. Ford of the USA, seeking a world-wide sporting image, tried for two years to win Le Mans using a British-designed rear/mid-engined 'coupé' and a relatively crude pushrod-overhead-valve V8 engine closely related to a production Detroit unit. Ford won the World Sports Car Championship (or the Constructors' Championship, as it had now been renamed) from 1966 to 1968. In the first two years it succeeded with huge 7-litre, overhead-valve V8s, relying on the old automotive adage that 'there is no substitute for cubic centimetres'. Running in the Group 7 class, Ford at last vanquished the 'prototypes' with their 3-litre overhead-camshaft motors of advanced design. By 1968 the regulations had been changed to admit 'sport' models with engines up to 5 litres, provided that their valve-gear was of the simple pushrod-and-rocker type.

Under the new regulations Ford raced 5-litre GT40s under the banner of the JW Automotive Team, run by Le Mans expert John Wyer who had masterminded Aston Martin's championship win in 1959. Ford won Le Mans in 1968 with a simple 5-litre V8, but it was only 72 km (45 miles) ahead of the advanced 2.2-litre Porsche 907 prototype at the end of 24 hours.

The 1970s

The prestigious German marque dominated the championship races from 1970 to 1972 with its 4.5-litre, 12-cylinder Type 917. It was a highly complex rear/mid-engined car with horizontally opposed, air-cooled motor, fuel

injection, twin-overhead-camshafts for each bank of cylinders, dual ignition, titanium connecting rods, and an output in the early stages of development of 540 bhp. Later versions, turbocharged for Can-Am racing, developed no less than 900 bhp!

The 917 won Porsche's first-ever Le Mans in 1970 – after 20 years of trying – and the cars were virtually invincible while the factory stayed in racing. The 917 ran in Group 4 Sports category, which admitted high-performance cars and included all equipment normally provided on road vehicles, with at least two seats. No engine restrictions were imposed, and at least 25 had to have been made.

The almost unbeatable Porsche 917s were

effectively outlawed in 1972, however, when the Constructors' Championship regulations were substantially changed to include a new Group 5 for sports cars with no production minimum but an engine capacity limit of 3 litres. The limit coincided with that of Formula 1, and it came as no surprise when Formula 1 engines appeared in the new category. Ferrari and Matra used their 12-cylinder *grand-prix* engines, and Lola and Mirage joined in with detuned versions of the Ford-Cosworth DFV V8. Ferrari's horizontally opposed, water-cooled, unsupercharged unit developed about 150 bhp per litre, and the Matra water-cooled V12 produced 415 bhp in Le Mans form, which was remarkable for long-distance racing en-

A 1966 Ford GT40 Mk 2, culmination of the American company's huge investment in a world-beating sports car for endurance races. The car, with a 7-litre engine developing over 400 bhp, took first, second, and third places at Le Mans in 1966; a Mk 4, with 500 hp, came first the following year, averaging 218.2 km/h (135.5 mph).

A 1970 Porsche 917K, with a 4.5-litre, flat-12 engine of 520 bhp. The car is in the colours of the Gulf/JWA team, whose seven championship victories out of 10 helped to give Porsche the 1970 world title. A similar car running for a Salzburg team also won the Le Mans that year — the marque's first outright victory in the 24-hour race.

gines. Ferrari won the 1972 World Constructors' Championship, but Matra finished first and second at Le Mans.

The Matra proved marginally faster than Ferrari in 1973, and the French marque won the championship, although the Italian cars were generally more reliable; the Cosworth-engined Mirages won the Spa 24-hours. Matra repeated its championship win in 1974, sweeping all before it, and once again humbling the Ferraris. Another Italian horizontally opposed 12-cylinder car, the Alfa Romeo 33TT, had exhibited speed on occasions but not reliability, and in a crisis year for the state-sponsored company the cars were withdrawn as the season progressed.

With Matra out of 1975 sports-car racing, Alfa Romeo returned and took up the championship with its rear/mid-engined, unsupercharged 12-cylinder *boxermotor*. The main opposition came from Alpine-Renault's experimental turbocharged 2-litre V6 and Porsche's old 908s, re-engined with turbocharged versions of the durable air-cooled flat-six. Turbocharging, a 'free' supercharging system which forces gas into the engine cylinders by means of an exhaust-driven compressor, increases power output by at least a third, and does not rob the engine of power as does a mechanically-driven supercharger.

Le Mans' race committee refused to abide by the FIA rules in 1975 and adopted its own regulations, but it still attracted a top selection of cars in the following four years. Porsche won the Sports Car Championship and Le Mans in 1976, extracting a reliable 530 bhp from its 2.2-litre, air-cooled flat-six. But it was apparent that Renault was making big strides with its own 2-litre, watercooled, turbocharged V6.

Porsche and Renault withdrew from the Sports Car Championship in 1977 which was won by Alfa Romeo with its 12-cylinder *boxermotor*, but without serious opposition. Real interest now centred on the non-championship

Below Martini-Porsche 935 Turbos, with bodywork based on the 911 road car and 330 hp flat-six engines, have been dominant in long-distance races in the 1970s. The inset shows Jochen Mass and Jacky Ickx's car at the 1976 Silverstone 6-hour Race; at bottom a similar car goes into Druid's at Brands Hatch during the 1974 British Airways 1,000 km race.

Above The Renault-Mirage M9 turbocharged V6 car, driven by Jacques Laffite, Vern Schuppan, and Sam Posey, that came tenth at Le Mans in 1978. A similarly engined Renault Alpine A 442 B Turbo, with Didier Pironi and Jean-Pierre Jaussaud at the wheel, took first place.

Le Mans, where the turbocharged Porsches and Alpine-Renaults were locked in battle. Once again the German marque won. For 1978 Renault made a huge effort, spending enormous sums of money and entering several variations on the turbocharged theme. It beat Porsche fair and square with the 2-litre V6.

The victory brought into focus the enormous strides that had been made since Levassor's Panhard had won the Paris–Bordeaux–Paris race in 1895. The 1.2-litre twin-cylinder German engine of the Panhard had developed 3.3 bhp per litre: the 1978 Le Mans Alpine-Renault's turbocharged 2-litre V6 produced 260 bhp per litre. The Renault averaged 210 km/h (131 mph) for 24 hours! Turbocharging is already well established in Porsche and Saab production cars, and no doubt sports-car racing will add much to the designers' knowledge of this promising boost to piston-engine power.

As we have seen, motor racing in its earliest days was essentially for ordinary 'production' cars. The history of racing can be seen as progress towards specialization of cars and events. The trend has been away from production models towards cars that are purpose-built for specific types of event; the most extreme examples are, of course, *grand-prix* racing cars and the highly developed 'sports cars' that compete at Le Mans. As each such shift towards specialization has occurred, it has opened a gap in motor sport for production models – cars that, however modified, are based substantially on those for sale to the public.

Today this gap is filled by production- and saloon-car racing, which have their origins in the British Racing Drivers' Club's International Trophy meeting at Silverstone in 1949. The first of these events laid down no specific regulations regarding homologation (numbers of cars built) or their tuning. In fact, the Jaguar XK120s driven by Leslie Johnson and Peter Walker, who claimed the first two places in that one-hour race, were not strictly production vehicles, since delivery of the XKs had not begun by then. With the very fast Jaguar XKs also winning in 1950 and 1951 it was not surprising that saloon cars soon disappeared from these production-car races. In 1952, therefore, the Silverstone International Trophy programme included the first race purely for saloons.

Stirling Moss's lumbering Jaguar Mk 7 comfortably won the 17-lap race of 80 km (50 miles). Next came Ken Wharton's Healey-Elliott and Sidney Allard's 3.6-litre Allard PI. Jaguar domination of the Silverstone International saloon-car races was unbroken during the 1950s, first with the Mk 7 and later with the smaller 2.4 and 3.4 Mk 1 saloons. Drivers such as Moss, Ian Appleyard, Mike Hawthorn, Ivor Bueb, and Walt Hansgen triumphed for Jaguar in this era, and when the Mk 1 was replaced by the 3.8 Mk 2, more Jaguar victories were gained by Colin Chapman, Roy Salvadori, Sir Gawaine Baillie, Graham Hill, and Mike Parkes. While Jaguars dominated saloon-car events overall, competition between individual Jaguar drivers was intense, as it was in the smaller-car classes between the likes of Austin A30s, A35s, Standard Tens, Fords, Sunbeam Rapiers, Riley One-Point-Fives, and MG Magnettes.

Although factory-supported saloons were more advanced than those entered privately, the races of the 1950s were contested by cars far closer to the true production specifications than the Group 1 touring cars that race today in the British car championship. In that decade, too, lessons learnt from circuit racing were incorporated in ordinary production cars to a

greater degree than happens now. Nowadays, manufacturers prefer to enter their production-based saloons in international rallies rather than in circuit races.

A championship for saloons

The success of saloon-car racing led to the first British Saloon Car Championship in 1958. It was run by the British Racing and Sports Car Club to their own regulations. The championship ended in a tie between Jack Sears (Austin A105) and Tommy Sopwith (Jaguar 3.4). In an unusual method of deciding the winner, the two drivers competed in a drive-off against each other in Riley One-Point-Fives. There were two races, in between which they swopped cars. Each driver won one race, but Sears took the title with an aggregate time of 1.6 seconds less than Sopwith's. The following year the championship was enlarged and new regulations adopted, permitting more liberal engine tuning. A works-supported Ford Zephyr driven by Jeff Uren won the series.

The arrival of the BMC Mini in 1959 provided an enormous fillip to the sport. The British 1961 Saloon Car Championship was won by John Whitmore's Mini Cooper – and 17 years later the 1978 title was won by Richard Longman's Leyland Mini 1275GT. During the intervening seasons the Mini provided immense enjoyment for thousands of competitors and spectators in every conceivable form of motor sport.

Above Jaguar dominated British saloon-car racing in the 1950s, and won every international Production Car race at Silverstone's major meetings in 1952–3. Stirling Moss, one of several *grand-prix* drivers racing in Jaguars during this decade, is seen here cornering in one of the compact Jaguar 3.4-litre Mark III saloons at Silverstone in 1960.

As well as winning the British championship, Minis have also claimed three European saloon-car titles.

In the 1961 BRDC Silverstone International, Dan Gurney's 6.7-litre Chevrolet Impala signalled a trend towards big, powerful American cars that would develop in saloon-car racing through the 1960s. Although it failed to win, the big Impala had superior speed to the previously all-conquering Jaguars and shattered the lap record. For 1963 John Willment acquired a 6.9-litre V8 Ford Galaxie, and the May International Trophy provided a historic result: for the first time since the opening saloon event in the 1952 International Trophy race, Jaguars were beaten. The victor was Jack Sears in the Willment Galaxie.

Ford's British family saloon, the Cortina, was to become the greatest threat to the Detroit cars. The Willment Cortina GTs were supplemented by Colin Chapman's Ford Lotus-Cortinas, and in the mid-1960s Jim Clark and Graham Hill led the British Lotus-Cortina attack on the Sears, Gurney, and Jack Brabham Galaxies. The Galaxies were replaced by the smaller 4.7-litre (American) Ford Mustangs in 1965, and Roy Pierpoint won the British championship in one of these powerful cars.

In 1966 British saloon-car racing became more competitive still with the change of regulations from FIA Group 2 to Group 5. The new rules permitted complete freedom as far as brakes were concerned, and although the original (production) engines had to be used and the location of the camshaft remained unaltered, the scope for adaptation was great and resulted in highly developed power units with alloy-heads, dry sumps, and fuel injection. Production transmission cases had to be retained, but both BMC and Ford fitted their competition gearboxes with five speeds instead of the original four, and limited-slip differentials (reducing back-wheel spin) began to appear.

Racing steadily became faster and more spectacular in the mid-1960s. The American Ford Falcons, with their many glass-fibre body parts, became the cars to beat, and only the magnificent driving of Jim Clark in the works Lotus-Cortina prevented total domination by the American saloons. The Broadspeed Ford Anglias proved equally dominant in the 1-litre group, however, and John Fitzpatrick won the championship in one of Ralph Broad's cars.

The early 1970s saw the British Touring Car Championship run to a Group 2 formula featuring cars of widely different size and engine capacity. Frank Gardner, an Australian stalwart of the British Saloon Car Championship for several years, drove an SCA Freight-sponsored Chevrolet Camaro Z28, powered by a 5.7-litre V8 engine, in the 1971 season. Here he leads the late Gerry Birrell in a German-built Ford Capri RS2600 of 2.9 litres and John Fitzpatrick in a 1.7-litre Ford Escort RS1600 out of a corner at Brands Hatch.

Brian 'Yogi' Muir, another leading Australian driver, was sponsored in the early 1970s by Wiggins Teape, who also gave substantial support to the British Saloon Car Championship. After driving a Camaro in 1970–1, Muir switched to a factory-supported Ford Capri RS2600, in which he is seen here taking the hairpin at Mallory Park, Leicestershire, in 1972.

Technical development in Group 5 saloon-car racing reached almost ludicrous proportions in 1967 when Ford's Mk 2 Lotus-Cortina featured Cosworth's new Formula 2 racing-car engine which developed 210 bhp. But Frank Gardner's 4.7-litre Ford Falcon Sprint, run by Alan Mann, won the championship. A year later Cortinas were replaced by the new Ford Escorts, and Gardner's Alan Mann Escort won the series outright. Ford's domination of the Group 5 championship was impressive. But in 1969, the last year of the Group 5 British Saloon Car Championship, Alec Poole's 970 cc Mini Cooper S amassed sufficient points to claim the title.

The 1970s
The RAC British saloon series reverted to the Group 2 formula from 1970 until 1973. While liberal enough in terms of modifications, the rules did not allow completely different cylinders or non-homologated transmissions to be fitted. George Bevan's remarkably quick little Hillman Imps, driven by Bill McGovern, won the championship outright in 1970, 1971, and 1972 – much to the annoyance of the circuit promoters, who were trying to promote Group 2 saloon-car racing as spectacular and fast with big, powerful cars.

When the Ford Falcons became ineligible in the early 1970s, domination passed to the Ford Mustangs and Chevrolet Camaros. Frank Gardner was so monotonously successful with his American machines that many people became convinced that the big-engined North American cars would have to be banned from Group 1.

Meanwhile, at club level, production-saloon-

car racing was proving immensely successful, and so it was not surprising when, in 1974, the RAC British Saloon Car Championship was run for the Group 1 Production Car Formula. Limited to cars in 'showroom condition', the formula restored a sense of proportion to saloon-car racing by strictly limiting the modifications allowed to engine, suspension, brakes, and bodywork. The new series attracted a far greater variety of cars than before, and also much-needed support from manufacturers. Leyland entered motor racing with the Triumph Dolomite Sprints, Chrysler UK with Avenger GTs, and there were works-supported BMWs and Ford Capris. However, the Chevrolet Camaros of Richard Lloyd and Stuart Graham continued to dominate Group 1 in 1974–5.

In 1976 the championship was limited to 3-litres maximum, making the big American cars ineligible. The consequence of this has been that 3-litre Ford Capris have dominated the large class of the saloon-car championship, with an occasional showing by BMW. The smaller (2-litre) Broadspeed-prepared Dolomite Sprints have proved immensely fast and have often challenged Capris for outright victory. They claimed the British Saloon Car Championship in 1975 when Andy Rouse was driving. The Chrysler Avenger driven by Bernard Unett won the championship outright in 1974, 1976, and 1977, and from the same small class Richard Longman's Mini won the series in 1978.

American saloon racing
The National Association for Stock Car Automobile Racing (NASCAR) organizes saloon-car racing in the United States – the term 'stock car' having a different meaning there from that in Britain. Indianapolis aside, NASCAR's Winston Cup Grand National Championship is the most successful form of motor racing in the United States. More than £2 million is offered in prize money every year, many of the races are televized, and hundreds of the most powerful 'stockers' hurtle along at average speeds of up to 240 km/h (150 mph).

NASCAR owes its success to the entertainment value of its events. Racing excitement and spectacle come first, and engineering developments are of secondary importance. Organizers concentrate on making the cars strong and safe, and as evenly matched as possible. If any model begins to dominate events the rule-makers 'handicap' it by imposing restrictions to lessen its performance.

A good example of this occurred before the start of the 1978 season with the announcement of specifications for a new restrictor plate for the all-conquering 1976 Chevrolet Chevelle Laguna SS. The new regulations reduced the

Chevelle's throttle-bore diameter, severely limiting any reworking of the carburettor internals, and narrowed the fuel line between the carburettor and the intake manifold. The intention was to make the Chevelle less competitive, to encourage other models to enter.

Yet the change to new models has been more apparent than real because these cars have also been General Motors products of similar track and wheelbase to those of the Chevelle. Indeed, the Oldsmobiles and Buicks which superseded the Chevrolet have even been allowed to use the same 5,866 cc Chevrolet V8 engine equipped with the carburettor and restrictor plate used by the Chevelle.

NASCAR promoters have another gimmick in case their restrictor plates are not immediately effective. If a car builds up a substantial lead during a race, the track officials wave yellow caution flags that oblige the cars to slow down – and the field bunches up again.

The next few years will bring changes to NASCAR as American manufacturers move towards the production of smaller cars. The association expects to have substantially altered its regulations by 1981. It may well be that the way NASCAR deals with the move towards smaller cars and other likely restrictions on fuel consumption will serve as a model for the rest of the motor-sporting fraternity as worldwide petrol shortages begin to bite.

No comparison can be drawn between the spectacle of saloon-car racing in Europe and that in America. The European saloon races are hindered by numerous complicated regulations. The high-spots of international saloon-car endurance racing in Europe have been few and far between. The best period came in 1973 with the exciting battles between lightweight Ford Capris from Germany and the winged BMW CSLs. A brief resurgence of interest came in 1977 with Leyland's Jaguar XJ12 coupé, but the car was forced into retirement at the end of an unsuccessful season. Manufacturers have hitherto shown little interest in the European touring-car championship, and in the 1978 season privately owned, out-of-date BMW CSLs claimed the honours.

The finest season so far of the European Touring Car Championship was 1973, which saw a series of exciting duels between the closely matched BMW CLSs and Ford Capris. The championship was eventually won for BMW by the Dutch driver Toine Hezemans, who is seen here leading the Touring Car event at Zandvoort followed by one of his main rivals, the *grand-prix* driver Jochen Mass, in a German-built Capri.

Left The free-for-all regulations for Saloon Car racing at club level in the 1970s gave rise to some freakish hybrids. Typical of these was Colin Hawker's Volkswagen fastback, which was powered by a rear-mounted Cosworth DFV engine from a Tyrell Formula 1 *grand-prix* car.

Below The highlight of NASCAR racing in the United States is the February meeting at Daytona, Florida (seen here during a 1972 event). Speeds at Daytona nowadays reach more than 320 km/h (200 mph).

Manufacturers' support

However, the situation seems likely to improve. Ford, Leyland, and Volkswagen were supporting the British Group 1 championship and, with the Fédération International de l'Automobile (FIA) also adopting a Group 1 championship for the first time in 1979, other manufacturers were likely to follow suit. The success of Group 1 racing is vital if manufacturer's support is to be retained.

Participation in saloon-car racing can alter, sometimes dramatically, the public's view of a company's cars. This has been the experience of Ford in Britain (although, like many other companies, Ford is now seeking to capitalize on public interest through rallies rather than circuit events). Leyland was quick to react with national advertizing to announce the victory in the 1978 British Saloon Car Championship by Richard Longman's Mini 1275GT. There is, indeed, no better method of discovering the qualities and weaknesses of a family saloon than by pushing it to the limit in competitive events.

Private entrants continue to provide the backbone of saloon-car racing at all levels. The cash required varies enormously, from about £30,000 for a season of Group 1 racing to £2,000 for a first season of Mini racing.

Europe's largest saloon-car race is the Spa 24-hours, a magnificent endurance event held on the great Belgian circuit. It was once the main contest in the Group 2 European touring-car championship, but the discrepancy in performance between BMWs or Fords and the little Renaults or Skodas proved to be too dangerous, so the event has been run in recent years to its own set of production-car regulations on lines

similar to those of the British Saloon Car Championship. It is the greatest event in the European saloon-car calendar, and it is promoted with the same kind of ballyhoo as that which attracts the crowds to the NASCAR races in the United States.

European saloon-car categories

Even saloon-car racing, then, has followed the historical trend of increasing specialization and modification in search of faster cars. The main European categories are as follows:

European Group 1 Open to current-production saloons; four capacity classes up to 3,000 cc. Limited modifications permitted to engine, brakes, and suspension. The British Saloon Car Championship is run to the same rules.

European Group 2 A more extreme category, allowing greater modification of engine, suspension, and brakes, and wheels up to 400 mm (16 in) wide. No capacity limit. Cars must be production-based, with at least 1,000 identical models produced in the same year.

British Club Production Saloon Cars The most stringent production-car category, permitting only listed modifications for normal road-going models plus a few others concerned with safety; 3,000 cc capacity limit.

One-make Saloon-car Formulas Mainly club-level events for models at various stages of tuning. There are series events for Ford Escorts, Renault 5s, Leyland Minis, VW Golfs, BMWs, and others.

Special Saloon Cars These are production-based hybrids in which only the exterior body-work shape must be unaltered; supercharging and turbocharging permitted. Typical examples: Ford BDA-engined Hillman Imps, Chevrolet-engined Volkswagens, and Ford V6-engined Skodas.

Europe's most demanding Saloon Car race is the Spa 24 Hours. Run on the famous Belgian circuit of Spa-Francorchamps, it attracts by far the largest crowds of any European Saloon Car event. During the early 1970s the speed differentials between the various classes became dangerous, and when three drivers were killed during the 1973 race the most highly modified cars were banned. The race is now run according to a stringent production-car formula

28 Rallies and Marathons

Historically, a motor-car rally has been difficult to define, so varied have been the events that could loosely be grouped under this heading. In the earliest days of motoring, any event – whether a race, a reliability trial, or what we would now call a rally – posed the fundamental problem of whether the cars would prove reliable enough to finish at all. As performance, strength, and mechanical reliability improved, however, the essential differences between a race and a rally began to evolve.

The first true rally was the German Herkomer Trophy of 1904. It established the classic rally format by setting up a series of control points along the route at which each driver had to report, and by stipulating the average speed that the cars had to maintain between each point. The Herkomer was joined in 1908 by the much more arduous Prinz Heinrichfahrt (Prince Henry Trial); the latter, however, was to develop later into a fully fledged sports-car race (*see* Chapter 24). The event that first captured the imagination of the public at large, and that

has continued to the present day, was the Monte Carlo Rally, inaugurated in 1911.

Origin of the Monte Carlo Rally

The Monte owed its birth to the Société des Bains de Mer at Monaco, which decided that, since cars were becoming popular, and since Monte Carlo was virtually empty in the out-of-season period from January to March, it should organize a rally to attract visitors at that time of year. The first Monte, therefore, was merely a promotional idea, and it attracted only 20 starters. Another Monte was held in 1912, but then there was a big gap, to 1924, before the event took its familiar place in the sporting calendar. In essence, the event is still run in its original form: cars from starting points all over Europe (and occasionally even farther afield) converge on a meeting point, and pour into Monaco over roads that may be covered in ice and snow.

Since the 1920s the accent has shifted from reliability, comfort, and a *concours d'élégance* to

Below The Herkomer Trophy, which was officially described as a long-distance regularity trial for touring cars, was the earliest event to establish modern rally-type regulations. Here a FIAT 7.4-litre tourer leaves a control point during the 1906 Herkomer.

outright performance. By the 1930s speed tests in Monaco were needed to separate the field; by the 1940s high-speed regularity runs in the mountains above the town had been added; and by the 1960s flat-out special stages were adopted. The object, though, has always been to attract entries from far and wide to the principality.

The 1937 rally was altogether typical, with starts from John O'Groats, Gibraltar, Valencia, Stavanger (Norway), Umeå (Sweden), Tallinn (Estonia, now part of the Soviet Union), Amsterdam, Bucharest, Athens, and Palermo. The meeting point was Avignon, about 210 km (130 miles) to the west of Monaco. Bonus marks were allowed for the choice of a climatically difficult route, intermediate controls were established at major cities on the way, and almost every sporting-minded manufacturer in the business entered cars.

Town-to-town schedules were imposed, usually requiring average speeds of about 50 km/h (31 mph); but by the 1950s this was not stringent enough to produce penalties. Rallying fashion meant that speed tests were needed, and so special stages were introduced in 1961. A special stage is nothing less than a flat-out dash between two points, often 30 or 40 km (18 or 25 miles) apart, usually over ice-covered roads, where the clock is the arbiter and where a competitor races alone.

Rallies evolve

On events all round the world, the trend in the 1930s and 1940s was to make rally routes more demanding, and no organizer was content until he could include high mountain passes, difficult route finding, rough or 'colonial' roads, and sections which required crews to drive as fast as they could against the clock. Although at club level strict time-keeping and difficult navigation were the most important features until the 1970s, big international rallies like the Alpine Trial and the Marathon de la Route (better known as the Liège–Rome–Liège), which both blossomed in the 1930s, demanded speed, endurance, and occasional bursts of flat-out hill-climbing in speed tests.

The other type of rallying – rough, tough, long, and ultimately destructive – developed in the 1950s with events such as the East African Safari and the Round Australia Trial. These routed the cars over primitive (and sometimes non-existent) tracks, deliberately set unattainable average speeds, and placed their controls in such a way as to extract the highest possible lateness penalties. Great strength and durability were required of cars and crews, who had to balance speed against possible damage to their vehicles.

Real red-blooded rallying was centred on Europe from the 1930s to the 1950s, for traffic laws weighed heavily against open-road sport in North America, and the lack of passable roads hampered rallying in other parts of the world. Even so, the events which made up the European rally championship were all different.

Apart from the Monte, the major French event was the Coupe des Alpes (Alpine Rally), in which route-finding was easy, but in which the terrain of the French, Italian, and Swiss mountains made the required average speeds very difficult to maintain. In the Alpine almost every section was difficult to complete in the time allowed; *sélectives* were more difficult still, while the *épreuves* were outright speed tests, usually hill climbs of famous passes.

The Liège–Rome-Liège, promoted by a Belgian club, directed cars on a serpentine tour of several countries, including the Alps of France and Italy. It went on for four days virtually non-stop and gave little chance of rest for cars or crews. The Liège relied on endurance (human

Left Competitors stuck on an Austrian pass during the 1912 Monte Carlo Rally. The open car and female passenger reflect the fact that, in those early days, the event was regarded by many as an adventurous holiday jaunt rather than as a serious competition. Nonetheless, this, the second Monte to be staged, attracted 87 entrants, including some from the distant starting point of St Petersburg (Leningrad).

Above Paddy Hopkirk winning the 1964 Monte Carlo Rally in his Mini-Cooper S. Minis dominated European rallies in the mid-1960s and won the Monte again in 1965 and 1967.

Below A Citroën DS19 negotiating an icy corner at night on the Col de Turini, north-east of Nice, during a late-1960s Monte Carlo Rally.

and mechanical) to sort out the field, and usually only a few exhausted crews crawled back to Belgium and the finish of the event. Controls (where crews had to stop and wait if they had gained on the schedule, or where they lost marks if they were late, which was far commoner) came thick and fast. It was often impossible even for the experts to pace themselves from one day to the next. Indeed, as the years passed, the Liège became progressively more of a race than a rally. The last event, the Spa–Sofia–Liège, was held in 1964.

Other events, the RAC and Tulip rallies in particular, retained the traditional approach. Both included easy sections of long-distance motoring from town to town. In the Tulip bore-

dom was dispelled by including high-speed hill climbs, while in the RAC there were bouts of night navigation and map-reading or intricate driving tests where low-speed manoeuvrability and braking were at a premium.

Post-war developments

The modern breed of rallying was first established in Scandinavia in the 1950s. In Sweden (the Midnight Sun rally) and in Finland (the Thousand Lakes rally), speed tests were run on loose-surfaced tracks, often through quite dense forest. These special stages were time trials with impossible target average speeds; the routes were often unknown to the drivers beforehand, and the terrain invariably put enormous strains on the suspensions and structures of the cars.

In rallies of this type, the drivers rarely see their rivals during the speed tests. The cars leave the start at one-minute intervals, and their times are not officially published until hours (or even days) later. One of the most important jobs of the co-driver of each car is to discover at each checkpoint his own time and the times of his main rivals.

During the 1960s more and more rallies were obliged to stage their speed sections on private roads. The British RAC rally became a 'stage' event in 1961, and it is now probably the most important rally of this kind in the world.

Several other European events came to prominence in the 1960s, and most of them were modelled on one or other of the classic events. The Acropolis Rally, held in Greece, is an attractive amalgam of the Liège's rough roads, the Midnight Sun's stages, and the high temperatures of the Adriatic countries. The San Remo Rally (once called the Rally of the Flowers) is based on the Italian riviera, but it includes a good deal of mountainous terrain immediately to the north. One of the most popular rallies is the Tour de Corse, which takes place entirely on the Mediterranean island of Corsica, and is all over within 24 hours. It became internationally popular in the 1960s and is now one of the most demanding in the world. Special stages using public roads closed for the occasion come thick and fast, and the overall time schedule is so tight that liaison sections are often extremely difficult as well. Almost any stop for servicing or repairs means a time loss (and, therefore, a penalty). The winner usually has a combination of well-practised crew, a reliable car, and an efficient support team.

Europe has dominated the rally scene for many years, although rallying has become increasingly popular elsewhere in recent years. Rallies qualifying for the World Championship

Left The Alpine Rally routed cars over many of the highest and most difficult passes in the Alps. The picture shows an Adler taking a hairpin on the formidable Stelvio Pass, west of Bolzano, in the 1934 event; Adler won the 2-litre team award.

In the 1950s and 1960s the Safari organizers insisted on standard production cars being used, although they allowed drivers to fit shields to protect the underbody of the cars. In recent years the event has been thrown open to the ultra-fast European type of rally car. But the challenge of the rally remains as formidable as ever, due not only to the terrain but also to the climate. Tropical storms can reduce dusty tracks to impassable mud within minutes; the water in river fords can rise by feet in a matter of hours; and both rally cars and support vehicles can become marooned for days.

The Safari is the most famous of such events, but rallies in Australia (the Round Australia Trial) and South Africa (Roof of Africa) follow the same pattern. The roads in these countries are constantly improving, and even the daunting Safari is becoming much more of a latter-day Liège–Sofia–Liège than its originators could ever have imagined.

The biggest, rarest, and (in publicity terms) the most prestigious of all events are the transcontinental marathons. Derided by many as expensive bonanzas, they provide an enormous challenge to men and machines. Probably the first of all was the Pekin-to-Paris event of 1907 (won by Prince Scipione Borghese's Itala), but the first modern marathon was the London to Sydney in 1968. Sponsored by British and Australian newspapers, this rally led crews across Europe, the Middle East, and India to Bombay, where they boarded a ship for Perth, then resumed the contest in a dash across Australia to Sydney. Andrew Cowan (Hillman Hunter) won that first event. He repeated the feat in 1977, driving a Mercedes-Benz, and took the 1978 Round South America tour in another Mercedes-Benz.

in North America (the Press-on-Regardless, the Rideau Lakes, and the Quebec) all use the European format of easy, non-competitive road sections linking flat-out special stages, usually on loose-surfaced tracks or on tarmac roads on private land. Even in New Zealand (the South Pacific) and Australia (the Southern Cross) the rallies are similar, although they tend to be much longer and with more gruelling stages.

Safaris and marathons

The other face of rallying is the long-distance event, usually over primitive 'roads', in which stamina and durability of both drivers and cars are as important as sheer performance. The first of such rallies was the East African Safari, inaugurated in 1953 and taking in Kenya, Uganda, and Tanganyika; it is now known merely as the 'Safari' and is confined to Kenya. In the 1950s the roads were so poor that cars could fall not merely minutes but days behind schedule. Then, as now, there was no need for special stages, as the overall time schedule was quite impossible to achieve. Set speeds were high and have repeatedly been raised to keep ahead of the power and strength of modern cars, and control points are numerous.

Below The Marathon de la Route was one of the toughest and fastest European rallies of its day — a brutal test of endurance for cars and drivers. Here an Austin-Healey 3000, one of the most formidable rally cars of the 1960s, speeds through a rough-surfaced bend near San Stefano di Cadore (east of Cortina) in the Spa-Sofia-Liège event of 1963.

Above A Saab 93 high in the Italian Alps during the 1958 Sestriere Rally. During the 1950s the Sestriere was the principal Italian event (it was combined with the San Remo to form the Italian Rally in 1970), and Saabs, in the hands of skilful Scandinavian drivers, were becoming a major force.

Left Erik Carlsson, one of the greatest Swedish rally drivers, in his Saab 96 during the 1964 RAC Rally – an event he had won in 1960–2. The present character of the RAC dates from 1961, when Forestry Commission tracks were made available for high-speed special stages.

Right Rally cars are now so noisy that driver and co-driver require intercom sets to converse with each other. This Daf co-driver's head-set is neatly built into his crash helmet.

Marathons tend to be pioneering events over roads rarely used by private cars, through frontiers often otherwise closed, and through great extremes of climate. It is not just the competition but the possible rewards from publicity that attract big entries. Factory teams often shun these events because chance (or luck) plays so great a part; nevertheless, well-prepared factory teams have in fact reaped the major successes – Ford in the London to Mexico in 1970, and Mercedes-Benz in the Round South America tour in 1978. In general, costs are so high, and the time required for preparation so long, that it is difficult to justify staging more than one of these events every two years; but in the old sense of rallying – contending with the elements, the unknown, and the problems of vehicle durability – they undoubtedly have their attraction.

The rally car today

As rallies have become specialized, so too have the cars. In the 1920s and 1930s the cars were virtually standard production models that had been carefully prepared – and often fitted with special equipment with an eye to winning one of the 'comfort' or *concours d'élégance* awards that the organizers usually included among the prizes. Then, as now, there were class divisions according to engine size and vehicle type. After World War II production sports cars became dominant, and when factory teams came on the scene these cars tended to become very specialized. Rules had to be drawn up to ensure that expensive 'one-off' machines were not entered, usually by requiring a minimum number of identical machines to have been built and sold to the public.

So the modern system of 'homologation'

Above During the 1970s the Ferrari-engined Lancia Stratos, a car specially designed for the purpose, became one of the most successful of all rally cars over almost every kind of terrain. Here Robin Ulyate, driving a works-team Stratos, corners in a road-turned-river in the 1977 Safari Rally.

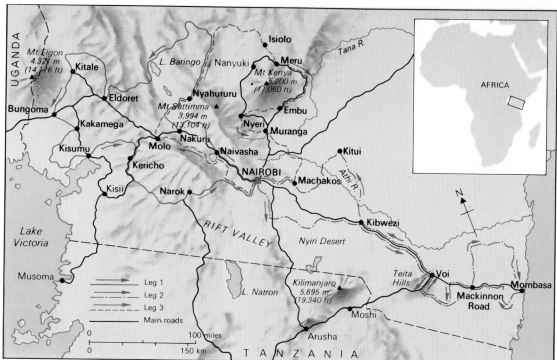

Right The formidable three-leg route of the 1978 Safari Rally. Each leg started and finished in the Kenya capital, Nairobi.

The Fiat 131 Abarth rally car owes little to the ordinary production 131. It has a 2-litre, twin-overhead-cam engine, a five-speed gearbox, independent suspension all round, and uses glass-fibre or light-alloy body panels to reduce weight.

pleted, with hundreds of dimensions and dozens of pictures, along with the declaration that the required number of the model has been built.

Modern rally cars are often hand-built, starting from bare body shells, in a process that may take several weeks. They have to be enormously strong, very fast and versatile, and easily repaired 'in the field'. Leading cars, such as the Ford Escort RS 1800 and Fiat 131 Abarth, have between 240 and 260 bhp available from their 2-litre engines.

Because of the nature of most rallying tracks, undersides have to be strong and protection equipment has been developed continuously since the 1940s. Extensive skid shielding is needed under engine sumps, gearboxes, and final drive casings; bodies, suspension links, and braking systems are all reinforced. Inside the cars, bulky, heavy, but effective roll cages are used, while other safety features include ring-main fire-extinguisher installations and foam-filled bag-type fuel tanks The overall result is a rally car looking superficially like the production machine from which it has been developed, but immensely strong and safe, with great acceleration up to speeds of about 180 km/h (112 mph), and with agile roadholding and handling.

Drivers and support teams

In the early days of rallying there were few stars who could be compared in fame with *grand-prix* drivers. In the years following World War II, one of the best and most consistently successful was Ian Appleyard, who usually drove Jaguar XK sports cars. Since the mid-1950s Scandinavian drivers have dominated the major events. Erik Carlsson from Sweden was one of the first and greatest; since his day many others, notably Rauno Aaltonen, Timo Mäkinen, Björn Waldegaard, and Hannu Mikkola have all proved that familiarity with the northern forests and exceptional skill on snow- or ice-covered surfaces are keys to success. From Britain Paddy Hopkirk and Roger Clark, from Italy Sandro Munari, and from France René Trautmann have all been consistently successful. Among several notable women drivers, Carlsson's wife Pat, sister of Stirling Moss, has been outstanding.

evolved. It is administered by the Commission Sportive Internationale from Paris. There are various groups based on the numbers of a model built in 12 months. Group 1 cars, for instance, are saloons of which 5,000 must have been built, while Group 4 cars qualify if 400 have been made. To gain approval (no car can compete in international events until 'homologated') a detailed standard form must be com-

Skilled mechanics and support teams make this exciting and colourful sport possible. Their skill in the workshop is taken for granted: it is their resourcefulness in repairing battered and broken cars at the roadside, often in minutes, usually in the dark, and invariably in the most primitive conditions, which is so special. No modern factory team of drivers could survive without them, and complex two-way radio

networks keep them in touch with their cars.

Co-drivers also contribute a vital expertise. In all but a few events, competitors are allowed to familiarize themselves with the routes beforehand, and crews spend a great deal of time on the speed sections before the event is actually held. Co-drivers make route notes for their own guidance and 'pace notes' of the special stages. During the event the driver and co-driver wear helmets fitted with intercom systems which are needed because of the high noise level inside the car. The co-driver spends much of his time reading to the driver from his notes, which describe every bend or other significant feature on the route.

The co-driver must also be a car manager. He must choose the time and place to fit or discard special tyres, the time to re-fuel, and the time to carry extra supplies; he must arrange for service and repairs, find food for the driver, and take the wheel when his partner needs a rest.

Above The Porsche 911 series has succeeded alike in rallies and major sports-car races. Here Björn Waldegaard, one of the most successful Scandinavian rally drivers of the past 20 years, corners his 911 in the 1978 Safari Rally.

Right Hannu Mikkola, the Finnish ace, winning the 1978 RAC Rally. His Ford RS1800 looks like an ordinary Escort but has a 2-litre, 16-valve, twin-cam engine developing 270 bhp; it proved to be the outstanding British rally car of the 1970s.

29 Hill Climbs

Hill climbing evolved naturally out of conventional motor racing. Even before the turn of the century, races incorporated many main-road hills as part of the testing nature of the course. It was not long before groups of enthusiasts decided that hill-climbing could provide exciting sport on its own account. Moreover, at an amateur level it was simple and cheap to organize and a whole series of events could be completed within the course of a day.

One of the earliest officially organized hill climbs took place in 1897 when, as the final stage of the Marseilles–Nice–La Turbie road race, a timed climb was staged. It started on the Moyenne Corniche in Nice and finished in the shadow of the Trophée des Alpes in La Turbie village. This event is historic in another sense: it is the only major race to have been won by a steam car, a De Dion-Bouton brake driven by Comte Gaston de Chasseloup-Laubat. La Turbie was to become inextricably linked with Edwardian motoring, for it became an integral part of Nice Week, when the rich disported themselves in the latest products of the best manufacturers in speed trials on the Promenade des Anglais.

Very soon hill races were being staged all over France and in neighbouring countries. There were events at Laffrey, Gaillon, the long slog up to the observatory of Mont Ventoux, and Val Suzon. It is difficult to avoid hills in Switzerland, and one of the better known climbs at the turn of the century was the one up to St Cergue from Trelex, near Geneva. In Italy the 22 km (13.5 mile) hill climb up Mount Cenis from Suza (west of Turin) to the Italian-French border was to become a classic of its kind.

Above Vincenzo Lancia takes a 14-litre, four-cylinder FIAT around a hairpin at Mont Cenis in 1904. Lancia was a racing driver for the FIAT works team until 1908 – a year after he had produced his first cars.

Below A 16/20 hp Sunbeam tourer at Shelsley Walsh. The picture was taken shortly after the famous uphill sprint course was opened in 1905.

British venues

In England things were different because of the ban on motor racing on public roads; but so far as the law was concerned there seemed to be no objection to staging timed climbs up little-used hill roads.

The British climbs were of necessity very short, being mostly in the nature of sprints, and they set a pattern which persists to this day. Shelsley Walsh, founded in 1905 and one of the most famous of British climbs, was held on private land in Worcestershire. A mere 915 m (1,000 yd) long, it has been the scene of intense rivalries and was the focal point of British hill climbing in the 1920s and 1930s. In the early days it had to take its place in the calendar with venues such as Kop Hill, Aston Clinton, South Harting, Laindon, Spread Eagle, Angel Bank (near Birmingham), and the Rest-and-be-Thankful in Scotland. In 1924 there were no less than 34 different venues scattered all over Britain.

There was little spectator control at these early events, a local constable usually being the only official present. On the whole, however, hill climbing was considered to be a fairly safe sport. But in 1925 at a Kop Hill meeting Francis Giveen, an inexperienced driver who had bought Raymand Mays' very fast Brescia Bugatti, ran into some spectators and broke an onlooker's leg. The meeting was abandoned at once, and shortly afterwards it was announced that no further permits would be issued for speed events on public roads. Thenceforward Shelsley Walsh came to rank as a venue almost as important as Brooklands in the eyes of motor racing enthusiasts. In its heyday Shelsley was about the only place in England where one

Left Alessandro Cagno in a FIAT 100 hp racing car after completing the Mont Ventoux climb in 19 min 13 sec in 1905. The present record is 10 min 0.5 sec set by Peter Schetty (Ferrari 212E) in 1969.

Right A Vauxhall Prince Henry 3-litre tourer at Shelsley Walsh in 1912–3. One of the most successful hill-climb cars of its day, the Prince Henry's design inspired the legendary Vauxhall 30/98 of 1913.

Below The 5.1-litre, six-cylinder Delage (seen here at a British vintage-car event) was designed specially for hill-climb events in 1922. René Thomas used it to win the Mont Ventoux event in 1922 and 1923, and to break the record at La Turbie in 1923 and 1924.

could see a racing car in action on a road, as distinct from a track.

After the 1925 ban a few new venues were discovered by enthusiasts – some up the drives of loftily situated country houses. A typical, and famous, example is Prescott, which was discovered by L. T. C. Rolt on behalf of the Vintage Sports Car Club and was used by the Bugatti Owners' Club. After 1945 the old Rest-and-be-Thankful climb, west of Arrochar, was briefly revived and became the longest British hill-climb course. It is now no longer used, but there are more than a dozen locations where the British Hill Climb Championship can be contested.

The short British hill climbs bred a special kind of motor car. In its great days Shelsley attracted a host of specials, many of them based on the chassis of the old GN Light Car. The

Above left The 4-cylinder Bugatti Type 13 Brescia was another hill-climb special of the early 1920s. This particular car is a survivor from Raymond Mays' famous stable.

Left Rudolf Caracciola, in a Mercedes-Benz W25 *grand-prix* car, breaking the Klausen hill-climb record in 1934. This climb was reckoned to be one of the most difficult in Europe.

Above The first Porsche, the 356 introduced in 1950, was designed for sports events, and works and privately owned models were entered in hill-climb events from the earliest days. This 356 is at the start of the Gaisberg climb, near Salzburg, one of the fastest European championship courses.

essentials required of a sprint hill-climb car were light weight, a quick gearchange, plenty of grip, and a torquey engine. The GN frame was light to the point of fragility, the solid back axle needed no self-locking differential to prevent a rear wheel spinning, and the multiple chain drive with selection of the appropriate ratio by dog clutches was just about the quickest gear shift available in the days of crash gearboxes. Moreover, it was possible to install almost any car engine between the simple parallel-frame members. Favourite engines included the big GN twin-overhead-camshaft racing units; alternatives included the twin-cylinder JAP, the six-cylinder AC unit, and variations of the 1,500 cc side-valve Anzani.

The most successful hill-climb cars in the 1920s and 1930s, however, were not GN-based. Raymond Mays, who possessed the ideal temperament for these sprints, scored many successes in Brescia Bugattis, AC specials, the Villiers-supercharged 3-litre Vauxhall, the Invicta, and the ERA built in his own garage at Bourne. Hans Stuck, the great European hill-climb champion, paid a short visit to England in 1930 and in his 3-litre Austro-Daimler set a time of 42.4 seconds at Shelsley which the locals were unable to better for three years.

At the present time in Britain, as in Europe, the ideal car has been found to be one which has the standard circuit-racing configuration, with the engine behind the driver and the power transmitted to the ground via wide racing tyres. The main modifications are to the gearing and the seating position, which is a little more upright. The speeds, even at Shelsley, are high enough to justify the use of wings. The Shelsley record is at present held by A. Douglas-Osborn in a Pilbeam R22 in a time of 27.35 seconds.

The inter-war years in Europe

European hill climbing, being permitted on roads normally open to the public, changed its pattern very little over the years. Between the wars the typical course varied between 5.5 km (3.5 miles) and 32 km (20 miles) of mountain roads. The cars were, and still are, modified formula or sports racing cars. There have been

Prescott Hill nowadays features climbs organized by the Bugatti Owners' Club. One of the regular competitors there in recent years has been Murray Rainey in this 1936 Alfa Romeo 8C (eight-cylinder) 'special'.

the odd specials, such as the four-wheel-drive Bugatti and, latterly, the Ferguson, but drivers are more used to two-wheel drive and the European championship is usually won with this configuration.

During the period of German domination in *grand-prix* racing in the late 1930s the European Hill Climb Championship had great propaganda value. Both Mercedes-Benz and Auto Union built special cars and used their best drivers in the qualifying events. Each country had its championship hill, and they were all difficult. Possibly the hardest of all was the Klausen, in Switzerland. It was about 21 km (13 miles) long with more than 100 bends and corners, including 20 hairpins. In 1934 Rudolf Caracciola in a Mercedes-Benz climbed this hill in 15 minutes 22 seconds in wet and mist. Somewhat shorter in length, but with just as many bends and hairpins, is the Stelvio climb in the Italian Alto Adige. It has the highest finishing line in Europe at 2,428 m (7,965 ft) above sea level. In the 1930s Stelvio could usually be relied on to favour the Italian Alfa Romeos, which were lighter and more manoeuvrable than the powerful German racers; but the Germans normally got their own back on their home ground at Freiburg. This course, opened in 1925, is still used for the European Mountain Championship. Relatively short by continental standards, it is 11 km (6.9 miles) long with 170 bends. Austria's pre-war venue was the Gross-glockner pass, part of a toll road 19.5 km (12 miles) long with a total rise of 1,593 m (5,226 ft). The French championship course was at Mont Ventoux, which was first raced in 1902. Other venues counting for the title were at Kesselberg in Germany and Tatra in Czechoslovakia.

The post-war years

Modern European mountain racing is much less tense than it was in those nationalistic pre-war days, when political insignia were prominent amid the grey dust and white racing helmets. Yet manufacturers still maintain keen interest in this branch of motor racing. Many of the venues have changed: Freiburg still stands for Germany, but Italy has been using the Trento–Bondone climb for several years; Andorra now stages an event in the Pyrenees, and others are held at Ampus, Dobratsch, Montseny, Estrala, Copa Sila, Mont-Dore, and St Ursanne-les-Rangiers.

Perhaps the most exciting period for postwar hill climbing in Europe was the late 1950s and early 1960s when Porsche, Ferrari, Abarth, and Maserati strove for dominance. Climbing mountains in fast sports cars has a long tradition in Germany, so it is not surprising that Porsche was the most dominant marque during

this period, although Maserati, with Willy Daetwyler of Switzerland at the wheel, gained the championship in 1957 and Ludovico Scarfiotti won with a 2-litre V6 Ferrari in 1962.

With the increase in traffic since the war, passes such as the Grossglockner, Klausen, Maloja, and Stelvio have been lost to hill climbers. The climbs are now between 5 and 13 km (3 and 8 miles) long. The post-war championship proper was inaugurated in 1957. Two litres was the capacity limit for racing cars, with 3 litres for sports cars. Apart from Heini Walter in 1960 and 1961, all the winners have been *grand-prix* drivers. Wolfgang ('Taffy') von Trips and Jean Behra, both in Porsches, fought for the title in 1958; Trips won although Jo Bonnier and Hans Herrmann in Borgwards pushed him hard. In ensuing years competition came from Abarth, sponsored by Fiat, and a host of private entrants in various types of ex-formula machinery. Ferrari had the final say in that era when Peter Schetty went round the hill climb circuit in his Ferrari 212E and established a set of new records, many of which still stand.

In the United States the sport has never achieved a development and popularity to compare with that in Europe, although the Sports Car Club of America includes some hill climbs in its calendar of events. The best-known event, which can claim a sporting history as long as some of Europe's famous venues, is at Pike's Peak. This mountain of some 4,300 m (14,110 ft) has the highest finishing line in the world. The climb is up a private dirt road 20 km (12.4 miles) long. The Unser family has made something of a monopoly of this event. Louis Unser won nine climbs between 1934 and 1953; Peter Unser won twice, in 1964 and 1965; and his brother Bobby has no fewer than 11 wins to his credit.

Right Porsche dominated European mountain-racing for many years after its first championship in 1959. One of the marque's best years was 1967, when Ruedi Lins, seen here on the Gaisburg in his Porsche Carrera 6, took the Sport category, and other Porsche models won the Racing and Grand Touring titles.

Below A break in Porsche's championship successes came in 1962, when Ludovico Scarfiotti took the title with four wins and a second place in this works-prepared Ferrari Dino 2-litre V6. Here he is in the Swiss Mountain Grand Prix on the Ollon–Villers climb, south-east of Lausanne.

Ever since the 1890s cars have kindled the competitive instinct of drivers. In most sports events, then as now, success has required a wide range of engineering, design, and performance virtues in competition cars. This chapter is concerned with a very specialized motor sport in which pure, straight-line acceleration, above all else, separates winners from losers. Britain took the lead in this field, which we now call sprinting, in the early years of this century. Many of the old venues have fallen into disuse or have been acquired for other purposes, but new ones, most notably Santa Pod Raceway in Bedfordshire, have come into being in more recent times.

In the United States the sport began in southern California in the 1930s, and from the beginning was dominated by cars, whereas in Britain early sprinting was more of a motor-cycle sport. The Americans raced 'souped-up' Ford Roadsters and Model Ts, three or four abreast, up and down the San Fernando Valley. There were no such things as driving licences or tests in those days, and often local police actively participated in or even helped to organize the events.

The post-war years

Drag racing developed fully only in the years after World War II. The Americans took an early lead when a group of now-famous engine specialists in this field – men such as Ed Iskenderian, Fred Offenhauser, Phil Weiand, and Vic Edelbrock – and other enthusiasts formed the Southern California Timing Association (SCTA), which was dedicated to improving safety and organizing proper venues and races. *Hot Rod* magazine, founded in 1947, helped to launch the National Hot Rod Association (NHRA), whose aims are to promote safety, provide tracks, and advise on technical developments.

One of the first NHRA sponsored meetings was held at Santa Ana, California, in 1950. It was a success, and the sport has never looked back. Regional divisions were formed within the NHRA; rules and classes were formulated; and the engineering and design of the cars developed rapidly. From these early beginnings have evolved national competition events in America in which more than 1,200 cars enter for the big meetings, which are attended by crowds of 150,000 and more.

The nature of the sport

There are two distinct types of race – sprinting and drag racing. The distance for the main international events of both types is now $\frac{1}{4}$ mile (402.3 m). Competitors start from a stationary position at a designated mark, accelerate over

Don 'Big Daddy' Garlits, one of the greatest American drag-racing drivers, has been in the sport for more than 25 years. Among innovations he introduced to the sport are rear-mounted engines in Top Fuel cars and the use of aerodynamic wings over the rear tyres.

the quarter mile, and elapsed times and terminal speeds are recorded electronically. In sprinting each competitor races against the clock rather than another driver, the fastest time deciding the winner of each round (heat). Then the round winners advance to the next round (or rounds) until an eventual winner emerges with the fastest time in the final round. In drag racing competitors start together (unless they are handicapped) and the first past the finish line is declared the round winner.

To ensure fair and equal starts, a run-in 100 mm (4 in) before the start beam is allowed. When a competitor crosses the beam, photo-electric cells are actuated. If a competitor's run-in is outside this limit his time is disqualified; if he leaves too early, known as 'red-lighting', the race goes to his opponent provided the latter completes his run.

In sprinting, the start beam consists of one pair of photo-electric cells per lane; the timing clocks are actuated when the beam is broken by the front of the machine. Drag racing is perhaps more refined in that two additional cells are situated actually on the start line. When staging (lining up for the start) the two machines are allowed to edge forward, one at a time. A timing light system clearly visible to competitors indicates when the first beam is broken by giving a yellow, 'pre-staged' signal. The first machine continues to edge forward slowly until the driver sees the second yellow light, indicating that he is 'staged'. This means that the frontmost part of the car has broken the beam. A third beam becomes visible if the car is 'overstaged' (too far forward). If the driver fails to correct his position within a certain time, a red light will show he is disqualified. His competitor then has a similar procedure to go through, but once the first driver is staged the other must be similarly placed within 20 to 30 seconds.

With both drivers staged the automatic systems then show the drivers first one yellow light, then a second yellow light, and than a green light, whereupon both start their run. If a driver anticipates the final 'green' and moves too soon, a red light shows in his lane indicating an automatic win for his opponent. There are similar beams in each lane at the finish line; the breaking of the beams by the cars automatically triggers the timing clocks. Another measuring device is the 'speed trap', which consists of two further beams – one 20 m (66 ft) before the finish beam, the other 20 m beyond it. The time the car takes to break both beams gives its terminal speed. (This speed is of interest to drivers and spectators, but only the elapsed time determines the winner.)

Drag racing has overtaken sprinting in

Above The Chrysler Hemi engine in Gene Snow's Plymouth Arrow Funny Car. Most dragsters in the top classes use super-charged, nitro-burning engines based on the Hemi.

Below Dennis Priddle, one of the most successful drivers of nitro-burning Funny Cars. His protective gear includes multi-layered, fire-resistant suit and gloves, and a face mask with two air filters. Although dragster engines frequently catch fire or explode, serious injuries are rare in this sport.

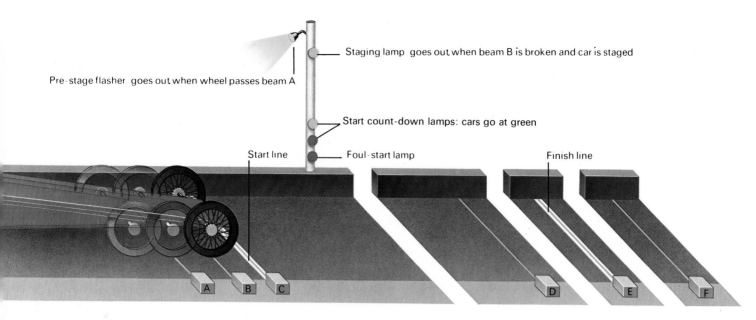

Pre-stage flasher goes out when wheel passes beam A

Staging lamp goes out when beam B is broken and car is staged

Start count-down lamps: cars go at green

Start line

Foul-start lamp

Finish line

A   B   C

D   E   F

Above Drag-strip start and finish. A to F are photo-electric beams. Car, edging towards start line, is staged when front wheels break beam B. Elapsed time is measured by beams B and E; terminal speed by D and F, sited 20 m (66 ft) either side of finish line.

Below Don Prudhomme, seen here in his Plymouth Arrow Funny Car *The Snake*, has won more major titles in US national events than any other drag-strip driver.

spectator interest, mainly because the cars race against each other as well as against the clock. The big meetings are now very slickly organized, with a race occurring every six or seven seconds. The fastest cars can complete the quarter mile in a little over five seconds, achieving 'terminals' of more than 400 km/h (250 mph). Such a performance involves acceleration from 0 to 160 km/h (0 to 100 mph) in 1 to 1.5 seconds, and requires engines developing at least 2,000 bhp.

Specialized machinery

In the years immediately after World War II, development of the cars was very much a do-it-yourself activity, practised in the main on a trial-and-error basis rather than on formal engineering principles. But the more gifted designers and tuners soon established a reputation, and before long they began to produce new or modified components for sale to fellow enthusiasts. Most of the now-legendary names in American drag-racing began in this modest way – Ed Iskenderian and his camshafts, Phil Weiand (manifolds), Fred Offenhauser (engines) and many others. Today there are 'speed shops' where you can buy over-the-counter engine and body parts and complete design plans.

By the mid-1950s the big four American car makers – Chrysler, Ford, General Motors, and American Motors – realized that publicity gained by their machinery winning national drag races could boost sales of production cars by tens of thousands. So backing for racers was introduced. The big four manufacturers started to develop and make, in limited quantities, higher performance engines and transmission/drive-train combinations for the performance-minded youth market. Famous examples of this era include the Corvette Stingray, the late-1960s Pontiac GTO, Dodge Challenger, Plymouth Barracuda, and Ford Mustang. Some of these cars were producing, ex-factory, 400 to 500 hp from engines of 6 or 7 litres. Generally, straight-line performance was dominant: the suspension, braking, and handling of these cars were greatly inferior to those of the specialized European models, although in recent years they have improved considerably.

In drag racing the 'flatheads' (side-valve engines) developed before World War II were superseded by the more efficient overhead-valve engines. The single most important engine ever produced for drag-racing cars was the Chrysler Hemi engine. (The car manufacturers discovered the virtues of the cross-flow, hemispherical combustion chamber only after it had become commonplace on motor-cycles.) The original Hemi, developed in 1951, was of 6,420 cc. But it was the 'late-model' eight-cylinder Hemi of 6,980 cc, developed in 1963, that became the 'building block' of the sport, winning its first race, the Daytona 500, in February 1964. Since then it has dominated virtually every major drag race until the present day. This steel motor is usually equipped with a special crankshaft, giving a longer stroke length with a standard con-rod – whence the term 'stroker-crank'. As a consequence, Hemis displacing over 8,200 cc are now commonplace.

The engines are fitted with aluminium or magnesium superchargers on the manifold, and use fuel-injection instead of carburettors. Instead of petrol they burn a mixture of nitro-methane (72 to 94 per cent) and methanol, which is much richer in oxygen. They develop about 2,200 hp. The most prominent racing-engine builders in this field are Keith Black Racing Engines, Ed Pink Enterprises, Sid Waterman, John Rodeck, and Ed Donovan. A custom-built engine/blower combination from one of these specialists would cost anything up to £7,500 ($15,000).

Car categories

One of the attractions of drag racing is that virtually anyone with a production car can enter and win races. This ensures a plentiful supply of new talent entering the sport, which has classes for everything from production vehicles to out-and-out racing machinery. The main categories are as follows:

Production Must be factory produced and fitted with standard seats, trim, and electric systems. Original bodies with a few modifications (for safety reasons) and factory options are permitted.

Street Unrestricted as to modifications, but must be 'street legal' (permitted to travel on public roads).

Modified Major modifications permitted, such as racing clutches and gearboxes; engines other than original equipment can be fitted; minimum wheelbase 1.8 m (72 in).

Competition Altered Racing machinery only, divided into junior, middle, and senior classes; multiple carburettors or fuel injection allowed, but not superchargers. Where class record is over 240 km/h (150 mph), parachutes must be fitted to assist stopping.

Dragster Junior, middle, and senior classes. Single-seat, extended-wheelbase cars; motor-cycle front wheels allowed; one or two engines permitted.

Pro-Stock Production-car 'facsimiles' fitted with racing carburetted/injected engines and transmissions; bodies can be of glass-fibre or acid-dipped to reduce weight.

Pro-Comp Dragster or altered configuration, or facsimile; glass-fibre bodies; choice of superchargers running on methanol or injectors running on nitro-methane.

Funny Car Full racing machinery; any engine/fuel combination; removable glass-fibre bodies with surface resemblance to production vehicles.

Top Fuel Stretched-wheelbase dragsters; no restrictions.

In the top classes, the use of a blower (supercharger) is the commonest way to obtain extra

Above Danny Townsend runs his Fiat Topolino-bodied car, with injected Chevrolet engine, in the Competition class, where a variety of body forms is permitted.

Below 'Wild Bill' Shrewsbury travelling the full quarter mile on his rear wheels. Steering is by separate brakes on each rear wheel.

Above British driver Reg Hazzleton does a burn-out in his Pro-Comp *Thunderbird*. Burn-outs deposit a film of rubber on the track, so improving tyre grip.

Above Mickey Naylor's Top Fuel *Medicine Man* comes to grief at Santa Pod in September 1978. Shortly after this picture was taken, the dragster rolled over six times at speed before stopping; Naylor emerged unhurt.

power. Gains of 50 to 100 per cent with a blower are quite common, as they are with the more-recent turbochargers.

Nitrous oxide (N_2O) injection is also used for power boosting. Similar principles apply. N_2O is very rich in oxygen, so an N_2O-plus-air mixture can burn more fuel than air by itself. The fuel is simply metered into the inlet manifold from a pressurized container stowed in a convenient place. Few engine modifications are required and power gains of up to 50 or 60 per cent can be achieved.

Mechanical developments

In the last 15 years drag-racing design has progressed considerably, especially in the Top Fuel and Funny Car classes. In the early 1960s Top Fuel dragsters ran iron-block, nitro-burning, supercharged engines of 6,425 cc to 7,000 cc with front-mounted motors and wheelbases of 3.5 to 4 m (140 to 160 in). Today the frames have stretched to 5.6 to 6 m (220 to 240 in), monstrous all-aluminium engines of 7,850–8,520 cc are installed behind the driver, and the blown, nitro-burning motors deliver well in excess of 2,000 bhp.

The main reason for the switch from front- to rear-mounted engines was one of safety. It was introduced internationally by one of the sport's great innovators, the American Don Garlits. Because the engines in a top competitive event are highly stressed and often running at the limit of mechanical strength, they often explode or catch fire. Garlits was involved in many such incidents in the 1960s. In one of them the resulting explosion cut his dragster in half and took off three of his toes. While recovering in hospital he designed a longer chassis with the engine mounted behind the driver – a safer position in the event of fire. This innovation was at first treated with considerable scepticism, but Garlits went on to win many races

and the Top Fuel Championship, setting new speed records. Today almost all the Top Fuel drivers in the United States and Britain use rear-mounted engines.

In the 1960s drag racers used no gearbox, there being direct drive between the engine and rear wheels. Owing to the enormous power of the engines, drivers had to spin their rear tyres all the way from the start line to the finish, otherwise they would have snapped the drive shaft or rear axle. Although tyre spinning was spectacular, with clouds of smoke trailing behind the cars, it was wasteful of engine power. It was also wasteful of 'slicks' – the 380 mm (15 in) wide, treadless rear tyres. Today special 'slider' clutches and two-speed racing transmissions make tyre spin unnecessary except before the start in the 'burn-out' area, where the drivers do it deliberately to heat the tyre rubber in order to improve its grip on the road.

A Funny Car is basically a shorter-wheelbase – 5 to 5.5 m (200 to 220 in) – Top Fuel dragster with an all-enclosing glass-fibre body. Because of space limitations, these cars have to be front-motored, making them perhaps the most spectacular to watch. Being of shorter wheelbase and therefore less stable, 'floppers', as they are known, often give spectacular runs, veering from side to side as the drivers fight to keep the machines on the strip.

Safety

A great deal of attention is paid to safety in this most explosive of sports. Indeed, in spite of the speeds and dangers involved, drag racing has a better accident record than any other motor sport. Drivers must sit in chrome/molybdenum, aircraft-quality, all-enclosing chassis, with double upright roll cages extending some 250 mm (10 in) in front of the driver's helmet. Fire extinguishers must be fitted; full safety harnesses have to pass stringent tests; and drivers are required to wear firesuits of seven to nine layers of non-flammable material, as well as gloves and flame-proof face masks. Other features include explosion-proof clutches encased in scatterproof bell housings and emergency blow-off valves on the engine.

The effectiveness of these safety regulations, pioneered by the Speciality Equipment Manufacturers' Association in the United States, is impressive. In 1977 at Santa Pod, for instance, Owen Hayward's *Houndog* Funny Car got out of control at almost 290 km/h (180 mph) and hit the safety barriers. The car was completely destroyed after turning five somersaults, yet because of the safety equipment, particularly the roll cage, Owen was pulled dazed but unhurt from the wreckage.

The sport today

Drag racing as we know it today began in the United States and it is there that the sport – heavily sponsored and advertised – is seen at its most colourful. Moreover, the numbers of competitors in major events is far greater in America than elsewhere. It is quite common for Top Fuel, Funny Car, and Pro-Comp classes to field 60 to 70 cars trying to qualify for the 16-car finals in each class.

A great deal of money is involved in mounting events on this scale. The most powerful drag cars can cost more than £18,000 each, and each machine needs to be backed up by spare engines, transmissions, and the like. Even so, the cost of running a dragster for a season is considerably lower than the cost of fielding a *grand-prix* car. And the top drivers, with their win and contingency money topped up by personal sponsorship, can earn more than £75,000 a season.

For the teams with little or no sponsorship, however, the costs can be daunting. In Britain a pair of rear slicks (treadless tyres) can cost about £400 and are usually good for only 20 full-bore runs. Nitromethane costs £12 a gallon, and in a single quarter-mile dash preceded by a couple of tyre-warming burnouts a supercharged dragster will consume six to eight gallons.

At the big meetings there is often a variety of supporting 'turns'. A typical example is wheel-standing, in which cars with engines mounted right at the back drive the full quarter mile on the rear wheels only. The driver looks through transparent floor panels and steers the car by differential braking on each wheel.

Another demonstration class is cars powered by jet engines, often with reheat (afterburning) for a sudden increase of power. There are few sights as awesome as a jet car at night, complete with afterburner, trailing fire out of the back as

Above Shirley Muldowney became Top Fuel World Champion in the United States in 1977 – the first woman to do so. Here she deploys her parachute at the end of a run at Indianapolis.

Below 'Slammin' Sammy Miller in *Vanishing Point* achieving the fastest-ever run in Britain in September 1978: elapsed time 4.34 seconds; terminal speed 467.9 km/h (290.6 mph). His rocket engine, burning hydrogen peroxide fuel, developed some 2,270 kg (5,000 lb) thrust.

it revs to 40,000 rpm on the start line prior to 'launch'.

Because of their superior power/weight ratio there is little to touch the hydrogen peroxide rocket-powered vehicles for sheer acceleration. At a concentration of 85–90 per cent, the fuel must be handled with extreme care – it is said that a teacupful could demolish the average house – and is stored in stainless-steel containers. Hydrogen peroxide liberates an enormous amount of oxygen, and when passed over a nickel-silver catalyst mesh in a stainless-steel pressure chamber it generates instant steam and thrust. A rocket engine nominally rated at 2,250 kg (4,950 lb) thrust takes up less space and is lighter than the automatic transmission of a typical motor car. The Americans have quite a number of rocket-powered dragsters, funny cars, and even karts. They regularly achieve elapsed times of less than 4.5 seconds, with terminal speeds of more than 545 km/h (340 mph).

Drag racing has come a long way since its tentative beginnings in the 1930s. Apart from the United States and Britain it is now very popular in Canada, Mexico, Puerto Rico, Sweden, Norway, France, Germany, Holland, Iran, South Africa, New Zealand, and Australia. The next logical step forward will be the organization of a world championship.

The biggest advances to come in the next decade will probably be in chassis and tyre technology. There is already a surplus of power; the problem is to keep it firmly on the tarmac. By 1985 even internal-combustion-engined machines should be achieving elapsed times approaching 4.5 seconds.

31 Record Breakers

The pursuit of speed and endurance records began soon after motor cars appeared on public roads. At that time, in the last two decades of the 19th century, there was considerable rivalry between the petrol, steam, and electric systems of propulsion. Perhaps the first meetings to establish a speed record were those in 1899 between Comte Gaston de Chasseloup-Laubat and Camille Jenatzy, both driving electric cars. Jenatzy won this series of races, and his cigar-shaped *Jamais Contente* became the first car to exceed one mile a minute when he attained a speed of 105.9 km/h (65.75 mph).

Once 100 km/h had been achieved, the next targets attempted were 100 km (62 miles) in the hour and 100 mph (161 km/h) over the flying kilometre. The first offical timing of 100 km within the hour was made at the 1904 Circuit des Ardennes race when Arthur Duray, in a Darracq, covered the first lap of the 119 km (74 mile) circuit in 72 minutes. The same year Louis Rigolly, driving a Gobron-Brillié, became the first man to top 100 mph (161 km/h) with a speed of 166.6 km/h (103.5 mph).

One hundred miles in the hour, however, was much more difficult, and it had to await the building of Brooklands track in Britain in 1907. Once the track was open the battle was on, with the honours eventually going to Percy Lambert driving a 4.5-litre Talbot on 9 February 1913. By that time the official distance for the land-speed record had been increased from a kilometre to a mile, and the first holder over the new distance was L. G. Hornsted in a 21.5-litre Benz at 199.8 km/h (124.1 mph) in 1914.

Any record claimed by the Americans in

Above Camille Jenatzy aboard the electric-powered *Jamais Contente* in which he became the first driver to exceed one mile a minute in 1899. Probably the earliest aerodynamically efficient car in the world, its electric engines were geared directly to the rear axle.

Below A 1920 Sunbeam V12, 350 hp racer at Brooklands. Malcolm Campbell used one of these cars at Pendine Sands to raise the land speed record to 235.32 km/h (146.16 mph) in 1924.

those days was regarded in Europe with distrust, yet there is little doubt that the first man to exceed 120 mph (193 km/h) was the extraordinarily courageous Fred Marriott, who put the boiler pressure of his Stanley steam car up to 1,000 lb/sq in at the 1906 Ormond Beach speed meeting and was accurately timed at 205.5 km/h (127.4 mph). The Americans claim that the first man to exceed 150 mph (241 km/h) was Tommy Milton in a Duesenberg with 156 mph (251 km/h) in 1920; but the Association Internationale des Automobiles Clubs Reconnus, the international body, withheld recognition of Milton's achievement. The officially ratified record was achieved by Malcolm Campbell's V12 350 hp Sunbeam on Pendine Sands in Wales in 1925.

Daytona and Bonneville

As cars got faster and more specialized it became increasingly difficult to find suitable venues for speed-record attempts. The last land speed record at Brooklands was set in 1922, and the record breakers then started to look for long beaches, taking a tip from the Americans who had held speed weeks from the turn of the century on the lengthy Ormond Beach at Daytona, Florida. Henry Segrave used Southport Sands for his 244 km/h (152 mph) record in 1926, but Malcolm Campbell preferred Pendine Sands in South Wales because it was longer. J. G. Parry Thomas also used Pendine, but he lost his life there in 1927 when attempting to break the land-speed record.

After that Daytona became the favoured venue, and in 1927 Segrave was the first to exceed 200 mph (322 km/h) there in a twin-engined Sunbeam. Daytona was nearly ideal, but it began to look narrow to the drivers when

Major Henry Segrave's 1,000 hp Sunbeam, using two 22.4-litre Sunbeam aero-engines, in which he set a land speed record of 328.10 km/h (203.79 mph) at Daytona Beach in March 1927. Although best known as a land-speed-record contender, Segrave was also an outstanding *grand-prix* and sports-car driver in the early 1920s.

speeds began to approach 480 km/h (300 mph). The highest speed achieved at Daytona was 445.4 km/h (276.8 mph) by Campbell in 1935.

Attention then switched to a large area of salt flats at Bonneville in Utah. The flats dry up in the summer to leave a hard, smooth, level surface. Campbell was the first to break the record there, in 1935, attaining a speed of 485 km/h (301.1 mph) in his famous *Bluebird*. A fortnight before the outbreak of World War II, John Cobb set a new record of 595.2 km/h (369.7 mph) in a car designed, as was *Bluebird*, by Reid Railton.

Since World War II, the land-speed records have been dominated by Americans, latterly driving machines powered by turbojet or rocket engines. In 1965 Craig Breedlove raised the record to 966.9 km/h (600.6 mph) with his jet-powered *Spirit of America*. The present holder of the record is Gary Gabelich, who in 1970 achieved a speed of 1,015.8 km/h (629.79 mph) at Utah in his rocket-powered *Blue Flame* which developed 7,260 kg (16,000 lb) thrust.

Small-car record breakers

The rocket-powered monsters can scarcely be regarded as motor cars. Far more interesting work has been done over the years exploring the possibilities of small piston engines. Between the wars speed-record-breaking was a natural activity for the new breed of baby cars. Herbert Austin, who had raced in the Gordon Bennett Trophy races in a Wolseley of his own design, was not slow to exploit racing and record breaking as a medium to prove that his 'little one' was a serious motor car.

The first racing appearance of the Austin Seven was at the 1923 Brooklands Easter meeting, where it won the small car handicap. Captain A. C. R. Waite, Austin's son-in-law, was in charge of the factory's competition department, and he set his sights on 160 km/h (100 mph) for the 750 cc baby. By continuous development over a period of eight years, during which the Austin Seven supercharged racers covered themselves with glory, the car

Left The Irving Special *Golden Arrow*, powered by a 930 hp Napier engine, in which Segrave broke the land speed record at 372.62 km/h (231.44 mph) at Daytona in March 1929. On his return to England Segrave was knighted, but he lost his life the following year in the course of setting a world water-speed record on Lake Windermere, Westmorland.

Right German cars were involved in various attempts on world speed class records during the 1930s. Here Rudolf Caracciola in his *Rennlimousin* — basically a 430 bhp Mercedes W25 *grand-prix* car with enclosed cockpit — attempts a class record on the Avus circuit in 1935.

Below During the 1930s the most successful land-speed-record breaker in the small-car field was Major 'Goldie' Gardner in MG 'specials'. He is seen here in his crowning pre-war achievement — the flying-start kilometre record of 327.70 km/h (203.54 mph) in the 1,100 cc MG EX135 on the Dessau *Autobahn* (south-west of Berlin) in 1939.

was ready to take the honour of being the first small car to exceed 100 mph.

In fact, that record was established by a 750 cc MG M-Type, driven by George Eyston, in 1931. Eyston used the same car to achieve 160 km (100 miles) in one hour. Later, he used a similar car in achieving a 750 cc record of two miles in one minute – 193.2 km/h (120 mph).

The greatest of all the record-breaking MGs was a racer based on a Magic Magnette of the early 1930s. In 1937 it was acquired by Major 'Goldie' Gardner and in the following year, with a new body designed by Reid Railton, it registered an astonishing 302 km/h (187.6 mph). The engine was then reworked, a new supercharger was fitted, and the car was taken to the newly opened Dessau track in Germany. There it comfortably turned in 327.6 km/h (203.5 mph) to take the speed record for cars of less than 1 litre. Overnight two MG engineers, Sid Enever and 'Jacko' Jackson, bored out the engine to bring it over 1,100 cc, and it took the 1,500 cc record at the same speed. Later this car, running on three of its six cylinders, took the 500 cc record to 247.8 km/h (154 mph). Later still it was fitted with a prototype four-cylinder XK100 engine and broke further records in class E (1,500–2,000 cc). Gardner certainly got his moneysworth from that chassis.

The MGs mentioned above were all attempting international class records, in which each class corresponds to a particular engine-capacity range. Over the years there have been many outstanding performances by individual cars or drivers. In 1933, for instance, a 10 hp Citroën christened *Petite Rosalie* was driven a total distance of 301,875 km (187,500 miles) at an average speed of 93.4 km/h (58 mph) and in the process broke almost 300 international class records.

Right Craig Breedlove's second jet-powered *Spirit of America*, in which he broke the 600 mph barrier in 1965; his actual speed was 966.97 km/h (600.60 mph). Many people do not regard the American turbojet- or rocket-powered record breakers as authentic cars because their engines do not drive the road wheels.

Left Craig Breedlove's first *Spirit of America* achieved 847.31 km/h (526.28 mph) at Bonneville in 1964. Moments after this picture was taken the parachute brakes were torn away from the car, which ended up in a deep pool of water. Since the vehicle had three wheels rather than four. Breedlove was accorded not the car but the motor-cycle record.

Right The world land speed record stands at 1,015.8 km/h (629.79 mph), achieved at Bonneville in 1970 by Gary Gabelich, a drag-racing driver, in *Blue Flame*. The vehicle was powered by a rocket motor burning liquid propane and hydrogen peroxide, and delivering about 7,260 kg (16,000 lb) thrust.

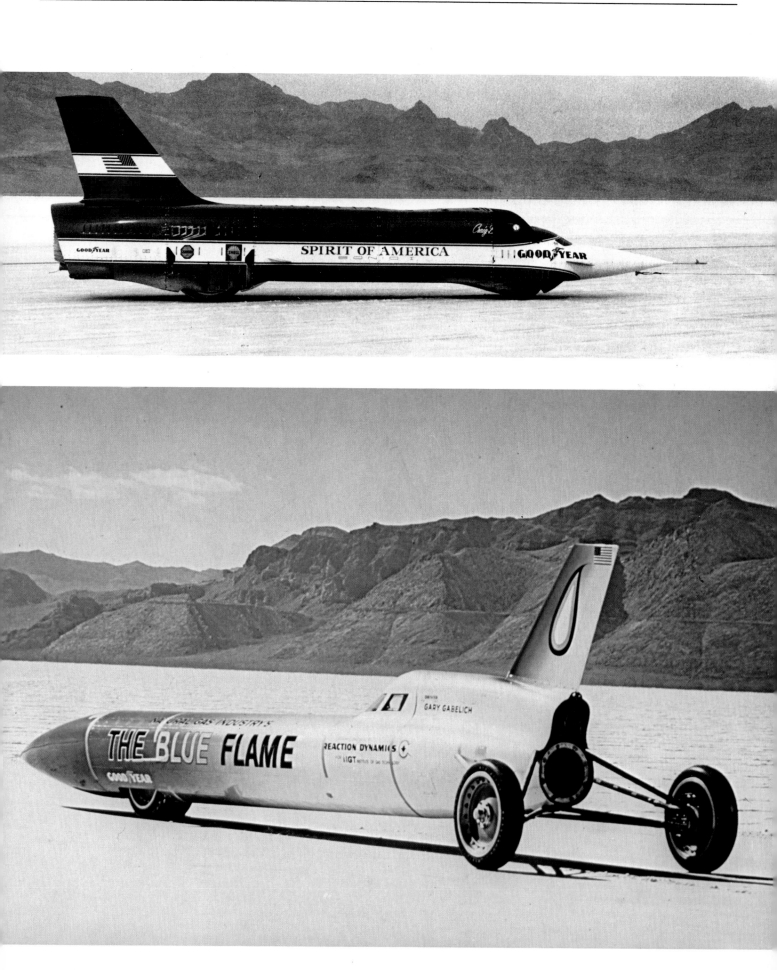

Motor-racing venues can take two forms: they can consist of linked stretches of roads that at other times are open to public traffic (the Monaco Grand Prix course is of this type); or they may be specially designed tracks used exclusively for sport (as in the case of Silverstone or the Indianapolis Speedway). The term 'circuit' can be applied to both forms: it is used in connection with events consisting of more than one lap of a specified course.

The first important event of this kind appears to have been the 1902 Circuit des Ardennes, run over six laps of a 119 km (74 mile) circuit linking Bastogne, Martelange, Habay, and Neufchâteau in the rolling Ardennes hills of southern Belgium. It was won by Charles Jarrott driving a Panhard. His average speed of 87 km/h (54 mph) was all the more impressive because he had never seen the circuit before, and had learnt it by following the wheel tracks of the other competitors. The Circuit des Ardennes was run on a number of occasions up to 1914, but not always over the same route. In the 1902 race there was no crowd control, and spectators lined the streets, presenting a danger to both themselves and the contestants.

Concern for spectators came when the Automobile Club de France organized the French Grand Prix of 1906. It appears to have been the first race at which covered stands were erected, and there was adequate spectator protection in all the villages and towns along the route. Taking a tip from the German Kaiserpreis of the year before, the organizers dug a tunnel under the track to save spectators from having to cross the road.

An equally auspicious event in the same year was the first Targa Florio, organized by Vincenzo Florio, a great enthusiast who had already been responsible for a number of races bearing his name in Brescia. Conducted over three laps of the Grande Madonie circuit in the Madonie mountains to the east of Palermo, Sicily, it featured 1,006 corners per lap and had a total distance of 445 km (277 miles). The 1906 race was an impromptu affair between 10 of Florio's friends or guests. The prize was a solid-gold embossed plaque weighing several pounds: no wonder there were more than 50 entries for the 1907 event! The main problem for the organizers of the race was not so much crowd control as the activities of bandits in the more remote parts of the circuit. The Targa soon became one of the most prestigious events in the sporting calendar, and grandstands and permanent pits were eventually erected near the little town of Cerda.

There were two Madonie circuits in general use, the Grande and the Piccolo; there was also a Medio Madonie. They measured, respec-

tively, 148.7 km (92.2 miles), 71.4 km (44.7 miles) and 108 km (67.1 miles). Before 1914 the Grande Madonie was the rule; there were also races right around Sicily in 1912, 1913, and 1914. After World War I the Medio Madonie saw all the great drivers of the period in action and the Targa Florio became the most important sports-car event in the world, with drivers such as André Boillot, Count Masetti, Wilhelm Werner, Achille Varzi, Albert Divo, and the great Tazio Nuvolari among the winners. The Grande Madonie was used just once more in 1931, when Nuvolari won; thereafter the Piccolo Madonie became the favoured circuit. After 1945 there were Italo-German duels on many occasions, especially between Ferrari and Porsche. Until the death of Florio the race was conducted with great ceremony and cars were started through a trellis-work gate decked with branches of orange and lemon trees. The Targa came to an end when a prohibition was placed on racing through the narrow streets of towns on the route. In its whole history there was only one fatality, to Count Masetti in a Delage in 1925.

Brooklands

As auspicious as the inauguration of the Targa Florio, especially to the speed-starved British, was the opening of the Brooklands track at Weybridge, Hampshire. Hugh Fortescue Locke-King had been a spectator at the first Targa Florio and was depressed to find not a single British car present. He put this down to the prohibition of road racing in England and was wise enough to see that this was placing the nascent British industry at a considerable disadvantage. He realized that Britain needed a

Above Vincenzo Trucco (Isotta-Fraschini) at the start of the third Targa Florio in 1908. The main stands at that time were at Buonfornello, west of Campofelice; after 1921 they were at Cerda. Trucco's average speed over three laps of the very difficult 148.7 km (92.2-mile) Grande Madonie circuit was 59.9 km/h (37.1 mph).

Above right The map shows the three circuits of the Targa Florio in the Madonie mountains of northern Sicily. From 1951 onward only the Piccolo Madonie was used.

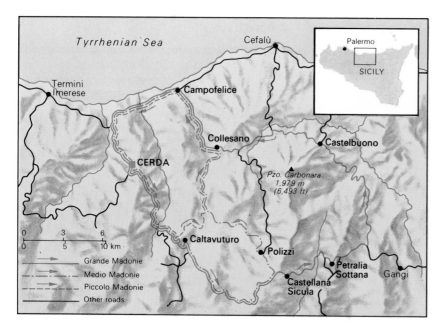

place where cars could be tested at high speed. With encouragement from Lord Northcliffe and Lord Montagu of Beaulieu, he commissioned a concrete track in the shape of an ovoid saucer, with banked bends and a length of 5.2 km (3.2 miles), of which 3 km (2 miles) was straight.

The first race meeting was held in July 1907, although before that it had been used by S.F. Edge in a Napier Sixty to establish a 24-hour speed record (the great weight of the Napier on the newly laid concrete was blamed for the bumps for which Brooklands became·notorious). Despite the protests of local inhabitants at the noise, which caused a prohibition of night events, Brooklands became the home of British motor racing. It was the scene of the first 100 miles (160 km) in an hour and the place where hundreds of records were established by small-capacity cars. There was nothing like it anywhere in the world until the construction of Montlhéry circuit. It will always be remembered for the Double Twelve Hour race, the JCC 200, the 1,000 Mile race, and John Cobb's records in the Napier-Railton, which in 1935 set the lap record at 230.9 km/h (143.4 mph). The cost of repairing the track after World War II would have been prohibitive, and it was sold to the resident aircraft firm of Vickers.

Indianapolis Speedway

It is not certain whether the American Carl G. Fisher ever saw Brooklands, but he watched the 1905 Gordon-Bennett race and went back to the United States resolved to give his country a circuit on which cars could be raced and tested. The result was the Indianapolis Speedway, constructed by a consortium consisting of Fisher, Arthur Newby of the National Vehicle

Company, and Frank Wheeler of the Wheeler-Schebler Carburettor Company. The chosen site was a plot of land 1.6 by 0.8 km (1 mile by $\frac{1}{2}$ mile) near the city of Indianapolis, Indiana. On it they built a 4 km (2.5 mile) rectangular track with gently banked corners – the angle was slightly more than 9 degrees – surfaced with a compound of limestone and tar on a gravel bed. The official opening was on 19 August 1909, with a meeting combining motor-cycles and cars. Everything went well until the cars got going, when the track surface broke up and the racing had to be called off. The Speedway Corporation resurfaced the entire track with paving bricks, and from that time on the 'Brickyard' became part of the American sporting heritage.

The first 500 Mile race was held there on 30 May 1911, and since that time there have been only six years in which the event has not been held (two during World War I and four during World War II). The policy from the outset was just one race a year; but it has become the richest in the world, with a purse of more than $1 million (£500,000) and enormous exploitation fees possible for successful drivers. For many years 'Indy' was the preserve of front-engined racers powered by Miller or Offenhauser engines, but Wilbur Shaw in a Maserati 8CTF managed to overcome them in 1939 and 1940. Engines began to move behind the driver after Jim Clark won in 1965 with a Ford V8-powered rear-engined Lotus. In that race Clark lifted the race average above 150 mph (241.40 km/h) for the first time.

Below The first major event at the newly opened track at Brooklands in 1907 was S. F. Edge's successful attack on the 24-hour record. He is seen here in his stripped-down 60 hp Napier six-cylinder tourer before the start; the other two Napiers were used as pace cars. Edge averaged 106.1 km/h (65.9 mph).

Above Line up at the start of the first motor-car race at Indianapolis Speedway in August 1909. The event was won by Bob Burman and Lewis Strang in car number 34 (Buick).

Right The Citroën 8CV *Petite Rosalie II* at Montlhéry in 1933, where it ran for 133 days and broke 296 world class records.

Below Map of Montlhéry oval and road circuit. The connecting links (bretelles) allow different lap lengths.

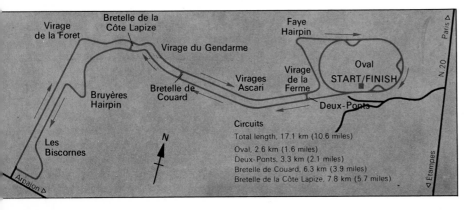

Circuits

Total length, 17.1 km (10.6 miles)

Oval, 2.6 km (1.6 miles)
Deux-Ponts, 3.3 km (2.1 miles)
Bretelle de Couard, 6.3 km (3.9 miles)
Bretelle de la Côte Lapize, 7.8 km (5.7 miles)

Montlhéry

The fact that big races were run on public-road courses held back the construction of a permanent, continuous-high-speed circuit in France until 1924. That year M. Lamblin, a manufacturer of radiators, acquired a 4,855 hectare (12,000 acre) estate to the south of Paris between the villages of Montlhéry and Linas on which he constructed a reinforced-concrete, banked oval of 2.6 km (1.6 miles). It had two well-calculated bankings connected by straights. With so much land available, he added a 14.5 km (9-mile) road circuit as well.

Montlhéry had a number of advantages over Brooklands. In particular it had a smoother surface; and, because there were no noise restrictions, round-the-clock racing was possible. Indeed, all the great endurance-event drivers between the wars used Montlhéry for attempts on the 24-hour record. The whole range of motor racing has been seen there, from cyclecar races to the French Grand Prix.

Monza

Two years before Montlhéry was built the Italians had established their own permanent circuit, or set of circuits, in the royal park at Monza on the northern outskirts of Milan. Initially there was a 4.5 km (2.8 mile) banked oval and a 5.4 km (3.42 mile) road circuit, which could be combined to form a 10 km (6.2 mile) mixed circuit. Two other circuits were added later, the 6.8 km (4.2 mile) Florio circuit and the 4 km (2.4 mile) Short Florio circuit. During World War II the circuits were all but destroyed and it was not until 1948 that the road section could be rebuilt. The banked section was reconstructed in 1955, but by then it was unsuitable for modern *grand-prix* cars. Although the 1955 and 1956 Italian GPs were held on the mixed circuit, manufacturers rebelled when an attempt to use it again was made in 1960. But before 1939 Monza was the venue for practically every Italian Grand Prix, and it was the setting for the Two Worlds Trophy in 1956 and 1957 when a number of Indianapolis cars and drivers matched their cars with similar vehicles hastily concocted by the Europeans. The banked circuit was used on this occasion. Otherwise its main use has been for production-car record breaking.

Monza has been the scene of some particularly unfortunate accidents. In 1928 Ernesto Materassi's Talbot left the track, killing the driver and 20 spectators. Count Louis Zborowski was killed in a works Mercedes on the Lesmo bend in 1924. In 1933 Baconin Borzacchini and Giuseppe Campari died when their cars spun on oil dropped by a Duesenberg in the heats of the

Monza Grand Prix, and Count Stanislas Czaykowski was killed in the 1933 final. In 1961 'Taffy' von Trips died in an accident which also claimed a number of spectators. And in 1978 Ronnie Peterson died after his Lotus was involved in a pile-up soon after the start of the Italian Grand Prix.

German circuits

The first high-speed German circuit was the Avus, near Berlin, which was started in 1913 but not completed until 1920. Originally it consisted of two parallel straights connected by a tight bend at the southern end and a more gentle loop at the northern; the total length was 20 km (12.4 miles). Only twice, in 1926 and 1959, has the German Grand Prix been held there, but a series of races called the Avusrennen was staged annually before World War II, and in the late 1930s it provided a venue for exhibiting the Mercedes-Benz and Auto Union racers. Bernd Rosemeyer's lap record of 276.3 km/h (171.7 mph), achieved in 1937 in an ultra-streamlined Auto Union, established Avus as the fastest track in the world. As a result of the war it bestrode different political zones and was reduced in length to 8.2 km (5.1 miles). Avus was notorious for the brick-surfaced north-end banking constructed in 1927; it was lethal in the wet, and no driver who had raced there shed any tears when it was knocked down in 1967, and the track became part of the *Autobahn* system.

Germany's most attractive circuit is undoubtedly the Nürburgring in the Eifel mountains, built between 1925 and 1927 to ease unemployment in the area. It consists of two loops of road winding over the hills above the Ahr valley near the tiny town of Adenau. The little medieval castle of Nürburg dominates the start and finish area; the pits are located in the middle of an out-and-return loop. The Nordschleife (northern loop) measures 22.8 km (14.1 miles). Apart from numerous uphill and downhill corners and fast bends, it features the Karrusel – a concrete-surfaced ditch on the inside of a bend just wide enough to take a single car. Some say that it was not even paved in the early days, when a few brave competitors used it as a banking to get through the corner more quickly. The Südschleife is 7.75 km (4.8 miles) long and is not much used nowadays, although the 1960 Formula II German Grand Prix was staged on it.

The two greatest German races, the *grand prix* and the 1,000 km (621 mile) sports-car event, were staged at the Nürburgring for many years, and the latter still is; the *grand prix* however, has moved to the circuit at Hockenheim (between Karlsruhe and Mannheim).

Le Mans

The great circuit of Le Mans is by far the most famous in France. The city of Le Mans – the country's insurance centre – has had associations with motor sport since the early years of this century; as we have seen, the world's first *grand prix* was staged there, over a circuit of more than 100 km (62 miles) that included the towns of St Calais and Ferté Bernard to the east.

The present circuit, to the south of the city, was first used in 1920. It took much the same route as it does now, except that it included a hairpin bend at Pontlieue, on the outskirts of Le Mans. In 1929 a bypass was built to skirt the centre of Pontlieue; it cut the length of the circuit from 17.2 km (10.7 miles) to 16.2 km (10.1 miles). In 1932 the Automobile Club de l'Ouest bought land to build the section from the Dunlop bridge through the Esses to la Terte

Monza, the home of Italian *grand-prix* racing since 1922, includes a banked section as well as a road circuit. The combination is dangerously unsuitable for modern *grand-prix* cars, which require different suspension settings for banked and normal circuits. As a result only the road circuit has been used for the Italian Grand Prix since 1959. The picture shows the banking during the 1955 event, which was dominated by Mercedes-Benz; the winner was number 18, driven by Juan Manuel Fangio.

Rouge, which further reduced the distance to 13.3 km (8.3 miles). The only subsequent change, apart from widening the pit area after the 1955 disaster in which more than 100 spectators were killed, has been to introduce the Virage Ford in the straight on the western section between the White House and the pits. It was donated in 1968 by the Ford Motor company to celebrate its wins there and to reduce the speed of the cars through the pit area.

The feature of the Le Mans circuit which makes it so challenging is the long Mulsanne straight from Le Tertre Rouge southward to the village of Mulsanne. Although it has one testing bend, speeds reach about 320 km/h (200 mph) in the straight, and there is a right-angle bend at the end which puts enormous loads on brakes.

Monaco

Antony Noghès of the Société des Bains de Mer of Monaco and the Automobile Club de Monaco were jointly responsible for founding a *grand prix* for the principality in 1929. The little 3 km (1.9 mile) circuit in Monte Carlo is one of the most picturesque and exciting in Europe. The start was originally located on the Quai d'Albert alongside the harbour on one side of a dual carriageway. The cars would then pile into the Gasholder hairpin before rushing back along the opposite carriageway and up the hill to the Casino, where they would plunge down the narrow defile below the Hotel Metropole, round the Mirabeau and Station corners, and enter the curving tunnel which took them back to the harbour. They returned to the start area through Tabac Corner, so-called because of a tiny tobacconist's shop set into the harbour wall. A multiple crash at the Gasholder hairpin in 1961 caused the start to be moved to the landward side of the dual carriageway; otherwise the only change has been the diversion caused by a new swimming pool that projects into the harbour.

The first Monaco Grand Prix was won by William Grover in a Type 35B Bugatti; that marque dominated the race until 1932, when Nuvolari won in an Alfa Romeo Monza. There has been only one fatal accident, in 1967, when Lorenzo Bandini overturned at the chicane that had been erected to slow the cars after they emerged from the tunnel.

Spa-Francorchamps

The Belgians were motor racing almost as soon as the French, and most of their important events were centred then, as now, on the town of Spa, about 30 km (18½ miles) south-east of Liège. The Spa-Francorchamps circuit is a few miles east of Spa and is based on the villages of Francorchamps, Malmedy, and Stavelot.

Above Looking north towards the pits and grandstands of the Le Mans circuit. Motor racing's worst disaster occurred here during the 1955 24-hour race, when Pierre Levegh's Mercedes-Benz 300SLR hit an Austin-Healey on the 42nd lap and crashed into the crowd opposite the pits. As a result the Virage Ford — the kink in the circuit immediately before the straight leading to the pits — was introduced to reduce speeds through the grandstand area.

Right Map of Le Mans circuit. The city and its southern suburb Pontlieue are immediately to the north of the map area.

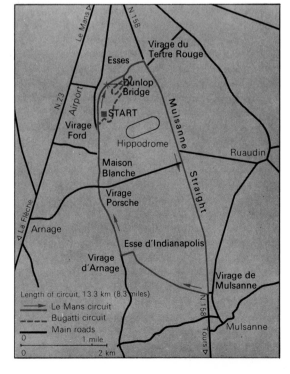

Some 14 km (8.7 miles) long, it is the fastest European road circuit now in use, and as long ago as 1970 was lapped at 258.2 km/h (160.5 mph) by Pedro Rodrigues in a Porsche 917 sports prototype. Although the Belgian Grand Prix has been moved to the rather characterless circuit of Zolder, among the sand dunes near Hasselt, the classic 1,000 km (621 mile) sports-car race continues to be held at Spa-Francorchamps, as is the 24-hour race.

Zandfoort

Zandfoort circuit in the Netherlands was built partly on coast roads constructed by the German army in World War II. Johnny Hugenholtz designed the track and invited the British Racing Drivers' Club to organize the first meeting in 1948. Formula I races have been staged on this sandy circuit since 1950, when Louis Rosier in a 4.5-litre Lago-Talbot was the first victor.

Austrian circuits

Austria has had two important circuits at Zeltweg, south-west of Vienna. The older one was on a military airfield where sports-car races and then Formula II events were held in the late 1950s and early 1960s. The Austrians were eventually allocated a championship *grand prix* in 1964 on this original circuit, which was only 3.2 km (1.9 miles) long and had a rough surface. Since 1969 the Austrian Grand Prix has been held on the newer Österreichring, a 5.7 km (3.6 mile) circuit built in the hills behind the old one. Winding over a saddle in the mountains, it measures up fully to modern safety requirements.

British circuits

Although none of the British circuits is comparable in quality or historical associations with the greatest ones on the continent, a few deserve to be singled out. When Donington Park, 16 km (10 miles) from Derby, opened its gates in 1934, British enthusiasts were elated, for it provided genuine road racing for the first time in England (TT races having been confined to the Isle of Man and Northern Ireland). At first it measured only 3.5 km (2.2 miles) but an extension incorporating a downhill hairpin at the Melbourne end of the circuit increased the lap to 4 km (2.5 miles). Donington Park was quickly espoused by the Junior Car Club and the British Racing Drivers' Club from Brooklands, which staged the Nuffield and Empire Trophy races there. But its greatest moments came with the participation of the German Mercedes-Benz and Auto Union teams in the 1937 and 1938 Donington Grands Prix.

After World War II a determined effort was made to develop a circuit suitable for *grand-prix* racing. Neither Donington Park nor Brooklands would have been adequate; in any case, both were out of commission. The choice fell on a site at Silverstone, in Northampton-shire, and the RAC devised a 4.7 km (2.9 mile) circuit that was the setting for the first post-war British Grand Prix in 1948. Since that time it has been the home of British motor racing, and it is owned and administered by the British Racing Drivers' Club. Production-car racing began at Silverstone in 1949, and nowadays the BRDC organizes the British Grand Prix in conjunction with the RAC. The privilege of staging the race is shared today with the Brands Hatch circuit near Wrotham, in Kent. Silverstone put motor racing on the map in post-war Britain and paved the way for the nation's strong position in the sport today.

Right The very testing 'around-the-houses' circuit at Monaco, the most glamorous of the European *grand-prix* venues. The picture shows the Ancienne Gare (Old Station) hairpin in Monte Carlo.

Below Map of Monaco circuit. Until 1961 the start was on the east lane of the dual carriageway.

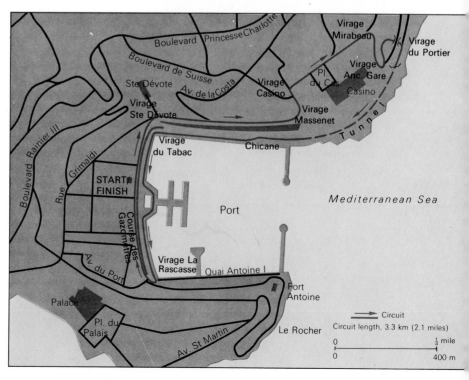

Nostalgia

33 Old-Car Clubs

Old-car clubs are today an increasingly significant part of the motoring scene. They play a vital role in keeping historic vehicles on the road by stimulating enthusiasm, providing spare parts and specialist advice, and organizing events of all kinds. The British have long been noted for their sentimental enthusiasm for old cars. In more recent years the enthusiasm has spread to many European countries, most notably West Germany, the Netherlands, and Switzerland. Today, especially in the field of restoration, the Americans are pre-eminent. Their interests include not only great American cars of the past, such as Duesenberg and Cord, but also several British sports-car marques; American clubs devoted to the latter have close ties with their British counterparts.

The now-defunct tabloid the *Daily Sketch* was indirectly responsible for forming the world's first old-car organization, the Veteran Car Club, in 1930. Three years previously, in 1927, the newspaper had staged its first 'Old Crocks' Run' from London to Brighton, to commemorate the original Emancipation Run of 1896. Similar events were held again in 1928 and 1929, and in the following year the Royal Automobile Club was persuaded to take over the organization of the run. It was after this event, on 23 November 1930, that the Veteran Car Club was founded, appropriately enough at Brighton, by three enthusiasts: S.C.H. (Sammy) Davis, racing driver and Sports Editor of the *Autocar*, Jackie Masters, and John Wylie. The club confirmed the informal but generally

Above 1903 De Dion-Bouton, a beautifully maintained veteran car.

Preceding two pages The Veteran Cars section of Lips Autotron Automuseum at Drunen, near Hertogenbosch, in the Netherlands.

Below A Lancia Lambda of the mid-1920s — one of the most sought-after Italian vintage sports cars.

accepted definition of a 'veteran' as a car that was built on or before 31 December 1904. Only vehicles manufactured by this date were to be eligible for the London to Brighton Run. The event has continued to be organized by the RAC since 1930.

By 1939 there were about 250 veteran-car enthusiasts owning some 150 cars, and the VCC's role as a preserver of historic vehicles was clearly established. In 1943, however, the club took a significant step by extending membership to owner's of vehicles manufactured before the end of 1916, and later before the end of 1918, in view of the number of historic vehicles that were threatened by the World War II drive for scrap metal. These later cars were eligible for all club events, with the exception of the London to Brighton Run.

The creation and success of the VCC inspired the formation of the Vintage Sports Car Club in 1934. Indeed, its original title was *Veteran* Sports Car Club, but it was later changed to *Vintage* in deference to the VCC. The first meeting of the VSCC was held on 23 October 1934, the intention initially being to restrict membership to the owners of light vintage sports cars. The club was founded largely as a reaction against the declining standards of sports-car design in the early 1930s, but such was the interest it generated that entry was extended to *all* cars provided they had been manufactured earlier than five years prior to 1 January 1935. So the definition of the vintage era was established for the first time.

It was not until the end of World War II that another change was made to the VSCC's eligibility rules. At the annual meeting held in September 1945 it was decided to create a category for those marques or models which, in the club's view, had maintained the traditions

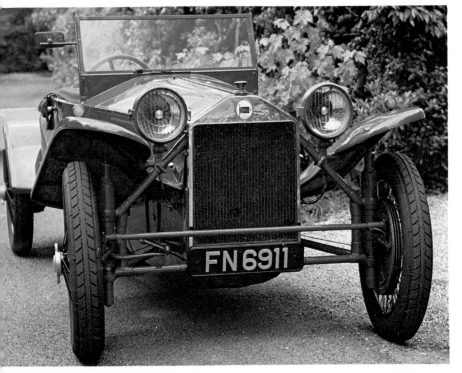

of vintage craftsmanship into the 1930s. This permitted the inclusion of several post-1930 Alvis, Lagonda, Rolls-Royce, and Invicta cars, and also the K3, Q, R, C, M, J3 and J4 models of the MG, spanning the years 1929–35. A full list of approved makes was issued by the club in 1963. Before then, Post Vintage Thoroughbreds (PVT), as these post-1930 cars were called, had been individually considered for inclusion on an *ad hoc* basis by the club's committee. A rather surprising inclusion was the Citroën 7CV *traction-avant* (front-wheel-drive) of 1934 – an outstanding model in design and road-holding, but unquestionably neither vintage nor a sports car. (The fact that many VSCC members happened to own these cars no doubt helped to persuade the committee to include it among the PVT.)

Above A young enthusiast admires a 1933, 1.5-litre model at an Aston Martin Owners' Club meeting. Many sports cars of the 1930s had anti-stone guards on the headlamps and radiator.

Below The instrument panel of a supercharged 1932 MG J2 Midget. The octagonal shape of the instruments was inspired by that of the marque's radiator badge.

One-make clubs
The success of the VCC and VSCC led to the founding of a number of clubs, each devoted to a single marque. One of the best known to have survived from the 1930s is the Bentley Drivers' Club, created some four years after the demise of W.O. Bentley's company in 1931. Its founder-members included owners of no less than 27 Bentleys. Although membership was originally confined to the products of the old Cricklewood factory, the club later agreed to admit owners of Bentleys manufactured by Rolls-Royce at Derby (and later Crewe).

One of the earlier one-make clubs in Britain was formed in 1929 to cater for enthusiastic owners of that exciting and distinctive French racing and sports-car marque, the Bugatti. The club gradually grew in strength and in 1937, in order to provide itself with a hill-climb course, purchased the grounds of Prescott House in the Gloucestershire Cotswolds. Club members were

greatly honoured in 1939 when they were presented with a racing car by the Bugatti factory; the vehicle was intended for the use of members who could not afford such a car of their own. In fact, ownership of this Bugatti proved something of an embarrassment, owing to the difficulty of deciding who was to be allowed to drive the car – a potent Type 51 *grand-prix* model; eventually, and with great reluctance, the BOC decided to sell it in 1943.

The world's largest one-make car club also has its roots in pre-war days. The MG Car Club was founded in 1931. Its first honorary secretary was John Thornley, who had joined the MG Car Company in the same year (21 years later he was to become MG's general manager). The club's activities were by no means confined to the British Isles, however. In 1939 the first overseas centre was established in Ceylon, soon to be followed by an American one. Membership grew apace and by September 1938 it stood at 1,500. After the war these figures continued to soar, and when Wilson McComb took over as general secretary in 1963 membership was around 10,000.

Most of the one-make clubs mentioned so far cater for sports cars, but the distinction of being the oldest one-make club in the world must go to the Jowett Car Club. It was founded in 1922 for owners of that tough, sturdy little car from Idle, Yorkshire, powered by an almost veteran flat-twin engine – 'the little engine with the big pull' as the manufacturers proudly described it.

After World War II there was a rapid expansion of car clubs. Amongst the one-make organizations created in the late 1940s were the AC Owners' Club and the re-formed Aston

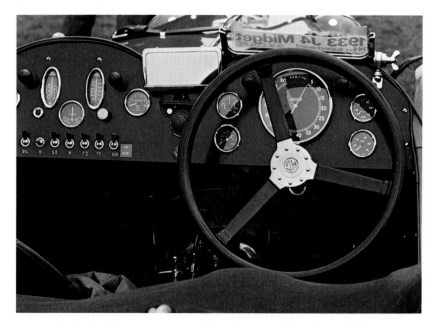

A quartet of SS two-seaters at a club meeting at Donington Park in 1938. The car on the left is an SS90 with 2.5-litre engine, which first appeared in 1935; the others are SS Jaguar 100s, with a similar short chassis but a 3.5-litre engine.

Club is typical of a group that caters for a small number of cars. Gordon-Keebles were in production between 1964 and 1967, during which time only 99 cars were made – fast, handsome GT coupés powered by a 5.4-litre Chevrolet engine. The club was founded in 1970; it has accounted for all but six of the total production, and is consequently *the* source of information about every aspect of the marque.

As more makes are collected more clubs are created to cater for the new owners. These include in recent years the Morris Minor Owners' Club and organizations for the Sunbeam Alpine (1953–7) and the Triumph Mayflower (1950–3).

Car-club activities

Much work is involved in running a club, particularly in its formative months, and it requires a dedicated team of volunteers. As clubs grow their organization becomes more professional; and as their finances grow they are usually able to employ a full-time secretary. This improves the running and efficiency of the club and often allows a professionally produced magazine to be circulated to members. The magazine is the life blood of any club and usually contains news of past and future events, restoration advice, and a historical section based on research by a club historian or registrar. Clubs soon build up an excellent fund of knowledge about their marques and become centres for documentation, accumulating handbooks, sales literature, photographs, and much else.

A club's most important role, however, is to keep the cars in good running order. For this reason, practically all clubs have a spares registrar, whose job is to ensure that the types of spares that are in constant demand by members – cylinder-head gaskets, valves, pistons, and clutch and brake parts – are in good supply. Sometimes there is no shortage of parts, particularly if the model has only recently ceased production; but if the club is dealing with a vehicle that was made in small numbers many years ago, the availability of spare parts is a major problem. Members banding together can order parts in batches, and items such as pistons, gaskets, camshafts, and even complete cylinder blocks can be specially produced if there is sufficient demand.

The spares registrar keeps on the lookout for unexpected supplies of spare parts; it is by no means unknown, for example, for tons of spares to be offered for sale when an old garage is closing down. The registrar must move quickly and make an offer, otherwise the valuable spares will be sold for their scrap value. In many instances the work of the spares registrar has

Martin Owners' Club, which had been founded in 1935. Again the accent was on sports cars, but 1952 saw the creation of the Bullnose Morris Club catering for those distinctive Morrises, first launched in 1913, which were best-selling cars in Britain in the 1920s. Another mass producer of the inter-war years, Austin, was represented by the creation of the Vintage Austin Register in 1958 for the larger and somewhat pedestrian models of the 1920s; the phenomenally successful Baby Austin was already catered for by the 750 Motor Club, which placed greater emphasis on competitive activities. By 1959 the one-make clubs embraced such marques as Daimler, Humber, Fiat, Riley, and Lancia.

As the movement gathered momentum, clubs were established to cater for post-war cars. Typical of these is the Jaguar Drivers' Club, founded in 1956. It was originally created mainly for the owners of XK models, and went through a revitalization in the late 1960s when a separate XK register was formed. The club now contains a number of registers: the SS register caters for all the pre-XK-engined cars; there are others for the Mark I and II cars, the E-Type, S-Type, and SJ models. Thus the JDC, like many similar clubs, caters for recent examples of the marque, and this has helped to forge a strong bond between the club and the Jaguar factory. An annual rally is held at the Coventry works and the club and manufacturer cooperate in finding spare parts for obsolete models.

If the Jaguar Drivers' Club is typical of a one-make club for a car made in relatively large numbers, then the Gordon-Keeble Owners'

Left A legendary (and now rare and almost priceless) Duesenberg Model SJ at an American club meeting. Introduced in 1932, its supercharged 6.9-litre, straight-eight Lycoming engine developed 320 hp — almost unprecedented for a road car at that time.

Below An Autojumble in the grounds of the National Motor Museum at Beaulieu, Hampshire. Thousands of spare parts, servicing and repair manuals, and motoring books are on sale, and the event attracts collectors and other enthusiasts from all over the world.

turned into a full-time job, and a number of firms who supply spare parts for notable post-war makes (which are now known in Britain as 'classics') began life as sections of one-make clubs or registers.

Another source of spare parts, for both clubs and individual members, is the increasingly popular autojumbles. To the uninitiated such sales look like a large collection of wooden tables covered with assorted piles of scrap iron, but nothing could be further from the truth. At these events enthusiasts have an opportunity to seek out spare parts for their particular vehicle, find a component of an original tool kit, or dig out an original handbook. The largest event of this type in Britain is the annual Auto-jumble held at the National Motor Museum at Beaulieu, Hampshire. In 1978 no less than 18,000 enthusiasts attended from all over the world. Smaller events are now held in all parts of the country, often by one-make car clubs.

Car clubs have played a vital part in the preservation of our historic vehicles. And what has happened in England has been copied throughout the world. Today the old-car movement has never been stronger. The thousands of gleaming veteran, vintage, post-vintage and classic cars to be seen at rallies and meetings in all parts of the world fully vindicate the dedication of the pioneers of the 1930s.

As we have seen, the 'old crocks' London-to-Brighton commemoration runs of the late 1920s played an important role in the foundation of the Veteran Car Club. But exactly what did these runs commemorate? The development of the motor car in Britain lagged behind that in Germany and France during the late 19th century owing at least in part to legislation that positively discouraged the use of mechanically propelled vehicles on public roads. Some of the more punitive restrictions were removed from the statute book by the Locomotives on the Highway Act, which became law on 14 November 1896. A key provision of the Act was that 'locomotives' of less than 6,600 kg (3 tons) unladen weight were not to be regarded as 'light' vehicles, and that therefore it was no longer required that a man walk in front of them to alert other road users of their approach. The Act also established a maximum permissible speed of 22.5 km/h (14 mph), although the Local Government Board reduced this to 19.3 km/h (12 mph). The passing of the Act was regarded as a great victory by the motoring lobby, and Harry Lawson – head of the British Motor Syndicate and most vociferous member of the lobby – decided to organize a procession of horseless carriages from London to Brighton on what he termed 'Emancipation Day'.

Two Panhard-Levassors outside the Hotel Metropole in Northumberland Avenue before the start of the original London-to-Brighton Emancipation Run in November 1896. Harry Lawson, the event's organizer, is with his wife in the leading car; Charles McRobie Turrell and Jack Dring are in the other car.

Participants in the event assembled at Hyde Park Corner, in London, on the morning of 14 November. The opening ceremony was enlivened by the Earl of Winchelsea tearing up a red flag – a gesture whose symbolism lost some of its force in the fact that the man formerly required to precede a car on public roads had not been obliged to carry a flag since 1878. Nonetheless, the run to Brighton captured the imagination of the motoring public, and today the annual commemoration on a Sunday in November remains one of the most important events in the veteran-car calendar. The sight of several score geriatric cars putt-putting their way along the Brighton road undoubtedly strikes a warm spark in the minds of the motoring public – a fact amply demonstrated by the enormous success of the film *Genevieve*, made in 1954 (it was discovered too late that the car driven by Kenneth More in the film, a four-seat Spyker made in Amsterdam, was ineligible since it dated from 1905). The London-to-Brighton run is the exemplar of hundreds of events of this kind that are now held all over the world.

The Itala and Seaman trophies

Also of historic interest, but featuring genuine races rather than runs, are the meetings held by the Vintage Sports Car Club. Perhaps the two most outstanding events of a busy calendar are the G.P. Itala Trophy race for vintage racing cars, which is held at the Silverstone racing circuit, Northamptonshire, and the Richard Seaman Trophy race for the later historic racing machinery.

The Itala Trophy is an award that was presented to the club in 1947 by R. Wil-de-Gose, who had competed with a 1908 Grand Prix Itala at Brooklands in pre-war days. In recent years the race has been dominated by two marques: Bentley and Bugatti. It is difficult to imagine two greater automotive extremes. The big green Bentleys are always a delight to watch, their lazy, unstressed engines burbling round the Silverstone circuit and often putting up deceptively fast lap times. The consistently reliable performances of these cars are a reminder of how important reliability was in W.O. Bentley's design philosophy – a virtue rewarded by the marque's success in the Le Mans 24-hour races during the 1920s. The French Bugattis look small in comparison, but the two-seaters, in particular the Type 35 in its various forms, remain for many enthusiasts the definitive expressions of what vintage racing cars should look like. Their small straight-eight engines need to work much harder than those of the larger Bentleys, and the characteristic high-pitched scream of the supercharged Type 35s is

as unmistakable a sign of Bugattis at work, as are the famous horseshoe-shaped radiator cowl and eight-spoked cast-aluminium road wheels.

The Richard Seaman Trophy is held in memory of an outstanding British driver who joined the all-conquering Mercedes-Benz racing team and died after crashing at the 1939 Belgian Grand Prix at Spa. The trophy, for which historic racing cars compete, is the one that Seaman was awarded for his third place in the 1938 Donington Grand Prix at the wheel of a Mercedes-Benz; it was presented to the Vintage Sports Car Club in 1950 by his friend, the motor racing photographer George Monkhouse.

Held at Oulton Park circuit in Cheshire, the event has for long been dominated by ERAs, except for a brief period when more modern racing cars were given their head. ERAs (the

Above A 3-litre Bentley of the 1920s putting on an impressive display at a recent VSCC Itala Trophy meeting at Silverstone.

Below Bugatti Type 35 and 37 *grand-prix* cars have often disputed domination of the Itala Trophy race with Bentleys in recent years. The black spot visible on the car's bonnet is a hole for the supercharger's relief valve.

initials stand for English Racing Automobiles) did well in *voiturette* racing in the mid-1930s; they were Britain's major cars of the period – though they were of course no match for the much more powerful Mercedes-Benz and Auto Union *grand-prix* racers. In the 1,500 cc class, however, they scored many successes in the hands of Raymond Mays (one of the ERA's designers), 'B. Bira' (a Thai prince), Richard Seaman, Arthur Dobson, Lord Howe, and others. They are single seaters, powered by either 1.5- or 2.5-litre six-cylinder engines based on a Riley unit tuned and supercharged to a high degree. Acceleration is aided by the use of a pre-selector gearbox, and seeing a gaggle of ERAs leave the start line at the beginning of a race is a sight not to be missed. The VSCC deserves great credit for organizing events that allow these cars to be fielded competitively: of the 16 examples built before World War II, no fewer than 15 are still running.

Other events

In recent years the growth of the one-make car clubs has resulted in the proliferation of marque-anniversary events of one kind and another. A typical example of such events was the rally that took place in France in 1974 to

celebrate the 50th anniversary of the introduction of the Bugatti Type 35. This great racing car was first seen in public at the French Grand Prix held at Lyons in 1924, and 50 years later scores of surviving examples returned to the circuit in a splendid tribute to the car and its creator, Ettore Bugatti.

Another significant commemoration occurred in 1978, when Britain's Austin-Healey clubs celebrated the 25th anniversary of the introduction of the 'Big Healey', as the Austin-Healey 100 and its successor, the 3000, are affectionately known. These low-slung two seaters, produced by the British Motor Corporation from 1953 until 1968, were among the most successful British rally cars in the early 1960s; the celebrations made a fitting tribute to the principle guest, the designer Donald Healey, who was himself a notable rally driver in the 1930s.

In addition to gatherings that can be linked to a specific historic occasion, many car clubs organize an event known as a *concours d'élégance*. This is essentially a static gathering, the cars being lined up and examined by a team of experts, who have to decide which vehicle is in the best condition. Great importance is attached to a car's fidelity to its original specification

ERAs on the front rows of the grid at a meeting for vintage and historic cars at Oulton Park, Cheshire. The car in the foreground, nicknamed *Remus*, was one of several ERAs raced by 'B. Bira' (Prince Birabongse Bhanuban of Thailand) in 1935–47 for the White Mouse Stable.

and bodywork; if restoration has been carried out the correct materials and finishes must have been used. For example, in the 1920s almost all cars had leather upholstery. It is almost inevitable that, on a 50- or 60-year-old car, the original leather will have deteriorated and needed to be replaced. If the owner of the car in question has used a modern synthetic material instead of leather he will loose marks when the judges come to evaluate his car. Similarly, nickel plate was used extensively for brightwork in the vintage era, chromium plate appearing only at the end of the 1920s. If an owner inadvertently chromes parts of the car

that were originally nickel plated he will also be penalized. Not surprisingly there is plenty of friendly rivalry between owners. These events are very popular amongst both enthusiasts and members of the public, for a colourful collection of historic vehicles in sparkling condition is a very beautiful sight.

Concours d'élégance are usually advertised in local newspapers or specialist magazines and are held on most weekends during the summer months. Often not only cars but historic commercial vehicles, motor-cycles. tractors, and bicycles will be represented, making a fascinating exhibition of the machines of yesterday.

An impressive line-up of 1950s models at an Aston Martin Owners' Club *concours d'élégance.* at which the condition and authenticity of bodywork, interior furnishing, engine, and even small elements of trim are vital to success.

35 Restoration and Collections

Buying old motor cars and restoring them to their original condition has never been more popular than it is today. It can, indeed, be a very lucrative occupation, for extravagant sums regularly change hands at some of the larger auctions for veteran and vintage cars. It was not always so. Before World War II it was possible to buy some of the greatest vintage sports and racing cars at what today would be considered giveaway prices. In 1938, for instance, an issue of *Motor Sport* advertised a short-chassis Lancia Lambda, one of the finest Italian cars of the 1920s, for £15; one of the legendary Vauxhall 30/98s for £27 10s; and a Bentley Speed Six – perhaps the finest of W.O.'s designs, and the type that won the Le Mans 24-hour race in 1929 and 1930 – for a mere £37 10s. If the very cream of vintage machinery was available second-hand for such derisory sums in 1938, the little mass-produced cars of the 1920s – the Austins, Morrises, and Clynos – must have been worth little more than scrap. Indeed, thousands of them, as well as many more-illustrious cars, *were* sold for scrap, especially during World War II; and this, of course, was responsible for conferring on them a rarity value that inflation and the growing numbers of collectors and restorers have multiplied to the present astonishing levels. Today, for instance, an authentic Bentley Speed Six would fetch about £20,000.

Anyone seeking to buy an old car nowadays is in very much the same position as the collector of works of art: the quality of what he will be able to acquire will almost invariably depend on how much money he is prepared to invest. On the other hand, just as the art collector is occasionally lucky enough to discover (and quickly buy) a valuable old painting stored in somebody's attic, so do car collectors from time to time come across bargains in out-of-the-way places. The barns and other out-buildings of farms have yielded a number of interesting car-collector's items in recent years. Service garages in rural areas have been another source of valuable finds – although with the enormous rise in the market value of old cars, such sources have been fully explored in the last decade.

One of the most notable achievements in recent years was the discovery of the car in which J. G. Parry Thomas, a notable designer and driver in the 1920s, attempted to break the world land-speed record in March 1927. The car, designed and built by Parry Thomas himself, and named *Babs*, was a huge, streamlined monster powered by an American Liberty V12 aero-engine of 27-litres capacity. The record attempt was made on Pendine Sands in South Wales, and it ended in gruesome tragedy when

the car crashed at almost 274 km/h (170 mph) and decapitated the driver. The car was not removed from the sands but buried on the spot. In 1969 Owen Wyn Owen, a lecturer at Bangor University, obtained permission to search for the car, and he eventually discovered and exhumed it. *Babs* proved to be in surprisingly good condition after being buried for 42 years, only its aluminium components being severely corroded. The car is still in the process of restoration.

As we saw in Chapter 33, it is not only veteran and vintage cars that are sought by the collector today. With the passage of time, many

A beautifully restored Spyker of 1904 at the Lips museum. One of the few Dutch marques, Spyker ceased production in 1925.

Below The dashboard of a De Diétrich of 1902–3, emphasizing the beauty as well as the importance of authentic components in the restoration of old cars.

of the most interesting models produced since World War II have become collector's items and have been given the title of classic cars. Initially, it was post-war sports cars that attracted most interest, notably the Jaguar XK series (1949–60), the MG TC, TD, and TF models (1946–55), the Aston Martin DB2 (with a W.O. Bentley-designed engine), DB2/4, and DB4 produced from 1949 to 1963, and the Austin-Healey 100 and 3000 (1953–68). The owner of a well-maintained example of any of these models with the original bodywork in mint condition is the proud possessor not merely of a fine car but of an extremely valuable and rapidly appreciating investment.

Buying and restoration

For most enthusiastic beginners, answering an advertisement in one of the specialist magazines is the commonest way of acquiring an interesting old car. The popularity of and the commercial significance of the market for old cars is such that a number of magazines catering for enthusiasts have been successfully established in Britain, the United States, and elsewhere during the last decade. The magazines regularly include features on the history of particular marques and models, practical advice on restoration, announcements and reports of club events, and advertisements offering or seeking cars and spare parts.

The buyer of a car should preferably already have a detailed knowledge of the particular model. He would also be well advised to talk to a member of the relevant one-make club, who will be able to advise on any particular snags about the model (including problems with the availability of certain spare parts); indeed, if the model is exceedingly rare, club members may well be familiar with the history of the individual car in question. As in any other activity in which a good deal of money may change hands, the novice needs to be on his guard. Nowadays, almost any car that is more than 10 years old is likely to be described as a 'classic'. On the other hand, a modest start to a collection can be made with one of the less-expensive but authentic classics, such as a Morris Minor (1948–70), or an Austin-Healey Sprite (1958–71).

Another way of buying an interesting old car is at one of the many auctions that are becoming increasingly popular. These auctions – and especially those at the big West End sale-rooms in London – tend to attract the more expensive type of car, and are often attended by collectors from all over the world; but it is sometimes possible to pick up a bargain among the cheaper offerings that tend to be overshadowed by the more exotic machines. But if

Left and below This 1930 Austin Seven Chummy was recently rescued from a garage where it had stood unused for 36 years. The pictures show it before and after restoration. Note the horn projecting from the side of the scuttle.

Left An immaculately restored Ford Model A roadster of about 1930. New and replica spares are readily available for popular cars of this type and age.

The Panther Lima appeals to lovers of traditional open-air motoring. The late-1930s body style (making considerable use of glass-fibre panels) clothes a modern 2.3-litre engine, floor pan, suspension, and steering from Vauxhall.

you are buying your first old car it is not advisable to look for it at an auction. It will tend only to highlight your lack of experience, and it is very easy to get carried away in the excitement of the bidding.

Of course, many old cars are not in particularly good condition when rescued from a damp garage or barn or a less-than-careful owner; but as an increasing number of cars are being collected, the number of specialist firms that will undertake work on them is also growing. There are companies that will completely rebuild an engine, make new parts, and restore the bodywork (or if necessary make a completely new one). There are also firms who will supply the type of electric cable used in the 1920s, provide the original type of cast-aluminium number plate, faithfully reproduce the correct nickel finish on the brightwork, and paint the bodywork in one of the correct colour shades for the model and year. Serious restoration work requires this kind of attention to the smallest details. Failure to do so will mean that the car will stand no chance of success if it is entered in a *concours d'élégance*, and its value as an investment will be greatly affected. Maintaining the authenticity of the breed – from the overall design to the most mundane details of coachwork or mechanical fixings – is one of the most important roles of the one-make clubs.

The problem of authenticity has become exacerbated in recent years by the very existence of specialized firms devoted to rebuilding engines and bodies. Many such firms have made a vital contribution to the car-collecting scene, and full restoration of some of the finest veteran and vintage machines would have been im-

possible without them. By the same token, it has now become possible to build what might pass for a veteran car from scratch, and an increasing number of such 'replicas', as they are called, have appeared in recent years. Many are fairly accurate reproductions of the original designs; others consist of, say, an exact copy of a vintage body clothing a modern frame and mechanical parts. Replicas have their place, but they are of little interest to the serious collector. Specialist firms have also prospered in the craze for 'customized' cars, which are essentially one-off designs built to the buyer's specifications. They are mentioned here simply because in many examples the bodywork styles hark back to the veteran or vintage period.

Nostalgia for older – and therefore, in some people's eyes, better or more carefree – days has also led to the emergence of a number of small firms using traditional methods of construction, such as hand-made coachwork, to create new cars based loosely on the designs of highly regarded models of the past. There is no pretence that such cars are replicas: they are entirely new models, and they are offered for sale in the same way – though not in the same numbers – as are the latest products of any other motor manufacturer. They do, of course, appeal to a very limited public, not least because, being hand-assembled by skilled craftsmen, they are extremely expensive. Among the best-known of these manufacturers in Britain is Panther West Wind, whose products include the J72, with bodywork reminiscent of the SS100 two-seater (1938–40), a precursor of the Jaguar; the De Ville, which harks back in appearance and opulence to the stupendous Bugatti Royale (1929); and the Lima, a small two-seater of late 1930s style. In some respects the Lima is the most interesting of the three. Stylistically, it draws inspiration from a period rather than from a specific model. It has successfully married a traditional form with modern techniques: the bodywork is of glass-fibre and, in one version, its engine (based on a Vauxhall 2.3-litre unit) is turbocharged.

Car museums

There is no better way of getting an idea of the evolution of the motor car than by visiting a motor museum. There are hundreds of such establishments, large and small, all over the world. Many of the major general museums also have departments devoted to motor-vehicle exhibits. Notable examples include the Conservatoire National des Arts et Métiers in Paris, which includes Cugnot's steam wagon of 1770 and Bollée's *L'Obéissante* steam carriage of 1873; the Science Museum, London; and the Smithsonian Institution in Washington, D.C.

It would be impossible to describe all the fine motor museums in the compass of this chapter, but the following are a few of the most notable in North America and Europe.

The first major establishment in the United States to feature historic cars was the Henry Ford Museum, which was opened in the company's headquarters city of Dearborn, Michigan, in 1929 to mark the 50th anniversary of Thomas Edison's invention of the electric lamp. The museum's primary purpose was and is to exhibit North American artefacts of past and present – a purpose that seems to fly in the face of Henry Ford's famous dictum that 'history is bunk'. The core of the original vehicle collection was acquired in curious circumstances. The cars had been collected and displayed by a Californian in the early 1920s. When the local Ford representative called on him with the proposal that he should present the collection to the new museum, the owner dropped dead on the spot. The resourceful Ford man comforted the widow, supervised arrangements for the funeral, bought the collection, and dispatched it to Dearborn in 56 freight wagons. The collection was opened to the public in 1933, and today contains hundreds of cars and horse-drawn vehicles; two notable exhibits are Henry Ford's vast 999 racer, a clutchless and gearless machine in which Ford attained a speed of 147 km/h (91.4 mph) in 1904, and the 1928 Franklin Airman 3.9-litre sedan once owned by the aviator Charles Lindbergh.

Fittingly for the greatest motoring nation on earth, the United States has the largest car museum in the world – Harrah's Automobile Collection at Reno, Nevada. It had its beginnings in 1948 when William Harrah, who had made a fortune out of an enormous casino complex at Reno, bought a 1911 Maxwell; it was joined soon afterwards by a Ford Model T of the same vintage and an even earlier Olds Curved Dash runabout. Within a few years the collection had expanded to such an extent that Harrah decided to open a public museum. Today it contains more than 1,100 cars on display. Perhaps the outstanding exhibits are two Bugatti Royales (only six of these gigantic 12.7-litre, 250 hp cars were made, in 1932–3); and the Thomas Flyer K-6-70 model that won the New York-to-Paris race of 1908.

Other fine American collections are at the Indianapolis Speedway, Indiana, at the Long Island Automotive Museum, Glencove, New York, and at Costa Mesa, near Long Beach, California, where a magnificent display of historic racing and sports cars has been assembled by Briggs Cunningham, himself a distinguished sports-car driver and designer.

There are a number of very fine motor

museums in Europe. Among the best is the Museo dell'Automobile, in Turin, which traces its origins back to the Turin motor show of 1933 for which Count Carlo Biscaretti Di Ruffia, son of one of the founders of the Fiat company, assembled a collection of historic vehicles. He added to the collection during the next decade, but it was not until 1957 that a company was set up by the Agnelli family, the owners of Fiat, to establish and operate the museum; the collection was opened to the public in 1960. Two of its most important exhibits are the 7.4-litre Itala tourer that won the Pekin-to-Paris

Above Harrah's Automobile Collection at Reno: behind the 1929 Mercedes-Benz SSK with British 'Corsica' coachwork can be seen one of the museum's two priceless Bugatti Royales.

Below A 1906 Panhard *grand-prix* car at the Schlumpf collection at Malmerspach, France.

Left A typical product of the French motor industry in the late Edwardian era, when Renault was becoming the largest car manufacturer in Europe. Note the car's 'coal-scuttle bonnet, for long characteristic of the marque, and the contemporary Motor Union, RAC, and AA badges on the bulkhead.

race of 1907 and the massive 8-litre FIAT racer in which the great Felice Nazzaro won the French Grand Prix the same year.

The most recent of the great collections to be opened to the public in France is the Schlumpf collection at Malmerspach in Alsace. The collection was acquired in somewhat mysterious circumstances by the Schlumpf brothers and was discovered only in 1977. The museum is a treasure-house of more than 600 cars of great historic interest; in particular it contains over 100 Bugattis — the most important assemblage of this marque under one roof.

Among a host of other important European motor museums are a number assembled by manufacturers and devoted to individual marques. Among the most interesting of these are the Autobiographie Renault, in Paris; the Daimler-Benz Museum at Unterturkheim, Stuttgart; the BMW Museum at Munich; the Museo Alfa Romeo at Arese, near Milan; the Museo Lancia at Turin; and the Centro Storico Fiat at the company's headquarters in Turin.

In Britain the largest and best-known collection is the National Motor Museum at Beaulieu, Hampshire. It was in 1952 that Lord Montagu of Beaulieu decided to open a museum in memory of his father, the Hon. John Scott-

Montagu, a pioneer motorist who introduced the Prince of Wales (later Edward VII) to the pleasures of motoring. The museum contains more than 100 cars together with an impressive collection of motor-cycles. Perhaps the most outstanding exhibits are the land speed record cars. They include the 350 hp Sunbeam with which Kenelm Lee Guinness established a new world land-speed record of 215.2 km/h (133.7 mph) in 1922; Major Henry Segrave's 1,000 hp Sunbeam; and the beautiful *Golden Arrow*, in which Segrave raised the record in 1929 to 372.6 km/h (231.4 mph). In addition to the exhibits there is an excellent library of books and magazines relating to the history of the motor car, together with a collection of historic photographs.

There are many smaller motor museums scattered throughout Britain, including excellent local collections at Birmingham (Museum of Science and Industry) and Glasgow. One of the newest is near Bridgnorth, Shropshire; its centrepiece is the 24-litre Napier-Railton in which John Cobb established the lap record of 230.9 km/h (143.4 mph) at Brooklands in 1935.

Probably the best racing-car collection is at Donington Park racing circuit in Derbyshire.

Pre-World War II exhibits include a straight-eight Maserati 8CM, an Alfa Romeo P3 Monoposto racer of 1932, and a 1936 Austin racer with a 750 cc twin-overhead-camshaft engine. Post-war racers include the very successful Ferrari 4.5-litre V12, a 1958 Vanwall (the marque won the Manufacturers' Championship that year), and a mid-1960s Ferguson P99 with four-wheel drive. (The Ferguson layout, tried on *grand-prix* and Indianapolis 500 cars, promised excellent road-holding and speed but did not survive the 1960s in racing cars.) Donington Park was the venue for the Donington Park Grands Prix of 1937 and 1938, dominated by Mercedes-Benz and Auto Union teams, and is Britain's only surviving pre-war racing circuit. Many of the racing cars in the collection are regularly run on the track. The exhibits at Donington Park also include a collection of historic vehicles owned by British Leyland. The oldest is an Aveling and Porter steam roller of 1882, and there is also an 1896 Leyland steam-powered lawn mower. The cars include an Alvis 10/30 of 1920, the year the first models bearing this famous name went into production; a 1922 Standard 13.9 hp SL04; a Leyland Eight, one of the most expensive and powerful British cars of the early 1920s, designed by J. G. Parry Thomas; and many other historic British models.

Land speed record cars at the National Motor Museum, Beaulieu. In the foreground, from left: Kenelm Lee Guinness's 350 hp Sunbeam (1922); Major Henry Segrave's *Golden Arrow* (1929); Segrave's 1000 hp Sunbeam (1927); Donald Campbell's Proteus *Bluebird* (1964).

Index

Page numbers in *italics* refer to captions.

Acknowledgments

The publishers thank the following individuals and organisations for their kind permission to reproduce the photographs in this book:

John S. Adams 2–3; All-Sport (Tony Duffy) 175 below; *Autocar* 67 below right; Automobile Association 85 above right; BL 54 above left, 84 below left, 94, 102 above left; Bosch 48; Neil Bruce 143, 146 above and below right; Chrysler United Kingdom Limited 137 above; Collection: The Museum of Modern Art, New York 71 below right; Daimler-Benz AG Bildarchiv 6–7; Edward Eves 200 above left, 206 right; Ford Motor Company Limited 58–63, 191; GKN 46 below right, 47; Lawrie Gatehouse 210–15; General Motors 142 above, 157 below right; G.N. Georgano 89 above right; Geoffrey Goddard 174 above, below and centre, 226, 227; Fay Goodwin 72; Goodyear Tyre and Rubber Company Limited 221 below; C.W.P. Hampton (Nicky Wright) 140 above right; Hong Kong Government Information Service 70 below right; *Illustrated London News* 44; Keystone 184 above; Howard Kingsnorth 78–9 below centre; John Laing and Sons 77 below left; Lincoln Owners' Club 139 below right; London Art Technical Drawings Limited 149 above left, 203 above and below right; Lotus Cars 96 above, 128–9; Mansell Collection 73 above and below right; Mazda 95 above right; Mercedes-Benz (United Kingdom) Limited 157 above right; Metropolitan Police (Roger Millington) 86 below right, 87; Michelin Tyre Company Limited 216 above; Roger Millington 64–5, 71 above right, 82 above left; Pete Myers 8–9, 11 below right, 12, 17 above right, 31 below right, 84 above left, 103, 139 above right, 152 below; National Motor Museum 81 above right, 138, 178 below, 183 above and below, 216 below, 217, 218, 222, 233 below, 243; Doug Nye 173 above; Orbis 22 above right, 26 above right; Panther West Wind 240; Popperfoto 75 below right; Plessey 79 above right; Press Association 79 below right; Peter Roberts Collection endpapers, 10, 13 above, below left and right, 14 above and below, 16, 17 below, 18–21, 24 above and below, 25 above and below right, centre, 27 above left, 28 below, 30 below right, 31 above right, 33 above left and right, 34–43, 46 above, 50, 51 below right, 55 below left and right, 56, 57 above left, 66, 67 above right, 68, 69 above and below right, 74 above and below left, 75 above right, 78 above left, 80 above and below right, 83 above right, 85 below left, 88, 92, 93 above right, 97 above right, 99 above and below right, 100, 102 below left, 111, 130, 131, 132 above and below left, 133 above left and below right, 134 above and below left, 135 above right and below, 136, 137 above right, 140 above left and below right, 141 above and below right, 145 above right, 148, 149 below right, 150, 151 above, 153 above and below left, 154, 155 below right, 156 above and below left, 158–9, 160–70, 175 above and below, 173 below, 175 above, 178 above, 179–82, 185 above and below, 187, 189 above, 190, 192–9, 200 below left and right, 202, 204–6, 207, 219–21, 223–5, 230 above, 231 above and below, 232, 233 above, 234–9, 241–2; Peter Roberts Collection (Donington Collection) 32; (Lips Autodrome) 22 below right, 26 above left, 29 above, 228–9; (Mercedes-Benz Bildarchiv) 30 above right; (*Punch*) 86 above right; Rolls Royce 29 below right; Royal Automobile Club: painting by F. Gordon Crosby (photo: Pete Myers) 171; Science Museum (London): painting by Cuneo (photo: Pete Myers) 11 above right; Gerald Scott (Nicky Wright) 230 below; Shell 81 above right, 82 below right; Jerry Sloniger 208, 209; Smiths Industries Limited 48–9 above; Jasper Spencer-Smith 152 above; Tony Stone Associates 27 below right, 33 below right, 76–7; Colin Taylor 189, 201; Les Thacker 188; Transport and Road Research Laboratory 79 left; Triplex Safety Glass Company Limited 49 above and below left; Mirielle Vautier (De Nanxe) 45; Vauxhall Motors Limited 51 above right, 93 below left, 95 below right; Volkswagen 54 above right, 57, 96 below left; Volvo 89 below right, 97 below right; Nicky Wright 145 above, 147, 151 below right, 78 above right; Zefa/Eric Carle 83 below right; Zefa/J. Pfaff 70 above; Zefa/A. Thill 176.

Illustrators

Christian Baker, R John Way, Venner Artists. Maps by Terry Allen Designs/Nick Skelton/Roger Courthold/Nigel Waller.